SELF-DEFENCE AGAINST NON-STATE ACTORS

In this book, self-defence against non-State actors is examined by three scholars whose geographical, professional, theoretical, and methodological backgrounds and outlooks differ greatly. Their trialogue is framed by an introduction and a conclusion by the series editors. The novel scholarly format accommodates the pluralism and value changes of the current era, a shifting world order with a rise in nationalism and populism. It brings to light the cultural, professional and political pluralism which characterises international legal scholarship and exploits this pluralism as a heuristic device. This multiperspectivism exposes how political factors and intellectual styles influence the scholarly approaches and legal answers. The trialogical structure encourages its participants to decentre their perspectives. By explicitly focussing on the authors' divergence and disagreement, a richer understanding of self-defence against non-State actors is achieved, and the legal challenges and possible ways ahead are identified.

Mary Ellen O'Connell is the Robert and Marion Short Professor of Law and is Research Professor of International Dispute Resolution at the Kroc Institute for International Peace Studies, University of Notre Dame, Indiana. She was previously a vice president of the American Society of International Law and chaired the Use of Force Committee of the International Law Association. She has also practised law with the Washington, DC-based law firm, Covington & Burling.

Christian J. Tams is Professor of International Law at the University of Glasgow, where he directs the Research Group on International Law, Conflict and Security. His academic work focuses on the use of force, investment law and international courts and tribunals. In addition to his academic work, Professor Tams regularly advises States and other actors in matters of international law and is an academic member of Matrix Chambers, London. Over the course of the last fifteen years, he has acted in proceedings before the International Court of Justice, the International Tribunal for the Law of the Sea, the Iran–US Claims Tribunal, as well as arbitral tribunals (ICSID, PCA, ICC).

Dire Tladi is Professor of International Law at the University of Pretoria. He is a member of the UN International Law Commission and is Special Rapporteur on Peremptory Norms of General International Law (Jus Cogens) as well as a member of the Institut de Droit International. He is former Deputy Legal Adviser of the South Africa Department of Foreign Affairs and was previously legal adviser to the South African Mission to the United Nations in New York, including during its 2011–12 tenure on the UN Security Council. He also served as Special Adviser to the South African Foreign Minister.

MAX PLANCK TRIALOGUES ON THE LAW OF PEACE AND WAR

In a *Max Planck Trialogue*, three authors discuss one topic within the international law surrounding armed conflict. Each trio is composed so as to engage different modes of legal thinking, intellectual paradigms, regional backgrounds and professional specialisation. By bringing the pluralism of premises and methods to the fore, the *Trialogues* facilitate the emergence and global refinement of common legal understandings.

Series Editors

Professor Anne Peters
Max Planck Institute for Comparative Public Law and International Law

Dr Christian Marxsen
Max Planck Institute for Comparative Public Law and International Law

Self-Defence against Non-State Actors

Volume 1

MARY ELLEN O'CONNELL
University of Notre Dame, Indiana

CHRISTIAN J. TAMS
University of Glasgow

DIRE TLADI
University of Pretoria

CAMBRIDGE
UNIVERSITY PRESS

University Printing House, Cambridge, CB2 8BS, United Kingdom

One Liberty Plaza, 20th Floor, New York, NY 10006, USA

477 Williamstown Road, Port Melbourne, VIC 3207, Australia

314–321, 3rd Floor, Plot 3, Splendor Forum, Jasola District Centre, New Delhi – 110025, India

79 Anson Road, #06–04/06, Singapore 079906

Cambridge University Press is part of the University of Cambridge.

It furthers the University's mission by disseminating knowledge in the pursuit of education, learning, and research at the highest international levels of excellence.

www.cambridge.org
Information on this title: www.cambridge.org/9781107190740
DOI: 10.1017/9781108120173

First published 2019

Printed and bound in Great Britain by Clays Ltd, Elcograf S.p.A.

A catalogue record for this publication is available from the British Library.

Library of Congress Cataloging-in-Publication Data
NAMES: O'Connell, Mary Ellen, 1958– | Tams, Christian J. | Tladi, Dire.
TITLE: Self-defence against non-state actors / Mary-Ellen O'Connell, University of Notre Dame, Indiana; Christian Tams, University of Glasgow; Dire Tladi, University of Pretoria.
DESCRIPTION: Cambridge, United Kingdom ; New York, NY, USA : Cambridge University Press, 2019. | Series: Max Planck Trialogues on the Law of Peace and War; volume 1
IDENTIFIERS: LCCN 2018053751 | ISBN 9781107190740
SUBJECTS: LCSH: Self-defense (International law) | Non-state actors (International relations)
CLASSIFICATION: LCC KZ4043 .S439 2019 | DDC 341.6/8–dc23
LC record available at https://lccn.loc.gov/2018053751

ISBN 978-1-107-19074-0 Hardback
ISBN 978-1-316-64112-5 Paperback

Contents

Introduction to the Series: Trialogical International Law
Anne Peters   *page* xi

    I.   The Pluralistic Structure and Self-Contradictory Substance
         of International Law   xii
   II.   Multiperspectivism   xiv
  III.   The Timing of the Trialogues: Pressure on International
         Law's Universality   xvi
  IV.   Problematising National Perspectives on Questions of the
         Law *Contra Bellum* and *In Bello*   xviii
   V.   Bottom-Up Universalisation   xx
  VI.   Contributing to the Self-Reflexivity of International Legal
         Scholarship   xxiv

Introduction: Dilution of Self-Defence and its Discontents   1
Christian Marxsen and Anne Peters

    I.   The Controversy Around Self-Defence against Non-State
         Actors   2
   II.   Revival of the Debate since 2014   7
  III.   Three Perspectives in a Trialogue   10

1.   **The Use of Force in Self-Defence against Non-State Actors,**
     Decline of Collective Security and the Rise of Unilateralism:
     Whither International Law?   14
     Dire Tladi

    I.   Introduction   14
        A.   Importance and Controversy of the Law on the Use
            of Force   14

| | | B. | The Role of Policy Considerations | 17 |

B.   The Role of Policy Considerations   17

C.   The Purpose of the Chapter   19

II.   Prohibition on the Use of Force   22

A.   A Brief Historical Context   22

B.   The Content and Status of the Prohibition   23

III.   International Peace and Security Architecture   28

A.   The Charter as an Instrument for Collective Security   28

B.   Institutional Framework for Peace and Security under the Charter   30

IV.   The Law on Self-Defence   36

A.   General Framework   36

B.   The Permissibility of Unilateral Use of Force against Non-State Actors   37

C.   The Proposition that Unilateral Force can be used Extraterritorially in Self-Defence against Non-State Actors   42

D.   The Rules for Interpreting and Identifying the Scope of Self-Defence in Respect of Non-State Actors   48

V.   Evaluation of the Scope of the Right of Self-Defence   52

A.   The 'Inherent Right': Pre-Existing Rules of Customary International Law   52

B.   Armed Attack does not mean Armed Attack by a State   54

VI.   Unilateral or Collective Security: The Intersection of Law and Policy   81

A.   Scope and Limits of the Law of Self-Defence against Non-State Actors   81

B.   Do Current Circumstances Call for a New Approach?   82

VII.   Summary and Conclusions   87

2.   Self-Defence against Non-State Actors: Making Sense of the 'Armed Attack' Requirement   90
Christian J. Tams

I.   Introduction   90

II.   Setting the Stage   94

A.   A Problem of Force in International Relations   95

B.   A Question of Self-Defence   98

C.   A Question of Treaty Law   104

III.   The 'Armed Attack' Requirement: Making Sense of the Treaty Text   112

A.   '... the ordinary meaning to be given to the terms of
the treaty ...'   112
B.   '... in their context ...'   114
C.   '... and in the light of its object and purpose'   120
D.   The Preparatory Work of the Treaty and the
Circumstances of its Conclusion   123
E.   The Text of Article 51: Where Do We Stand?   124
IV.   'Meaning Through Deeds': Subsequent Practice in
Application of the 'Armed Attack' Requirement   125
A.   Subsequent Practice in Treaty Interpretation   125
B.   The General Framework: An Inter-State Reading of
Self-Defence   129
C.   Particular Instances of Self-Defence (1946–Late 1980s):
A Plea for Nuance   136
D.   Post-Cold War Practice: Gradual, Palpable Change   142
E.   Subsequent Practice: Where Do We Stand?   158
V.   Assessment and Concluding Thoughts   164
A.   The Case for Asymmetrical Self-Defence   164
B.   Implications   169

3.   **Self-Defence, Pernicious Doctrines, Peremptory Norms**   174
Mary Ellen O'Connell

I.   Introduction   174
II.   Evidence of the Durable Meaning of Self-Defence   179
A.   The Terms of the Charter   180
B.   The Drafting History of the Charter   183
C.   The Understanding in UN Organs   186
III.   Three Pernicious Doctrines of Expansive Self-Defence 212
A.   Inherent/Imminent   214
B.   Terrorism/War   218
C.   Unable/Unwilling   224
IV.   The Prohibition on the Use of Force as *Ius Cogens*   228
A.   The Methodology of *Ius Cogens*   229
B.   History, Morality, Natural Law   236
C.   The Implications of *Ius Cogens* Status for
Self-Defence   244
V.   Conclusion   253

**Conclusion: Self-Defence against Non-State Actors –
The Way Ahead**   258
Christian Marxsen and Anne Peters

   I.   Different Modes of Engaging with the International
         Law on Self-Defence   258
  II.   Handling the Sources of Self-Defence   260
 III.   Moral Values and *Ius Cogens*   262
 IV.   The Indeterminacy of the Law on Self-Defence   264
  V.   How Does the Law of Self-Defence Change?   269
       A.   Change of the Charter Law   270
       B.   Change of the Customary International Law on
           Self-Defence   274
       C.   The Law in Transition   276
 VI.   Conclusion   277

Index   282

Introduction to the Series: Trialogical International Law
Anne Peters[*]

This book is the inaugural volume of the series 'Max Planck Trialogues on the Law of Peace and War'. The books in this series each treat one single topic in the area of the law surrounding armed conflict (*ius contra bellum, ius in bello* and *ius post bellum*). The volumes take up classical subjects but will also react to recent challenges. The idea is that within one book, the chosen topic is examined by three scholars whose geographical, professional, theoretical, and methodological backgrounds and outlooks differ greatly. They write on one and the same issue, approaching it from their own distinct perspective, and responding to each other.

The objective is to bring to light the cultural, professional, and political pluralism which characterises international legal scholarship, and to exploit this pluralism as a heuristic device. So the core method of the 'Max Planck Trialogues on the Law of Peace and War' is to positively acknowledge the diversity of perspectives, and to make constructive use of them (multiperspectivism). The direct meeting of divergent views should expose – more clearly than the usual business of argument and response in separate publications – that and how the political as well as regional factors and accompanying intellectual styles influence the scholarly approach taken and the legal answers given. By inviting the participants of the Trialogue to a conversation, and by explicitly focussing on their divergence and disagreement (or their complementarity and synergies), a decentring of perspectives might be facilitated. This should ultimately contribute to a richer understanding of the set of international legal questions tackled in each volume.

The Trialogue format suggests itself in the law surrounding armed conflict, because this field of international law is characterised by deep controversies.

[*] The author thanks Dr Christian Marxsen and the participants of the research seminar at the Max Planck Institute for Comparative Public Law and International Law for helpful comments on a prior version of this text.

It touches the core principles of international law and relates to questions which are existential for States. The exact balance that is struck between, for example, sovereignty and human rights, or between the territorial integrity of one State and the security concerns of another, directly affects the material interests of States. Thus, the legal choices to be made are deeply value-loaded and connect to underlying political and theoretical preferences. This diversity of opinions and assessments cannot be easily reconciled, nor can 'correct' solutions be found by means of doctrinally exact and rigid legal scholarship. Rather, the divergent legal assessments of situations surrounding armed conflicts are, as a matter of fact, profoundly rooted in the plurality of theoretical and practical approaches that can be found in the reality of international relations. Such plurality also governs and should continue to govern scholarly approaches.

But I submit that this praise of pluralism does not contradict or overtake the scholarly ideal of intersubjective comprehensibility. Academic works aim, or at least should aim, for universal intersubjective comprehensibility, allowing scholars with diverging geographical, educational, or theoretical backgrounds to understand an argument or a research finding – regardless of sex, nationality or religion. Global intersubjectivity in turn requires a transnational academic legal discourse whose participants accept that arguments are sound only if they are fit for universal application. But of course the global inter-subjective comprehensibility and replicability depends on the premises and methods, which first of all should be made the explicit object of scholarly reflection. The purpose of the Trialogue is exactly to do this job.

I. THE PLURALISTIC STRUCTURE AND SELF-CONTRADICTORY SUBSTANCE OF INTERNATIONAL LAW

It is a truism that international law is in structural terms 'pluralistic', being

> *fragmented* (with no necessary coherence across international law as a whole), *decentralized* (where many centres and processes exist to create and interpret law), *contingent* (norms do not exist *a priori* but emerge from an engagement with the particular circumstances of their invocation, including agents and context), and *deliberative* (law is not so much a series of commands as a space in which meaning is collectively created in relation to social practices).[1]

---

[1] René Provost, 'Interpretation in International Law as a Transcultural Project', in Andrea Bianchi, Daniel Peat and Matthew Windsor (eds.), *Interpretation in International Law* (Oxford: Oxford University Press, 2015), 290–308 (304) (emphasis in original).

Besides possessing these peculiar structural features, the content or substance of international law is marked by internal tensions and even contradictions. These are more pronounced than is usual in domestic legal orders. The reasons partly overlap with the pluralistic structure just mentioned. They are the absence of a unitary law-maker, the diplomatic technique of drafting treaty texts vaguely and ambigiously in order to facilitate agreeement, the multiplicity of law-interpreting actors, the scarcity of case-law that could clarify and settle understandings, and the lack of an apex court to harmonise the law. An important factor is also international law's evolution through accretion, in which new layers of legal principles and mechanisms have been added on top of older ones without being able to clear the table of the remnants of the old. The law of self-defence is a good example.[2] One of its precursors is the police-type action against criminals and pirates (itself a survivor of the mid-nineteenth century) which only partly occurred outside the territory of the reacting State, and which was often taken against foreign ships on the high seas. The legal good protected then was typically the lives and property of nationals – as opposed to national security looked after by national self-defence in the modern sense. Also, the legal consequence was distinct: the use of force was excused or tolerated as opposed to fully justified. The remnants of mid-nineteenth century police-type action against pirates and other criminals continue to fester and, one might say, 'infect' (in any case confuse) the contemporary debate on self-defence.

Martti Koskenniemi has argued that the 'fluidity' resulting from the said tensions are a crucial factor of the success of international law because they contribute not only to its factual acceptance by the participants whose interests and preferences diverge so starkly, but even to the normative acceptability of international law.[3] Both the pluralistic structure of international law and the

[2]   Tadashi Mori, *Origins of the Right of Self-Defence in International Law: From the Caroline Incident to the United Nations Charter* (Leiden/Boston, MA: Brill Nijhoff, 2018), passim.

[3]   Martti Koskenniemi, *From Apology to Utopia: The Structure of International Legal Argument* (Cambridge: Cambridge University Press, 2nd edn., 2005), 590: 'The articulation of the experience of fluidity ... [of the international legal discourse] is much stronger (and in a philosophical sense, more "fundamental") [than mere semantic openness] and states that even where there is no semantic ambivalence whatsoever, international law remains indeterminate because it is based on contradictory premises and seeks to regulate a future in regard to which even single actors' preferences remain unsettled. To say this is not to say much more than that international law emerges from a political process whose participants have contradictory priorities and rarely know with clarity how such priorities should be turned into directives to deal with an uncertain future.' Koskenniemi's point is 'not that all of this should be thought of as a scandal or (even less) a structural "deficiency" but that indeterminacy is an absolutely central aspect of international law's acceptability' (*ibid.*, 591).

'fluidity' of international legal argument can be teased out and better understood through a trialogical method, as shall be explained now.

II. MULTIPERSPECTIVISM

The Trialogue-method builds on critical legal studies to the extent that those
have recognised '*problems of perspective* as a central and determinative element in the discourse' of law.[4] International law is (as is all law) a social fact
which is continuously and recursively created by social agents.[5] International
law exists first of all in the beliefs and through the meaning ascribed to acts of
law-makers and law-appliers. (These acts may then have physical manifesta-
tions which produce significant physical effects. For example, bombing a site
under the heading of self-defence will destroy buildings and lives.)

Philosophers of science have long asserted that scientific findings are
influenced by the perspective of the researcher.[6] For example, Hilary
Putnam has claimed that '[t]here is no God's Eye point of view that we can
know or usefully imagine', but only 'the various points of view of actual
persons reflecting various interests and purposes that their descriptions and
theories subserve'.[7] Notably, feminists have further developed this insight into
a standpoint epistemology which endorses situated knowledge(s)[8] and thus
seeks to avoid a 'totalising' single vision, on the one hand, and a sterile and
unsustainable epistemic relativism, on the other.[9]

Along these lines of thought we must acknowledge that legal concepts to
some extent depend on the (diverging) perspectives of those who create, apply,

---

[4] Günter Frankenberg, 'Critical Comparisons: Re-Thinking Comparative Law', *Harvard
    International Law Journal* 26 (1985), 411–55 (411) (emphasis added; with a view to comparative
    law, not international law).
[5] Anthony Giddens has called this 'structuration'. According to Giddens, social structures are
    created recursively. They result from patterns in agency, which are constrained by social
    structures, which result from agency, and so on. In and through their activities agents repro-
    duce the conditions that make these activities possible. See Anthony Giddens,
    The Constitution of Society: Outline of the Theory of Structuration (Cambridge: Polity Press,
    1984), 2. I thank Tom Sparks for this reference.
[6] Gert König, 'Perspektive, Perspektivismus, perspektivisch, I. Philosophie; Theleologie; Geistes-
    und Naturwissenschaften', in Joachim Ritter, Karlfried Gründer and Gottfried Gabriel (eds.),
    Historisches Wörterbuch der Philosophie (Basel: Schwabe & Co. AG Verlag, 1989), vol. VII,
    363–75.
[7] Hilary Putnam, *Reason, Truth and History* (Cambridge: Cambridge University Press, 2nd edn.,
    1997), 50.
[8] Seminally, Donna Haraway, 'Situated Knowledges: The Science Question in Feminism and
    the Privilege of Partial Perspective', *Feminist Studies* 14 (1988), 575–99.
[9] See for a short and accessible refutation of epistemic relativism, John Searle, 'Why Should You
    Believe It?', *The New York Review of Books*, vol. 56, no. 14 (24 September 2009).

interpret and criticise the law. Law is therefore inevitably a multi-perspectival phenomenon. Kaarlo Tuori has spelled this insight out for transnational (or international) law:

> [P]erspectivism is an inherent feature of all law. Legal actors always approach the law from a particular perspective, which inevitably affects what they identify as law and how they interpret and apply it ... Law exists only as identified and interpreted by situated legal actors: that is, legal actors embedded in a particular social and cultural context. Although a general characteristic of law, perspectivism is particularly pronounced in transnational law ... This is due to the great variety of legal actors and the great variety of the situatedness of these actors.[10]

The Trialogues seek to build on and take advantage of this perspectivism. Their multiperspectivism highlights 'the importance of seeing international law and international issues through the eyes of others'.[11] The trialogical setting seeks to encourage situated participants to become more sharply aware of how some arguments might be viewed differently from another perspective. This approach aligns with Yasuaki Onuma's call for a 'transcivilization perspective', which the Japanese scholar defined as follows:

> The transcivilizational perspective is a perspective from which people see, sense, (re)cognize, interpret, assess, and seek to propose solutions for the ideas, activities, phenomena and problems transcending national boundaries by adopting a cognitive and evaluative framework based on the recognition of the plurality of civilizations and cultures that have long existed throughout history ... The transcivilizational perspective sounds new, but it is not. It is a re-conceptualization of an already existing perspective from which people see trans-boundary or global affairs in terms of civilizations, including cultures and religions.[12]

The Trialogues are a conscious attempt to pluralise the relevant interpretive communities[13] around concrete international legal problems. This scheme acknowledges 'the polycentric and polyphonic nature of the interpretive

---

[10] Kaarlo Tuori, *European Constitutionalism* (Cambridge: Cambridge University Press, 2015), 78.

[11] Anthea Roberts, *Is International Law International?* (Oxford: Oxford University Press, 2017), 320.

[12] Yasuaki Onuma, *International Law in a Transcivilizational World* (Cambridge: Cambridge University Press, 2017), 19–20.

[13] Stanley Fish, *Is There a Text in this Class? The Authority of Interpretive Communities* (Cambridge, MA: Harvard University Press, 2nd edn., 1982). See, for the application of this concept to the interpretation of international treaties, Ian Johnstone, 'Treaty Interpretation: The Authority of Interpretive Communities', *Michigan Journal of International Law* 12 (1991),

process in international law'.[14] Indeed, the three voices in a Trialogue might be in harmony or in dissonance. Inevitably, the polyphony (to stick to the image) is less pronounced than ideal because the Trialogues are conducted in English. This language comes with a certain, historically impregnated writing and speaking style and carries the baggage of legal concepts stemming from the various English-speaking national traditions. It might even promote the trend towards a more case-oriented, less systematic, in short 'Anglo-Saxon' style of legal reasoning. For sure, its use is a significant competitive disadvantage for non-native speakers. Being aware of the cultural losses caused by English monolingualism, also in the Trialogue exercise, we do not see a feasible alternative.[15] We nevertheless hope to uphold some degree of transculturalism in the Trialogues.

The trialogical method bears a family resemblance with René Provost's 'interpretation in international law as a transcultural project'. Provost has concluded that the pluralistic nature of international law forces us to recognise pluralistic interpretive communities as well. He suggests 'that approaches relying on a concept such as *the* interpretive community fail to support the normative claim embodied in international law. Instead, a thicker understanding of the interpretive process projects a pluralistic construction of international law that can more accurately capture the promise and limits of that regime.'[16] The intention of the Trialogues is to beef up the interpretive process in that sense.

III. THE TIMING OF THE TRIALOGUES: PRESSURE ON INTERNATIONAL LAW'S UNIVERSALITY

International law aspires to be universal but carries a historical baggage of Eurocentrism.[17] 'In a system with the limited heritage but universalist pretensions of international law', the 'importance of accomodating legal pluralism within international legal discourse' cannot be overstated.[18] This has

---

371–419. See further Andrea Bianchi, *International Law Theories: An Inquiry Into Different Ways of Thinking* (Oxford: Oxford University Press, 2016), 306.

[14] Provost, 'Interpretation in International Law as a Transcultural Project' 2015 (n. 1), 303.

[15] Gleider I. Hernández, 'On Multilingualism and the International Legal Process', in Hélène Ruiz Fabri *et al.* (eds.), *Select Proceedings of the European Society of International Law* (Oxford: Hart, 2010), vol. II, 441–60.

[16] Provost, 'Interpretation in International Law as a Transcultural Project' 2015 (n. 1), 303–4 (emphasis added).

[17] Bardo Fassbender and Anne Peters, 'Introduction: Towards a Global History of International Law', in Bardo Fassbender and Anne Peters (eds.), *Oxford Handbook of the History of International Law* (Oxford: Oxford University Press, 2012), 1–24.

[18] Hernández, 'On Multilingualism and the International Legal Process' 2010 (n. 15), 457.

become all the more relevant in times of a global change of order.[19] Currently, the economic, political, military, and ideational dominance of the West is challenged not only by the rising States of the Global South and Asia but also by business enterprises, new regional organisations, and criminal networks which all unfold global action taking off from bases in various regions of the world.[20]

Because the international legal order 'feeds on preconditions which itself cannot guarantee'[21] (such as shared ethical norms, sufficient channels of communication, or the absence of unacceptable wealth disparities across the globe), it is inevitably affected by these changes. Most commonly, the macro-transformation of the international order is attributed to the ongoing redistribution and dispersion of political and economic power. But it also results from intellectual and moral factors which differ in the various regions of the world, ranging from resentment against 'Western' interference in the Middle East and Asia over the perception of being left behind and lack of prospects for a decent life in the Global South, up to the fear of losing privileges and wealth by the inhabitants of rich industrial States. The power shifts and the traction of anti-globalist ideas are likely to increase the ever-latent pressure on the universality of international law.[22] And if the international legal order feeds on preconditions which itself cannot guarantee, this means that international legal scholarship, too, must come to grips with pre-conditions and side-conditions over which it has no control.[23] Its methods must also react to changing environments.

[19] Charles A. Kupchan, *No One's World: The West, the Rising Rest, and the Coming Global Turn* (Oxford: Oxford University Press, 2013). For the consequences for international law William Burke-White, 'Power Shifts: Structural Realignment and Substantive Pluralism', *Harvard Journal of International Law* 56 (2015), 1–79.
[20] Rana Dasgupta, 'The Demise of the Nation State', *The Guardian*, 5th April 2018.
[21] See, with regard to States (the most powerful entities in the international legal order), Ernst Wolfgang Böckenförde's statement: 'Der freiheitliche, säkularisierte Staat lebt von Voraussetzungen, die er selbst nicht garantieren kann'; Ernst Wolfgang Böckenförde, 'Entstehung des Staates als Vorgang der Säkularisation', in *Säkularisation und Utopie: Ebracher Studien, Ernst Forsthoff zum 65. Geburtstag* (Stuttgart: Kohlhammer, 1967), 75–94 (93); reprinted in Ernst Wolfgang Böckenförde, *Recht, Staat, Freiheit: Studien zur Rechtsphilosophie, Staatstheorie und Verfassungsgeschichte* (Frankfurt a. M.: Suhrkamp, 1991), 92–114; an English translation is forthcoming in Mirjam Künkler and Tine Stein (eds.), *Religion, Law, and Democracy: Selected Writings of Ernst-Wolfgang Böckenförde* (Oxford: Oxford University Press, 2019).
[22] See Roberts, *Is International Law International?* 2017 (n. 11), 289.
[23] Anne Peters, 'The Rise and Decline of the International Rule of Law and the Job of Scholars', in Heike Krieger, Georg Nolte and Andreas Zimmermann (eds.), *The International Rule of Law: Rise or Decline?* (Oxford: Oxford University Press, forthcoming).

In our 'post truth age', the standpoint epistemology mentioned above[24] has been hijacked by right-wing parties and populists and has thereby muted the critical camps' emancipatory aspirations.[25] A reappraisal of the value and importance of an (at least procedural and discursive) legal universalism therefore seems urgent. At this juncture, the Trialogue-method actively embraces a culture-based moderate moral relativism as an appropriate attitude and as a useful starting point for scholarly debates in our pluralist, divided, multicultural world. It makes use of the 'situationality' of international legal actors. 'Situationality' expresses that the law-applier and law-interpreter are '*not absolutely constrained* by contexts and circumstances that can never be overcome' while steering away from 'falling into relativist particularisms or homogenising universalism'.[26] Utilising perspectivism and situationality, the Trialogues might modestly contribute to the attempt to build a bottom-up legal universalism without plunging into legal absolutism. Starting from the pragmatic assumption that people can make moral and learning experiences which force them to step out of the moral and epistemic framework they are used to, a Trialogue is one way to tease this out.

IV. PROBLEMATISING NATIONAL PERSPECTIVES ON QUESTIONS OF THE LAW *CONTRA BELLUM* AND *IN BELLO*

The different nationalities of the Trialogue participants are not their only marker of diversity, but they are an important one. We invite authors with different national backgrounds because we acknowledge that the domestic legal training, the domestic legal culture, and the political (often regionally informed) worldview of scholars influences their approach to international legal problems. In this regard, the Trialogues are in line with the current investigations into 'comparative international law' which include notably empirical research on the national education material, style and case-material used in textbooks, citation practices, and the like.[27]

---

[24] Haraway, 'Situated Knowledges' 1988 (n. 8).

[25] Albrecht Koschorke, 'Die akademische Linke hat sich selbst dekonstruiert. Es ist Zeit, die Begriffe neu zu justieren', *Neue Zürcher Zeitung*, 18 April 2018.

[26] Outi Korhonen, *International Law Situated: An Analysis of the Lawyer's Stance Towards Culture, History and Community* (The Hague: Kluwer Law International, 2000), 8–10 (emphasis added).

[27] Roberts, *Is International Law International?* 2017 (n. 11). Anthea Roberts, Paul B. Stephan, Pierre-Hugues Verdier and Mila Versteeg (eds.), *Comparative International Law* (Oxford: Oxford University Press, 2018). The study of the reception of international law in the different legal orders of the world, and the shaping of international law by the different States is part of the original mission of the Max Planck Institute for Comparative Public Law and

By highlighting different nationally coloured approaches, the Trialogues seek to problematise 'epistemic nationalism'. With this I mean the twofold phenomenon that international legal scholars often espouse positions which can be linked to their prior education in their domestic legal system and/or which serve a national interest.[28] The first variant, thinking along one's familiar legal tradition, often occurs unconsciously, while the second variant, supporting one's home country, may happen either deliberately or unwittingly. A parallel issue is the persistent segregation of research institutions along national lines. It is for that reason, too, that we nowadays doubt that the 'invisible college of international lawyers', as invoked by Oscar Schachter in the 1970s,[29] is really a global college. It rather seems to be an elite college of scholars of the developed world, a college in which academics from the so-called Global South are relegated to the role of the eternal students.

I think that the exposure of the fragility of the universality of international legal scholarship is apt to contribute to the constant work of building and rebuilding a universal international law. This stands in contrast to the early twentieth century's scholarly quest for a radical detachment from one's national background. George Scelle, for example, had still linked the surpassing of the national (and in his time probably intensely nationalist) perspective to the object of his discipline: 'Scientific objectivity must dispel ... every subjective point of view and, in particular, ... every national point of view from legal education ... The only ideal we should nurture is the objective of

International Law in Heidelberg. See for an original theoretical approach (without the empirical research programme) Mireille Delmas-Marty, 'Comparative Law and International Law: Methods for Ordering Pluralism', *University of Tokyo Journal of Law and Politics* 3 (2006), 43–59. See also Emmanuelle Jouannet, 'French and American Perspectives on International Law: Legal Cultures and International Law', *Maine Law Review* 58 (2006), 291–601; Martti Koskenniemi, 'The Case for Comparative International Law', *Finnish Yearbook of International Law* 20 (2009), 1–8. See with a focus on the Cold War claims of particular regional and strongly politicised approaches to international law (notably Soviet international law) Boris N. Mamlyuk and Ugo Mattei, 'Comparative International Law', *Brooklyn Journal of International Law* 36 (2011), 385–452.

[28] Anne Peters, 'Die Zukunft der Völkerrechtswissenschaft: Wider den epistemischen Nationalismus', *Heidelberg Journal of International Law* 67 (2007), 721–76; Anne Peters, 'International Legal Scholarship Under Challenge', in Jean D'Aspremont, Tarcisio Gazzini, André Nollkaemper and Wouter Werner (eds.), *International Law as a Profession* (Cambridge: Cambridge University Press, 2017), 117–59 (118–26).

[29] Oscar Schachter, 'The Invisible College of International Lawyers', *Northwestern University Law Review* 72 (1977), 217–26: '[T]he professional community of international lawyers ... constitutes a kind of invisible college dedicated to a common intellectual enterprise.' The expression 'Invisible College' was used by Robert Boyle in 1646 in relation to a predecessor society to the *Royal Society*, which was founded in 1660 (see Robert Lomas, *The Invisible College* (London: Headline, 2002), 63; *The New Encyclopedia Britannica*, 32 vols. (Chicago, IL: Encyclopedia Britannica, 15th edn., 2002), vol. X, 220).

law itself, being an ideal in so far as it can never be attained: the creation of peace between human beings.'[30]

Speaking up against Scelle on this point, I suggest that while scholars of international law should avoid outright nationalism, it is not desirable and not even possible to clinically strip off their particular points of view which root in and are informed by specific educational backgrounds, political and cultural traditions, and a general embeddedness in national discourses. On the contrary, I think that scholars can and should proactively make use of their diverse backgrounds by enriching international legal scholarship with a comparative law dimension. The espousal of the Trialogues' participants' national *Vorverständnis* should ultimately contribute to working towards Scelle's ideal of peace.

V. BOTTOM-UP UNIVERSALISATION

Presupposing that the *raison d'être* of international law is to govern relationships between political actors dispersed on the entire globe and to provide a common language and culture, international law must be universal (providing rules which apply to *all*). The fulfilment of the said functions requires distinguishing sharply between a welcome plurality of perspectives (including the possibility of diverging interpretations), on the one hand, and an undesirable plurality of *different rules* for different players even if these are similarly situated, on the other.

Take an example from the law on the use of force, the 'unwilling or unable' standard for identifying States from whose territory terror attacks have been launched and against which self-defensive action should then be allowed. It cannot be applied across the board. International order would be destroyed if *all* States (and not only the powerful ones which arrogate themselves the privilege to apply these standards against others) relied on it because this would lead to a very high rate of military activities by numerous States against numerous others.[31] This means that the 'unwilling or unable'

---

[30]   Georges Scelle, *Précis de Droit des Gens: Principes et Systématique*, 2 vols. (Paris: Recueil Sirey, 1932), vol. I, ix. Author's translation of the original: 'L'objectivité scientifique doit bannir d'un enseignement juridique tout idéal extra-juridique, toute "croyance", toute aspiration affective, tout point de vue subjectif et, notamment, dans notre domaine, les points de vue nationaux –, tout sentiment en un mot, si élevé, si légitime ou si profond soit-il. Le seul idéal qu'on puisse contempler c'est le "but", idéal aussi, puisque jamais atteint, que se propose le Droit: l'établissement de la paix entre les hommes.'

[31]   See Jutta Brunnée and Stephen Toope, 'Self-Defence against Non-State Actors: Are Powerful States Willing but Unable to Change International Law?', *International and Comparative Law Quarterly* 67 (2018), 263–86 (285).

standard is not universalisable. It can only function if it is used very sparingly. This means *de facto* (due to the uneven technical and financial capacities of States) that it will result in a restraint and disciplining tool on many weak States (especially those in which significant terrorist groups are based) and as an empowering device of some States with the sufficient military capacities to strike. Such a multi-class or two-speed model of international law may be acceptable for very limited and select issues, or as a temporary device allowing for experimentation on a small scale, but should not be allowed to affect core principles of international law, because that would erode the quality of international law as a worldwide normative system. (For example, already the two-class regime of the Nuclear Non-Proliferation Treaty faces increasing scepticism.)

I submit that the aspiration to a discursive, procedural and bottom-up universalism in international legal scholarship is not logically or intrinsically a 'false' universalism which merely camouflages particular interests. This submission does not neglect or reject the critical analysis of the operationalisation of international law's claim to universality as a mode of power.[32] It is a historical fact that such hegemonic camouflage has often occurred and continues to happen not only in real international relations but also in scholarship – both in the discourse and in its outside features, for example in the way careers are managed and projects are organised and financed. Critical scholars such as Sundhya Pahuja find that 'even if the claim to universality is a familiar mode of power, it is nevertheless an unstable one, for it is always implanted with the seeds of its own excess.' But 'a universal orientation is unavoidable if there is to be law.'[33] Ultimately, Pahuja acknowledges, the universal and the particular depend on each other. They are constructed in relation to each other, leading to a 'critical instability' of international law.[34]

The conscious advertisement of multiperspectivism does not, in itself, call into question the necessity of universalising international law. Multiperspectivism might, on the contrary, be seen 'as not threatening international law but as contributing to its refinement'.[35] Mathias Forteau has pointed out with regard to the recently touted discipline of comparative international law that such an

---

[32] Sundhya Pahuja, *Decolonising International Law Development: Economic Growth and the Politics of Universality* (Cambridge: Cambridge University Press, 2011), 252–7.
[33] *Ibid.*, 41.
[34] *Ibid.*, 25.
[35] With a view to comparative international law: Mathias Forteau, 'Comparative International Law within, not against, International Law', in Roberts, Stephan, Verdier and Versteeg, Comparative International Law 2018 (n. 27), 161–79 (179).

ecumenical conclusion depends heavily on the way diversity is approached. So far as diversity is assessed with the specific purpose of reaching a consensus on the definition of international, common rules, comparative international law harmoniously supplements international law. On the other hand, if comparative international law were to be designed as a way to claim the existence of specific approaches to international law, there is a risk that it would eventually lead to the disintegration of the core idea of international law as the common law humankind.[36]

More profoundly, multiperspectivism is distinct from espousing epistemic or moral relativism.[37] Multiperspectivism is independent from, or neutral towards, what Karl Popper has called the framework-theory (and the accompaniyng framework-relativism[38]). The framework-theory forms the backbone of critical legal theory. It holds that there is no external point of reference beyond the frameworks from which the meaning of words, the truth of propositions and the validity of ethical norms can be judged. Therefore, legal language, thought and judgment are trapped within inescapable epistemic, linguistic, cultural and moral frames of reference.[39] Frameworks are institutionalised so that researchers are dominated 'by a grid of concepts, research techniques, professional ethics, and politics, by which the prevailing culture imposes on the individual scholar

---

[36] *Ibid.*

[37] I cannot fully discuss the merits and problems of moral and epistemic relativism in this contribution. But I am sympathetic to discourse theory's attempt to demonstrate that engaging in a discourse implies recognition of some universal moral norms. See generally Karl-Otto Apel, *Transformation der Philosophie, vol. II: Das Apriori der Kommunikationsgemeinschaft* (Frankfurt a. M.: Suhrkamp, 1973), 400, 420–5; Jürgen Habermas, 'Diskursethik – Notizen zu einem Begründungsprogramm', in *Moralbewußtsein und kommunikatives Handeln* (Frankfurt a. M.: Suhrkamp, 1st edn., 1983), 53–125 (105). Jürgen Habermas, 'Erläuterungen zur Diskursethik', in *Erläuterungen zur Diskursethik* (Frankfurt a. M.: Suhrkamp, 2nd edn., 1992), 119–226 (195). See for an analysis and criticism of the philosophical foundations of Habermas' universal pragmatics Christian Marxsen, *Geltung und Macht – Jürgen Habermas' Theorie von Recht, Staat und Demokratie* (Munich: Wilhelm Fink, 2011), 68–88. See, for a brilliant application of discourse theory to the international legal discourse, Ingo Venzke, *How Interpretation Makes International Law* (Oxford: Oxford University Press, 2012).

[38] Karl Popper has defined framework-relativism as 'the doctrine that truth is relative to our intellectual background, which is supposed to determine somehow the framework within which we are able to think: that truth may change from one framework to another' (Karl Popper, *The Myth of the Framework: In Defence of Science and Rationality* (London: Routledge, 1994), 33).

[39] Seminally François Lyotard, *La Condition Postmoderne: Rapport sur le Savoir* (Paris: Édition de Minuit, 1979). Lyotard identifies as characteristics of the post-modern era the obsoleteness of meta-narrratives, which were in modern times used to legitimise institutions, social and political practices, ethics and modes of thought. From the obsoleteness of meta-narratives results the irresolvable incommensurability of language games, which make consensual notions of truth and justice impossible.

its canons of how legal scholarship is to be conducted'.[40] The gist here lies not in the hardly deniable proposition that throughout history and geography we have a plurality of epistemic, normative and cultural frameworks. The gist lies in the assertion that these frameworks are *incommensurable*.[41] The Trialogues attempt to test the alleged incommensurability in a real setting.

Moreover, a Trialogue can be seen as an exercise in intercultural hermeneutics[42] in which the conversation or 'dialogue' between the legal material (texts) and their readers (scholars)[43] is explicitly loaded with the concept of culture (including legal culture[44]), because the three readers are selected so as to represent different cultures. In interpreting the texts of international law (both the primary material, for example the treaties and soft law texts themselves, and the scholarly secondary material) the cultural 'Other' embodied therein is in principle not different from the intra-cultural or historical 'Other'. The cultural distance can be revealed, described and conveyed through interpretation. Intercultural hermeneutics thus presuppose, search, find and enlarge the overlaps between different cultures and philosophies. These overlaps make cross-cultural communication and understanding possible – also on questions of international law.[45] The Trialogues indeed aspire to identify the existence or absence of an 'overlapping consensus' on international legal principles.[46] It will remain to be seen whether the

[40] Günter Frankenberg, 'Stranger than Paradise: Identity and Politics in Comparative Law', *Utah Law Review* 2 (1997), 259–74 (270).

[41] See, for a critique of the incommensurability thesis, Anne Peters and Heiner Schwenke, 'Comparative Law Beyond Post-Modernism', *International and Comparative Law Quarterly* 49 (2000), 800–34.

[42] Elmar Holenstein, 'Intra- und interkulturelle Hermeneutik', in *Kulturphilosophische Perspektiven* (Frankfurt a. M.: Suhrkamp, 1998), 257–87. See for practical application Fred Edmund Jandt, *An Introduction to Intercultural Communication: Identities in a Global Community* (Los Angeles, CA: SAGE, 8th edn., 2016).

[43] See for a 'dialogical' (or 'conversational') hermeneutics Alexandra Kemmerer, 'Chapter 22: Sources in the Meta-Theory of International Law: Hermeneutical Conversations', in Samantha Besson and Jean D'Aspremont (eds.), *The Oxford Handbook on the Sources of International Law* (Oxford: Oxford University Press, 2017), 469–90. The dialogue or conversation mentioned is between the reader and the text, and points to the reader's self-reflexive positititioning in his/her changing environment (which includes the others members of the interpretive community).

[44] See, for a critical overview of the term's usage, Ralf Michaels, 'Rechtskultur', in Jürgen Basedow, Klaus J. Hopt and Reinhard Zimmermann (eds.), *Handwörterbuch des Europäischen Privatrechts* (Tübingen: Mohr Siebeck, 2009).

[45] Axel Horstmann, 'Interkulturelle Hermeneutik: Eine neue Theorie des Verstehens?', *Deutsche Zeitschrift für Philosophie* 47 (1999), 427–48 (438).

[46] See *mutatis mutandis* John Rawls, 'The Idea of an Overlapping Consensus', *Oxford Journal of Legal Studies* 7 (1987), 1–25 (Rawls conceptualised this for societies 'with a democratic tradition confronted by the fact of pluralism').

Trialogues make a contribution, in a discursive process, to universalising the legal ideas surrounding the *ius contra bellum* and *in bello*.

Ideally, this project could be complemented by anthropological research trying to ascertain the validity of moral norms empirically with a view to actual moral attitudes of people. Along this vein, Gregory Shaffer and the 'new legal realists' call for empirical, social-science based studies in order

> to uncover new vantages and perspectives through empirical engagement, *permitting our incoming predisposition (inevitable no matter how neutral we aim to be) to be challenged and potentially transformed* ... This approach is particularly important for the analysis of international law in a world characterized by constituencies with differing priorities, perspectives, and opportunities to be heard in which the most read and influential international law scholarship tends to be written by those from particular backgrounds working in a particular language, English.[47]

Empirical studies are helpful to shake and challenge predispositions, but will do the job only if they are informed by a conceptual framework which proactively foregrounds pluralism. On the basis of such a conceptualisation and method, universalism would not be based on an *a priori* reasoning, but it would be an *ex post* universalism based on empirical data.[48]

VI. CONTRIBUTING TO THE SELF-REFLEXIVITY OF INTERNATIONAL LEGAL SCHOLARSHIP

Scholars of international law should not harbour illusions about the relevance of their contributions to international law. They cannot make law – just as lepidopterists cannot make butterflies.[49] Because scholars have no law-making and no law-destroying authority themselves, it depends on the persuasiveness of their arguments whether these will be taken up by the political actors or not. But however weak the power of the argument is, academics have a (modest) role to play, not as architects of the international

---

[47] Gregory Shaffer, 'New Legal Realism and International Law', in Heinz Klug and Sally Engle Merry (eds.), *The New Legal Realism, vol. II: Studying Law Globally* (New York: Cambridge University Press, 2016), 145–59 (146) (emphasis added).

[48] See for an empirical study the World Values Survey, a global network of social scientists studying changing values and their impact on social and political life, available at www.worldvaluessurvey.org.

[49] Jörg Kammerhofer, 'Lawmaking by Scholars', in Catherine Brölmann and Yannick Radi (eds.), *Research Handbook on the Theory and Practice of International Lawmaking* (Cheltenham/Northampton, MA: Edward Elgar Publishing, 2016), 305–25 (305).

legal order but rather as 'caretakers' of the fragile autonomy and universality of international law.[50]

The Trialogues are in line with the current trend of increased self-circumspection of international legal scholarship, which may be taken as a sign of crisis but which probably helps to improve the enterprise.[51] The Trialogues might contribute to the self-reflexivity as called for by Andrew Lang and Susan Marks, who find that

> by showing how our professional sensibilities are entrenched, transmitted and propagated through disciplinary habits of thought, assumptions, and dispositions, we are brought face to face with the processes through which we are ourselves enrolled in, and shaped by, the collectively produced disciplinary structures we inhabit. This can encourage us to engage with these processes in a more reflexive and critical way.[52]

The direct confrontation in the Trialogue workshops is expected to provoke a 'comitted argument'[53] by the discussants, to borrow Owen Fiss' phrase. The set-up is more conducive to engaged scholarship than to armchair international law.

Michael Bohlander demonstrated how the language and different legal educations of the legal actors influence the operation of international criminal law, and he praised these influences as an asset: '[I]t would be dreadful if the entire human intellectual enterprise were to be guided by the same intellectual style.'[54] Along this line, the Trialogues should uphold intellectual 'stylistic' diversity and ultimately work against an intellectual monoculture.

---

[50] Richard Collins and Alexandra Bohm, 'International Law as Professional Practice', in D'Aspremont, Gazzini, Nollkaemper and Werner, *International Law as a Profession* 2017 (n. 28), 67–92 (88).

[51] D'Aspremont, Gazzini, Nollkaemper and Werner, *International Law as a Profession* 2017 (n. 28).

[52] Andrew Lang and Susan Marks, 'People with Projects: Writing the Lives of International Lawyers', *Temple International And Comparative Law Journal* 27 (2013), 437–53 (449).

[53] Owen Fiss, 'The Varieties of Positivism', *Yale Law Journal* 90 (1981), 1007–16 (1009).

[54] Michael Bohlander, 'Language, Culture, Legal Traditions, and International Criminal Justice', *Journal of International Criminal Justice* 12 (2014), 491–513 (21).

Introduction

Dilution of Self-Defence and its Discontents

Christian Marxsen and Anne Peters

Self-defence against non-State actors, such as pirates and ships carrying letters of marque with deliberately ambiguous links to sovereign States, was the cardinal issue that framed and propelled the rise of modern international law. After the adoption of the UN Charter, the concept of self-defence has been sharpened to mean first of all the situation that one State defends itself against an ongoing armed attack by another State. However, the concept has remained controversial at the margins.

This book is about the major controversy related to the transnational activities of armed non-State groups.[1] Terrorist organisations have become a major security concern for States in all parts of the world. Terrorism has been qualified by the Security Council as 'one of the most serious threats to international peace and security'.[2] Recurring strikes by armed terror groups raise the questions of whether and when such resort to armed force by non-State actors triggers the right to self-defence under international law.[3]

The international lawfulness of military reactions against physical violence exercised by non-State actors but unequivocally imputable to another State is fairly easy to assess. In terms of the International Court of Justice's *Nicaragua* judgment, attacks by non-State armed groups are attributable to a State when that State has sent them or when the latter is 'substantially involved' (referring

---

[1] The other major uncertainty concerns the temporal dimension of self-defence, which has become more acute in the nuclear age with the dangers of total destruction. The question is whether self-defence is or should be admissible against imminent (as opposed to ongoing) attacks, or even against more remote, future threats such as those emanating from the proliferation of weapons of mass destruction.

[2] SC Res. 2178 of 24 September 2014.

[3] The question has become a standard textbook problem but remains unresolved (see Christian Henderson, *The Use of Force and International Law* (Cambridge: Cambridge University Press, 2018), chapter 8, 308–46, specifically devoted to the use of force against non-State actors).

to Article 3 lit. g of the General Assembly Definition on Aggression (3314) of 1974).[4] An alternative criterion figuring prominently in the international legal debates lies in the standard of 'effective control', which is the general standard for attribution in the international rules on State responsibility.[5] Where imputation is possible under these standards, the attacked State may take necessary and proportionate action against the State from whose territory the non-State actors operate, because the acts of the non-State actors are – from a legal perspective – those of the State.

I. THE CONTROVERSY AROUND SELF-DEFENCE AGAINST NON-STATE ACTORS

The controversial constellation is defensive action taken against an – as Dire Tladi calls it in this volume – 'innocent State',[6] that is a State to which the military operation of an armed group is not imputable under the acknowledged principles. This scenario raises the questions of whether a lower degree of State involvement is or should be sufficient to allow for self-defence affecting that 'innocent' State, and whether imputation to the territorial State matters at all.

It is by no means a new phenomenon that States use military force against non-State actors which operate independently from or at least not under the actual control of another State. In this book, Christian Tams reminds us of various instances since the 1940s. He pleads for acknowledging the nuances in the law which was – so he claims – not as straightforwardly State-oriented as standard narratives would have us believe.[7] However, while States did defend themselves against non-State actors by military means, these hardly triggered any international legal debate. Legal writings in the early days of the Charter did not take up the issue at length, but largely presupposed a State-oriented reading of the rules on self-defence.[8] While in the following decades a few especially affected States such as Israel took a clear position on

---

[4]   ICJ, *Military and Paramilitary Activities in and against Nicaragua* (Nicaragua v. United States), Merits, Judgment of 27 June 1986, ICJ Reports 1986, 14, para. 195.

[5]   *Ibid.*, paras. 115 and 109; ICJ, *Case Concerning Application of the Convention on the Prevention and Punishment of the Crime of Genocide* (Bosnia and Herzegovina v. Serbia and Montenegro), Judgment of 26 February 2007, ICJ Reports 2007, 43, paras. 398 *et seq.* In this sense, see also ILC Articles on the Responsibility of States for Internationally Wrongful Acts, *Yearbook of the International Law Commission*, 2001, vol. II, Part Two, 31 *et seq.*, Article 8.

[6]   Tladi in this volume, 20.

[7]   Tams in this volume, 136.

[8]   See Tladi, 43–8, and Tams, 129, in this volume.

the issue,[9] the underlying general question was not made a direct subject of controversy.

This changed significantly with the terrorist attacks of 9/11 in 2001 and with the subsequent military interventions. These events are often seen as constituting a 'true turning point' in the debate on the international law of self-defence.[10] Since the military intervention of the United States and its allies in Afghanistan in 2001, self-defence – and especially against non-State actors – figures as a, if not the, controversial issue of international peace and security law.[11] The primary target of the United States was the terrorist organisation Al-Qaeda. The US army intervened in Afghanistan, which the US accused of allowing 'the parts of Afghanistan that it controls to be used by this organization as a base of operation'.[12] As Afghanistan did not have 'effective control' over Al-Qaeda, the traditional criteria of imputation would not have allowed defensive action against its territory. Many observers interpret the US intervention and the international reactions to that intervention as triggers of a sudden shift in the law, partly described as a case of 'instant custom'.[13]

Those assuming such a shift in the law mainly point to Security Council resolutions 1368 and 1373 of September 2001.[14] These resolutions mention the inherent right of self-defence in their preambles before condemning the terrorist attacks of 9/11. While self-defence does not need a licence by

---

[9] See Tom Ruys, *'Armed Attack' and Article 51 of the UN Charter: Evolutions in Customary Law and Practice* (Cambridge: Cambridge University Press, 2010), 401–2. See, for a discussion of State practice, Tams in this volume, 136–42.

[10] Tom Ruys, 'Crossing the Thin Blue Line: An Inquiry into Israel's Recourse to Self-Defense against Hezbollah', *Stanford Journal of International Law* 43 (2007), 265–94 (280). See, for a prominent analysis written at that time, Thomas M. Franck, 'Terrorism and the Right of Self-Defense', *American Journal of International Law* 95 (2001), 839–43. See also Michael Wood, 'International Law and the Use of Force: What Happens in Practice?', *Indian Journal of International Law* 53 (2013), 345–67 (356).

[11] In a recent book devoted to the political functions of international law, Ian Hurd specifically focuses on the expansion of self-defence for illustrating that international law has lost its constraining power; Ian Hurd, *How to do Things with Law* (Oxford: Oxford University Press, 2017), chapter 4 'The Permissive Power of the Ban on War', 58–81. The law of self-defence is a 'law that cannot be broken' or 'infrangible law' (*ibid.*, 79) – and that is, we might add, no law at all.

[12] UN Doc. S/2001/946, 7 October 2001 (USA).

[13] Christine Gray, 'The Use of Force and the International Legal Order', in Malcom D. Evans (ed.), *International Law* (Oxford: Oxford University Press, 2nd edn., 2006), 589–619 (602); Yutaka Arai-Takahashi, 'Shifting Boundaries of the Right of Self-Defence – Appraising the Impact of the September 11 Attacks on Jus Ad Bellum', *International Lawyer* 36 (2002), 1081–1102 (1094–1095); Benjamin Langille, 'It's Instant Custom: How the Bush Doctrine Became Law After the Terrorist Attacks of September 11, 2001', *Boston College International and Comparative Law Review* 26 (2003), 145–56.

[14] SC Res. 1368 of 12 September 2011; SC Res. 1373 of 28 September 2011.

the Security Council, and although the Council cannot unilaterally change the law of the Charter, its explicit classification of a terrorist threat as an armed attack would have contributed to the formation of a novel interpretation and *opinio iuris* in this direction.[15] Many observers interpret the resolutions' language as an endorsement by the Security Council of a right to self-defence against the non-State group Al-Qaeda.[16] Along the same line, the international support for the US, in combination with the absence of a condemnation of the military intervention in Afghanistan, is interpreted as acquiescence, or at least as a toleration, of a broader legal rule on self-defence.[17]

The question, however, has remained controversial. Critics of the extended notion of self-defence insist that the Security resolutions of 2001 only mention the right to self-defence without passing a judgment on its lawful use in the concrete case of the strikes against Al-Qaeda on Afghan territory.[18] Besides, the international reactions to the invasion in Afghanistan, especially Ad the laconism or muteness of many States, have been interpreted in different ways. The opponents of the broader reading of self-defence explain the silence of many States as a politically motivated restraint that was not intended to have an influence on the law and thus does not express any *opinio iuris*.[19]

The case-law of the International Court of Justice has not settled the issue. While the *Advisory Opinion on the Israeli Wall* of 2004 is mostly read as

---

[15] Jost Delbrück, 'The Fight against Global Terrorism: Self-Defense or Collective Security as International Police Action: Some Comments on the International Legal Implications of the "War against Terrorism"', *German Yearbook of International Law* 44 (2001) 9–24 (14, fn. 16). See also Monica Hakimi, 'The *Jus ad Bellum*'s Regulatory Form', *American Journal of International Law* 112 (2018), 151–190, on the Security Council employing what she calls 'informal regulation' that does not authorise but 'condones' specific uses of military force and thereby confers legitimacy. Hakimi considers Resolutions 1368 and 2249 as examples for this novel type of regulation that might help preserve the *ius contra bellum*'s relevance (*ibid.*, 165–6 and 187–9).

[16] Davis Brown, 'Use of Force against Terrorism After September 11th: State Responsibility, Self-Defense and Other Responses', *Cardozo Journal of International & Comparative Law* 11 (2003), 1–54 (29); Nicholas Tsagourias, 'Cyber-Attack, Self-Defence and the Problem of Attribution', *Journal of Conflict and Security Law* 17.2 (2012), 229–44 (243); Anders Henriksen, 'Jus Ad Bellum and American Targeted Use of Force to Fight Terrorism Around the World', *Journal of Conflict and Security Law* 19 (2014), 211–50 (225).

[17] Steven R. Ratner, 'Jus Ad Bellum and Jus in Bello after September 11', *American Journal of International Law* 96 (2002), 905–21 (910).

[18] Alain Pellet and Sarah Pellet, 'The Aftermath of September 11', *Tilburg Foreign Law Review* 10 (2002), 64–75 (71–3).

[19] Dire Tladi, 'The Nonconsenting Innocent State: The Problem with Bethlehem's Principle 12', *American Journal of International Law* 107 (2013), 570–6 (574–5).

leaning towards a State-oriented reading of self-defence,[20] the ICJ judgment in *Congo v. Uganda* of 2005 gave room for much debate.[21] For many readers, this judgment signalled that the ICJ was open for accepting self-defence against non-State actors.[22]

International legal scholars and practitioners have developed a number of proposals for dealing with self-defence against non-State actors: the Chatham House Principles,[23] the Leiden Policy Recommendations,[24] and the Bethlehem Principles.[25] These sets of principles and recommendations purport to describe actual State practice and the current state of the law and (partly) make *de lege ferenda* proposals.[26] While they significantly diverge in their details, these proposals all assume that self-defence against non-State actors on the territory of a non-consenting State is lawful (or in the process of

---

[20] See ICJ, *Legal Consequences of the Construction of a Wall in the Occupied Palestinian Territory*, Advisory Opinion, ICJ Reports 2004, 136, para. 139. In his declaration to the *Wall* opinion, Judge Buergenthal had called the majority's focus on State attacks a 'legally dubious conclusion', based on a 'formalistic approach' of the Court (ICJ, *ibid.*, Declaration of Judge Buergenthal, ICJ Reports 2004, 240, paras. 5 and 6). Other observers read the Advisory Opinion as having *left open* the question of whether self-defence against a non-State actor can be lawful. See, for discussion and diverging interpretations of the *Wall* opinion, Tladi, 56–7, and Tams, 156–8, in this volume. The prior judgment ICJ, *Case Concerning Oil Platforms* (Islamic Republic of Iran v. United States of America), ICJ Reports 2003, 161, paras. 51 and 61, is also relevant in this context. It implies that attacks must be imputed to a State (in this case to Iran).

[21] See ICJ, *Armed Activities on the Territory of the Congo* (Democratic Republic of the Congo v. Uganda), Judgment, ICJ Reports 2005, 168, paras. 146–7. Here the Court first stated in para. 146 that the acts of armed bands or irregulars against Uganda were not attributable to the DRC. In view of this, the ICJ then found in para. 147 that there is 'no need to respond to the contentions of the Parties as to whether and under what conditions contemporary international law provides for a right of self-defence against large-scale attacks by irregular forces'.

[22] See, for opposing interpretations of the decision, Tladi, 57–9, and Tams, 157–8, in this volume.

[23] 'The Chatham House Principles of International Law on the Use of Force in Self-Defence', *International and Comparative Law Quarterly* 55 (2006), 963–72.

[24] 'Leiden Policy Recommendations on Counter-Terrorism and International Law', *Netherlands International Law Review* 57 (2010), 531–50.

[25] Daniel Bethlehem, 'Self-Defense against an Imminent or Actual Armed Attack by Nonstate Actors', *American Journal of International Law* 106 (2012), 770–7 (the 'Bethlehem Principles'; with 'Principles Relevant to the Scope of a State's Right of Self-Defense against an Imminent or Actual Armed Attack by Nonstate Actors' at 775). See the response by Elizabeth Wilmshurst and Michael Wood, 'Self-Defense against Nonstate Actors: Reflections on the "Bethlehem Principles"', *American Journal of International Law* 107 (2013), 390–5; see also Daniel Bethlehem, 'Principles of Self-Defense: A Brief Response', *American Journal of International Law* 107 (2013), 579–85.

[26] The Chatham House Principles (n. 23) claim to be a statement of international law 'properly understood' (963), whereas the Leiden Policy Recommendations (n. 24) also aim to 'highlight areas in which greater consensus needs to be pursued at the international level' (540), and the Bethlehem Principles (n. 25) acknowledge that they not reflect 'a settled view of any state' (773). See, for discussion, Tladi in this volume, 38–42.

becoming the law, or should be allowed) in situations where the territorial
State is either unwilling or unable to prevent attacks by non-State actors
emanating from its territory.[27]

Many scholarly writings of the post-9/11 era, however, have remained more
cautious. A general undertone of the debate has been an acknowledgement
of a certain tendency towards a broader reading of self-defence, while
formulations have often remained far from unequivocally postulating such
an understanding. In that sense, commentators have stated, for example, that
an extensive interpretation of self-defence 'appears to be gaining ground',[28]
and that a 'trend ... clearly [points] towards the establishment of an even
further-reaching responsibility of the host state based on the mere toleration
or harbouring of terrorists.'[29] Christian Tams held in an earlier article that
'the international community today is much less likely to deny' a State's
invocation of self-defence against attacks not imputable to a State.[30] Claus
Kress found that an 'alleged right of self-defence in case of a non-State armed
attack now occupies a place within the "light grey" area of the international
law on the use of force'.[31] Thus, even positions generally agreeing that the
solely State-centred reading of self-defence had come under immense pressure were hesitant to outrightly assume that a clear shift in the law had
already taken place.

---

[27] The Leiden Policy Recommendations (n. 24) state: 'The territorial State's consent to military
action is required, except where the territorial State is unable or unwilling itself to deal with
the terrorist attacks' (540); the Chatham House Principles (n. 23) hold: 'If the right of self-
defence in such a case is to be exercised in the territory of another State, it must be evident that
that State is unable or unwilling to deal with the non-State actors itself, and that it is necessary
to use force from outside to deal with the threat in circumstances where the consent of the
territorial State cannot be obtained' (969); the Bethlehem Principles (n. 25) deal with the
'unwilling or unable' standard in principles 11 and 12. See critically on this body of literature
Jutta Brunnée and Stephen Toope, 'Self-Defence against Non-State Actors: Are Powerful
States Willing but Unable to Change International Law?', *International and Comparative Law
Quarterly* 67 (2018), 263–86 (275), diagnosing 'a curious interplay amongst State officials,
former officials writing in their personal capacity and some academic commentators, whereby
a small group tries to expand its influence by constantly cross-referencing each other'.

[28] Jutta Brunnée and Stephen Toope, *Legitimacy and Legality in International Law* (Cambridge:
Cambridge University Press, 2010), 296.

[29] Carsten Stahn, 'Terrorist Acts as "Armed Attack": The Right to Self-Defense, Article 51(1/2) of
the UN Charter, and International Terrorism', *Fletcher Forum of World Affairs* 27 (2003),
35–54 (47).

[30] Christian J. Tams, 'The Use of Force against Terrorists', *European Journal of International
Law* 20 (2009), 359–97 (381).

[31] Claus Kreß, 'Major Post-Westphalian Shifts and Some Important Neo-Westphalian
Hesitations in the State Practice on the International Law on the Use of Force', *Journal on
the Use of Force and International Law* 1 (2014), 11–54 (53). His paper was published before self-
defence was claimed against ISIS by the US and other States, which started in September 2014.

II. REVIVAL OF THE DEBATE SINCE 2014

The debate about whether and under what conditions self-defence is lawful against (certain types of) non-State attacks has received renewed attention since 2014 due to the interventions of numerous States in the armed conflict in Syria. In this context, a number of States – notably the United States, Turkey, the United Kingdom, and France – have claimed to act in individual self-defence against Islamist terrorist groups, above all against the group Islamic State of Iraq and Syria (ISIS).[32] Some States alternatively or additionally relied on the collective self-defence of Iraq,[33] and thus presupposed that Iraq was suffering an armed attack in the sense of Article 51 of the UN Charter.

The Security Council has assumed an equivocal position on interventions in Syria. In its Resolution 2249, it 'calls upon' member States to participate in the fight against ISIS, but did not itself authorise an intervention under Chapter VII of the UN Charter.[34] Furthermore, the Council did not even mention self-defence (not even in the preamble) – unlike in its Resolution 1368 after 9/11. It limited its 'call' to measures 'in compliance with international law'.[35] This reference to 'international law' can be read in various ways. It is at first sight a reminder that any reaction must be lawful. It might also be a veiled reference to the law of self-defence, avoiding an explicit mentioning, so as to escape a repetition of the post-9/11 controversy regarding whether the Security Council had endorsed the American claim of self-defence or not. The Security Council thereby left the controversial question of self-defence against non-State actors to the interpretation of the States. Unsurprisingly, the (probably deliberately) cryptic resolution has been interpreted both ways, as remaining within the boundaries of the established State-centred law, on the one hand,[36] and as embracing a broadened understanding of self-defence, on the other.[37]

---

[32]   UN Doc. S/2014/695, 23 September 2014 (USA); UN Doc. S/2015/563, 24 July 2015 (Turkey); UN Doc. S/2015/688, 7 September 2015 (UK); UN Doc. S/2015/745, 8 September 2015 (France).

[33]   See UN Doc. S/2014/695, 23 September 2014 (USA); UN Doc. S/2015/563, 24 July 2015 (Turkey); UN Doc. S/2014/851, 25 November 2015 (UK); UN Doc. S/2016/523, 9 June 2016 (Belgium); UN Doc. S/2015/693, 9 September 2015 (Australia); UN Doc. S/2016/132, 10 February 2016 (The Netherlands); UN Doc. S/2016/513, 3 June 2016 (Norway); UN Doc. S/2015/221, 31 March 2015 (Canada); UN Doc. S/2015/946, 10 December 2015 (Germany); UN Doc. S/2016/34, 13 January 2016 (Denmark).

[34]   SC Res. 2249 of 20 November 2015, para. 5.

[35]   *Ibid.*

[36]   See Tladi in this volume, 73–6; see also O'Connell in this volume, 211.

[37]   See e.g. Michael P. Scharf, 'How the War against ISIS Changed International Law', *Case Western Reserve Journal of International Law* 48 (2016), 15–67 (66): 'Despite its ambiguity,

Among the intervening States, the conditions of lawful self-defence are far from agreed. Rather, the participating States have invoked diverse rationales for their interventions, ranging from the 'unwilling or unable' standard (proclaimed by the United States, Australia, Canada and Turkey)[38] to the criterion of effective territorial control (emphasised by Belgium and Germany).[39] In the course of the conflict in Syria, the extended understanding of self-defence has not only been invoked against ISIS. Turkey has also claimed to act in self-defence against the Kurdish militia YPG. In its operation 'Olive Branch', commenced in January 2018, Turkey claimed the right to defend itself against the 'threat from the Syria-based terrorist organizations, among which Deash and the PKK/KCK Syria affiliate, PYD/YPG, are at the top of the list'.[40]

Some observers have interpreted recent State activity in Syria as giving the 'final push' to a change in the law.[41] In view of significant State practice supporting a broader understanding of self-defence, and in view of widespread scholarly endorsement of this broad reading,[42] it partly seemed as if, in the words of van Steenberghe, 'the orthodoxy on the law on the use of force has

---

Resolution 2249 will likely be viewed as confirming that use of force in self-defense is now permissible against non-State actors where the territorial State is unable to suppress the threat that they pose.' Michael Wood, 'The Use of Force in 2015 with Particular Reference to Syria', Hebrew University of Jerusalem Legal Studies Research Paper Series 16-05 (2016), 8: '[I]t is difficult to read the resolution otherwise than as an endorsement . . . of the use of force in self-defence against an ongoing or imminent armed attack by Da'esh, a non-State actor.'

[38] See UN Doc. S/2014/695, 23 September 2014 (USA); UN Doc. S/2015/563, 24 July 2015 (Turkey); UN Doc. S/2015/221, 31 March 2015 (Canada); UN Doc. S/2015/693, 9 September 2015 (Australia).

[39] UN Doc. S/2016/523, 9 June 2016 (Belgium); UN Doc. S/2015/946, 10 December 2015 (Germany).

[40] UN Doc. S/2018/53, 22 January 2018 (Turkey); see the critical analysis of Anne Peters, 'The Turkish Operation in Afrin (Syria) and the Silence of the Lambs', *EJIL Talk!*, 30 January 2018, available at www.ejiltalk.org/the-turkish-operation-in-afrin-syria-and-the-sile nce-of-the-lambs.

[41] Scharf, 'How the War against ISIS Changed International Law' 2016 (n. 37), 66.

[42] See e.g. Kimberley N. Trapp, 'Back to Basics: Necessity, Proportionality, and the Right of Self-Defence against Non-State Terrorist Actors', *International and Comparative Law Quarterly* 56 (2007), 141–56 (147); Noam Lubell, *Extraterritorial Use of Force against Non-State Actors* (Oxford: Oxford University Press, 2010), 42; Yoram Dinstein, *War Aggression and Self-Defence* (Cambridge: Cambridge University Press, 5th edn., 2012), 227–30; Ashley Deeks, 'Unwilling or Unable: Toward a Normative Framework for Extra-Territorial Self-Defense', *Virginia Journal of International Law* 52 (2012), 483–550 (486); Wood, 'The Use of Force in 2015' 2016 (n. 37), 1, 8; see also the five contributions (Frowein, Oellers-Frahm, Kouzigou, Keinan, Tams) in the section 'expansionist positions' in Anne Peters and Christian Marxsen (guest eds.), 'Self-Defence against Non-State Actors: Impulses from the Max Planck Trialogues on the Law of Peace and War', *Heidelberg Journal of International Law* 77 (2017), 1–93 (15–45).

dramatically switched from a restrictivist to an expansionist perspective.'[43] However, pronounced scepticism towards the broader reading,[44] notably against the 'unwilling or unable' formula,[45] persists. An important academic action was the 'Plea against the Abusive Invocation of Self-Defence as a Response to Terrorism', initiated by Olivier Corten in 2016, which found the support of more than 240 international lawyers and professors from a wide range of countries.[46] The plea explicitly rejects the 'unable' part of the 'unwilling or unable' doctrine[47] and perceives 'a serious risk of self-defence becoming an alibi, used systematically to justify the unilateral launching of military operations around the world'.[48] Further commentators criticise the 'unable or unwilling' standard from the perspective of weaker States, and in particular the Global South, as 'ignoring the unequal international environment in which the doctrine operates'.[49] This doctrine will not apply in powerful States, but it is a legal framework for what Jochen von Bernstorff has called the 'semi-periphery'-States 'that do not belong to the inner circle or are not powerful enough to resist the application of the regime'.[50] In this vein, the 'unwilling or unable' standard has been especially criticised from a post-colonial perspective as a vehicle for 'reintroduc[ing] a hierarchy of States in the operation of *jus ad bellum*' –

[43] Raphaël van Steenberghe, 'The Law of Self-Defense and the New Argumentative Landscape on the Expansionists' Side', *Leiden Journal of International Law* 29 (2016), 43–65 (43). The terms 'restrictivist' and 'expansionist' are meanwhile widely used, although they are controversial and might be criticised for their evaluative overtones.

[44] Peter Hilpold, 'The Applicability of Article 51 UN Charter to Asymmetric Wars', in Hans-Joachim Heintze and Pierre Thielbörger (eds.), *From Cold War to Cyber War: The Evolution of the International Law of Peace and Armed Conflict over the Last 25 Years* (Cham: Springer, 2016), 127–35 (129); Jochen von Bernstorff, 'Drone Strikes, Terrorism and the Zombie: On the Construction of an Administrative Law of Transnational Executions', *ESIL Reflections*, 5(7) (2016), available at www.esil-sedi.eu/node/1368; see also the eight contributions (Corten, Christakis, Oesterdahl, Kawagishi, Urs, Giacco, Sjöstedt, and Hartwig) in the section 'restrictivist positions' in Peters and Marxsen, 'Self-Defence against Non-State Actors' 2017 (n. 42), 15–45.

[45] See, for a lucid critique from a Fullerian perspective, Brunnée and Toope, 'Self-Defence against Non-State Actors' 2018 (n. 27); Olivier Corten, 'The "Unwilling or Unable" Test: Has It Been, and Could It Be, Accepted?', *Leiden Journal of International Law* 29 (2016), 777–99; Paulina Starski, 'Right to Self-Defense, Attribution and the Non-State Actor: Birth of the "Unable or Unwilling" Standard?', *Heidelberg Journal of International Law* 75 (2015), 455–501 (496–97).

[46] http://cdi.ulb.ac.be/wp-content/uploads/2016/06/Liste-prof-et-assistants-oct.pdf.

[47] 'A Plea against the Abusive Invocation of Self-Defence as a Response to Terrorism, 6 October 2016, available at http://cdi.ulb.ac.be/contre-invocation-abusive-de-legitime-defen se-faire-face-defi-terrorisme: '[T]he mere fact that, despite its efforts, a State is unable to put an end to terrorist activities on its territory is insufficient to justify bombing that State's territory without its consent.'

[48] *Ibid.*

[49] Dawood I. Ahmed, 'Defending Weak States against the Unwilling or Unable Doctrine of Self-Defense', *Journal of International Law and International Relations* 9 (2013), 1–37 (36).

[50] von Bernstorff, 'Drone Strikes, Terrorism and the Zombie' 2016 (n. 44).

a hierarchy that echoes 'the infamous nineteenth-century distinction between civilized, semi-civilized and uncivilized states'.[51]

III. THREE PERSPECTIVES IN A TRIALOGUE

Against this background, this Trialogue raises a seemingly simple yet complex set of interrelated questions. Does international law as it stands allow for self-defence against non-State actors on the territory of a non-consenting State? Has an evolution of the law occurred in this regard, and, if yes, when and how? Assuming there has been legal evolution, what does this mean in terms of legal policy? What are the repercussions for the entire regime of the *ius contra bellum*, and for the international legal order at large?

The first two questions are primarily doctrinal, about the current state of law and the modes of legal change. Answering them requires an engagement with the doctrines on the sources of international law and hence with recent State practice. The aim is to identify whether and to what extent the numerous proposals and normative claims about self-defence that have been brought up in practice and theory have actually solidified into hard international rules and generally accepted interpretations.

As explained in the Introduction to the series, it is the characteristic feature of a Trialogue to approach the research questions from three perspectives which differ in terms of regional background, technical method, and world-view of the discussants.[52] Dire Tladi was invited to the Trialogue for his unique experience as a South African scholar and Professor of International Law at the University of Pretoria who has, at the same time, significant experience in the practice of international law. In addition to his academic appointments and scholarly work, he has served as the Principal State Law Adviser for International Law for the South African Department of International Relations and Cooperation and as legal adviser to the South African Permanent Mission to the United Nations. Moreover, he is a member of the International Law Commission and its Special Rapporteur on Peremptory Norms of General International Law (*Jus Cogens*). With such a background, Tladi is in a position to clearly assess the consequences of an extended reading of self-defence for States that are potentially not powerful enough to resist outside intervention in the fight against terrorism.

[51] Ntina Tzouvala, 'TWAIL and the "Unwilling or Unable" Doctrine: Continuities and Ruptures', *AJIL Unbound* 109 (2015), 266–70 (267).
[52] See Anne Peters, 'Trialogical International Law – Introduction to the Series', in this volume.

In his contribution to this Trialogue, Tladi espouses a 'positivist approach to the identification of the law',[53] aiming for the 'objectively correct interpretation' of the rules of international law on self-defence.[54] He offers an account of self-defence whose core is the embeddedness of this legal institution within a system of collective security. Tladi sets out the principles of the prohibition on the use of force and of collective security. Then, based on arguments of context and purpose, he advocates what has long been the largely uncontroversial interpretation, namely a State-centred reading of the rules on self-defence which requires attribution of the strikes by the non-State actors to a State. He accepts the possibility that State practice, whether as a constituent element of customary international law or as subsequent interpretation of article 51, can affect the State-centred interpretation of the law on self-defence. Having assessed the practice that is often put forward in support of a shift, including the interventions in Afghanistan and Syria, he concludes that the established notion of self-defence as requiring an armed attack from a State is still good law and has not been changed.

The second co-author of the Trialogue is Christian Tams, Professor of International Law at the University of Glasgow. Tams received his legal education in both Germany and the United Kingdom, and was invited to the Trialogue as someone who has been exposed to both the doctrinal rigour of the German legal system as well as to the case- and practice-oriented perspective commonly found in the Anglo-Saxon approach to international law.

Tams frames the issue of the legality of self-defence against non-State actors as a pure question of treaty interpretation, namely of the interpretation of the term 'armed attack' contained in Article 51 of the UN Charter. Tams essentially follows the structure of Articles 31 and 32 VCLT as a guideline to interpretation and provides a rich discussion of the wording, context, object and purpose as well as the preparatory work. His main focus rests on a discussion of practice since 1945. He embraces what he has described elsewhere as 'the uncertainty of old', arguing that self-defence against non-State actors has always been present in international practice since the foundation of the UN.[55] Tams rejects what he calls the 'popular narrative'. According to that narrative, the 'law of self-defence was "sufficiently clear"' until the 1990s or even until 2001, when (potentially)

---

[53] Tladi in this volume, 21.
[54] Tladi in this volume, 17.
[55] Christian Tams, 'Embracing the Uncertainty of Old: Armed Attacks by Non-State Actors prior to 9/11', *Heidelberg Journal of International Law* 77 (2017), 61–4.

a sudden shift in practice and law was triggered by the events of 9/11.[56] Tams thus departs from a different starting point than Tladi for his legal assessment. In Tams' view, we should not presume a basically unequivocal old State-centred law whose changes we ought to discuss in light of recent State practice based on new legal justifications. Rather, State practice, e.g. in Afghanistan and Syria, only carries on and has thereby intensified the legal justifications that were present before. The law was – so Tams argues – uncertain in the first place. Therefore, importantly, the standards for the operation of 'a change in the law' are significantly different from, if not actually lower than for, constellations in which an old rule was clear and strong. In discussing recent events as 'subsequent practice' (in the sense of Article 31(3)(b) VCLT) against the backdrop of 'the uncertainty of old', Tams arrives at the conclusion that international law in principle does allow for self-defence actions to be taken against non-State actors, independently of any attribution to a State.

The third co-author of the Trialogue is Mary Ellen O'Connell, Professor of International Law at the University of Notre Dame in the United States. She received her legal education in the United Kingdom and the US, and has specialised in the law of the use of force and has, *inter alia*, chaired the Use of Force Committee of the International Law Association and was a professional military educator for the US Department of Defense in Germany for several years. We invited her to the Trialogue for her normative approach to international law, at the core of which is a strong sceptical attitude toward the utility and morality of using military force.

Mary Ellen O'Connell's reading of the UN Charter is underpinned by natural law theory that she regards as the basis of the prohibition on the use of force. She generally shares Dire Tladi's argumentative direction by rejecting an extended reading of self-defence. She identifies and discusses three 'pernicious doctrines of expansive self-defence',[57] namely the assertion of a right to defend oneself against imminent attacks, the treatment of terrorist crimes as armed attacks, and the assertion of the 'unwilling or unable' doctrine to satisfy or substitute for the requirements of attribution or consent. With Dire Tladi, and in contrast to Christian Tams, she shares the assumption of a clear State-oriented character of the *ius contra bellum*. In contrast to Tladi, however, her main argument does not rest on an interpretation of recent State practice. Rather, central to O'Connell's argument is what she defines as the natural law/*ius cogens* character of

---

[56] Tams in this volume, 136.
[57] O'Connell in this volume, section III, 212–28.

the prohibition on the use of force and its exceptions. In her understanding, the *ius cogens* character restricts the possibility of derogation. This means that the prohibition may not be reduced or diluted by means of subsequent practice; and this guarantees that the law is not affected by contrary practice.

We hope that the readers of the three contributions will, not least through the numerous cross-references, be able to trace the trialogical exchange of arguments and considerations, and sense not only the tensions and undercurrents but also identify the concessions and winning arguments, and ultimately be empowered to form a better informed view on the legality, the politics, and the morality of self-defence against non-State actors.

1

The Use of Force in Self-Defence against Non-State Actors, Decline of Collective Security and the Rise of Unilateralism: Whither International Law?

Dire Tladi

I. INTRODUCTION

A. *Importance and Controversy of the Law on the Use of Force*

This Trialogue concerns the use of force in self-defence against non-State actors in the territory of third States under international law. International law relating to the use of force, in particular international law on the rules of self-defence, is immensely important. It is immensely important because one of the most fundamental objectives of modern international law, and an over-riding objective of the UN Charter, is the prevention of war.[1] International law on the use of force provides the framework within which the objective recited in the preamble of the UN Charter to 'save succeeding generations from the scourge of war' is pursued by the United Nations. Having clear and precise scope and limits of this law is necessary to achieving this lofty objective. Yet the importance of the international law on the use of force is matched by the controversy surrounding the very scope and limits of the law on the use of force.

In many ways, as will become clear in the course of this chapter, the controversy is centred not so much around the use of force *per se*, but rather on the right to use force unilaterally. Collective use of force in accordance with the Charter of the United Nations – in principle this refers to the use of force authorised by the UN Security Council – does not raise the same controversies as those raised in this chapter. This is not to say that collective

---

[1] See Nikolas Stürchler, *The Threat of Force in International Law* (Cambridge: Cambridge University Press, 2007), 267. See also Marcelo Kohen, 'The Use of Force by the United States After the End of the Cold War, and its Impact on International Law', in Michael Byers and Georg Nolte (eds.), *United States Hegemony and the Foundations of International Law* (Cambridge: Cambridge University Press, 2003), 197–231 (197).

use of force does not raise controversies at all, for it surely does. Whether the Council has unlimited power to authorise force, who may be the addressees of the authorisation, under what circumstances force may be authorised and for what purpose are some of the issues that have been the subject of much intellectual discourse over the course of the UN Charter's existence.[2] Similarly, the very question of what constitutes 'collective use of force', beyond explicit authorisation of the UN Security Council, remains an issue of debate. Can, for example, action under the North Atlantic Treaty Organisation (NATO), or the African Union (AU) without UN Security Council authorisation qualify as collective measures under the Charter?[3] These issues, interesting though they are, fall beyond the scope of this contribution. Instead, the controversy that this chapter concerns itself with is that relating to the unilateral use of force.

The controversy surrounding the law on the unilateral use of force is manifested in different ways. None, however, is as pronounced as the controversies concerning the unilateral use of force in self-defence. The debate concerning humanitarian intervention is, for example, largely *passé*, since the concept is rejected by a large majority of States.[4] The controversy concerning the right to use force unilaterally in self-defence raises questions concerning the requirements for self-defence, the precise limits of which appear sufficiently malleable to attract widely divergent approaches.[5] Some scholars and States adopt a generous and permissive approach to the law on self-defence, granting States a comparatively large margin to decide when, how and under

---

[2]   See, e.g. Dan Sarooshi, *The United Nations and the Development of Collective Security: The Delegation by the UN Security Council of its Chapter VII Powers* (Oxford: Clarendon Press, 1999).

[3]   See, e.g. Article 4(h) AU Constitutive Act of 2002. See also AU Decision on the Operationalisation of the African Capacity for Immediate Response to Crisis, Assembly/AU/Dec.515 (XXII), 30–31 January 2014.

[4]   The doctrine of the responsibility to protect is seen largely as a replacement of humanitarian intervention. However, responsibility to protect offers little value from a legal perspective since its invocation would require a UN Security Council authorisation. The legal justification, when force is used pursuant to responsibility to protect, would therefore be the authorisation by the United Nations. For discussion see Dire Tladi, 'The Intervention in Côte d'Ivoire (2011)', in Tom Ruys and Olivier Corten (eds.), *The Use of Force in International Law: A Case-Based Approach* (Oxford: Oxford University Press, 2018).

[5]   See Christine Gray, *International Law and the Use of Force* (Oxford: Oxford University Press, 3rd edn., 2008), 114, stating that the 'law on self-defence is the subject of the most fundamental disagreement between states and between writers'. See also Kimberley N. Trapp, 'Back to Basics: Necessity, Proportionality, and the Right of Self-Defence as against Non-State Terrorist Actors', *International and Comparative Law Quarterly* 56 (2007), 141–56 (141). See for further discussion Martin Dixon, *Textbook on International Law* (Oxford: Oxford University Press, 7th edn., 2013), 325.

what circumstances force may be used in self-defence, which in turn means a narrow approach to the prohibition on the use of force.[6] Others, on the other hand, adopt a more restrictive approach to the use of force in self-defence, which, in turn, implies a generous approach to the prohibition of the use of force. Commenting on the contrast between the restrictive and permissive approaches, Arimatsu and Schmitt state that there is

> inherent ambiguity in the law governing the use of force by States. Such ambiguity should not be surprising because States are caught on the horns of a dilemma. On the one hand, clear and restrictive norms serve to enhance international peace and security by limiting what States may do in terms of force. Yet, on the other, opacity benefits the State when it is facing threats.[7]

Very often, the question whether particular acts of self-defence are in conformity with international law is considered from the perspective of legal rules on proportionality and necessity,[8] and rules concerning anticipatory self-defence.[9] The latest, and perhaps most complicated, controversy surrounds the question of whether force may be used in self-defence against non-State actors in the territory of a third State. There is a growing trend, including in the writings of some commentators and the views and actions of some States, suggesting that force may be used against non-State actors in the

[6] See Lauri Hannikainen, 'The World After 11 September 2001: Is the Prohibition of the Use of Force Disintegrating?', in Jarna Petman and Jan Klabbers (eds.), *Nordic Cosmopolitanism: Essays in International Law for Martti Koskenniemi* (Leiden: Nijhoff, 2003), 445–68 (448) ('some States have interpreted the prohibition of the use of armed force and the right of self-defence liberally in such a way that they have multiple grounds to resort to armed force').

[7] Louise Arimatsu and Michael Schmitt, 'Attacking "Islamic State" and the Khorasan Group: Surveying the International Law Landscape', *Columbia Journal of Transnational Law Bulletin* 53 (2014), 1–29 (29).

[8] See, e.g., statements by Mr Gambari (on behalf of the Secretary-General), Mr Dolgov (Russia), Mr Mayoral (Argentina), Mr Liu Zhengmin (China), Mr Emyr Jones Perry (United Kingdom), Mr Ikouebe (Congo), Mr Mahiga (Tanzania), Ms Løj (Denmark), Mr Mlynàr (Slovakia), Mrs Papadopoulou (Greece) and Mr De la Sablière (France) during the UN Security Council Debate on the Situation in the Middle East and the Use of Force by Israel in Lebanon, on 14 July 2006, UN Doc. S/PV.5489. See also Gray, *International Law and the Use of Force* 2008 (n. 5), 149, 166; Albrecht Randelzhofer and Georg Nolte, 'Article 51', in Bruno Simma, Daniel-Erasmus Khan, Georg Nolte and Andreas Paulus (eds.), *The Charter of the United Nations: A Commentary* (Oxford: Oxford University Press, 3rd edn., 2012), vol. II, 1397–428 (1425). See generally Judith Gardam, *Necessity, Proportionality and the Use of Force by States* (Cambridge: Cambridge University Press, 2004).

[9] See for discussion Ian Brownlie, *Principles of Public International Law* (Oxford: Oxford University Press, 6th edn., 2003), 701; Peter Malanczuk, *Akehurst's Modern Introduction to International Law* (London: Routledge, 7th revised edn., 2003); Christine Gray, 'The Use of Force and the International Legal Order', in Malcolm D. Evans (ed.), *International Law* (Oxford: Oxford University Press, 4th edn., 2014), 618–48 (630).

territory of innocent third States.[10] It is this question that this Trialogue is concerned with.

When these various aspects affecting the scope of the prohibition on the use of force are placed in a single crucible, the possible interpretations of what is permissible under international law on the use of force become many – almost indeterminable. At the narrowest end of the spectrum, the use of force in self-defence would only be permitted in cases where an armed attack by a State has already commenced. At the other, more permissive, end of the spectrum, the use of force would be permitted where there is a possibility of an attack by a non-State actor operating on the territory of a third State. Between these possibilities, and taking into account the fact or circumstance specific dimensions pertaining to proportionality and necessity, there is a continuum of other options on the scope of the right to use force in self-defence. The argument in this contribution is that there is an objectively correct interpretation of the rules on the use of force which can be discovered by the proper application of the tools of interpretation and methodology of international law.[11]

B. The Role of Policy Considerations

While there is an objectively correct interpretation of the rules on the use of force, it is also true that law does not exist in a vacuum. Law exists in the real world, to curb real-world problems. Policy considerations, therefore, tend to play a significant role in the approach that States and commentators take with respect to law, in particular international law. This also applies to the law on the use of force and, in particular, the right to use force in self-defence. That policy considerations play a role, however, should not be taken to mean that law does not provide objectively correct answers or that the law is, so to speak, in the eye of the beholder. Such approaches risk undermining the rules of international law and the UN's objective to 'save succeeding generations from the scourge of war'.

Policy considerations have a direct influence on the content of objective law in a number of ways. Policy considerations may provide context for the interpretation of rules of law, whether this is through the 'object and purpose',

---

[10] See, e.g. Sean D. Murphy, 'Self-Defence and the Israeli Wall Advisory Opinion: An *Ipse Dixit* from the ICJ?', *American Journal of International Law* 99 (2005), 62–7 (62); Jordan Paust, 'Self-Defence Targeting of Non-State Actors and Permissibility of US Use of Drones in Pakistan', *Journal of Transnational Law and Policy* 19 (2010), 237–80 (237). See for comparison Christian Tams, 'The Use of Force against Terrorists', *European Journal of International Law* 20 (2009), 359–97 (359).

[11] See, e.g. Georg Nolte, 'Introduction', in Helmut Philipp Aust/Georg Nolte (eds.), *The Interpretation of International Law by Domestic Courts: Uniformity, Diversity, Convergence* (Oxford: Oxford University Press, 2016), 1–7 (3).

'context' or 'relevant rules of international law' elements of interpretation, or the assessment of practice, either for the purpose of treaty interpretation (cf. Article 31(3) of the Vienna Convention on the Law of Treaties –VCLT)[12] or formation of customary international law. More importantly, policy considerations influence how States behave and, consequently, will affect practice, which is central to both the evolution and interpretation of law. It is important to stress, however, that the policy considerations do not replace law, but rather influence its development and assessment.

One important policy consideration that may well influence the evolution of the law is the change in the nature of conflict from purely inter-State to intra-State conflict involving non-State actors and the growth of terrorism as a new threat to international stability. The terrorist attack of September 2001 in the territory of the United States has, largely because of US dominance in international affairs, caused a shift in strategies to combat terrorism.[13] More broadly, the emergence of non-State entities such as Al-Qaeda (responsible for those attacks in September 2001), Boko Haram, Al-Shabaab and more recently the Islamic State of Iraq and Syria (ISIS), has changed the nature of terrorism, and this *may* necessitate new strategies for confronting terrorism, including the use of force as a response strategy.[14] The rise in terrorism could be a basis for turning away from the prohibition of force as a legal norm. As a policy matter, it may well be asked why a State like Nigeria should not have the right to use force against Boko Haram if it is operating from Cameroon or the Central African Republic to launch attacks in its territory. As a policy question it may also be asked whether non-State actors operating in failed States should be permitted to carry out 'armed attacks' against innocent third States without consequences because rules of international law permit the use of force in defence only against culpable States. Should, in the light of these realities (situation on the ground), States be afforded a greater margin to unilaterally use force 'in self-defence'?

---

[12] Vienna Convention on the Law of Treaties, 23 May 1969, 1155 UNTS 331.

[13] Speaking in the aftermath of the 11 September 2001 attacks, the UN Secretary-General called terrorism 'a global menace' that called for 'a united, global response'. See 'True Faith is Respectful, Compassionate, Devoid of Hatred, Says Secretary-General at Temple Emanu-El in New York', UN Press Release SG/SM/7962/Rev.1 of 18 September 2001.

[14] See Eric Rosand, 'The UN Response to the Evolving Threat of Global Terrorism: Institutional Reform, Rivalry or Renewal?', in Peter G. Danchin and Horst Fischer (eds.), *United Nations Reform and the New Collective Security* (Cambridge: Cambridge University Press, 2010), 250–81 (250), who notes that terrorism itself is not a new phenomenon. Rather, he observes, what has changed 'is the dramatic increase in the number of terrorist attacks around the globe by stateless international groups, including Islamists terrorists groups'. See also Lindsay Moir, *Reappraising the Resort to Force: International Law, Jus ad Bellum and the War on Terror* (Oxford: Hart, 2010), 1.

These policy considerations, flowing from 'facts on the ground', can have three different possible impacts on the law.[15] First, they may suggest a need to elastically interpret the rules of the Charter to enable a broader interpretation of the rules. Second, they may require us to jettison altogether the rules of law relating to the use of force to permit a completely unrestrained right to use force unilaterally. Glennon, for example, has asserted that given the realities on the ground, the insistence on the rules of international law on the use of force is 'illusory'.[16] A third possibility is the argument that, independent of the growth in terrorism, the rules of international law on the use of force in self-defence have always been permissive.

These realities on the ground could influence policy positions concerning how broad or narrow to interpret the law on the use force in self-defence. To influence the development (or evolution) of international law, however, requires that they also influence the practice of States. In other words, it is not enough to show that policy or normative considerations require a particular – narrow or broad – interpretation of the rules on the use of force in self-defence. To influence the development of the law, it is necessary to show that these policy and normative considerations have influenced the practice of States, either for the purpose of the formation of customary international law or treaty interpretation.

C. The Purpose of the Chapter

This chapter of the Trialogue focuses on a specific problem,[17] namely whether international law permits the use of force in self-defence in the territory of

---

[15] See, e.g. Tams, 'The Use of Force against Terrorists' 2009 (n. 10), especially at 381.

[16] See, e.g. Michael J. Glennon, 'The Fog of Law: Self-Defence, Inherence, and Incoherence in Article 51 of the United Nations Charter', *Harvard Journal of Law and Public Policy* 25 (2001/2), 539–58 (549): 'The international system has come to subsist in a parallel universe of two systems, one *de jure*, the other *de facto*. The *de jure* system consists of illusory rules that would govern the use of force among states in a platonic world of forms, a world that does not exist. The *de facto* system consists of actual practice in the real world, a world in which states weigh costs against benefits in regular disregard of the rules solemnly proclaimed in the all-but-ignored *de jure* system. This decaying *de jure* catechism is overly schematised and scholastic, disconnected from state behaviour, and unrealistic in its aspirations for state conduct.' See also Thomas M. Franck, 'What Happens Now? The United Nations After Iraq', *American Journal of International Law* 97 (2003), 607–20 (608); Peter G. Danchin, 'Things Fall Apart: The Concept of Collective Security in International Law', in Danchin and Fischer, United Nations Reform (n. 14), 35–75 (53), described commentators such as Glennon as 'representing or sympathetic to the interests of the bigger or more powerful states', who assert that 'international law [. . . is] founded on "speculative utopias", and thus too far removed from the factual realities of politics'.

[17] This contribution provides an expanded account of the views of the author in publications and articles as follows: Dire Tladi, 'The Nonconsenting Innocent State: The Problem with Bethlehem's Principle 12', *American Journal of International Law* 107 (2013), 570–6;

a State that has not consented and to which the actions of the non-State actors cannot be attributed – referred to in a previous contribution by the author as 'innocent States'.[18] The phrase 'innocent State' in this context means nothing more than a State on which an armed attack cannot be attributed. The relevant States may be less than innocent in general (they may even be generally 'evil'). Their 'innocence' in this regard is a shorthand denoting only that they are 'innocent' of the acts of the non-State actor, or that the acts of the non-State actor are not attributable to them.

Most authors agree that the starting point for any attempt to decipher the rules under international law relating to the use of force must be Article 2(4) and Article 51 of the UN Charter.[19] However, it is also important to understand these provisions as part of the larger system of collective security established under the Charter. Interpreting their precise scope and limits must, therefore, be informed by the context of the system of collective security. The collective security system will therefore be described with a view to providing context for the interpretation of the rules on the use of force in self-defence.

The next section seeks to identify core elements of the prohibition of the use of force. Section III provides a sketch of the collective security system established by the Charter, of which the prohibition of the use of force and the exception permitting the use of force in defence in Article 51 are a part. Section IV presents the arguments often advanced for an expansive reading of self-defence which would permit the right to use force against non-State actors in the territory of innocent third States. These arguments are based mainly on an assessment of practice. Section V evaluates the arguments for an expansive interpretation of self-defence based on the tools and methodology of interpretation under international law. Section VI considers the legal and policy implications of the opposing interpretations of the right to self-defence. This contribution makes the following conclusions. First, the practice often referred to in support of the expansive interpretation of self-defence cannot sustain the argument for an expansive interpretation. Second, the rules of interpretation support a narrow reading of self-defence in which attribution of the acts of non-State actors to the third State is required in order to allow for self-defence on the

Dire Tladi, 'The Use of Force in Self Defence against Non-State Actors in International Law: Recalling the Foundational Principles of International Law', *Zanzibar Yearbook of Law* 2 (2012), 71–87; Dire Tladi and Maryam Shaqra, 'Assessing the Legality of Coalition Air Strikes Targeting the Islamic State in Iraq and the Levant (ISIS) in Syria under International Law', *South African Yearbook of International Law* 40 (2015) 281–96; see also Dire Tladi on the Use of Force in Self-Defence against Non-State Actors, UN Audio-Visual Library, 10 April 2013.

[18] Tladi, 'The Nonconsenting Innocent State' 2013 (n. 17).
[19] See, e.g. Gray, *International Law and the Use of Force* 2008 (n. 5), 6.

territory of that third State. Third, the collective security system, established by the Charter, which seeks to prevent unilateral use of force, provides further support for an attribution-based approach to self-defence.

It is worth setting out, at the outset, the approach and normative premises from which the chapter proceeds. First, this chapter is grounded in a positivist approach to the identification of the law. In other words, as described above, policy considerations are relevant only to the extent that they are supported by the traditional materials for the identification and interpretation of law. Second, powerful States tend to seek to 'de-constrain' themselves from the shackles of law while leaving the illusion of the constraining power of law in order to constrain the less powerful.[20] I am thus concerned about – and thus seek to avoid – an interpretation of law that facilitates the 'de-constraining' through an expansive interpretation that may permit the limits of the right to use force in self-defence to be in the eye of the beholder and thus benefit the (militarily) powerful. The position, however, is not merely a policy preference, it is also one which is grounded in the law.

A final preliminary point concerning the approach in this chapter: I adopt a decidedly doctrinal approach to the question of the use of force against non-State actors and refuse to be engaged with what may be termed a 'fact or circumstance specific' approach. 'Fact or circumstance specific' approaches suggest that the dangers of a broad interpretation of the right to use force in self-defence against non-State actors can be addressed by reliance on concepts such as proportionality and necessity as requirements of self-defence. The problem with these approaches is that they assume, incorrectly in my view, that, in principle, international law permits the use of force in self-defence against non-State actors in the territory of non-consenting third States. The 'fact or circumstance specific' approaches obviate the need to address the principles of the prohibition on the use of force and places us on a slippery slope. It is a reflection of a trend to chip away at the legal principle itself and to leave us at the point where the law is really in the eye of the beholder. Where there are no principle constraints against the use of force, and the facts and circumstances constrain behaviour, it becomes easier, in politically conveni-ent circumstances, to suggest that the law permits a particular course of action. The reliance on facts or circumstance specific arguments is, in my view, the road to erosion of the law prohibiting the use of force.

---

[20] A related, but altogether different point, is reflected in Christian Marxsen, 'International Law in Crisis: Russia's Struggle for Recognition', *German Yearbook of International Law* 58 (2015), 11–48 (13). It is different because Russia cannot reasonably be described as 'less powerful'. But it is related because it seeks to show how arguments promoting permissiveness used by the 'more powerful' are resisted when used by the 'less powerful'.

II. PROHIBITION ON THE USE OF FORCE

A. *A Brief Historical Context*

It is now beyond dispute that international law prohibits the use of force and Article 2(4) of the Charter reflects the basic rule concerning the use of force. As with any other provision of any treaty, Article 2(4) of the Charter is to be interpreted using the rules of interpretation of international law. Nonetheless, to grasp the breadth (and limits) of the prohibition on the use of force requires an understanding of the historical evolution of the prohibition under international law. This historical evolution provides context to the rule in Article 2(4). Moreover, as will be seen below, a historical event, namely the *Caroline incident*, forms a central element of the argument in favour of permitting the use of force in self-defence against non-State actors in the territory of third States. It is therefore apposite to begin the analysis by a description of the history of the prohibition of the use of force in international law.

International law did not always prohibit the use of force as an instrument of foreign policy.[21] The *Caroline* incident should be seen in the light of the nature of pre-twentieth-century international law, based on a bundle of bilateral relations, in contrast to the new international law based on community values.[22] In this classical international law, States, as sovereign entities, were free to determine the nature of their international relations including by relying on the comparative advantage of military might.

The view that international law has always prohibited the resort to force is often based on the just war theory. Yet as Randelzhofer and Dörr correctly observe, 'the medieval theory of *bellum iustum* had been developed by theologians and was never a valid rule of public international law.'[23] For others, the widely cited *Caroline* incident– involving an exchange in 1842 between the United States and the United Kingdom on the use of force by the latter on the territory of the former – is often advanced as an illustration that the use of

---

[21]   For another view supporting the idea that international law has always prohibited the resort to force, see Mark W. Janis, *An Introduction to International Law* (New York: Aspen Publishers, 3rd edn., 1999), 168 *et seq.*

[22]   On the transition of international law from sovereignty-centred to a community-based, see Bruno Simma, 'From Bilateralism to Community Interests in International Law', *Recueil des Cours* 250 (1994), 217–384. See also John Dugard, 'The Future of International Law: A Human Rights Perspective – With Some Comments on the Leiden School of International Law', *Leiden Journal of International Law* 20 (2007), 729–39 (731); Emmanuelle Jouannet, 'Universalism and Imperialism: The True–False Paradox of International Law', *European Journal of International Law* 18 (2007), 379–407 (379).

[23]   Albrecht Randelzhofer and Oliver Dörr, 'Article 2(4)', in Simma, Khan, Nolte and Paulus, *The Charter of the United Nations* 2012 (n. 8), vol. I, 200–34 (204).

force was prohibited in the nineteenth century.[24] However, it is not at all clear that the exchange between Lord Ashburton, for the United Kingdom, and Daniel Webster, for the United States, was meant to convey *legal* propositions. Justification for the use of force, in particular self-defence, was often advanced for 'political expediency' and in 'order to secure moral high ground', rather than as a shield against legal wrongfulness.[25] In this regard, in the exchange Lord Ashburton declares that it should not be lightly assumed that the United Kingdom would 'provoke a great and powerful neighbour' – a clear appeal to the political and expediency.[26] Brownlie similarly states that the reference to the *Caroline* incident 'as the critical date for the customary international law' on self-defence is both 'anachronistic and indefensible'.[27] The position advanced by Randelzhofer and Dörr, that up and until 1919 public international law 'did not know any rules about when it [was] permissible to wage war' and that the use of force was 'permitted in the relations between States without any conditions',[28] is therefore the correct position in law.

B. The Content and Status of the Prohibition

The right to use force in self-defence is an exception to a general rule, namely the prohibition on the threat or use of force. The content of the exception – the right to use force in self-defence – can only be understood in the light of the general rule – the prohibition on the use of force.[29] While Randelzhofer and Dörr state that the two provisions 'do not exactly correspond to one another in scope', they do suggest the phrase 'armed attack', used in Article 51, is narrower

---

[24] The exchange between the United States and United Kingdom governments is reproduced in full in John B. Moore, *Digest of International Law as Embodied in Diplomatic Discussions, Treaties and Other International Agreements: Volume II* (Washington: US Government Printing Office, 1906), 409–13. An example of those who view the incident as constituting customary international law is Anthony Clarke Arend, 'International Law and Preemptive Use of Military Force', *The Washington Quarterly* 26 (2003), 89–103 (90). For similar suggestions, see Chris Richter, 'Pre-emptive Self-Defence, International Law and US Policy', *Dialogue* 1 (2003) 55–66 (57); Paust, 'Self-Defence Targeting of Non-State Actors' 2010 (n. 10), 241; Murphy, 'Self-Defence and the Israeli Wall Advisory Opinion' 2005 (n. 10), 65.

[25] Dire Tladi and John Dugard "The Use of Force by States" in John Dugard, Max du Plessis and Dire Tladi (eds.), *Dugard's International Law: A South African Perspective* (Cape Town: Juta, 5th edn., 2019), 729.

[26] Letter by Ashburton in Moore, *Digest of International Law* 1906 (n. 24), 412.

[27] Brownlie, *Principles of Public International Law* 2003 (n. 9), 701.

[28] Randelzhofer and Dörr, 'Article 2(4)' 2012 (n. 23), 204. See also Edward Gordon, 'Article 2(4) in Historical Context', *Yale Journal of International Law* 10 (1985), 271–8 (271). See further, W. Michael Reisman, 'Coercion and Self-Determination: Construing Charter Article 2(4)', *American Journal of International Law* 78 (1984), 642–5 (642).

[29] Randelzhofer and Dörr, 'Article 2(4)' 2012 (n. 23), 214, para. 15.

than the notion of 'use of force'.[30] Determining the scope of Article 2(4) can therefore be useful in identifying at least the limits of what is meant by 'armed attack' in Article 51. As a treaty rule, the prohibition on the use of force is to be found in Article 2(4) of the Charter of the United Nations. It provides as follows:

> All members shall refrain in their international relations from the threat or use of force against the territorial integrity or political independence of any State, or in any other manner inconsistent with the Purposes of the United Nations.

The ICJ, in the *Military and Paramilitary Activities* case, identified several key aspects of the prohibition. First, the Court made the distinction between, on the one hand, 'the most grave forms of the use of force' and, on the other hand, 'other less grave forms' of the use of force.[31] According to the Court, it is the former forms of the use of force – the most grave forms – that constitute an armed attack.[32] Other 'less grave forms' of the use of force remain, none-theless, prohibited by Article 2(4). It appears that the significance of the distinction by the Court is that the right to use of force in self-defence, in terms of Article 51 of the Charter, applies in respect to an armed attack, i.e. 'the most grave forms of the use of force' and not to 'other less grave forms'.[33] As a consequence of this distinction, the Court states that 'assistance to rebels ... in the form of provision of weapons or logistical support ... may be regarded as threat or use of force' but not armed attack.[34] Examples identified by the Court, and drawn from the UN Declaration on Principles of International Law concerning Friendly Relations and Cooperation among States, of 'less grave forms of the use of force', include 'organizing, or encouraging the organization of irregular forces ... for incursion into the territory of another State', 'instigating, assisting or parti-cipating in acts of civil strife or terrorist acts in another State or acquiescing in organized activities within its territory'.[35] These actions by a third State would amount to a violation of the prohibition of the use of force but would not rise to the level of an armed attack. The consequence of this appears to be that while such acts would be unlawful and thus entitle the affected State to

---

[30] Randelzhofer and Nolte, 'Article 51' 2012 (n. 8), 1401, para. 6.
[31] ICJ, *Military and Paramilitary Activities in and against Nicaragua* (Nicaragua v. United States), Merits, Judgment of 27 June 1986, ICJ Reports 1986, 14, para. 191.
[32] *Ibid.*
[33] See for a brief discussion Franck, 'What Happens Now?' 2003 (n. 16).
[34] ICJ, *Military and Paramilitary Activities* (n. 31), para. 197.
[35] *Ibid.*, para. 191.

invoke the responsibility of the State providing assistance, it would not entitle the affected State to use force in response.

Other international instruments contributing to an understanding of the prohibition on the use of force include Resolution 3314 (XXIX) on the definition of aggression[36] and the International Law Commission's 1996 Draft Code of Crimes against the Peace.[37] In its commentary to Draft Article 16 on the crime of aggression, the Commission notes that Article 16 refers to 'aggression committed by a State' and that the 'rule of international law which prohibits aggression by a State applies to the conduct of a State in relation to another State'.[38]

The prohibition on the use of force has been described variously as 'the central rule' of international law,[39] 'one of the cornerstones of the modern international law legal order',[40] and a 'basic rule of the Charter'.[41] The International Court of Justice has itself recognised the principle, not only as a 'cornerstone of the United Nations Charter',[42] but as a rule of customary international law.[43] Indeed, the prohibition on the use of force is generally accepted as a norm of *ius cogens*.[44] Already in 1966, the International Law Commission, while not venturing to provide details on *ius cogens*, was able to declare boldly that 'the law of the Charter concerning the prohibition of the use of force in itself constitutes a conspicuous example of a rule' of *ius cogens* in international law.[45] More ambiguously, the International Court of Justice in the

---

[36] Definition of Aggression, GA Res. 3314 (XXIX) of 14 December 1974. Article 1 of the Annex to the resolution defines aggression as 'the use of armed force by a State against the sovereignty, territorial integrity or political independence of another State or in any other manner inconsistent with the Charter of the United Nations', while Article 3 proceeds to identify particular acts which qualify as acts of aggression. These include 'invasion by armed force of a State', 'bombardment by the armed forces of a State . . . ' and 'the blockade of the ports or coasts of a State by armed forces'.

[37] ILC, 'Draft Code of Crimes against the Peace and Security of Mankind with Commentaries', *Yearbook of the International Law Commission*, 1996, Vol II, Part II.

[38] *Ibid.*, para. 4. See also Article 8*bis* of the Rome Statute of the International Criminal Court, which essentially repeats the text of the Annex to Resolution 3314 (Article 8*bis* has yet to enter into force).

[39] Gray, *International Law and the Use of Force* 2008 (n. 5), 31.

[40] Randelzhofer and Dörr, 'Article 2(4)' 2012 (n. 23), 203.

[41] Hannikainen, 'The World After 11 September 2001' 2003 (n. 6), 446.

[42] ICJ, *Case Concerning the Armed Activities in the Territory of the Congo* (Democratic Republic of the Congo v. Uganda), Judgment of 19 December 2005, ICJ Reports 2005, 168.

[43] ICJ, *Military and Paramilitary Activities* (n. 31), paras. 188 *et seq.*

[44] See, e.g. Alexander Orakhelashvili, 'The Impact of Peremptory Norms on the Interpretation and Application of United Nations Security Council Resolutions', *European Journal of International Law* 16 (2005), 59–88 (63) ('The prohibition of the use of force is undeniably peremptory'); Randelzhofer and Dörr, 'Article 2(4)' 2012 (n. 23), 203 and 231.

[45] ILC, 'Draft Articles on the Law of Treaties with Commentaries', *Yearbook of the International Law Commission* (1966), vol. II, Commentary to Draft Article 50, para. 1. See also 'Draft

Military and Paramilitary Activities case stated that the International Law Commission 'expressed the view that "the law of the Charter concerning the prohibition of the use of force itself constitutes a conspicuous example"' of a *ius cogens* norm.[46] There has been some debate as to whether, by this language, the Court was endorsing the view expressed by the Commission or whether the Court was being non-committal.[47] Whatever the reluctance of the Court to unambiguously declare the prohibition of the use of force as a peremptory norm of international law, it is now beyond dispute that the prohibition on the use of force is a norm of *ius cogens*.[48]

The questions of whether the prohibition on the use of force is *ius cogens* and, more to the point, whether it matters, are addressed in the two other

Articles on Responsibility of States for Internationally Wrongful Acts with Commentaries', *Yearbook of the International Law Commission* (2001), vol. I, part II, Commentary to Draft Article 26, para. 5 where the prohibition of 'aggression' is included as an example of a norm of *ius cogens* under international law. See also Fourth Report on Peremptory Norms of General International Law (Ius Cogens) by Special Rapporteur (Dire Tladi), UN Doc.A/CN.4/727, paras 62–8.

[46] ICJ, *Military and Paramilitary Activities* (n. 31), para. 190.

[47] See First Report on *Ius Cogens* by the Special Rapporteur (Dire Tladi), UN Doc. A/CN.4/693, 8 March 2016, para. 46. Cf. James Green, 'Questioning the Peremptory Status of the Prohibition of the Use of Force', *Michigan Journal of International Law* 32 (2011), 215–57 (215): 'It is the view of the present author that the Court concluded here that the prohibition of the use of the force was a peremptory norm, although it must be said that others have a different interpretation of this passage.'

[48] See, as an example of State practice confirming the *jus cogens* status of the prohibition of the use of force, statement of Pakistan, thirty-fourth session of the General Assembly, A/C.6/34/SR.22, para. 22. See also ILC, Articles on the Responsibility of States for Internationally Wrongful Acts, GAOR, 56th Sess., Suppl 10, 43 *et seq.*, para. 5 of the commentary to draft Article 26 ('The principle of the non-use of force, and its corollary, were *jus cogens* ... '). See also ICJ, *The Accordance with International Law of the Unilateral Declaration of Independence in Respect of Kosovo*, Advisory Opinion of 22 July 2010, ICJ Reports 2010, 403, para. 81, where the Court describes 'unlawful use of force or other egregious violations of norms of general international law' as *ius cogens*. See also ICJ, *Certain Activities Carried out by Nicaragua in the Border Area* (Costa Rica v. Nicaragua), Provisional Measures, Order of 8 March 2011, Separate Opinion of Judge *ad hoc* Dugard, ICJ Reports 2011, 60, para. 15; ICJ, *Case Concerning Oil Platforms* (Islamic Republic of Iran v. United States of America), Judgment of 6 November 2003, Separate Opinion of Judge Simma, ICJ Reports 2003, 161, para. 6 ('I find it regrettable that the Court has not mustered the courage of restating, and thus reconfirming, more fully fundamental principles of the law of the United Nations as well as customary international law (principles that in my view are of the nature of *jus cogens*) on the use of force, or rather the prohibition on armed force, in a context and at a time when such a reconfirmation is called for with the greatest urgency'). See especially ICJ, *Legal Consequences of the Construction of a Wall in the Occupied Palestinian Territory*, Advisory Opinion of 9 July 2004, Separate Opinion of Judge Elaraby, ICJ Reports 2004, 246, para. 3.1 ('The prohibition of the use of force, as enshrined in Article 2, paragraph 4, of the Charter, is no doubt the most important principle that emerged in the twentieth century. It is universally recognized as a *jus cogens* principle, a peremptory norm from which no derogation is permitted'). See further Moir, *Reappraising the Resort to Force* 2010 (n. 14), 9.

chapters in this Trialogue. For Mary Ellen O'Connell, the prohibition is *ius cogens* and the characterisation of the prohibition as *ius cogens* matters for the question under consideration, i.e., whether a State may use force in self-defence in the territory of third States. Christian Tams does not offer a view as to whether the prohibition is or is not *ius cogens*, but states merely that it is irrelevant for the determination of the question. I share, without hesitation, the view expressed by O'Connell that the prohibition falls within the ambit of norms of *ius cogens*. That said, whether identifying the prohibition as *ius cogens* or not matters for the question at issue in the Trialogue depends on *what* is characterised as *ius cogens*. If what is characterised as *ius cogens* is the prohibition of force itself, then it clearly matters. In the resolution of tension (rather than conflict) between a *ius cogens* norm (in this case the prohibition on the use of force) and another norm (in this case self-defence), it would be expected that the *ius cogens* norm would be given priority. Thus if the prohibition of the use of force is *ius cogens*, the right to use of force in self-defence would have to be strictly circumscribed so that it does not affect the core of the *ius cogens* norm. For that reason, if the *ius cogens* norm is the prohibition itself, then it would clearly have an important role to play in the interaction between the prohibition and the right to use of force in self-defence. However, if the *ius cogens* norm is, as the International Law Commission has described, 'the law of the Charter concerning the prohibition of the use of force', then the characterisation as *ius cogens* is significantly less important for the purposes of the question under consideration in the Trialogue.[49] This is because the 'law of the Charter concerning the prohibition of the use of force' includes not only the prohibition but all of the Charter provisions relating to the use of force, including the right to use of force in self-defence. In those circumstances, the characterisation of the law as *ius cogens* has no effect on the interaction between the prohibition of the use of force and the right to use force in self-defence.

While the prohibition of the use of force is central to the UN system and modern international law, it forms part of a broader law on peace and security. This broader law includes, as an exception to the prohibition on the use of force, the right to use force in self-defence. However, the 'law of the Charter' relating to the prohibition of the use of force is underpinned by the collective

---

[49] The International Law Commission has described the *ius cogens* norm as follows: 'the law of the Charter concerning the prohibition of the use of force in itself constitutes a conspicuous example of a rule having the character of *jus cogens*.' See ILC, 'Draft Articles on the Law of Treaties' 1966 (n. 45), Commentary to Article 50, para. 1. See also ILC, Articles on State Responsibility, *Yearbook of the International Law Commission* (2001), vol. II, Part II, Commentary to Draft Article 26, para. 5. This description was relied on by the International Court of Justice in ICJ, *Military and Paramilitary Activities* (n. 31), para. 190.

security framework of the United Nations. This collective security system is also relevant in circumscribing the relative scope of the right to use force in self-defence *vis-à-vis* the prohibition on the use of force. It is this collective security system that is addressed next.

III. INTERNATIONAL PEACE AND SECURITY ARCHITECTURE

A. The Charter as an Instrument for Collective Security

While most contributions (correctly) assert that the starting point for the assessment of the law on the use of force in self-defence is Articles 2(4) and 51 of the UN Charter, these provisions themselves, and the customary international law rules they reflect, must be understood in their context. That context, I suggest, is the collective security system established under the Charter. It should be taken into account in trying to identify the limits of the right to use of force in self-defence against non-State actors in the territory of third States.

The Charter attempts to give life to its inspirational call to 'save succeeding generations from the scourge of war' by providing both normative rules and institutional mechanisms for overseeing the normative rules. It begins, in Chapter I, by laying out a series of purposes and principles peppered with the objective of peace and security. It is not surprising that the first purpose, and arguably the most important purpose, of the United Nations, identified in Article 1(1), of the Charter is to 'maintain international peace and security'.[50] More significant is that to achieve this primary purpose, the Charter sets out as a secondary purpose the taking of 'effective collective measures for the prevention and removal of threats to the peace'. Thus, under the Charter the principal way to remove threats to peace, including armed aggression, is through 'collective measures'. As Kohen observes, in the system set up by the Charter 'the motto was "peace through collective security".'[51] Similarly, just after the adoption of the Charter and the creation of the United Nations, the opening line in an article by Hans Kelsen declared that collective security 'is the main purpose of the United Nations'.[52]

---

[50]   See, e.g. Jean E. Krasno, 'The UN Landscape: An Overview', in Jean E. Krasno (ed.), *The United Nations: Confronting the Challenges of a Global Society* (Boulder: Lynne Rienner, 2004), 3–18 (3). See also Thomas G. Weiss, David P. Forsythe, Roger A. Coate and Kelly-Kate Pease, *The United Nations and Changing World Politics* (Boulder: Westview Press, 6th edn., 2010), 4.

[51]   Kohen, 'The Use of Force by the United States After the End of the Cold War' 2003 (n. 1), 197.

[52]   Hans Kelsen, 'Collective Security and Collective Self-Defence under the Charter of the United Nations', *American Journal of International Law* 42 (1948), 783–96 (783).

According to this general framework, the prohibition of the use of force in Article 2(4) is the primary normative rule for the maintenance of international peace and security, and the principal response to its breach is through collective measures.[53] Danchin defines collective security as the agreement by States to 'abide by certain norms and rules and to maintain stability and, when necessary, band together to stop aggression'.[54] This definition has three elements: first, the reliance on legal norms; second, the appropriate forms of response to breaches of (or threats to) security; and third the rejection of self-help in favour of collective responses when breaches do happen.[55] The third element, 'the rejection of self-help', is particularly noteworthy.[56] Danchin draws his definition from Kupchan and Kupchan's definition.[57] It is also noteworthy that Kupchan and Kupchan, in setting out their definition, emphasise a clear contrast between collective security, on the one hand, and, on the other hand, 'self-help balancing predicated on the notion of each for his own'[58] and 'anarchy [where] states fend for themselves'.[59] Danchin places the system of collective security between a system of balance of power – 'every "man" for himself' – and a system of global government where States are deprived of their power to the use of force in favour of a global government that has complete monopoly over force.[60] Collective security, he states, 'sits uneasily between and incorporates elements of both' sides.[61] The system, he continues

> involves a centralization of authority over the use of force to the extent that states are deprived of the legal right to use violence at their own discretion. That states give up this discretion and agree to follow objective rules governing the threat and use of force requires an international organization with the authority not only to determine when resort to force is illegitimate but also to

---

[53] See, e.g., José E. Alvarez, 'Legal Perspectives', in Thomas G. Weiss and Sam Daws (eds.), *The Oxford Handbook on the United Nations* (Oxford: Oxford University Press, 2007), 58–81, (58).

[54] Danchin, 'Things Fall Apart' 2010 (n. 16).

[55] *Ibid.*

[56] See also Report of the Secretary-General's High Level Panel on Threats, Challenges and Change, *A More Secure World: Our Shared Responsibility* (New York: United Nations, 2004), 16, para. 24, which makes the empirical evaluation that '[n]o State, no matter how powerful, can by its own efforts alone make itself invulnerable to today's threats.'

[57] Charles A. Kupchan and Clifford A. Kupchan, 'The Promise of Collective Security', *International Security* 20 (1995), 52–61 (52).

[58] *Ibid.*

[59] *Ibid.*, 53.

[60] Danchin, 'Things Fall Apart' 2010 (n. 15), 41–2; Weiss, Forsythe, Coate and Pease, *The United Nations and Changing World Politics* 2010 (n. 50), 4–5.

[61] Danchin, 'Things Fall Apart' 2010 (n. 15), 42.

require states to collaborate under its discretion in suppressing such use of force.[62]

B. Institutional Framework for Peace and Security under the Charter

The view taken in this chapter, namely that the key to understanding the scope of the right in Article 51 is the collective security system set up by the Charter, necessitates that the organs and entities created by the Charter for carrying out its purposes are discussed. This is particularly true since one of the arguments for an expansive interpretation rests on the impotence or ineffectiveness of the collective security system.

The UN Charter establishes three principal organs relevant to the maintenance of international peace and security, namely the UN Security Council, the General Assembly and the International Court of Justice. While arguments can be made for a recognition of the role that other organs of the United Nations *can* play in the maintenance of international peace and security, it is realistic to limit ourselves to these three principal organs. Indeed, arguments can be made for the exclusion of the International Court of Justice, whose primary mandate is the resolution of disputes, since its contribution to peace and security is, in a sense, indirect.[63] Nonetheless, given the important contribution that the Court has made to understanding the content of the rules, it is worth including here. Its particular contribution, however, will be considered not in this section, but in section IV on the prohibition of the use of force and the section on self-defence.

The Security Council is the lynchpin of the collective security system established under the Charter. It has the primary responsibility for the maintenance of international peace and security, a responsibility conferred on it by and exercised on behalf of the members of the United Nations. In some sense, as observed by Anne Peters, Article 24(1) of the UN Charter operationalises, at least partly, the primary purpose of the United Nations to maintain (and restore in case of breach) international peace and security.[64] The specific

---

[62]   *Ibid.*, 42–3.

[63]   Weiss, Forsythe, Coate and Pease, *The United Nations and Changing World Politics* 2010 (n. 50), 7, for example, list only the Security Council and the General Assembly as the 'two central bodies to directly safeguard the peace'.

[64]   Anne Peters, 'Article 24: Functions and Powers', in Simma, Khan, Nolte and Paulus, *The Charter of the United Nations* 2012 (n. 8), vol. I, 761–854 (771), quoting Kenneth Manusama, *The United Nations Security Council in the Post-Cold War Era: Applying the Principle of Legality* (Leiden: Nijhoff, 2006).

powers granted to the Council to discharge its mandate for the maintenance of international peace and security are to be found in Chapters VI and VII.

While the Council has wide powers, for the purposes of the use of force and self-defence, two powers are of particular importance. First, the Security Council has the power to make a determination 'about the existence of any threat to the peace, breach of the peace, or an act of aggression'.[65] This means that, over and above whatever measures the Council may decide upon to restore or maintain peace, a determination by the Council of aggression is *relevant* in making a determination of whether the use of force is consistent or not with the prohibition in Article 2(4) of the Charter. Second, the Security Council is empowered to 'take such action by air, sea or land forces as may be necessary to maintain or restore international peace and security'.[66] Thus, as a measure of collective security, where use of force in contravention of Article 2(4) has taken place, the Council is empowered to make use of force necessary in response to the aggressive use of force. Of course, in practice, the Security Council hasn't used force itself but rather has authorised willing States to take action on its behalf.[67] And the idea, certainly as originally envisaged by the drafters of the Charter, was that the Council's use of force (or authorisation of the use of force) would 'be the main exception to the prohibition on force'.[68] The unilateral use of force in self-defence, in response to an armed attack emanating from the territory of a third State, should be understood in this context, i.e. as an exception to the exception where the main exception, namely collective use of force in response to aggression, has not occurred.

While it has sometimes been contended that the Security Council possesses exclusive powers in relation to peace and security, it is clear that the General Assembly also plays a role.[69] Moreover, the International Court of Justice has

---

[65] Article 39 UN Charter.

[66] Article 42 UN Charter.

[67] See Kohen, 'The Use of Force by the United States After the End of the Cold War' 2003 (n. 1), 215.

[68] See Tams, 'The Use of Force against Terrorists' 2009 (n. 10), 365.

[69] See Chittharanjan Felix Amerasinghe, 'The Charter *Travaux Preparatoires* and United Nations Power to Use Armed Force', *Canadian Yearbook of International Law* 4 (1966), 81–101 (82). See generally, for example, the personal account of the negotiations on the crime of aggression in the Rome Statute where the French and United Kingdom delegations consistently made the argument; in the words of Dire Tladi: 'The French and the United Kingdom delegations' articulation of the issue – articulated at various preparatory meetings for the Review Conference – was very strongly worded and to the effect that the Security Council has the exclusive mandate to determine the existence of an act of aggression' (Dire Tladi, 'Kampala, the International Criminal Court and the Adoption of a Definition of the Crime of Aggression: A Dream Deferred', *South African Yearbook of International Law* 35 (2010), 80–96 (81)). See for discussion Jost Delbrück, 'Functions and Powers: Article 24', in

explicitly held 'that Article 24 refers to a primary, but not necessarily exclusive competence' and continued to note that the General Assembly does have powers in relation to peace and security.[70] Articles 10, 11, 12 and 14 make plain that the General Assembly may consider any matter 'within the scope of' the Charter, including matters of peace and security. Indeed, by virtue of the fact that the General Assembly has the power to discuss 'any matter', while all other organs of the United Nations are limited to specific areas, it may be said that the General Assembly 'is given pride of place' in the structure of the United Nations.[71] While the scope of its mandate is wide, the General Assembly's powers in the areas in which it may 'act' are limited, first in the sense that it may only discuss and make recommendations, and second in the sense that it may not make recommendations where the Council is seized with the matter. Thus, while the General Assembly has pride of place by virtue of the breadth of the scope of its mandate, the Security Council can claim preeminence by virtue of the depth of its powers in the narrow area of its mandate.

To start with, the fact that the General Assembly can, according to the text of the Charter, do no more than discuss and make recommendations is a significant limitation on the mandate of the General Assembly with regards to peace and security. The second limitation is that the General Assembly may not make recommendations while the Security Council is exercising its functions in respect of any dispute or situation. This requirement may raise questions about precisely when the Council 'is exercising in respect of any dispute or situation [its] functions' (Article 12(1) of the Charter). Does this include any situation on the agenda of the Security Council, or only those situations in which the Council has adopted measures?[72] If it is the latter, do the measures have to be effective or recent? Moreover, does the fact that the Security Council is seized with a situation preclude recommendations on any issue relating to that situation, even issues tangential to the particular situation?

Bruno Simma (ed.), *The Charter of the United Nations: A Commentary* (Oxford: Oxford University Press, 1995), 397–407, (400 *et seq.*, especially 402: 'primary responsibility ... means that the [Security Council] shall have stronger powers than the other organs, namely the [General Assembly], even though the latter may also concern itself with questions of the maintenance of international peace and security'). See also Peters, 'Article 24' 2012 (n. 64), 767, and Kelsen, 'Collective Security and Collective Self-Defence' 1948 (n. 52), 786.

70   ICJ, *Wall Advisory Opinion* (n. 48), 136, para. 26.
71   Eckart Klein, 'Functions and Powers: Article 10', in Simma, Khan, Nolte and Paulus, *The Charter of the United Nations* 2012 (n. 8), vol. I, 461–90 (462).
72   See for discussion ICJ, *Wall* Advisory Opinion (n. 48), 27: ' ... both the General Assembly and the Security Council *initially* interpreted and applied Article 12 to the effect that the Assembly could not make a recommendation on a question concerning the maintenance of international peace and security while the matter remained on the Council's agenda' (emphasis added).

The practice of the UN reveals a rather flexible approach to the limitations on the General Assembly. The most direct example of the flexibility adopted by the General Assembly is the Uniting for Peace Resolution of November 1950.[73] While the Charter provides that the General Assembly may not make a recommendation on a matter under consideration by the Security Council, the Uniting for Peace Resolution provides that it may make such a recommendation where the Council 'fails to exercise its primary responsibility' due to 'the lack of unanimity of the permanent members'.[74] Furthermore, the resolution permits the authorisation by the General Assembly through recommendation of the use of force in response to aggression.[75] The International Court of Justice has already affirmed the legality and validity of the Uniting for Peace Resolution.[76] If, as appears to be the view of the Court, the Uniting for Peace Resolution is legal and valid, then presumably the use of force pursuant to an authorisation given under the Uniting for Peace Resolution would be justified, notwithstanding the apparently clear language of the Charter. Moreover, even outside of the Uniting for Peace Resolution, the practice of the General Assembly has been to consider and make recommendations on matters that are still on the agenda of the Security Council.[77] The situation in Syria – discussed more fully further below – provides an example of the General Assembly's assertion of powers even while the Security Council is seized with a situation and without relying on the Uniting for Peace Resolution.[78] In these resolutions the General Assembly did more than discuss; it made 'demands', 'called upon' and 'decided' various things concerning the situation in Syria.[79] Importantly, in each of the resolutions on the situation, the General Assembly makes a determination about the lawfulness of the conduct of the relevant parties

---

[73] *Ibid.*

[74] GA Res 377 (V) of 3 November 1950, para. 1.

[75] *Ibid.* The resolution provides that in the event of the Council failing to act, the General Assembly 'shall consider the matter immediately with a view to making appropriate recommendation to Members for collective measures, including in the case of breach of the peace or act of aggression the use of armed force when necessary . . .'.

[76] See ICJ, *Wall* Advisory Opinion (n. 48), paras. 19–36.

[77] See for discussion *ibid.*, paras. 27–8.

[78] The General Assembly, in the face of Russian vetoes in the Security Council, adopted several resolutions on the situation in Syria. See e.g. Situation of Human Rights in the Syrian Arab Republic, GA Res. 66/176 of 19 December 2011; The Situation in the Syrian Arab Republic, GA Res. 66/253A of 16 February 2012; The Situation in the Syrian Arab Republic, GA Res. 66/243B of 3 August 2012.

[79] GA Res. 66/176, for example, in addition to strongly condemning violence by the Syrian authorities (para. 1) also called upon the Syrian authorities 'to immediately put an end to all human suffering' (para. 2).

to the conflict.[80] While the General Assembly's mandate to authorise through recommendations the use of force may be in question,[81] what is not in question is that, in practice the Assembly, together with the Security Council, is able to make determinations about the lawfulness of the use of force in given circumstances and, in this way, contribute to an understanding of the law on the use of force.[82]

The effectiveness of the system of collective security described above is of course based on particular geopolitical considerations. In particular, the dynamics on the Security Council, especially between the permanent members of the Security Council, often determine whether the collective security system established by the United Nations is able to function effectively. Some have thus suggested that the scope of the rules relating to the right to use force unilaterally should be determined by the effectiveness of the collective security system at any given time. Gray, for example, observes that

> Many US commentators argued during the Cold War that the interpretation of Article 2(4) depended on the effective functioning of the UN collective security system, and therefore that the inability of the Security Council to act because of the veto of the permanent five meant that Article 2(4) should be read to allow the use of force to further 'world public order' or the principles of the United Nations.[83]

This view was also advanced by Judge Jennings in his dissenting opinion in the *Military and Paramilitary Activities* case, in which he stated that

---

[80]   See, e.g., para. 2 of GA Res. 66/253A in which the General Assembly '*Strongly condemns* the continued widespread and systematic violations of human rights and fundamental freedoms by the Syrian authorities . . . '.

[81]   See, e.g., Kelsen, 'Collective Security and Collective Self-Defence' 1948 (n. 52), 786, who states that the Charter 'authorizes the Security Council, and only the Security Council, not the individual members or any other central organ of the United Nations, to ascertain the existence of the conditions under which the use of force within the system of collective security may take place'.

[82]   See however, Kelsen, 'Collective Security and Collective Self-Defence' 1948 (n. 52), 796.

[83]   Gray, *International Law and the Use of Force* 2008 (n. 5), 31. See also, appearing on behalf of the United Kingdom in the *Corfu Channel* case and responding to Albania's rejoinder concerning self-defence in the framework of the law of the UN Charter, Sir Eric Beckett's statement that the 'Security Council of the United Nations can be rendered powerless by a single vote. Consequently, it is only natural that the rights of self-defence and self-help which are recognized in municipal law should have a somewhat greater importance in international law.' Statement by Sir Eric Beckett, Public Sitting of 12 November 1948, Morning session, International Court of Justice, Pleadings, Oral Arguments, Documents: The Corfu Channel Case Vol III, Oral Proceedings Part I. See further Hersch Lauterpacht, *Oppenheim's International Law, vol. II* (London: Longmans, 7th edn., 1952), 155.

the original scheme of the United Nations Charter, whereby force would be deployed by the United Nations itself, in accordance with the provisions of Chapter VII of the Charter, has never come into effect. Therefore, an essential element in the Charter is totally missing. In this situation it seems dangerous to define unnecessarily strictly the conditions for lawful self-defence, so as to leave a large area where both a forcible response to force is forbidden and yet the United Nations employment of force, which was intended to fill the gap, is absent.[84]

The Court itself, however, rejected this view, holding that the prohibition in Article 2(4) is 'not as such conditioned by the provisions relating to the collective security'.[85] The problem with the interpretation making the full scope of Article 2(4) dependent on the effective functioning of the Security Council is that it deprives the prohibition on the unilateral use of force of an objective, independent content. Its content will always oscillate between broad and narrow depending on the effectiveness of the collective security system at a particular point in time. As stated at the beginning, the rules prohibiting the use of force have an objective and determinable content and are not in the eyes of the beholder. At any rate, the argument must fail since, as described above, in the event that the Council fails to act because of the veto, the General Assembly, by virtue of the Uniting for Peace Resolution and/or the practice described above, can fulfil the collective security functions. At the very least, given the controversy of interpreting the Charter as permitting the General Assembly to authorise the use of force, the General Assembly can make a determination that the use of force in self-defence is permissible because a situation constitutes an armed attack or aggression.

This framework of collective security established by the United Nations, and centred around the Security Council with the General Assembly playing a secondary role, provides the principal mechanism for addressing threats to international peace and security, with the collective use of force under Article 42 being the principal exception to the prohibition on the use of force. Reliance on self-help, as a means to respond to aggressive use of force, should therefore be seen as an exception to this principal exception. As Kelsen observes, 'self-defense as a case of decentralized use of force is an exceptional and provisional interlude between an act of illegal use of force ... and the collective enforcement action.'[86] This framework for collective security,

---

[84] See ICJ, *Military and Paramilitary Activities* (n. 31), Dissenting Opinion of Judge Jennings, 543.

[85] See ICJ, *Military and Paramilitary Activities* (n. 31), para. 188.

[86] Kelsen, 'Collective Security and Collective Self-Defence' 1948 (n. 52), 785.

underpinned by the Security Council's primary responsibility, provides the context within which the rules relating to the use of force should be seen.

IV. THE LAW ON SELF-DEFENCE

A. *General Framework*

The right to unilaterally use force in self-defence should be understood in the broader context of the collective security framework set up under the Charter. Article 51 provides as follows:

> Nothing in the present Charter shall impair the inherent right of individual or collective self-defence if an armed attack occurs against a Member of the United Nations, until the Security Council has taken the measures necessary to maintain international peace and security. Measures taken by Members in the exercise of the right to self-defence shall be immediately reported to the Security Council and shall not in any way affect the authority and responsibility of the Security Council under the present Charter to take at any time such action as it deems necessary in order to maintain or restore international peace and security.

That Article 51 is situated in Chapter VII, the chapter wherein the primary powers of the Security Council are provided for, serves to reinforce that the right to use force in self-defence should be seen in the context of the collective security framework described in Section III above. Under this framework, there is a prohibition on the use of force reflected in Article 2(4) of the Charter. In the event that this prohibition is breached, collective action, principally under Chapter VII, is foreseen. Unilateral self-defence, therefore, is an exceptional and 'temporary right'.[87] Indeed the International Court of Justice has suggested that the requirement to report to the Council is a factor to be considered, even under customary international law, in assessing the lawfulness of self-defence.[88] As with the prohibition on the right to use of force, the right to unilateral use of force has also been recognised to exist in customary

---

[87] Moir, *Reappraising the Resort to Force* 2010 (n. 14), 10. See also Gray, *International Law and the Use of Force* 2008 (n. 5), 119 ('Article 51 assigns a central role to the Security Council: States are under a duty to report measures taken in the exercise of self-defence to the Security Council and the right to self-defence is temporary until the Security Council' acts.).

[88] See ICJ, *Military and Paramilitary Activities* (n. 31), para. 200. The Court there stated that failure to report may indicate whether a State truly believed that it was acting in self-defence. See also ICJ, *Armed Activities in the Territory of the Congo* (n. 42), para. 145, where the Court 'finds it obscure' that Uganda had not reported to the Security Council the matters requiring it to act in self-defence.

international law.[89] The content of both Article 51 and that customary international law on self-defence are co-extensive.

B. *The Permissibility of Unilateral Use of Force against Non-State Actors*

At face value one would expect that the law on the use of force, including rules on self-defence, is applicable to inter-State conflict. As Gray observes, the two provisions in the Charter regulating the unilateral use of force, Articles 2(4) and 51, 'are very much a response to the Second World War and are accordingly directed to inter-state conflict'.[90] Moreover, Article 2(4) of the Charter expressly applies to inter-State use of force. It prohibits 'Members', which are States, from using force 'against the territorial integrity or political independence of any State'. As suggested above, if Article 51 was intended to be an exception to Article 2(4), one would expect it to regulate similar conduct, i.e. permit what is ordinarily prohibited in Article 2(4) subject to the particular requirements laid down in its provision.[91] As Kelsen observed shortly after the adoption of the Charter, Article 51 'restricts the right to self-defence to the case of an "armed attack" actually made by one *state against another*'.[92] Even Tams, who supports the idea that under international law, as it now stands, the use of force in the territory of another State in response to an attack by a non-State is permissible, accepts that the dominant theory *used* to be contrary to the proposition he now supports.[93]

In recent years, however, there has been a trend, mainly in European and American literature, that advances a broad and permissive interpretation of Article 51 so as to permit the use of force in self-defence against non-State actors in the territory of third States. According to this trend, international law, as it currently stands, permits States to use force unilaterally, i.e. outside of the

---

[89] See, e.g. ICJ, *Military and Paramilitary Activities* (n. 31), paras. 193 *et seq.*, especially at para. 194. See for discussion Randelzhofer and Nolte, 'Article 51' 2012 (n. 8), 1403–4.

[90] Gray, *International Law and the Use of Force* 2008 (n. 5), 7. See Sean D. Murphy, 'Terrorism and the Concept of "Armed Attack" in Article 51 of the UN Charter', *Harvard Journal of International Law* 43 (2002), 41–52 (43), arguing the prohibition in Article 2(4) applies to 'force by one state against the other'.

[91] See Tams in this volume, 114.

[92] Kelsen, 'Collective Security and Collective Self-Defence' 1948 (n. 52), 791 (emphasis added).

[93] Tams, 'The Use of Force against Terrorists' 2009 (n. 10), 363, stating that the restrictive approach to the use of force in self-defence 'represented the dominant approach to the *jus ad bellum*' and 'was reflected in many of the influential writings of the time, such as the treatment of Articles 2(4), 39–43 and 51 UNC in the first editions of Charter commentaries by Cot/Pellet and Simma'.

collective security framework of the United Nations, against a non-State actor in the territory of a third State without the third State's consent.

While this broad and permissive interpretation has been propagated in literature,[94] it has also been advanced in at least three widely discussed policy-oriented documents. The first of these, the Chatham House Principles, was adopted in October 2005 by the International Law Programme at Chatham House, based on consultation with an eminent group of British international lawyers.[95] The second document, the Leiden Policy Recommendations (Leiden Recommendations), was adopted in April 2010 and 'emanated from a consultative process' led by leading Dutch jurists Nico Schrijver and Larissa van den Herik.[96] The participants in the adoption of the Leiden Recommendations were predominantly from Europe and North America,[97] and all of the participants in the group addressing the use of force for the Chatham House Principles were from Europe and North America.[98] Finally, the Bethlehem Principles are a set of principles put forward by Daniel Bethlehem.[99] Bethlehem declares that the Principles 'do not reflect the settled *view* of any state' and are 'published under [his] responsibility alone'.[100] He states, however, that they have 'been informed by detailed discussions over

---

[94] In addition to the authors cited in note 10 above, see also Michael Wood, 'International Law and the Use of Force: What Happens in Practice?', *Indian Journal of International Law* 53 (2013), 345–67 (345); Oscar Schachter, 'The Extraterritorial Use of Force against Terrorist Bases', *Houston Journal of International Law* 11 (1989), 309–16 (309); Theresa Reinold, 'State Weakness, Irregular Warfare, and the Right to Self-Defence Post 9/11', *American Journal of International Law* 105 (2011), 244–86 (244). See also Dugard, *International Law* 2011 (n. 25). It is interesting to note that Arimatsu and Schmitt, 'Attacking "Islamic State" and the Khorasan Group' 2014 (n. 7), declare, at 29, that 'they remain split' on the question of whether 'Article 51 and customary international law extends to non-State actors'.

[95] Principles of International Law on the Use of Force by States in Self-Defence (2005), available at www.chathamhouse.org/sites/files/chathamhouse/public/Research/International%20Law/ilpforce.doc. The expert participants include Frank Berman, Daniel Bethlehem, Christopher Greenwood, Vaughn Lowe, Philippe Sands, Malcolm Shaw, Elizabeth Wilmshurst and Michael Wood.

[96] Leiden Policy Recommendations on Counter-Terrorism and International Law (2010), available at www.grotiuscentre.org/resources/1/Leiden%20Policy%20Recommendations%20 1%20April%202010.pdf.

[97] Out of thirty-three participants only four were outside Europe or North America. These are Anton du Plessis (South Africa), Martin Ewi (Cameroon), David Kretzmer (Israel) and Claudia Martin (Argentina).

[98] They are Andrea Bianchi (Italy), Michael Wood (United Kingdom), Steven Ratner (United States), Elizabeth Wilmshurst (United Kingdom), Christian Tams (Germany) and Claus Kreß (Germany).

[99] Daniel Bethlehem, 'Principles Relevant to the Scope of a State's Right of Self-Defense against an Imminent or Actual Armed Attack by Nonstate Actors', *American Journal of International Law* 106 (2012), 769–70.

[100] *Ibid.*, 773 (emphasis added).

recent years with foreign ministry, defense ministry, and military legal advisers from a number of *states who have operational experience in these matters*'.[101] Given the views expressed above about the significance of geopolitical considerations, it will come as no surprise that the source of these documents – that is the geographical representativeness of its drafters – is an issue of concern for me.

The Chatham House Principles, while acknowledging that 'the law in this area is politically and legally contentious', declare that the Principles 'are intended to give a clear representation of the current principles and rules of international law'.[102] Principle 6 of the Chatham House Principles states that 'Article 51 is not confined to self-defence in response to attacks by States' and that the 'right to self-defence applies also to attacks by non-State actors.'[103] The commentary to Principle 6 asserts that there 'is no reason to limit a state's right to protect itself to an attack by another state'. In the view of the drafters, the 'source of the attack, whether state or non-state actor, is irrelevant to the right'. In particular, the commentary states that the 'right to use of force in self-defence is an inherent right and is not dependent upon any prior breach of international law by the state in the territory of which defensive force is used'. This would suggest that attribution of the conduct of non-State actors to the territorial State is not a necessary condition for the exercise of force in self-defence. The commentary to the Chatham House Principles attempts to mitigate the implications of Principle 6 by stating that while normal rules, such as proportionality and necessity, apply to the application of the Principles, special considerations are relevant in cases where the State on whose territory force is being used is not responsible for the armed attack. In particular, the commentary to Principle 6 states that, more so than with respect to an attack by a State, the attack by non-State actors 'must be large-scale' to qualify as an armed attack for the purposes of Article 51.[104] This mitigation amounts to the same fact or circumstance specific approach that I earlier rejected.

The use of force against terrorists is dealt with in Part II of the Leiden Recommendations.[105] As with the Chatham House Principles, it assumes that the position it postulates on the use of force reflects current international law. The introduction to the policy recommendation on the use of force states the principal aim of the policy recommendations on the use of force against

---

[101]   *Ibid.* (emphasis added).
[102]   Chatham House Principles (n. 95).
[103]   *Ibid.*, Principle 6.
[104]   *Ibid.*
[105]   Leiden Recommendations (n. 96), at 11 *et seq.*

terrorists as being 'to clarify the state of international law on the use of force against terrorists against the backdrop of recent practice'.[106] It declares that there 'is no need for new rules' in this area and that the 'framework laid down in the Charter is the cornerstone of the international legal regime on the use of force'.[107] However, it states that the Charter 'is not a static instrument' and must be 'interpreted in the light of practice and taking states' expectations into account'.[108] The Recommendations state that the right of self-defence in Article 51 'makes no reference to the source of the armed attack'.[109] It then proceeds to state that it 'is *now* well accepted that attacks by non-state actors, even when not acting on behalf of a state, can trigger a state's right' of self-defence.[110] As with the Chatham House Principles, the Leiden Recommendations make some attempt to mitigate against the implications of permitting a wide reading of 'armed attack', by stating that only 'large-scale attacks' of the non-State actor can form the basis of the right to use force in self-defence.[111]

Unlike the Leiden Recommendations and the Chatham House Principles, the Bethlehem Principles do not, at least not expressly, purport to represent the law as it stands. On the Principles' relationship with law, Bethlehem states that they are '*intended to work with* the grain of the UN Charter as well as customary international law, in which resides the inherent right of self-defence'.[112] The stated objective of the Bethlehem Principles is, it seems, to stay clear of the doctrinal debate, which he says 'has yet to produce a clear set of principles', in favour of a more 'strategic' and 'operational' approach.[113] He accepts that some of the principles he advances will 'undoubtedly prove controversial'.[114] It is interesting though, that the examples of those principles

---

[106] Ibid., para. 29.
[107] Ibid., para. 28.
[108] Ibid.
[109] Ibid., para. 38.
[110] Ibid. (emphasis added). While this proposition is stated as an obvious and incontrovertible fact beyond controversy, it is not clear that that authors really believe this to be the case. In 2014, in the margins of the Annual Meeting of the American Society of International Law, I was invited by the organisers of the Leiden Recommendations to participate in a closed, Chatham House rule meeting on the Recommendations on the Use of Force. The issues for discussions included questions of proportionality, imminence and necessity, but not the legality of the use of force on the territory of third States as such. When I raised that question, of whether it was permissible to use force in the territory of a third State, I was informed that the issue was not on the table since it would prove too complicated to resolve.
[111] Ibid., para. 39 ('In the case of an armed attack by terrorists that is not attributable to a state, Article 51 should be read to require that the attack be large-scale ...').
[112] Bethlehem, 'Principles Relevant to the Scope of a State's Right of Self-Defense against an Imminent or Actual Armed Attack by Nonstate Actors' 2012 (n. 99), 773 (emphasis added).
[113] Ibid.
[114] Ibid., 773-4.

that are likely to prove controversial do not include the proposition that force may be used in the territory of a third State. Bethlehem offers, as examples of the more controversial principles, the question of what is meant by imminence and who may be 'properly targeted within the non-state actor continuum of those planning, threatening, perpetrating, and providing material support to an armed attack'.[115]

While the Chatham House and Leiden Recommendations depart from the assumption that, as a general rule, a State can use force unilaterally in self-defence against non-State actors on the territory of a third State, the Bethlehem Principles move from the opposite premise. Principle 10 of the Principles state as follows:

> Subject to the following paragraphs, a state may not take armed action in self-defense against a non-state actor in the territory or within the jurisdiction of another state ('the third state') without the consent of that state.

Principles 11 and 12 provide exceptions to the basic rule in Principle 10. Principle 11 states that the requirement for consent does not apply 'in circumstances in which there is a reasonable basis for concluding that the third state is colluding with the non-state actor' or in cases where the third State is 'unwilling to effectively restrain' the non-State actor. Principle 11, in its essence, removes the requirement of consent where there is *some attribution*[116] of the armed attack by the non-State actor on the third State or, to put it another way, in cases where the third State is not innocent. Principle 12, in contrast, does apply to what we may term the 'innocent State'. It provides that the requirement for consent in Principle 10 does not apply where 'there is a reasonable and objective basis for concluding that the third State is unable to effectively restrain' the non-State actors. There are of course factual questions that may be asked about this principle. For example, it is not clear who determines whether there is a 'reasonable and objective basis' for making a decision that the third State is unable to restrain the non-State actors. It is also not clear whether the criteria 'unable to effectively restrain' is one of result or conduct. If it is the former, then in most instances the third State will be deemed to be unable unless the third State is able to stamp out attacks from the non-State actor. At any rate, for the purposes of this contribution, the essential point is that, according to the Bethlehem Principles, like the Chatham House Principles and the Leiden Recommendations, a State that is a victim of an

---

[115] *Ibid.*

[116] I say some attribution, because whether the unwillingness to constrain is sufficient for attribution may well be open to question. However, for the purposes of this contribution, it is unnecessary to resolve that question.

attack or a series of attacks from a non-State actor may launch military attacks in self-defence against that non-State actor on the territory of an innocent non-consenting third State if that third State is unable to restrain the non-State actor.

While the Bethlehem Principles have a different point of departure from the other documents, the basic tenets of the three sets of documents are the same. All three advance a proposition that permits, in principle, the use of force against non-State actors, in the territory of non-consenting third States on whom the armed activities of the non-State actors cannot be attributed – what this chapter has termed the 'innocent State'. Moreover, all three documents suggest that this proposition reflects the law under the Charter and customary international law or, in the case of the Bethlehem Principles, is at least not inconsistent with it. It is also worth pointing out that these instruments offer scant legal justification for the proposition. The Leiden Recommendations simply state the proposition 'is now well accepted' and that Article 51 'makes no reference to the source of the attack'.[117] The commentary to Principle 6 of the Chatham Principles does, however, offer some basis, albeit without much explanation. First, similar to the Leiden Recommendations, the commentary to Principle 6 states that there 'is nothing in the text of Article 51' to suggest that the right to self-defence applies only in the case of an armed attack from a State. It suggests that this conclusion can be supported with reference to the *Caroline* incident – the relevance of this incident is considered below. Second, it is suggested in the commentary to Principle 6 that 'State practice in this field, including the recent practice of the Security Council, gives . . . support' to the notion that self-defence is permissible in the territory of an innocent third State even if the attacks by non-State actors are not imputable to the State on whose territory force is to be used. Although the commentary to Principle 6 does not expand on these bases, they are, by and large, reflected in the literature supporting the proposition that force may be used in the territory of a non-consenting innocent State. I turn now to the literature in support of the central proposition advanced in these three documents.

C. The Proposition that Unilateral Force can be used Extraterritorially in Self-Defence against Non-State Actors

Several authors have sought to justify the proposition that, under international law as it stands, a State may use force in self-defence against a non-State actor in the territory of an innocent State without that State's consent. A survey of

---

[117]   Leiden Recommendations (n. 96), para. 38.

the literature and the reasons advanced reveals, similar to the commentary to Principle 6 of the Chatham House Principles, that the proposition is based on three mutually reinforcing pillars. First, the proposition is based on a literal reading of Article 51. Second, the proposition is based on the idea that pre-Charter customary international law continues to exist side by side with the UN Charter and that under the rules established under customary international law, the use of force against non-State actors was (and still is) permissible. Finally, the literature suggests that post-Charter practice supports the proposition that force may be used against non-State actors in the territory of a non-consenting innocent State.

The literal interpretation pillar of the argument is based on the fact that the words in Article 51 of the Charter do not limit the right of self-defence to an armed attack from a State. Paust captures the argument succinctly as follows:

> Article 51 of the Charter expressly affirms the right of a State to respond defensively 'if an armed attack occurs', and nothing in the language of Article 51 restricts the right to engage in self-defense measures to circumstances of armed attacks by a 'state'.[118]

According to Murphy, 'the "ordinary meaning" of the terms of Article 51 provide no basis for reading into the text a restriction on who the attacker must be.'[119] But in addition to 'ordinary meaning', Murphy also advances what might be seen as a contextual reading of Article 51 as supporting the proposition that a State may unilaterally use force in the territory of innocent third States without such States' consent. He suggests that since Article 2(4) of the Charter explicitly prohibits the use of force against 'the territorial integrity or independence *of any State*',[120] if the drafters of the Charter intended to limit Article 51 to inter-State relations that construct would be repeated in Article 51.[121] Paust adds that any other interpretation would be 'lacking in common sense' since it would suggest that a State being attacked by a non-State actor may 'only defend itself within its own borders'.[122] This ordinary meaning

---

[118] Paust, 'Self-Defence Targeting of Non-State Actors' 2010 (n. 10), 240–1. See also Murphy, 'Self-Defence and the Israeli Wall Advisory Opinion' 2005 (n. 10), 64. See also Murphy, 'Terrorism and the Concept of "Armed Attack" in Article 51 of the UN Charter' 2002 (n. 90), 50. See also Schachter, 'The Extraterritorial Use of Force against Terrorist Bases' 1989 (n. 94), 311. See Reinold, 'State Weakness, Irregular Warfare, and the Right to Self-Defence Post 9/11' 2011 (n. 94), 244.

[119] Murphy, 'Self-Defence and the Israeli Wall Advisory Opinion' 2005 (n. 10), 64.

[120] *Ibid.* (emphasis added).

[121] *Ibid.*, 64.

[122] Paust, 'Self-Defence Targeting of Non-State Actors' 2010 (n. 10), 241.

argument underlying the proposition is also reflected in various ways in certain instruments.[123]

The second argument based on customary international law also proceeds from the text of Article 51 of the Charter. The argument proceeds from the fact that the right to self-defence in Article 51 is described as 'inherent' and takes this to mean that the rules on self-defence under customary international law continue to apply notwithstanding the UN Charter. Murphy recalls that to fully understand the rule in Article 51 'requires looking beyond the language of that article' because 'Article 51 did not create a right on self-defence.'[124] Rather, he argues, Article 51 'preserved' a right 'that existed in customary international law' even before the adoption of the Charter.[125] Authors raising this point in support of the broad interpretation of the 'armed attack' requirement – and therefore in support of a permissive approach to the unilateral use of force against non-State actors – invariably point to the *Caroline* incident as the foundation of the argument on customary international law.[126]

The *Caroline* incident is described in many texts, so only a summary of the relevant facts is presented here.[127] In short, in the nineteenth century, while the territory of Canada was still under British control, insurgents trying to overthrow British rule often carried out attacks, sometimes from the territory of the United States. In 1837, the *Caroline*, a vessel used in one such attack, was destroyed by the United Kingdom while it was in US waters. The content of the exchange of letters between Daniel Webster, on behalf of the United States, and Lord

---

[123] The Leiden Recommendations (n. 96), for example, state that Article 51 'makes no reference to the source of the attack'. Similarly, the commentary to Principle 6 of the Chatham House Principles (n. 95) states that there 'is nothing in the text of Article 51' indicating that it applies only in the case of an armed attack from a State.

[124] Murphy, 'Self-Defence and the Israeli Wall Advisory Opinion' 2005 (n. 10), 64.

[125] *Ibid.*

[126] See, e.g. Murphy, 'Self-Defence and the Israeli Wall Advisory Opinion' 2005 (n. 10), 65, noting that in the *Caroline* incident the Governments of the United States and the United Kingdom 'settled upon the basic contours of the right of self-defence, contours that today remain the touchstone for most discourse on the subject'. See also Murphy, 'Terrorism and the Concept of "Armed Attack"' 2002 (n. 90), 50 ('The preeminent precedent regarding self-defence – the *Caroline* incident – stands out just for Secretary of State Webster's proposition that self-defence is only appropriate in cases of necessity . . . but also for the proposition that self-defence is permissible as a reaction to attacks by non-governmental entities . . . '). See also Reinold, 'State Weakness, Irregular Warfare, and the Right to Self-Defence Post 9/11' 2011 (n. 94), 247 ('The Webster formula from the *Caroline* incident of 1837 continues to be the authoritative statement on the right to anticipatory self-defence in customary international law').

[127] For a full description of the *Caroline* incident, see Abraham Sofaer, 'On the Necessity of Pre-Emption', *European Journal of International Law* 14 (2003), 209–26 (214–220); Paust, 'Self-Defence Targeting of Non-State Actors' 2010 (n. 10), 241–4.

Ashburton, on behalf of the United Kingdom, is what is referred to as establishing the law on self-defence in the *Caroline* incident.[128] In his letter to Webster offering an explanation for the United Kingdom's use of force against the *Caroline* while it was on US waters, Ashburton declares that there are 'possible cases in the relations of nations as of individuals, where necessity . . . may be pleaded'.[129] In response, Webster, while admitting the existence of self-defence, notes that it is 'confined to cases in which the "necessity of that self-defence is instant, overwhelming, and leaving no choice of means, and no moment for deliberation"'.[130] The *Caroline* incident is more often than not raised in the context of the requirements of necessity and imminence. However, in the context of the proposition relating to the use of force against non-State actors, it is pointed out that Webster in his retort made no issue of the fact that the actors responsible for the attacks in British Canada were non-State actors. Nor is there any indication that the United Kingdom had imputed the acts on the United States government. Therefore, it is suggested, both the United States and the United Kingdom accepted that the use of force in self-defence against non-State actors in the territory of a third State was possible even if the attack by non-State actors were not imputable to that third State.[131]

The third pillar supporting the proposition is to refer to certain post-Article 51 State practice which, it is argued, supports the proposition that current international law permits a State to use force in self-defence against a non-State actor in the territory of an innocent third State without that third State's consent. Explaining the central element of this pillar, Murphy states that 'whatever the original meaning of Article 51 might have been, subsequent state practice appears to support' the proposition that a State may use force against non-State actors in the territory of a third State.[132] Similarly, van Steenberghe states that 'recent practice greatly contributes to the evolution of the law of self-defence' and 'implies the recognition of the right to respond in self-defence to private armed attacks'.[133] The examples of State practice in these areas are too many to fully

---

[128] The exchange is reprinted in Moore, *Digest of International Law* 1906 (n. 24), 409–13.
[129] *Ibid.*, 411.
[130] *Ibid.*, 412.
[131] See also commentary to Principle 6 of the Chatham House Principles (n. 95), stating that the proposition that the States may use force in self-defence against non-State actors in the territory of non-consenting third States 'is supported by reference to the *Caroline* case; the criteria in *Caroline* were enunciated in the context of a marauding armed band, not orthodox state-to-state conflict'.
[132] Murphy, 'Self-Defence and the Israeli Wall Advisory Opinion' 2005 (n. 10), 67.
[133] Raphaël van Steenberghe, 'Self-Defence in Response to Attacks by Non-State Actors in the Light of Recent State Practice: A Step Forward', *Leiden Journal of International Law* 23 (2010), 183–208 (208).

discuss or cover at any length. I will focus, therefore, only on those examples of practice common to all publications supporting the proposition that the use of force in self-defence against non-State actors in the territory of innocent third States is permissible. These can be usefully divided into two categories.

The first category involves practice following (and in response to) the attacks of 11 September 2001 in the United States.[134] These attacks on US territory were carried out by a non-State actor, Al-Qaeda. In the aftermath of those attacks, the United States notified the Security Council on 7 October 2001 that it would be deploying forces in Afghanistan in the exercise of its right to self-defence. It is now a historical fact that the United States did indeed attack Afghanistan in what was known as Operation Enduring Freedom. Tams, in other works, suggested that Operation Enduring Freedom provides 'the most obvious piece of evidence' to support the proposition that unilateral force may be used in self-defence against non-State actors in the territory of innocent non-consenting third States.[135] Similarly, Paust states categorically that the October 2001 use of force by the United States in Afghanistan against Al-Qaeda 'was justified, and justifiable, as self-defence against on-going processes of armed attack on the United States ... '.[136] He clearly identifies the use of force against Al-Qaeda as an act of 'self-defence' and in response to an 'armed attack', thus bringing them within the ambit of Article 51.

Practice flowing from the 11 September 2001 attacks is also said to include the UN Security Council resolutions adopted in the aftermath of those terrorist attacks.[137] In the aftermath of the attacks, the UN Security Council adopted Resolutions 1368 and 1373 on 12 September and 28 September respectively. Both Resolutions include a preambular paragraph recognising 'the inherent right of individual or collective self-defence in accordance with the Charter'. These references, it is said, amount to a recognition by the UN Security Council that unilateral force may be used in self-defence against non-State actors in the territory of a non-consenting innocent third State.[138] Explaining the position, Murphy states that there is no language in the Resolutions that indicates that the initial attack 'must first be imputed to a State' before the right to use force in self-defence can be triggered.[139]

[134] See for full discussion Murphy, 'Terrorism and the Concept of "Armed Attack"' 2002 (n. 90).
[135] Tams, 'The Use of Force against Terrorists' 2009 (n. 10), 378.
[136] Paust, 'Self-Defence Targeting of Non-State Actors' 2010 (n. 10), 248.
[137] See, e.g. Wood, 'International Law and the Use of Force' 2013 (n. 94), 356. See also Bethlehem, 'Principles Relevant to the Scope of a State's Right of Self-Defense against an Imminent or Actual Armed Attack by Nonstate Actors' 2012 (n. 99), 774.
[138] See, e.g, Tams, 'The Use of Force against Terrorists' 2009 (n. 10), 377; Murphy, 'Self-Defence and the Israeli Wall Advisory Opinion' 2005 (n. 10), 67.
[139] Murphy, 'Self-Defence and the Israeli Wall Advisory Opinion' 2005 (n. 10), 67.

The second category of examples often advanced to justify the use of force in self-defence against non-State actors in the territory of non-consenting innocent third States involves other uses of force by States, claimed to be in self-defence, against non-State actors in the territory of third States.[140] The most common examples of such other cases include the use of force by Israel against Hezbollah in Lebanon in 2006 and the incursion by Turkey into northern Iraq in response to attacks by the Kurdistan Workers Party in 2006 and 2008 respectively.[141] There are, of course, many other cases of use of force against non-State actors that have been considered, but time and space permit only the consideration of these two cases as illustrative of the discussion.[142] Tams, for example, refers to the US bombardment of a pharmaceutical plant in Sudan in response to attacks on its embassies in Kenya and Tanzania, the Russian airstrikes in Georgia in response to Chechen rebel activity, and the Colombian use of force in 2008 against the FARC.[143] In this Trialogue, Tams (pp. 152–3) lists, without discussion, the following additional cases of 'cross-border raids in pursuit of rebels': Tajikistan in Afghanistan; Rwanda against the DRC; Senegal in Guinea Bissau; and Thailand in Myanmar. In her chapter in the Trialogue, O'Connell (pp. 176–7), for her part, identifies a series of US conduct, not so much as law-changing practice, but rather as examples of unlawful use of force. More recently, the use of force against ISIS provides a significant example of practice.[144]

---

[140]   See for discussion *ibid.*

[141]   These cases are discussed in van Steenberghe, 'Self-Defence in Response to Attacks by Non-State Actors' 2010 (n. 133).

[142]   For other examples included in the literature see, e.g., Trapp, 'Back to Basics' 2007 (n. 5), 147 *et seq.* discussing the Israeli rescue operation in Entebbe airport following the hijacking of a Tel Aviv bound aircraft and bombing of the Palestinian Liberation Organisation's Headquarters in Tunis in response to the killing of citizens in Cyprus. In addition, see Paust, 'Self-Defence Targeting of Non-State Actors' 2010 (n. 10), 247, discussing the pre-9/11 missile strikes against Al-Qaeda in Afghanistan in response to attacks on the US Embassy in Kenya. See also Moir, *Reappraising the Resort to Force* 2010 (n. 14), 26 *et seq.* See also, for example, Gray, *International Law and the Use of Force* 2008 (n. 5), 137, discussing, *inter alia*, Apartheid South Africa's use of force in several neighbouring States in response to what it argued were terrorist operations by the African National Congress. See also William C. Banks and Evan J. Criddle, 'Customary Constraints on the Use of Force: Article 51 with an American Accent', *Leiden Journal of International Law* 29 (2016), 67–93 (81), which examines the situation where the US launched attacks in Libya in response to the bombing of a Berlin night club in which an American soldier was killed.

[143]   Tams, 'The Use of Force against Terrorists' 2009 (n. 10), 380.

[144]   For discussion see Arimatsu and Schmitt, 'Attacking "Islamic State" and the Khorasan Group' 2014 (n. 7). See also Michael Wood, 'The Use of Force in 2015 with Particular Reference to Syria', Hebrew University of Jerusalem Legal Studies Research Paper Series 16-05 (2016).

D. The Rules for Interpreting and Identifying the Scope of Self-Defence in Respect of Non-State Actors

1. The General Rules of Treaty Interpretation

Given that the rules on self-defence exist both under customary international law and the Charter, the question arises whether the proper analysis should focus on one or the other. In my view, because the content of the customary and charter rules on self-defence are co-extensive and identical, it makes little difference where the focus lies, and the outcome of the analysis will be the same.

The question, though, is how to construct the relationship between the prohibition in Article 2(4) and the right in Article 51 of the Charter. My co-participants in the Trialogue adopt largely divergent approaches. Tams, on the one hand, employs a positivist approach, seeking to find meaning in the text and the practice of States. O'Connell, on the other hand, adopts a historical account, based on the tenets of natural law, to her analysis and places the right of self-defence in the context of the important and fundamental nature of the prohibition on the use of force. Her position is that because the prohibition on the use force is *ius cogens*, the right to self-defence, as an exception to that prohibition, cannot be subject to the ordinary rules of interpretation, such as the application of subsequent practice in a way that would reduce the scope of the *ius cogens* norm.[145] I adopt the approach that the traditional rules of interpretation, including practice, provide the path for finding the scope of self-defence.

The rules relevant to the interpretation of Article 51 are to be found in Article 31 of the VCLT. The primary rule of interpretation, found in Article 31(1) of the VCLT, is that words in a treaty must be given their ordinary meanings, in their context and in the light of the object and purpose of the treaty. The literal meaning of the words can, therefore, not be dispositive of the question whether a State can use force in self-defence against non-State actors in the territory of innocent non-consenting third States. The context in which those words are used, as well as the object and purpose of the treaty, give the text its meaning. Moreover, the VCLT provides for subsequent agreements and subsequent practice of the parties to a treaty to contribute to finding the meaning of the treaty provisions. Article 31(3)(a) provides that, in the interpretation of a treaty text, 'subsequent agreement between the parties regarding the interpretation of the treaty' shall be taken into account. Article 31(3)(b), on the other hand,

---

[145]   O'Connell in this volume, 244.

provides for the taking into account of 'subsequent practice in the application of the treaty which establishes the agreement of the parties regarding its interpretation'. Finally, Article 31(3)(c) provides for the taking into account of 'relevant rules of international law applicable in the relations between the parties'.

As shown above (Section IV.C), the proposition that the right to use force in self-defence extends to force against non-State actors operating on the territory of an innocent non-consenting State is based on three pillars. First, that the word 'inherent' in Article 51 means that the rules of self-defence in customary international law continue to apply and that these customary international law rules permit the use of force in self-defence against non-State actors in the territory of innocent non-consenting States. The second pillar is that the phrase 'armed attack' in Article 51 is not qualified by the requirement that the armed attack must emanate from a State. Finally, this proposition is based on post-Article 51 practice that is said to support the idea that the use of force in self-defence against non-State actors in the territory of innocent third States is permitted.

All three pillars, in some way, depend on an assessment of practice. The pillar based on the word 'inherent' seeks to invoke customary international law, in particular practice in the form of, *inter alia*, the *Caroline* incident, to support the proposition. The pillar based on the phrase 'armed attack', though essentially advancing a literal interpretation of the Charter, must also, out of necessity, rely on practice. Practice would be important to establish the meaning of the phrase 'armed attack'. Finally, and most obviously, the third pillar on post-Article 51 practice is, of course, based on practice in the form of post-Article 51 practice. Given the centrality of practice for the proposition, a brief description of the role of practice for the determination of the rules of international law on self-defence is appropriate before embarking on an evaluation of the three pillars of the proposition.

2. The Role of Practice in Evaluating the Proposition

Practice can, potentially, serve three roles in the evaluation of the proposition that international law permits the unilateral use of force in self-defence in the territory of an innocent non-consenting third State. First, practice can be advanced in support of a rule of customary international law, existing independent of (perhaps even in competition with) Article 51 of the Charter. Second, practice can be advanced in support of an existing rule of customary international law to be considered in the interpretation of Article 51 of the Charter under Article 31(3)(c) of the VCLT. Finally, practice can be advanced as subsequent practice in the interpretation of Article 51 under Article 31(3)(b) of the VCLT. To fulfil these respective roles, however, the relevant practice must meet certain requirements.

For practice to contribute to the formation of customary international law, it has to be widespread or general and must be settled.[146] In 2018, the ILC adopted a set of Draft Conclusions on the Identification of Customary International Law on first reading.[147] According to Draft Conclusion 8, the 'relevant practice must be general, meaning that it must be sufficiently widespread and representative, as well as consistent'.[148] Thus, in instances where the practice is limited to a few States, condonation by other States, if sufficiently wide, might be sufficient to establish that there is widespread practice. Conversely, widespread objection to or criticism of a practice would prevent the establishment of widespread practice for the purposes of formation of customary international law. It is worth pointing out in this regard that the ILC, in its Draft Conclusions on the Identification of Customary International Law, considered, and decided not to include, a provision to the effect that the practice of 'specially affected States' is more significant in the establishment of customary international law.[149] The attitude of the 'silent majority' – those States that neither engage in a practice nor respond to it – is thus of particular importance. Inaction on its own cannot, as a rule, be taken to mean acquiescence to a practice.[150] It has to be shown that inaction was deliberate and aimed at expressing acquiescence.

---

[146] ICJ, *Jurisdictional Immunities of the State* (Germany v. Italy: Greece intervening), Judgment of 3 February 2012, ICJ Reports 2012, 99, para. 55.

[147] ILC, Draft Conclusions on the Identification of Customary International Law (adopted on second reading), Report on the work of its seventieth session, UN Doc. A/73/10 (2018).

[148] See *ibid.*, Draft Conclusion 8, para. 1.

[149] In the second report on the Identification of Customary International Law, the Special Rapporteur, Michael Wood, proposed a Draft Conclusion to the effect that 'the practice of specially affected states' must be accorded greater weight ('In assessing practice, due regard is to be given to the practice of States whose interests are specially affected'). See Proposed Draft Conclusion 9 in Michael Wood, *Second Report on Identification of Customary International Law*, UN Doc. A/CN.4/672 (2014), 4, para. 59. See for a description of the debate within the Commission Dire Tladi, 'Progressive Development and Codification of International Law: The Work of the International Law Commission During its Sixty-Sixth Session', *South African Yearbook of International Law* 28 (2013), 124–43 (129–30). The Commission eventually decided to include language in the commentary to Draft 8 to the effect that 'the extent to which those States that are particularly involved in the relevant activity or are most likely to be concerned with the alleged rule ("specially affected States") have participated in the practice … it should however be made clear that the term "specially affected States" should not be taken to refer to the relative power of States.' See ILC, Draft Conclusions on the Identification of Customary International Law (n. 147), Commentary to Draft Conclusion 8, para. 4.

[150] ILC, Draft Conclusions on the Identification of Customary International Law (n. 147). Draft Conclusion 6, para. 1, states that practice 'may, under certain circumstances, include inaction'. In paragraph 3 of the Commentary to the Draft Conclusion, the Commission states the 'words "under certain circumstances" seek to caution, however, that only deliberate abstention from acting could serve such a role: the State in question ought to be conscious about refraining from acting in a given situation'.

In addition to the above, for practice to form the basis of a rule of customary international law, that practice must be accepted by the community of States as a whole as a rule of law – *opinio iuris sive necessitas*.[151] Whether evidence of *opinio iuris* is sufficient to meet this standard requires not only the belief of a few States that the practice constitutes a rule of customary international law, but this belief must also be widely held. The question of the silent majority is again important here. In the commentary to Draft Conclusion 9 of the Draft Conclusion on the Identification of Customary International Law, the ILC observed that the requirement of acceptance of law 'is to be sought with respect to both the States engaging in the relevant practice (action or inaction) and those in a position to react to it'.[152] More to the point, paragraph 3 of Draft Conclusion 10 states that silence will only constitute *opinio iuris* if the States 'were in a position to react and the circumstances called for some reaction'. Thus, international law as it currently stands requires widespread practice and acceptance as law. For these purposes, it is important, particularly where the practice is limited in extent, to also consider the reactions of other States to that practice.

Similarly, there are important requirements for reliance on subsequent practice as a tool for interpreting Article 51 of the Charter. The VCLT provides that subsequent practice 'shall be considered' in the interpretation of a treaty provision. However, it is only practice which 'establishes the agreement of the parties regarding [the treaty's] interpretation' that is to be considered under Article 31(3)(b). Thus, in order to constitute an authentic interpretation of parties under Article 31(3)(b) of the VCLT, it is not sufficient to show widespread agreement. Rather, it must be shown that the practice in question establishes the agreement of *all the parties* to the UN Charter as to the interpretation of Article 51. Moreover, the practice must establish the agreement of all the parties *regarding the interpretation of* Article 51. Political support of particular conduct in which force has been used is insufficient; the support should be linked to the interpretation of Article 51. Thus, even more than with the formation of customary international law, the attitude of the silent majority is an essential element of any attempt at establishing that a particular conduct, or series of actions, constitutes subsequent practice for the purposes of Article 31(3)(b) of the VCLT. More to the point, *any* expression of criticism or objection will most certainly inflict a deathblow on any attempt to advance conduct, or series of actions, as constitutive of subsequent practice for the purposes of Article 31(3)(b) of the VCLT.

---

[151] See ICJ, *North Sea Continental Shelf* (Federal Republic of Germany/Denmark; Federal Republic of Germany/Netherlands), Judgment of 20 February 1969, ICJ Reports 1969, 44, para. 77.

[152] ILC, Draft Conclusions on the Identification of Customary International Law (n. 147), Commentary to Draft Conclusion 9, para. 5.

Thus, in assessing practice, whether for the purposes of customary international law or treaty interpretation, it is important to also assess the response of other States. Finally, it may also be pointed out in this respect that judicial practice, particularly that of the International Court of Justice – though not State practice – may also serve as an important element for weighing the evidence for an interpretation of rules of international law, including the weight of certain conduct as practice, either for the purposes of customary international law or as an authentic interpretation of Article 51 of the Charter under Article 31(3)(b) of the VCLT.[153]

V. EVALUATION OF THE SCOPE OF THE RIGHT OF SELF-DEFENCE

I proceed now to consider each of the three pillars on which the proposition that States may use force unilaterally in self-defence against non-State actors in the territory of an innocent third State without that State's consent rests in turn. The main thrust of the first pillar is dependent on the identification of customary international law before the Charter and not on the interpretation of the Charter provisions. The second and third pillars both rely on the interpretation of the provisions of the Charter concerning the use of force.

A. The 'Inherent Right': Pre-Existing Rules of Customary International Law

The cogency of the first pillar – pre-Charter customary international law permitted the use of force against non-State actors – depends on several assumptions. The first, and least controversial assumption, is that a rule of customary international law continues to exist even if embodied in a treaty. First, this assumption seems to be borne out by the text of Article 51 of the Charter, which refers to the 'inherent right' of self-defence, suggesting that the right exists independent of the Charter. Second, in connection with the right to self-defence, the ICJ has recognised this principle stating that there 'can be no doubt that the issues of the use of force and collective self-defence … are issues which are regulated both by customary international law and by treaties, in particular the United Nations Charter'.[154]

---

[153]   Article 38(1)(d) of the Statute of the International Court of Justice; ILC, Draft Conclusions on the Identification of Customary International Law (n. 147), Draft Conclusion 13.

[154]   ICJ, *Military and Paramilitary Activities* (n. 31), para. 34. In a more general context see ICJ, *North Sea Continental Shelf* (n. 151), paras. 61 *et seq.*, especially para. 71.

A second assumption necessary for the cogency of the argument based on the pre-Charter customary international law is that the exchange between Ashburton and Webster in the *Caroline* incident constituted customary international law. However, this assumption is based on flawed logic. For the exchange in the *Caroline* incident to be formative (or even reflective of a rule of customary international law), the resort to force had to be prohibited under international law *at the time of the exchange*. Self-defence, as an exception *under international law*, can only make sense where *international law* prohibits the resort to force. Yet, as observed in Section II.A above, at the time of the *Caroline* incident international law did not prohibit the use of force. The justifications advanced by Ashburton for the attack on the *Caroline* appear, therefore, to be for 'political expediency' and 'in order to secure moral high ground' and not to provide a shield against legal wrongfulness.[155] If the use of force was not prohibited under international law and the justifications offered by Ashburton were not intended as legal justification, then the *Caroline* incident cannot be said to have been constitutive, or reflective, of customary international law. This is not to say that it could not have inspired, at a later date, the establishment of specific rules of customary international law on the right to self-defence. However, any such rules would need to be established through the normal process of the formation of customary international law and not through some nostalgic recollection of some incident that took place before the development of the law on self-defence. In other words, if the *Caroline* incident inspired the establishment of a new rule of customary international law, it would be necessary to show the existence of such a rule through evidence of the practice and *opinio iuris* inspired by the exchange.

A third assumption underlying the pre-Charter customary international law argument is that a single incident, involving only two States, can generate a rule of customary international law. It is not clear how the *Caroline* incident meets the requirements of a widespread or general practice. Those advancing it as constitutive of customary international law make no attempt to show acquiescence on the part of other States. The *Caroline* incident does not meet the generally accepted criteria for customary international law. As most recently captured by the ILC: 'the practice must be followed by a sufficiently large and representative number of States.'[156] Moreover, even if it could be said that the exchange between Ashburton and Webster constituted widespread, representative and consistent

---

[155] Tladi and Dugard, 'The Use of Force by States' 2018 (n. 25), 729.
[156] ILC, Draft Conclusions on the Identification of Customary International Law (n. 147), Draft Conclusion 8, para. 2.

practice, no evidence of acceptance of law has been illustrated by those relying on the exchange to suggest a rule of customary international law. Quite the contrary if, as illustrated in Section II.A, international law did not prohibit the use of force, then the exchange could not be evidence of an acceptance of law. Indeed it is not even clear that the authors of the exchange themselves consider themselves to be stating rules of international law.[157]

A fourth assumption underlying the argument that pre-Charter customary international law permitted the use of force in self-defence against non-State actors is that customary international law is static, and an exchange which may have reflected (or formed) a rule of customary international law in the period around 1840 when the incident occurred would still reflect customary international law of the twenty-first century. This assumption seems to ignore the dynamic nature of customary international law and that, whatever the law may have been at the time of the incident, world events since then have impacted on customary international law on the use of force so much so that to refer to an exchange of letters in 1842 as definitively reflecting rules of customary international law is highly questionable.[158]

The argument that pre-Charter international law permits the unilateral use of force in self-defence against non-State actors on the territory of a non-consenting innocent State is based on four assumptions about customary international law, three of which are erroneous. The standard in the *Caroline* incident could, of course, reflect a rule of customary international law *if* it can be shown to meet the normal requirements for the formation of customary international law. It must thus be assessed in the light of practice, in particular developments in the twentieth and twenty-first century.

B. *Armed Attack does not mean Armed Attack by a State*

1. A (fairly) Consistent Line of Reasoning by the International Court of Justice

Before engaging with the interpretation of the words 'armed attack' in Article 51, it is useful to describe what appears to be a consistent line of reasoning from the International Court of Justice concerning the meaning of those words. Judicial practice, particularly from the ICJ, may be useful as a subsidiary

---

[157] An indication that the statements were not intended to signify a legal position is Ashburton's remark that the United Kingdom would not 'provoke a great and powerful neighbour'. Letter by Ashburton in Moore, *Digest of International Law* 1906 (n. 24), 412.

[158] See Brownlie, *Principles of Public International Law* 2003 (n. 9), 701, describing such a view as 'anachronistic and indefensible'.

means of determining the appropriate interpretation of Article 51. Over the years there have been several judgments, advisory opinions and individual opinions of members of the Court that have shed light on the proper interpretation of the rules of Article 51 and the corresponding rule of customary international law. In general, it may be said that the Court has, over the years, interpreted the phrase 'armed attack' as meaning an attack by one State against another.

It should be said, however, that the proposition that an armed attack from a non-State may permit the attacked State to use force against that non-State actor in the territory of a third State has received some support in separate and dissenting opinions of some members of the Court. Although Judge Schwebel's dissenting opinion is, at least insofar as concerns the meaning of 'armed attack', a little less generous than the proposition, he does, based on the views on Sir Humphrey Waldock's Hague Lectures, conclude that the use of force in self-defence is permitted even in cases not involving armed attack – a view even broader than the proposition.[159] More relevant for the present discussion, Judge Buergenthal, in his declaration in the *Construction of the Wall* opinion, declares that the United Nations Charter in Article 51 does not make the exercise of the inherent right to self-defence 'dependent upon an armed attack by another State'.[160] Similarly, Judge Higgins, in her separate opinion, noted that there is 'nothing in the text of Article 51 that thus stipulates that self-defence is available only when an armed attack is made by a State'.[161]

The Court itself, however, has been fairly consistent in rejecting the proposition that a State may unilaterally use force in the territory of an innocent third State without that State's consent. This consistent line of reasoning can be traced back to the *Nicaragua* case. There the Court states that for a State to rely on self-defence under international law, that State must be a victim of an armed attack.[162] In addressing what constitutes an armed attack, the Court famously makes the following statement, which has been the subject of much discussion:

---

[159] See ICJ, *Military and Paramilitary Activities* (n. 31), Dissenting Opinion of Judge Schwebel, paras. 172–4. A similar, though not identical, view is expressed in the Separate Opinion of Judge Simma in ICJ, *Case Concerning Oil Platforms* (n. 48), para. 12, stating that 'defensive action – by force also short of Article 51' in response to 'smaller-scale use of force' is permitted.

[160] See ICJ, *Wall* Advisory Opinion (n. 48), Declaration of Judge Buergenthal, para. 6.

[161] ICJ, *Wall* Advisory Opinion (n. 48), Separate Opinion of Judge Higgins, para. 33. See also ICJ, *Armed Activities in the Territory of the Congo* (n. 42), Separate Opinion of Judge Simma, para. 12 ('if armed attacks are carried out by irregular forces from [the territory of a third], these activities are still armed attacks even if they cannot be attributed to the territorial State').

[162] ICJ, *Military and Paramilitary Activities* (n. 31), 195.

There appears now to be general agreement on the nature of the acts which can be treated as constituting armed attacks. In particular, it may be considered to be agreed that an armed attack must be understood as including not merely action by regular armed forces across an international border, but also 'the sending by or on behalf of a State of armed bands, groups, irregulars, or mercenaries, which carry out acts of armed force against another State of such gravity as to amount to' an actual armed attack conducted by regular forces, 'or its substantial involvement therein'. This description ... may be taken to reflect customary international law.[163]

It is clear that the Court considers that, as a general rule, an armed attack means an attack by one State against another. However, the Court considers that it is possible for an armed attack, justifying the use of force in self-defence, to occur in the case of attacks by non-State actors. However, for this possibility, the acts must be arising from the 'sending by' or must be 'on behalf of [the third] State'.[164] In other words, the acts in question must be imputable to a State to constitute an armed attack capable of forming the basis of unilateral use of force in self-defence. The Court, moreover, continues to significantly reduce the possibility of imputability. The Court states that the notion of armed attack does not include cases where acts of non-State actors result from 'assistance to [non-State actors] in the form of the provision of weapons or logistical or other support'.[165] For the Court, therefore, armed attacks by non-State actors, will, for the purposes of the law on self-defence, be imputable to a State if that State exercises effective control over the non-State actors.

The basic principle, articulated in the *Nicaragua* case has been reaffirmed in other judgments and opinions of the International Court of Justice. Although the issue of the author of the 'armed attack' was not central in the *Oil Platforms* case, the Court in that case also contributed to this consistent line of jurisprudence when it noted that for the United States to successfully claim self-defence against Iran, it had to show that 'attacks had been made upon it for which *Iran was responsible*'.[166] The issue was also addressed in the *Wall* advisory opinion, in particular on the question of whether Israel was entitled to rely on Article 51 in response to attacks from non-State actors in the Occupied Palestinian

---

[163]   *Ibid.*

[164]   See, however, the commentary to Principle 6 of the Chatham House Principles (n. 95) which interprets this quote from the *Nicaragua* case as suggesting that any attack from a non-State actor of sufficient gravity will constitute an armed attack. However, it is clear that for the Court, the gravity is an additional element. The first element, completely unaccounted for in commentary to Principle 6 is 'the sending by or on behalf of a State'.

[165]   See ICJ, *Military and Paramilitary Activities* (n. 31), 195.

[166]   ICJ, *Case Concerning Oil Platforms* (n. 48), para. 51 (emphasis added).

Territories. In the *Wall* advisory opinion, the Court confirmed that Article 51 of the Charter applies to cases of an 'armed attack by one State against another'.[167] The language in these cases is clear and unambiguous.

The *Armed Activities in the Territory of the Congo* case was seen, by those supporting the proposition that States can use force unilaterally in self-defence in the territory of third States, as an opportunity to 'correct' the judgments in the *Nicaragua*, *Oil Platforms* and *Wall* jurisprudence.[168] The Court, however, confirmed the fundamental element in its reasoning in these decisions, namely that the use of force in self-defence was impermissible against non-State actors on the territory of a non-consenting, third State. Dismissing Uganda's claim of self-defence, the Court observed that Uganda 'did not ever claim that it had been subjected to an armed attack by the armed forces of the DRC'.[169] The Court notes that, rather, the armed attack which was purportedly the basis of the unilateral use of force response was from a non-State actor – the Allied Democratic Forces (ADF).[170] Therefore, having found 'no satisfactory proof of the involvement in these attacks, direct or indirect, of the Government of the DRC', or that the attacks emanated 'from armed bands or irregulars sent by the DRC or on behalf of the DRC', the attacks by the ADF were not attributable to the DRC and therefore could not form the basis of unilateral use of force in self-defence in the territory of the DRC.[171] The Court, thus, clearly requires 'proof of the involvement' of the third State, whether direct or indirect, or proof that the non-State actors were 'sent by' or acted 'on behalf of' the State in question before self-defence would be permissible. A statement by the Court that it is unnecessary 'to respond to the contentions of the Parties' concerning 'conditions under which . . . international law provides for a right of self-defence against large-scale attacks by irregular forces' might suggest a departure from the strict attribution standard.[172] This latter statement, however is hardly a declaration of law. Moreover, reliance on it ignores the fact that the Court makes this statement in the context of its finding that 'the preconditions for the exercise of self-defence' did not exist in that case.[173] These preconditions are precisely that the acts of the non-State actors 'remained non-attributable to the DRC'.[174] But more than that, the quoted phrase is not a doctrinal statement

---

[167]   ICJ, *Wall* Advisory Opinion (n. 48), para. 139.
[168]   See generally ICJ, *Wall* Advisory Opinion (n. 48), Separate Opinion of Judge Kooijmans, and ICJ, *Armed Activities in the Territory of the Congo* (n. 42), Separate Opinion of Judge Simma.
[169]   ICJ, *Armed Activities in the Territory of the Congo* (n. 42), para. 146.
[170]   Ibid.
[171]   Ibid., paras. 146–7.
[172]   Ibid., para. 147.
[173]   Ibid.
[174]   Ibid., para. 146.

about law but is rather, on its face, concerned with the fact/circumstance specific issues that I have already deemed beyond the scope of this contribution.

It has also been suggested by Trapp that the decision of the Court in *Armed Activities in the Territory of the Congo* can be read as not requiring attribution for reliance on the right to use force on the territory of a third State.[175] This conclusion is based on an interesting, yet ultimately misleading, reading of the Court's decision in the *Armed Activities in the Territory of the Congo* case. The conclusion highlights that in *Armed Activities in the Territory of Congo* 'the Court emphasized that Uganda's defensive measures were carried out *against* the DRC.'[176] This argument suggests that had Uganda's use of force been directed at the ADF and not the DRC, then the Court would have found such unilateral use of force, in principle and subject to other requirements, permissible. With respect, this interpretation is only possible if one ignores a number of important factors.

First, it ignores the fact that the decision of the Court in *Armed Activities in the Territory of the Congo* is not given in a vacuum but rather is part of a consistent line of reasoning in which the Court has defined 'armed attack' as either an attack emanating from a State or one which can be attributed to a State. This definition in a consistent line of findings by the Court would be inconsistent with the novel interpretation advanced by Trapp, and it is inconceivable that the Court would make such a significant departure from its previously declared position in such a furtive manner. Second, this interesting reading of the Court's decision ignores the fact that the Court is fully aware of the criticism *from some quarters* – mainly 'Anglo-Saxon scholars'[177] – that has been levelled against its definition of armed attack. If the Court wanted to depart from its jurisprudence in response to this criticism it would have done so explicitly. Third, this novel interpretation would ignore the judicial dialogue involved in the International Court of Justice's deliberative process. Several judges wrote separate opinions in the *Armed Activities* case, in particular Simma and Kooijmans, specifically

---

175   See generally Trapp, 'Back to Basics' 2007 (n. 5), 144 *et seq*. See especially Kimberley Trapp, 'The Use of Force against Terrorists: A Reply to Christian J. Tams', *European Journal of International Law* 20 (2010), 1049–55 (1051), stating that 'a careful reading of the International Court of Justice's (ICJ's) jurisprudence reveals that it does not actually require armed attacks by non-State actors to be attributable to the host state before defensive force can be used against (and only against) those non-State actors in the host state's territory.'

176   Trapp, 'Back to Basics' 2007 (n. 5), 145.

177   Tom Ruys, '*Quo Vadit Jus Ad Bellum?* A Legal Analysis of Turkey's Military Operations against the PKK in Northern Iraq', *Melbourne Journal of International Law* 9 (2008), 334–64 (351).

criticising the Court for sticking with its *Military and Paramilitary Activities* case definition of armed attack.[178] The Court was therefore well aware that its dicta in *Armed Activities in the Territory of the Congo* case would be seen as endorsing its previous decisions, and it continued in that direction. Sean Murphy, in the context of the *Wall* opinion, also considers the possibility that the Court had departed from its position in the *Military and Paramilitary* case and correctly observes that assuming that the views of the judges writing separate opinions 'were made known to the Court in the course of the deliberations, as would normally be the case, the Court understood how this language was going to be interpreted' and it nonetheless 'chose to adopt that interpretation'.[179] If there were any ambiguity in the Court's decision – and I do not believe there is – such an ambiguity would have to be seen in the light of previous judgments. Given the practice of the Court of following its previous judgments, it has to be assumed that it has done so also in *Armed Activities in the Territory of the Congo* case. The correct description of the Court's position after the *Wall* opinion, *Oil Platforms* case and the *Armed Activities* case seems to be neatly summarised by Tom Ruys, who observes that in these cases and the advisory opinion, the Court 'sticks to the restrictive threshold spelled out in *Nicaragua*'.[180]

It is worth noting that attribution of the armed attack, as the basis for unilateral use of force in self-defence on the territory of a third State, was not questioned, even in Judge Schwebel's strongly worded dissent in *Nicaragua*.[181] In his dissent, Judge Schwebel states that the Court's conclusion 'that a State's assistance to foreign armed irregulars who seek to overthrow the government of another State' does not amount to an armed attack 'is inconsistent with generally accepted doctrine, law and practice as well'.[182] Judge Schwebel's conclusion in the *Nicaragua* case that there was an armed attack necessitating the use of force in self-defence is based on his view that there was a 'pervasive and prolonged support by the Nicaraguan Government of the insurgencies in El Salvador' which has 'been a major, perhaps the critical factor in the transformation of what . . . were largely sporadic if serious acts of

---

[178] See ICJ, *Wall* Advisory Opinion (n. 48), Separate of Opinion of Judge Kooijmans, and ICJ, *Armed Activities in the Territory of the Congo* (n. 42), Separate Opinion of Judge Simma. These opinions are discussed below at section V.B.3.

[179] Murphy, 'Self-Defence and the Israeli Wall Advisory Opinion' 2005 (n. 10), 63.

[180] Ruys, '*Quo Vadit Jus Ad Bellum?*' 2008 (n. 177), 356.

[181] See ICJ, *Military and Paramilitary Activities* (n. 31), Dissenting Opinion of Judge Schwebel, 160–1, for example, para. 155, describing the judgment of the Court as '[f]ar from contributing . . . to progressive development [on the critical question of whether aid to irregulars may be tantamount to an armed attack]', it amounts to 'a regressive development'.

[182] *Ibid.*, paras. 160–1.

insurgent terrorism into an organized and effective army of guerrillas'.[183] It is clear that in his view, aiding or supporting, including through the provision of weapons or logistical support, or the provision of a safe haven, may constitute the basis of attribution. Thus attribution as such was not questioned in his dissent. What he did question was the standard required by the majority, which he deemed unreasonably high. This view was similarly advanced by Judge *ad hoc* Kateka in the *Armed Activities in the Territory of the Congo* case.[184] Similarly Judge Koroma makes a distinction between two scenarios, namely a 'State's massive support for armed groups, including *deliberately* allowing them access to its territory' and a 'State's enabling groups of this type of act against another State'.[185] The former, he claims, constitutes an armed attack while the latter may not. While Judge Koroma suggests that this distinction is consistent with the standard set forth in *Nicaragua*, there is a significant difference. In the *Nicaragua* case the Court expressly excluded assistance and support from the ambit of armed attack, while Judge Koroma expressly includes assistance if it is 'massive' and done with deliberate intent to allow access. Moreover, even the second category of Judge Koroma should not be automatically excluded from the scope of armed attack. In placing this distinction in context, Judge Koroma states that 'if a State is *powerless* to put an end to the armed activities of rebel groups despite the fact that it opposes them, that is not tantamount to' an armed attack.[186] Clearly, then, Judge Koroma is excluding only innocent States from the ambit of States in whose territory force in self-defence may not be used.

In previous works, our co-participant in the Trialogue, Christian Tams, has similarly called for something between 'strict adherence' to attribution and 'a radical departure' from the *Nicaragua* test.[187] He suggests discarding the 'effective control' test of *Nicaragua* to a rule permitting the use of force in self-defence in the territory of a third State if that third State has supported or provided a safe haven for non-State actors engaged in acts of terrorism.[188] In many ways, this approach appears similar to the language of the US National Security Strategy of 2002, which declares that the United States will not distinguish 'between terrorists and those *who knowingly harbour or*

[183] *Ibid.*, para. 172.
[184] See ICJ, *Armed Activities in the Territory of the Congo* (n. 42), Dissenting Opinion of Judge *ad hoc* Kateka paras. 12–15.
[185] ICJ, *Armed Activities in the Territory of the Congo* (n. 42), Declaration of Judge Koroma, para. 9 (emphasis in original).
[186] *Ibid.* (emphasis added).
[187] Tams, 'The Use of Force against Terrorists' 2009 (n. 10), 385.
[188] *Ibid.*

provide aid to them"[189] – it is one that is still based on some attribution, even if not rising to the level of the *Nicaragua* test. Dismissing this approach, Trapp states that this approach is 'a long-rejected basis for attributing non-State conduct to a state'.[190] Advancing her test, which she seems to posit as more in line with an inter-State reading of Article 51, she suggests that if the third State 'is doing everything possible to prevent its territory from being used as a base for terrorist operations' then the use of force in self-defence in the territory of that State is not permissible.[191] If the third State is not doing everything possible, then unilateral force in self-defence on its territory is permitted. There is an internal inconsistency in the approach. On the one hand, according to Trapp, assisting and supporting is too loose a standard for attribution – after all, that is the principal reason why it is 'long-rejected' – while on the other hand an even looser standard of attribution, namely 'not doing everything possible' is advocated.

The approach of the Court, which clearly rejects that force can be used in the territory of a third State in response to attacks from non-State actors, has been fairly consistent. The Court's interpretation, particularly since it has not met with widespread objection from other States, should be highly persuasive in assessing whether an armed attack includes an attack from non-State actors. More importantly, the Court's approach is consistent with the interpretation of Article 51 under the VCLT.

2. Interpretation According to Article 31 of the VCLT

The second pillar on which the proposition that the unilateral use of force in self-defence against non-State actors in the territory of an innocent third State is permitted under international law rests is the text of Article 51, which provides that the right of self-defence may be exercised in the event that 'an armed attack' occurs. It is pointed out by those supporting the proposition that Article 51 does not provide that it has to be an armed attack by 'a State'. At first blush, this argument seems convincing. Treaty text however, as Article 51 is, cannot be interpreted only with reference to the literal meaning of the terms. The basic rule of treaty interpretation is that the terms of a treaty must be given their ordinary meaning, in their context and in the light of the object and purpose of the treaty.

---

[189] See *National Security Strategy of the United States of America* (September 2002). The quote can be found in chapter III, titled 'Strengthening Alliances to Defeat Global Terrorism and Work to Prevent Attacks against Us and Our Friends', at 5 (emphasis added).

[190] Trapp, 'The Use of Force against Terrorists' 2010 (n. 175), 1051.

[191] *Ibid.*, 1053.

We can find the context of Article 51 in several places in the Charter. The Charter as a whole forms part of the context within which Article 51 ought to be interpreted. In this regard, the fact that Article 2(4) and Article 51, 'are very much a response to the Second World War and are accordingly directed to inter-state conflict', is a contextual factor that suggests that Article 51 applies to an armed attack from a State.[192] In this regard, Article 51 is an exception to Article 2(4). Article 2(4) is concerned with inter-State use of force. As pointed out in Section IV.B, if Article 2(4) is concerned with inter-State use of force, it would be expected that Article 51, the exception thereto, would cover the same terrain. More to the point, the broad interpretation of 'armed attack' to include attacks from non-State actors with no State involvement would significantly reduce the scope of the prohibition on the use of force in the Charter. After all, it should be recalled that the right to use force in self-defence is an exception to the prohibition on the use of force. Exceptions should not be interpreted so broadly that they render meaningless the primary rule, in this case the prohibition on the use of force.[193] As Randelzhofer put it, while the UN Charter did not 'intend to exclude self-defence entirely', it 'restricted its scope considerably'.[194] The proposition that self-defence may be used against non-State actors in the territory of innocent third States would significantly expand, not restrict, the scope of the self-defence and, as a consequence, significantly restrict the prohibition on the use of force.

Moreover, if Article 2(4) applied to use of force between States, while Article 51 permitted the use of force against non-State actors in the territory of third States, this would result in the anomalous situation that acting consistently with Article 51 would result in a violation of Article 2(4) since, by definition, any use of force in the territory of a third State would infringe the territorial integrity of that State. The commentary to the Chatham Principles is illuminating in this respect. It states that the 'right to use of force in self-defence is an inherent right and is not dependent upon any prior breach of international law by the state in the territory of which defensive force is used'.[195] This reasoning seems to assume that somehow a non-State actor on the territory of a third State can be targeted without violating the territorial integrity and sovereignty

---

[192] Gray, *International Law and the Use of Force* 2008 (n. 5), 7.

[193] Oscar Schachter, 'Self-Defense and the Rule of Law', *American Journal of International Law* 83 (1989), 259–77 (266): 'Recognizing these rights [of self-defence] as exceptions to the general prohibition on force necessarily presupposes that the exercise of the right is limited by law. If this were not the case and each state remained free to decide for itself when and to what extent it may use force, the legal restraint on force would virtually disappear.'

[194] Albrecht Randelzhofer, 'Article 51', in Bruno Simma (ed.), *The United Nations Charter: A Commentary* (Oxford: Oxford University Press, 1994), 661–78 (663).

[195] Chatham House Principles (n. 95), commentary to principle 6.

of the third State. But of course that is not possible. Moreover, this seems to ignore that Article 51 does not exist in a vacuum but rather in the context of other principles of international law which are also contained in the Charter. How any interpretation of Article 51 interacts with and impacts on these other principles is important for determining the scope and limits of the right to self-defence.[196] These principles, apart from the prohibition on the use of force itself, include the respect for the territorial integrity and sovereignty of other States. It should be recalled, in this regard, that the use of force in the territory of another State, even if minimal, implies a violation of the third State's territorial integrity and sovereignty. These principles of sovereignty and the respect for territorial integrity remain central and foundational to the UN system and international law and are held as fundamental by the vast majority of the international community.[197] To the extent that we have, in recent decades, seen the erosion of these principles, this has been to prevent States from using the principles to harm their own peoples. Indeed, world leaders have, in the Declaration of the High Level Meeting of the General Assembly on the Rule of Law at the National and International Level, rededicated themselves to:

> support all efforts to uphold the sovereign equality of all States, to respect their territorial integrity and political independence, to refrain in [our] international relations from the threat or use of force in any manner inconsistent [with the Charter].[198]

An interpretation of Article 51 that permits the use of force in self-defence against the territory of an innocent non-consenting third State would be countenancing the violation of the third State's sovereignty and territorial integrity and would significantly impair these principles. Self-defence, when permitted under international law, amounts to an act of self-help in response to 'a violation of rights ... against the state responsible for the violation'.[199] To hold otherwise would impair the principles of territorial integrity and sovereignty. A contextual interpretation of the words 'armed attack' in Article 51 should take into account these principles of territorial integrity

---

[196] These other principles would be relevant, in particular, under Article 31(3)(c) VCLT.

[197] See, e.g., Final Document of the 17th Summit of Heads of State and Government of the Non-Aligned Movement, 17–18 September 2016, Island of Margarita, Venezuela, para. 5 ('To this end, the Movement will continue to uphold the principles of sovereignty ... territorial integrity and non-intervention ... ').

[198] See Declaration on the High Level Meeting of the General Assembly on the Rule of Law at the National and International Levels, UN Doc. A/Res/67/1, 24 September 2012, para. 3.

[199] Kelsen, 'Collective Security and Collective Self-Defence' 1948 (n. 52), 783.

and sovereignty. This context, in my view, supports an inter-State reading of Article 51 of the Charter.

In his chapter in the Trialogue, Tams advances an alternative contextual factor that he describes as 'more powerful', namely Articles 39 and 42.[200] He suggests that because Articles 39 and 42 have, through interpretation and practice, shed the original 'inter-State construction', Article 51 should be interpreted in a similar fashion. With respect, the argument simply does not follow. The expansive reading of Article 39 and 42 has been facilitated in part by the special powers of the Council and its primary mandate for the maintenance of international peace and security, powers and a mandate that States, acting unilaterally, simply do not have. To suggest, as this contextual interpretation might imply, that the scope of the rights of an individual State under Article 51 is the same as or even comparable to the scope of the powers of the Security Council in Chapter VII is wrong and dangerous. As Corten notes, to confer 'on every state the power to implement unilaterally its own conception of the necessities of the war against terror' would be to bypass 'if not simply ignore' the core ideal of collective security.[201]

Tams, also in this Trialogue, has suggested that object and purpose are less helpful for the interpretation of Article 51 because teleological arguments 'simply do not offer compelling arguments either way'.[202] However, the object and purpose of the Charter also, in my view, suggest a restrictive interpretation of the phrase 'armed attack'. The object and purpose of the Charter, simply put, are the prevention of wars and conflict. Interpreting Article 51 to permit the use of inter-State force in the territory of another State – thereby violating the third State's territorial integrity – is contrary to this purpose. It promotes rather than prevents war. Presumably, a third State on whose territory force is used would feel that the 'act of self-defence' against the non-State actor *on its territory* is a violation of the protection afforded to it by Article 2(4) potentially justifying (counter) resort to Article 51. This is precisely what the UN Charter seeks to prevent. Rather – and this contributes to both context and object and purpose – the Charter promotes a collective approach to peace and security. It is worth repeating that the very first purposes of the United Nations mentioned in the UN Charter are, firstly, to 'maintain international peace and security' and, secondly, to do so by taking 'effective collective measures for the prevention and removal of threats to peace'. Unilateral action which the broad

---

[200] Tams in this volume, 117.

[201] Olivier Corten, 'The "Unwilling or Unable Test": Has It Been, and Could It Be, Accepted?', *Leiden Journal of International Law* 29 (2016), 777–99.

[202] Tams in this volume, 123.

interpretation of 'armed attack' facilitates has a serious potential for escalation and therefore undermines this objective.

Tams scoffs at this, suggesting that it is 'too good to be true'.[203] He suggests that this is because, like many treaties, the Charter does not have 'one single, undiluted object and purpose' – it rather 'seeks to integrate competing goals into one overarching framework'.[204] Yet he offers no evidence of an object and purpose conflicting with the object and purpose to remove threats to peace through collective action. The reference in his contribution of the Trialogue to the changing nature of conflict, supported by the Secretary-General's report, *In Larger Freedom*, in no way diminishes or contradicts this object and purpose. The right to self-defence is a provision in the Charter – an exception at that – and is not, as appears to be suggested by Tams, an object and purpose.

Finally, until recently, the undisputed understanding of Article 51 was that it applied to a right of a State to respond to an armed attack from another State.[205] That this was the generally accepted view until recently seems to be accepted by Tams in his chapter where it is suggested that there has been a 'gradual shift' from the restrictive interpretation of 'armed attack' to a more expansive interpretation.[206] This is significant for interpretation, because it suggests that if there has been a shift, it is for those who are advocating a shift to show either that the context of the words in the Charter and/or its object and purpose have changed to such an extent as to warrant a new meaning being ascribed to the words. A reliance on the literal meaning of the words 'armed attack' is simply inadequate because the words themselves have not changed. To illustrate, if in 1980 'armed attack' was understood as 'armed attack by a State', shifting to a broader meaning would require more than pointing out that taken literally 'armed attack' does not exclude 'armed attack from a non-State actor'. Something else would need to be advanced to show why these words have now acquired a new meaning. By the same token, it is inadequate to rely, as Murphy does,[207] on the differences in the choices of words between Articles 2(4) and 51. After all, the language on which this argument is based has

---

[203] Tams in this volume, 121.

[204] Tams in this volume, 123.

[205] The classic position is articulated in Kelsen, 'Collective Security and Collective Self-Defence' 1948 (n. 52), 791. See also Peter Hilpold, 'The Applicability of Article 51 UN Charter to Asymmetric Wars', in Hans-Joachim Heintze and Pierre Thielbörger (eds.), *From Cold War to Cyber War: The Evolution of the International Law of Peace and Armed Conflict over the Last 25 Years* (Cham: Springer, 2016), 127–35 (128).

[206] Tams in this volume, 132.

[207] Murphy, 'Self-Defence and the Israeli Wall Advisory Opinion' 2005 (n. 10), 64. See also Tams in this volume, 116.

not changed from the days when 'armed attack' was understood as an 'armed attack from a State'.

It would seem that the only plausible factor that could have resulted in a shift is subsequent practice by States, so that ultimately the fate of the proposition that a State may use force in self-defence against a non-State actor depends on whether subsequent practice, which is the third pillar of the argument, has been such as to be evidence of an agreement between members of the United Nations that 'armed attack' now applies to armed attack from non-State actors. It is this third pillar to which the chapter now turns.

3. Contemporary Practice regarding the Proposition that Unilateral Force against Non-State Actors in the Territory of Third States is Permissible

The third pillar on which the proposition is based is that there are examples in contemporary practice of States using force against non-State actors, in self-defence, in the territory of innocent third States without the latter's consent. The examples mentioned in Section IV.C can be separated into two categories. The first category concerns practice emanating from and linked to the US response to the terrorist attacks on 11 September 2001. These, as discussed above, include the adoption of UN Security Council Resolutions 1368 and 1373 and the US war in Afghanistan. Examples of the second category include the Turkish incursion into northern Iraq in 2008 in response to attacks by the Kurdistan Workers Party, Israel's bombardment of Lebanon in response to attacks by Hezbollah and the more recent use of force in Syria. I turn now to these examples of practice, beginning with the 9/11-related practice.

The 9/11-related practice – both the US intervention in Afghanistan and the Security Council Resolutions 1368 and 1373 – have been advanced as sufficient to change the course of law.[208] Similarly, after noting that early on Article 51 was seen as being applicable to armed attacks by States, Hilpold declares that 'the situation changed radically' after 9/11 and that '[w]ithout doubt, Resolution 1368 ... was a watershed.'[209] Indeed, several individual opinions of the Court suggesting a departure from the *Nicaragua* test appear to indicate that the change in the law occurred as a consequence of the practice of the international community in response to the 9/11 attacks. This view can be

---

[208] See, e.g., Wood, 'International Law and the Use of Force' 2013 (n. 94), especially at 356.
[209] Hilpold, 'The Applicability of Article 51 UN Charter to Asymmetric Wars' 2016 (n. 205), 129.

observed in the approach of Judge Kooijmans in the *Wall* opinion.[210] He begins by noting that the statement by the majority that Article 51 applies 'in the case of an armed attack by one State against another State ... *is undoubtedly correct*'.[211] However, he continues, Security Council Resolutions 1368 and 1373 have added '*completely new elements*' which would permit the use of force in response to acts of terrorists 'without ascribing these acts of terrorism to a particular State'.[212] This new element, Judge Kooijmans observes, 'marks undeniably a new approach to the concept of self-defence'.[213] Judge Simma, in his separate opinion in the *Armed Activities in the Territory of the Congo* case, viewed this permissive approach to be new under international law.[214] These positions, reflected in individual opinions of the Court, seem to accept that prior to 9/11, international law required attribution – using the strict standards set in *Nicaragua* – for a State to use force against non-State actors on the territory of third States.

The post 9/11 attacks have provided the most solid basis for departing from the test set by the International Court of Justice in the *Nicaragua* case largely because the US intervention in Afghanistan was undertaken with virtually no condemnation by other States.[215] It is possible, however, that the lack of condemnation, particularly of the initiation of the US attacks on Afghan territory, was more out of a sense of solidarity with the United States than any belief in the legality of the action.[216] However, for the purposes of this chapter, I will assume that the lack of response was not merely out of politeness. Nonetheless, a careful assessment of the 9/11-related practice does not support the expansive interpretation of self-defence.

---

[210] ICJ, *Wall* Advisory Opinion (n. 48), Separate of Opinion of Judge Kooijmans.

[211] *Ibid.*, para. 35 (emphasis added).

[212] *Ibid.* (emphasis added). See also ICJ, *Armed Activities in the Territory of the Congo* (n. 42), Separate Opinion of Judge Simma, para. 11.

[213] *Ibid.* These views of Judge Kooijmans are reiterated in his Separate Opinion in ICJ, *Armed Activities in the Territory of the Congo* (n. 42), paras. 19–32.

[214] See ICJ, *Armed Activities in the Territory of the Congo* (n. 42), Separate Opinion of Judge Simma, para. 11, stating that the 'restrictive interpretation of Article 51 might well have reflected the state, or rather the prevailing interpretation, of the international law on self-defence for a long time. However, in the light of more recent developments ... it ought to be reconsidered, also by the Court.'

[215] See Paust, 'Self-Defence Targeting of Non-State Actors' 2010 (n. 10), 249, and Murphy, 'Self-Defence and the Israeli Wall Advisory Opinion' 2005 (n. 10), at 67.

[216] David Ray Griffin, for example, states that the question of the legality of the war in Afghanistan 'has been considered off-limits, not to be raised in polite company'. See David Ray Griffin, 'Did 9/11 Justify the War in Afghanistan? Using the McChrystal Moment to Raise a Forbidden Question', 25 June 2010, available at www.globalresearch.ca/did-9-11-justify-the-war-in-afghanistan/19891.

I begin, first, by addressing the attacks by the United States in Afghanistan – the most direct form of practice. As mentioned above, these attacks were scarcely, if at all, condemned. Yet it is not at all clear that the United States was attacking what *it saw as* an innocent State, pouring serious doubt on the applicability of that intervention as an example of practice in support of the proposition. It is now not seriously questioned that the 9/11 attacks were committed by Al-Qaeda, a non-State actor, and that the US responded by launching attacks in Afghanistan. Yet speeches by the then US President, George W. Bush, suggest that, at the time, the United States, rightly or wrongly, did not view Afghanistan as an innocent State as we have defined it. In a speech on the day of the attacks, Bush said that the US 'will make no distinction between the terrorists who committed these acts *and those who harbour them*'.[217] Nine days later, in an address to a joint sitting of Congress, he reaffirmed those comments, stating that by 'aiding and abetting murder, the Taliban regime is committing murder'.[218] More to the point, in this speech, Bush went as far as to say 'we condemn the Taliban regime'[219] – at the time the government of Afghanistan. Finally, emphasising that the Taliban itself would be targeted by US operations, Bush said the 'Taliban must act and act now' and hand over the terrorists 'or they will share in their fate.'[220] It is clear that the US, at the time of the discussion, saw Afghanistan as, to some extent, responsible for the attacks. There seems to be, thus, some form of attribution, at least in the view of the United States at the time. It is true that the standard of attribution is probably inconsistent with the standard put forward by the International Court of Justice in the *Nicaragua* case. The standard, rather, appears more akin to that advanced by Judge Schwebel in his dissenting opinion in the *Nicaragua* case. It will be recalled that Judge Schwebel criticised the Court's decision to exclude 'State's assistance to foreign armed irregulars' as a basis for permitting the use of force in self-defence in the territory of the third State.[221]

The above analysis does not concern the lawfulness or unlawfulness of the use of force in Afghanistan, or the correctness or incorrectness of the standard

---

[217] See '9/11 Address to the Nation: A Great People has been Moved to Defend a Great Nation', Speech by President George W. Bush on 11 September 2001, available at www.americanrhetoric.com/speeches/gwbush911addresstothenation.htm (emphasis added).
[218] Address by President George W. Bush to a Joint Sitting of Congress on 20 September 2011, available at www.americanrhetoric.com/speeches/gwbush911jointsessionspeech.htm.
[219] *Ibid.*
[220] *Ibid.*
[221] ICJ, *Military and Paramilitary Activities* (n. 31), Dissenting Opinion of Judge Schwebel, para. 155. See also ICJ, *Armed Activities in the Territory of the Congo* (n. 42), Dissenting Opinion of Judge *ad hoc* Kateka, paras. 12–15, and ICJ, *Armed Activities in the Territory of the Congo* (n. 42), Declaration of Judge Koroma, para. 9.

of attribution applied by the United States in the case of Afghanistan. The analysis serves only to show that US attacks in Afghanistan, in response to the 9/11 attacks, do not constitute appropriate evidence of State practice in support of the use of force against non-State actors in the territory of a non-consenting innocent State. To relate this to the Bethlehem Principles, the events surrounding the use of force by the United States in Afghanistan in response to Al-Qaeda's terrorist attacks in the United States on 9/11 are more closely explained in terms of Principle 11, i.e., where the third State is unwilling to act against the terrorist and is a 'colluding or harbouring' State.[222]

The UN Security Council resolutions that are often advanced to support the proposition, Resolutions 1368 and 1373, also do not, on proper construction, constitute evidence of practice supporting an expansive reading of the right to self-defence against non-State actors. First, these Resolutions simply, on their face, do not support the proposition. Both Resolutions include a preambular paragraph recognising the 'inherent right of individual or collective self-defence'. Murphy is, of course, correct to state that 'no language in the resolutions indicates that the Security Council believes that terrorist acts must first be imputed to a State so as to trigger the right to self-defence.'[223] This view was also expressed in the declaration by Judge Buergenthal in the *Construction of the Wall* advisory opinion. In that case Judge Buergenthal stated that in 'neither of these resolutions did the Security Council limit their application to terrorist attacks by State actors only, nor was an assumption to that effect implicit in these resolutions'.[224] Nonetheless, it is also true that these resolutions do not state, or imply, that the inherent right of self-defence permits the use of force in the territory of a State where the original attack could not, in any way, be attributable to the third State. The resolutions contain a condemnation of the terrorist attacks and a reaffirmation of the right to self-defence. In the context of the present discussion they do nothing more than that. They do not suggest that the inherent right of self-defence is exercisable against non-State actors – indeed they do not mention non-State actors at all, certainly not in the context of the inherent right to self-defence. Second, these resolutions do provide some context that *might* be read as setting a standard for attribution. Resolution 1368, for example, states that those 'responsible for aiding, supporting or harbouring the perpetrators, organisers and sponsors of these acts will be held accountable'.[225] The preamble of

---

[222] Bethlehem, 'Principles Relevant to the Scope of a State's Right of Self-Defense against an Imminent or Actual Armed Attack by Nonstate Actors' 2012 (n. 99), 776.
[223] Murphy, 'Self-Defence and the Israeli Wall Advisory Opinion' 2005 (n. 10), 67.
[224] See ICJ, *Wall* Advisory Opinion (n. 48), Declaration by Judge Buergenthal, para. 6.
[225] SC Res. 1368 of 12 September 2001, para. 3.

Resolution 1373, for its part, recalls that 'every State has the duty to refrain from organizing, instigating, assisting or participating in terrorist acts in another State . . .' This does not mean that the resolutions set a new standard of attribution different from that set in *Nicaragua*. The simple point being made here is that the speculative arguments concerning the import of the preambular paragraph ignore that these provisions might have assumed the role of a State so that the reference to the inherent right of self-defence in the preamble could be linked to this possibility. This of course is also speculation. It suffices to say that we can learn nothing about the permissibility of the use of force against non-State actors in innocent third States from the provisions of these resolutions.[226]

It also bears mentioning that the judgments of the International Court of Justice in the *Armed Activities in the Territory of the Congo* case and the *Oil Platforms* case, as well as the *Wall* advisory opinion, were all delivered after 9/11 and yet all maintained the reasoning in the *Military and Paramilitary Activities* case. Against this background, the observations of Hilpold that 'subsequent practice is inconclusive' and that the international community 'has demonstrated an extreme reluctance to depart from the existing cautious and restrictive approach in the interpretation and application of Article 51' appear to be correct.[227]

Of the Turkish use of force in the territory of Iraq in 2006 and 2008, van Steenberghe asserts 'most international reactions (*sic*) remained vague regarding the legal justification.'[228] However, a cursory troll of news reports at the time suggests that most States and international actors questioned the legality of the use of force even though expressing sympathy for the Turkish security concerns. The EU, for example, through its then High Representative for Foreign Affairs, Javier Solana, expressed understanding for the concerns of Turkey but stated that its chosen course of action was 'not the best response'.[229] This statement by

---

[226] It is perhaps also worth noting that nothing in the statements by the members of the Security Council upon adoption of the said resolutions suggested that the reference to the inherent right to defence was meant to suggest the right to use force in the territory of an innocent third State. See, e.g., Statements by the Members of the Security Council in the Verbatim Records of the 4330th Meeting of the UN Security Council on 12 September 2001, UN Doc. S/PV.4330, and the 4385th Meeting of the UN Security Council on 28 September 2001, UN Doc. S/PV.4385. There were no statements in connection with the adoption of the latter resolution.

[227] Hilpold, 'The Applicability of Article 51 UN Charter to Asymmetric Wars' 2016 (n. 205), 129.

[228] van Steenberghe, 'Self-Defence in Response to Attacks by Non-State Actors' 2010 (n. 133), 188. See also Ruys, '*Quo Vadit Jus Ad Bellum?*' 2008 (n. 177), 345 ('Similarly, third countries remained remarkably vague and refrained from explicitly pronouncing on the operation's lawfulness').

[229] Mark John, 'EU's Solana: Turkey Incursion "Not Best Response"', 22 February 2008, available at www.reuters.com/article/idUSL22479277.

the EU High Representative was not just a political statement, or one concerned only with policy preferences. Confirming that the statement was one informed by the applicable legal principles, Solana explained that the 'territorial integrity of Iraq [was] very important for' the EU.[230] Then United Nations Secretary-General, Ban Ki Moon, similarly said that while he was 'conscious of Turkey's concern', he appealed for the 'utmost restraint, and for respect of the border between Iraq and Turkey'.[231] Similarly, Stephen Smith, then Australian Foreign Minister, also called on 'Turkey to respect Iraq's Sovereignty and [to] retreat back over the border as soon as possible'.[232] A theme running through all of these statements is the acceptance of the seriousness of the attacks (by non-State actors) against Turkey, but a declaration that the attacks by the Kurdistan Workers Party cannot justify the violation of the territorial integrity of Iraq. Incidentally, Turkey itself never declared that it has the right to use force in self-defence against the Kurdistan Workers Party in Iraq for acts not attributable to Iraq.[233] In the light of this reaction, it is hard to see how this example, often advanced as State practice in support of the proposition, can be seen either as reflective of customary international law or as constituting subsequent practice for the purposes of interpretation.

With respect to the use of force by Israel against Lebanon in 2006, van Steenberghe explains that many States explicitly recognised the right of Israel to use force to defend itself.[234] The statements to which van Steenberghe refers were delivered in the course of a UN Security Council debate and can be easily accessed.[235] Argentina, for example, while acknowledging Israel's right to self-defence, insists that Israel should exercise the right 'in accordance with the law'.[236] Van Steenberghe suggests that this reference to international law

---

[230] *Ibid.* Although Ruys (in Ruys, *'Quo Vadit Jus Ad Bellum?'* 2008 (n. 177), 343) refers to an EU statement that seems to condemn the attacks on mainly political grounds, two points must be made about the said statement. First, the statement was issued prior to the attacks, in October 2007. Second, and most important, even in that statement, the EU Commission urged the Government of Turkey to 'solve the problem with cooperation and with *regard to international law*' (emphasis added).

[231] 'EU Voices Concern over Turkish Military Incursion into Iraq', *Deutsche Welle*, 22 February 2008, available at www.dw.com/en/eu-voices-concern-over-turkish-military-incursion-into-iraq/a-3143907.

[232] 'Australia Urges Turkey to Pull Troops From Iraqi Kurdistan', *Ekurd Daily*, 24 February 2008, available at http://ekurd.net/mismas/articles/misc2008/2/turkeykurdistan1684.htm.

[233] See for discussion Jutta Brunnée and Stephen J. Toope, *Legitimacy and Legality in International Law: An Interactional Account* (Cambridge: Cambridge University Press, 2010), 297–8.

[234] van Steenberghe, 'Self-Defence in Response to Attacks by Non-State Actors' 2010 (n. 133), 193.

[235] See UN Security Council Debate on the Situation in the Middle East (n. 8).

[236] Statement by Mr Mayoral, Representative of Argentina, in UN Security Council Debate on the Situation in the Middle East (n. 8), 9.

was directed only at the elements of proportionality and necessity.[237] Yet there is nothing in Argentina's statement to indicate that its concern is directed only at proportionality and necessity. It is true that the statement referred to – 'in particular, excessive force' – suggests a link with proportionality. However, the statement also listed, separately, 'the imposition of sea, air and land blockade' and the 'violations on the part of Israel along the Blue Line' as concerns.[238] These elements were not linked with the excessive use of force but rather concerned the use of force as such. The Russian statement similarly attacked both the proportionality and the use of force as such by describing the Israeli action as both 'disproportionate *and* inappropriate use of force that threatens the sovereignty and territorial integrity of Lebanon'.[239] Other statements were even clearer and more direct. The statement on behalf of Ghana declared that the use of force against 'a sovereign state is unacceptable'.[240] Even more explicit, Qatar recognised the right of Israel to self-defence, but nonetheless described Israeli attacks in Lebanon as a 'flagrant violation of the Charter of the United Nations and all international custom'.[241] China used similarly strong terms, describing the attacks as an act of 'armed aggression'.[242] It is true that in its statement, as with most other statements, there is reference to proportionality, but there is nothing in its statement to suggest its description of the act as 'aggression' is based solely on proportionality. Indeed, the statement by China identifies the violation of sovereignty as such as a major cause of concern.[243] Given the criticisms of the use of force by Israel and, in particular, its characterisation as a violation of the UN Charter and an aggression, it cannot form the basis of subsequent practice for the purposes of interpretation of the UN Charter nor can it be regarded as practice constitutive or reflective of customary international law.

Other incidents, not fully discussed here, are similarly not reflective of customary international law, nor can they constitute subsequent practice, since they have been similarly criticised. The US attacks against a pharmaceutical factory in

[237] van Steenberghe, 'Self-Defence in Response to Attacks by Non-State Actors' 2010 (n. 133), 193.
[238] Statement by Mr Mayoral, Representative of Argentina, in UN Security Council Debate on the Situation in the Middle East (n. 8), 9.
[239] Statement by Mr Dolgov, Representative of Russia, in UN Security Council Debate on the Situation in the Middle East (n. 8), 7 (emphasis added).
[240] Statement by Mr Effah-Apenteng, Representative of Ghana, in UN Security Council Debate on the Situation in the Middle East (n. 8), 8.
[241] Statement by Mr Al-Qahtani, Representative of Qatar, in UN Security Council Debate on the Situation in the Middle East (n. 8), 10.
[242] Statement by Mr Liu Zhengmin, Representative of China, in UN Security Council Debate on the Situation in the Middle East (n. 8), 11.
[243] *Ibid.*

Sudan, in response to bombings of American embassies in Kenya and Tanzania, are a case in point. The Arab League, for example, declared the attack as 'an attack on Sudan's sovereignty'.[244] Tams, in addition to the examples discussed above, refers to the Iranian attacks in Iraq against the Mujahedin-e Khalq Organisation, Russian attacks in Georgia against Chechen rebels as well as Colombian forces against FARC rebels in Ecuador.[245] He concludes that for the most part these acts of force were met with 'mixed reactions' from third States.[246] If Tams' assessment is correct that the examples he cites were met with 'mixed reactions' then that already precludes their interpretative value as subsequent practice because they cannot be deemed as establishing the agreement of the members of the United Nations as to the interpretation of Article 51. Indeed, in the case of the Colombian use of force, the Permanent Council of the Organisation of American States determined that that action amounted to 'a violation of the sovereignty and territorial integrity of Ecuador and of principles of international law'.[247] Thus, there may well have been examples of States using force on the territory of another in response to attacks by non-State actors. However, given the at best 'mixed' and at worst 'negative' reaction, the acts cannot form the basis of relevant practice, either for the purposes of sustaining a customary international law rule permitting such use or as subsequent practice for the interpretation of Article 51.

The situation in Syria provides the most recent example of practice that may be advanced in support of the proposition for an expansive interpretation of the right to self-defence against non-State actors. That situation is a very complicated one, involving interrelated conflicts implicating a number of non-State actors and several States.[248] The non-State actors include the

[244] Karl Vick, 'US, Sudan Trade Claims on Factory', *Washington Post*, 25 August 1998, available at www.washingtonpost.com/archive/politics/1998/08/25/us-sudan-trade-claims-on-factory/b8 5afb93-83fb-4186-a49d-e5cb08oao187. The reaction to the attacks was divided, largely, along ideological lines. For a list of which states supported and which denounced the attack, see 'US Allies Back Muslim Strikes, Yeltsin Sides with Muslims', *The Irish Times*, 22 August 1998, available at www.irishtimes.com/news/us-allies-back-missile-strikes-yeltsin-sides-with-mus lims-1.185482.
[245] Tams, 'The Use of Force against Terrorists' 2009 (n. 10), 379–80.
[246] *Ibid*. While he does not arrive at the same conclusion concerning the Iranian attacks in Iraq, it is clear that Iran itself held the view that Iraq was complicit in those attacks. See Amin Tarzi and Darby Parliament, 'Missile Messages: Iran Strikes MKO Bases in Iraq', *The Non-Proliferation Review* 8 (2001), 125–33 (128), where Iran is reported to have written as follows to the UN Security Council: 'these limited and appropriate operations were aimed at halting the attacks against Iran launched by the' MKO.
[247] Permanent Council of American States, Convocation of the Meeting of Consultations of Ministers of Foreign Affairs and Appointment of a Commission, 5 March 2008, CP/Res.930 (1632/08).
[248] Wood, 'The Use of Force in 2015' 2016 (n. 144), 5.

Syrian anti-government forces, which itself consists of several separate groups, while the States involved include Syria, Iraq, Turkey, a US-led coalition of States and Russia. The Russian use of force in Syria (like the coalition use of force in Iraq) against ISIS is therefore excluded from the analysis below.

ISIS is a non-State actor that operates, in addition to other places, in Syria. It has been said to be responsible for terrorist attacks in several places, in particular in Europe, the United States and the Middle East. However, its acts are not attributable to Syria. Thus any use of force without the consent of Syria, against ISIS on the territory of Syria would fall squarely within the parameters of the proposition, namely the use of force against non-State actors in the territory of innocent, non-consenting third States. In addition to the United States, other States, like the United Kingdom, France, Belgium, Germany, Canada and Australia, have been engaged militarily in Syria against ISIS.[249] While the number of States involved in the attacks in Syria is impressive, the question is whether this constitutes practice sufficient to advance a particular interpretation of Article 51. In addition to these acts of force undertaken by individual States, the UN Security Council passed a resolution, UN Security Council Resolution 2249, invoking language similar to language used when the Council authorises the use of force. This Resolution has already attracted some attention.[250] What contribution, if any, do Resolution 2249 and the various acts by individual States operating in Syria make to the question on the use of force against non-State actors on the territory of third States?

It is useful to begin by reflecting on the key use of force-related language in Resolution 2249. As Wood notes, the language is complicated, indicating 'tough negotiations'.[251] While it is true that the Council does not expressly state that it is acting under Chapter VII, this is, in the greater scheme of things, immaterial. What is important is the language used in operative paragraph 5. There the Resolution

> *Calls upon* Member States that have the capacity to do so to take all necessary measures, in compliance with international law, in particular with the

---

[249] See UN Doc. S/2014/695, 23 September 2014 (USA); UN Doc. S/2014/851, 25 November 2015 (UK); UN Doc. S/2015/745, 8 September 2015 (France); UN Doc S/2016/523, 9 June 2016 (Belgium); UN Doc. S/2015/946, 10 December 2015 (Germany); UN Doc. S/2015/221, 31 March 2015 (Canada); UN Doc. S/2015/693, 9 September 2015 (Australia).

[250] SC Res. 2249 of 20 November 2015. See for an interesting discussion of the resolution, Dapo Akande and Marko Milanovic, 'The Constructive Ambiguity of the Security Council's ISIS Resolution', *EJIL Talk!*, 21 November 2015, available at www.ejiltalk.org/the-constructive-ambiguity-of-the-security-councils-isis-resolution.

[251] Wood, 'The Use of Force in 2015' 2016 (n. 144), 7.

United Nations Charter, as well as international human rights . . . on the territory under the control of ISIL also known as Da'esh, in Syria and Iraq . . .

A few preliminary points about some of the language in the paragraph are necessary. 'All necessary means' or, in this case, 'measures' as a rule includes the use of force. The 'territory under the control of [ISIS]' includes Syria. The Resolution therefore '[c]alls upon States that have the capacity to do so' to undertake military action in Syria against ISIS. However, the Resolution does not authorise the use of force. In UN language, 'calls upon' is, at best, encouragement. To authorise the use of force, the Resolution would use the verb 'Decide' or 'Authorize'.[252] Nonetheless, it has been suggested that, though not authorising the use of force, Resolution 2249 provides 'political support for military action'.[253] Wood goes further, suggesting that the Resolution is not only politically important but that it is legally important.[254] Even more pertinently for the purposes of the central question posed in this contribution, he suggests that 'it is difficult to read the resolution otherwise than as an endorsement . . . of the use of force in self-defence against' a non-State actor in the territory of a third State – in this case against ISIS in Syria.[255]

It is hard to argue that an encouragement to use force does not amount to the endorsement of such use of force. However, the Resolution does not encourage or endorse *all* uses of force against ISIS on the territory under the control of ISIS. The Resolution only encourages and endorses the use of force 'in compliance with international law'. It is not clear why the Resolution cannot be read as encouraging the use of force with the consent of the territorial States in question, i.e. Iraq and Syria. If, as I have argued, international law at the time of the adoption of Resolution 2249 did not permit the use of force against non-State actors on the territory of innocent third States, then Resolution 2249 would have no impact on that law, nor would it endorse, even as an exceptional measure, the use of force without the consent of the territorial State unless the conduct of ISIS were attributable to that State. That would be the effect of the phrase 'in compliance with international law'. The statement of Russia made it abundantly clear that Resolution 2249 was to have no impact on the current state of the law, stating that the Resolution was 'a political appeal' and did not 'change . . . the legal principles underlying the

---

[252] See, e.g., SC Res. 1973 of 17 March 2011, paras. 4, 6 and 8.

[253] Akande and Milanovic, 'The Constructive Ambiguity of the Security Council's ISIS Resolution' 2015 (n. 250).

[254] Wood, 'The Use of Force in 2015' 2016 (n. 144), 8.

[255] *Ibid.*

fight against terrorism'.[256] Of course, States have already relied on the Resolution in justifying the use of force on the territory of Syria.[257] The Resolution itself, however, has no effect whatsoever on the law regarding the use of force against non-State actors in the territory of third States.

While Resolution 2249 did not, itself, authorise the use of force, many States have used force in Syria against ISIS without the consent of Syria. In determining whether this use of force is relevant for identifying the scope of self-defence, it should be noted that the relevance of this operational 'conduct on the ground' depends not only on reactions to it, but also on the justifications for such use of force.[258] It is only if the justifications advanced are consistent that we can say that the practice 'establishes the agreement of the' States 'as to the interpretation of' Article 51 of the UN Charter.[259] For surely, if the various States advance different bases for their conduct, even if the conduct is the same, it cannot be evidence of established agreement as to the meaning of Article 51 and therefore cannot affect the interpretation of Article 51.[260]

It is clear that all the States using force in Syria adopt the position that taking such action is lawful. Some of the States operating there, it seems, have adopted Bethlehem's 'unwilling or unable' test.[261] The United States, for example, declares that 'when ... the government of the territory where the threat is located is unwilling or unable to prevent the use of its territory' for attacks, then it is entitled to have recourse to the right to use force in self-defence.[262] Australia has, similarly, advanced the 'unwilling or unable' test as the basis for the use of force under Article 51.[263] However, other States have advanced altogether different approaches that would seem to suggest

[256] Statement by Mr Churkin, Representative of the Russian Federation, during the 7565th Meeting of the Security Council, 20 November 2015, UN Doc. S/PV.7565.
[257] See e.g. UN Doc. S/2015/946, 10 December 2015 (Germany); UN Doc. S/2016/523, 9 June 2016 (Belgium); UN Doc. S/2016/513, 3 June 2016 (Norway). See also Akande and Milanovic, 'The Constructive Ambiguity of the Security Council's ISIS Resolution' 2015 (n. 250): 'The US coalition will no doubt claim that Resolution 2249 implicitly validates or confirms the legality of their current actions.'
[258] See for an assessment Corten, 'The "Unwilling or Unable Test"' 2016 (n. 201).
[259] See in particular ILC, Draft Conclusions on Subsequent Agreements and Subsequent Practice in Relation to the Interpretation of Treaties (adopted on second reading), Report on the work of its seventieth session, UN Doc A/73/10 (2018), Draft Conclusion 10(1).
[260] *Ibid.*, commentary to Draft Conclusion 10, para. 3.
[261] See Corten, 'The "Unwilling or Unable Test"' 2016 (n. 201), 780, who states that only four out of the States that submitted the letter relied on the 'unwilling or unable test', suggesting that there is a lack of common *opinio iuris* in favour of the 'unwilling or unable' test.
[262] UN Doc. S/2014/695, 23 September 2014 (United States).
[263] UN Doc. S/2015/693, 9 September 2015 (Australia); see also UN Doc. S/2015/563, 24 July 2015 (Turkey); UN Doc. S/2015/221, 31 March 2015 (Canada).

disagreement, or at best discomfort, with the 'unwilling or unable' test. Germany, for example, without referring at all to the 'unwilling or unable' test in the knowledge that other States before it had relied on that test, chose to rely, instead, on the fact that ISIS 'occupied a certain part of the Syrian territory', thus treating *that part* of Syrian territory as the territory of ISIS and not of Syria.[264] To be sure, this itself is a controversial assessment, but one that falls beyond the scope of this chapter. Belgium's letter is even more revealing of a distancing from the 'unwilling or unable' test.[265] Not only does Belgium rely, like Germany, on the fact that ISIS has 'occupied a certain part of the Syrian territory' and the government of Syria 'does not exercise effective control' over these parts, it also states that 'this is an exceptional situation.'[266] Like the German statement, the Belgian letter seems to suggest that it is using force against the government in control of a territory. But more importantly, the invocation of the exceptional nature of the circumstances is an indication that it does not view its conduct as a law-making or law-transforming conduct, whether for the purposes of customary international law or treaty interpretation. In addition there are those States that have taken action in Syria and, while fully aware that there are different interpretations to Article 51 and that States taking action have advanced different legal bases for their actions, that have advanced no legal interpretation of Article 51, suggesting that they are non-committal about the legal interpretation of Article 51.[267] And other States, notably Norway and Denmark, referred ambiguously to the fact that ISIS has established 'a safe haven' in Syria.[268]

To form the basis of subsequent practice in the interpretation of Article 51 of the Charter under Article 31(3)(b) of the VCLT, it is not sufficient that there is a common political purpose with respect to action to be taken in a particular case – as there seems to be, at least with respect to the States taking measures in Syria. There should also be a clear meeting of minds as to the interpretation of Article 51. While, at least in the case of Syria, there seems to be a number of States that have converged on the 'unwilling or unable' standard for the use of force in self-defence, this is not the case for all States. Some States also taking action in Syria, notably Germany and Belgium, have sought to clearly distance themselves from the broad 'unwilling and unable' test and have,

---

[264] UN Doc. S/2015/946, 10 December 2015 (Germany).
[265] UN Doc. S/2016/523, 9 June 2016 (Belgium).
[266] *Ibid.*
[267] See e.g. UN Doc. S/2015/745, 8 September 2015 (France); UN Doc. S/2014/851, 25 November 2015 (UK).
[268] See UN Doc. S/2016/34, 13 January 2016 (Denmark); UN Doc. S/2016/513, 3 June 2016 (Norway).

instead, referred to a more narrow 'where the State does not have effective control of its territory' test. Furthermore, other States have not advanced an interpretation of Article 51, suggesting that their conduct is not based on an interpretation of Article 51. When one considers that many more States have not expressed themselves at all, the disparate understandings of the basis for action in Syria by those that have taken measures in Syria hardly serve as 'establishing the agreement of' UN member States as to the interpretation of Article 51.

Finally, some States have questioned, at least implicitly, the legality of the use of force in Syria without the consent of the Government. Corten identifies, for example, in addition to Syria, a number of States, including Venezuela, Russia, Ecuador, Cuba, Iran, China, Chad, South Africa, India, Belarus and Argentina, that criticised the military action in Syria without its consent as a violation of its sovereignty.[269] For its part, the Non-Aligned Movement, a group comprising 120 States, though not commenting specifically on the use of force in Syria, has expressed concern about the trend to use extra-territorial force against non-State actors as part of the 'war on terror'. The Non-Aligned Movement (NAM) accordingly

> *Reject[s]* actions and measures, the use or threat of use of force in particular by armed forces, which violate the UN Charter and international law … under the pretext of combating terrorism.[270]

The language, of course, is not express. But it does serve to highlight the discomfort of a large number of States – States which have not participated in the actions in Syria – with the extraterritorial use of force to combat terrorism. More directly, a number of States, including the thirty-three States making up the Community of Latin American and Carribean States, have questioned the consistency with international law of the various letters sent to the President of the Security Council in support of the use of force in Syria.[271] This suggests that this large group of States does not share the interpretation that Article

---

[269] See Corten, 'The "Unwilling or Unable Test"' 2016 (n. 201), 788–9.
[270] Final Document of the 17th Summit of Heads of State and Government of the Non-Aligned Movement (n. 197), para. 258.34.
[271] See, e.g. Statement of the Permanent Mission of the Republic of El Salvador on behalf of the Community of Latin American and Carribean States (CELAC) during the United Nations' Special Committee on the Charter of the United Nations and the Strengthening of the Role of Organisation, New York, 20–28 February 2018, available at https://celac.rree.gob.sv/wp-content/uploads/2018/02/Statement-CELAC-Charter-Committee-Feb-2018.pdf ('CELAC has noted an increase in the number of letters addressed to the President of the Security Council under Article 51 of the Charter regarding military action, in the context of counterterrorism. As it has been noted before by the Group, this is an issue of concern … There are also underlying concerns stemming from attempts to reinterpret the law on self-defense and *de facto* expand an exception to the general prohibition to the use of force

51 permits the use of force against terrorists (non-State actors) in the territory of innocent non-consenting States. Indeed, in 2012 the NAM confirmed that

> consistent with the practice of the United Nations and international law, as pronounced by the ICJ, Article 51 of the UN Charter is *restrictive* and should not be re-written or re-interpreted.[272]

The views of such a large majority of parties to the UN Charter, expressed subsequent to the operations in Syria, can surely not be ignored in determining whether those operations reflect the agreement of the parties to the Charter as to its interpretation.

The conflict in Syria is important for at least two other reasons. First, it shows the fallacy of the arguments that a broad interpretation of self-defence is necessary because of the weakness of the collective security architecture. That within a matter of days following the attacks in Paris on 18 November 2016 the Security Council was able to adopt a resolution containing language referencing the use of force illustrates that the Council *can* and *has* acted in response to international threats. There were, of course, dynamics that prevented the adoption of a full use of force authorisation. Whatever these were, it is clear

---

contained in article 2.4 ...'). See also the statement by the Permanent Mission of the Republic of El Salvador on behalf of the Community of Latin American and Carribean States (CELAC) during the UN General Assembly Sixth Committee Consideration of the Agenda Item Measures to Eliminate International Terrorism, 2 October 2017 (A/C.6/72/SR.1) at para. 30 and the statement of the Permanent Mission of Brazil during the UN Sixth Committee consideration of the Agenda Item Measures to Eliminate International Terrorism, 2–4 October 2017 (A/C.6/72/SR.4) at para. 32 ('... there are underlying concerns stemming from attempts to reinterpret the law regarding the content and the scope of self-defence, especially *on* its applicability in relation to non state actors. However difficult, we should not shy away from discussing critical legal issues involving the use of force. Some interpretations regarding the scope and content of self-defence arising from counter-terrorism scenarios might not be adequate or advisable, as they might set dangerous precedent. Silence regarding these interpretations, such as the so-called "unwilling or unable doctrine", should not be understood as acquiessence or as proof of *opinio iuris*'). See also UN Doc. S/PV.8175, 6 February 2018, in which Mexico stated that it was concerned by the 'continuous references to Article 51 of the Charter of the United Nations by some States to address threats to international peace and security with military action, especially against non-State actors. Mexico is troubled that such a practice, coupled with the ambiguous language of recent Council resolutions, runs the risk of a de facto broadening of exceptions to the general prohibition on the use of force, as set out in Article 2, paragraph 4, of the Charter of the United Nations, in an irregular manner'. See also the statement of Brazil at the Security Council Debate on Upholding International Law within the Context of the Maintenance of International Peace and Security of 17 May 2018, UN Doc. S/PV.8262, 44: 'Some have been arguing that self-defence could be applied as a response to non-State actors, sometimes adding as a condition the criterion of unwillingness or inability on the part of the territorial State. Brazil does not agree with such interpretations.'

[272] *Ibid.*, para. 25.3 (emphasis added).

that when the Council is committed against a common threat, even well-documented differences between its permanent members will not prevent action to address the common threat.

Second, as a policy point, ISIS does not only operate from Iraq and Syria. To the extent that it has operatives in the territories of various European territories and that the relevant European States are not able to stamp out these activities, it would not be far-fetched to suggest that such States are 'unable' to effectively deal with the threat from ISIS. Would that (should that) justify any State that has suffered attacks by ISIS to use force on these European States' territories against ISIS? Further, does that not risk the type of escalation that our collective security system – underpinned by the prohibition on the use of force, with the exception of collective measures under Chapter VII of the Charter and, in urgent cases, the use of necessary force in self-defence – was designed to avoid? Is it not better, in such circumstances, to allow the Security Council or the General Assembly under the Uniting for Peace Resolution to exercise the mandate under the Charter to the best possible extent? It is of course true, as is arguably the case with terrorism and ISIS in particular, that measures adopted by the Security Council may not be sufficient, or be deemed sufficient by other States. But is that not the nature of the collectivity? That sometimes measures are more and sometimes less than what we, individually, may desire? To decide that we reserve the right – when such measures do not go as far as we would wish, or when they go further than we would prefer – to engage in unilateral action is to undermine that collective security system. This is so particularly when the very States that reserve the right to 'go at it alone' without the collective also have disproportionate influence on the Security Council – in terms of the States exercising force on the territory of Syria against ISIS without the consent of Syria, this would include the United States, France and the United Kingdom. This is the very constellation described by the proverb of eating one's cake and having it.

While there are many examples of incidents of States using force in the territory of third States in response to attacks from non-State actors, many of these qualitatively are not able to form the basis of either interpretative State practice or form the basis of a rule of customary international law because of the negative reaction from other States. Other cases advanced in support of a broad interpretation of self-defence, in particular the 9/11-related practice, appear to be based on attribution and can therefore not form the basis of the right to use force in the territory of an innocent third State. The Syria-related cases cannot form the basis of the expansive interpretation because they do not establish the agreement of the actors concerning the interpretation of Article 51. Contemporary practice does not, therefore, as is sometimes argued, form

The Use of Force in Self-Defence 81

the basis of an expansive interpretation of Article 51 which would permit the use of force against non-State actors in the territory of innocent third States.

VI. UNILATERAL OR COLLECTIVE SECURITY: THE INTERSECTION OF LAW AND POLICY

A. Scope and Limits of the Law of Self-Defence against Non-State Actors

The above analysis has illustrated a number of points concerning the law on the use of force against non-State actors. First, as a rule, a State may only use force in self-defence against another State in response to an armed attack from that State. Thus, at least as a general rule, a State may not invoke the right to self-defence as a justification for the use of force in the territory of a third State in response to acts performed by non-State actors. This view is supported by an interpretation of Article 51 of the Charter based on Article 31(1) of the VCLT, and there does not appear to be subsequent practice within the meaning of Article 31(1)(b) of the VCLT to lead to a contrary conclusion. Second, the fact that, as a general rule, a State may not use force in self-defence in response to an armed attack, does not mean that a State is prohibited from using force against non-State actors in the territory of a third State in all circumstances. In addition to the case where the third State has given consent, a State may use force in self-defence against non-State actors in the territory of the third State if acts of the non-State actor can be attributed to the third State.

While the basic rule articulated above is, to my mind, relatively clear, the application of the rule is less clear. In particular, an issue that arises in connection with this basic articulation of the law as it stands is: what is the standard of attribution that is required? Must the non-State actor be acting on behalf of the third State concerned or be sent by the third State for the armed acts of that non-State actor to be the basis for self-defence under Article 51, as seems to be the requirement under *Nicaragua*? Or is it sufficient for the third State to have assisted or harboured the non-State actor? The law articulated by the International Court of Justice, and which has yet to be overturned by any clear, consistent practice of States, appears to be that the non-State actors must have been sent by, or acting on behalf of, the third State. Whether, as a normative question, this standard ought to be reconsidered, is discussed below (section VI.B). Whatever the standard of attribution is, what should not be debatable, as a matter of law at least, is that some level of attribution is required before a State may exercise the right of self-defence against a non-State actor on the territory of a non-consenting third State. This basic rule reflects an equilibrium in the Charter that ought not to be lightly disturbed:

allowing one State to exercise its right under Article 51 means that another State will lose protection offered under Article 2(4), and this requires that the latter State has done something to justify this loss.

B. Do Current Circumstances Call for a New Approach?

As discussed above, there are new realities on the ground, in particular the rise in terrorism and the ability of terrorist groups to carry out large scale attacks, coupled with the existence of territories over which States may not have control.[273] These new realities might, it may be suggested, require that States should have greater leeway to protect themselves from incidents of terrorism. Schachter states, in this regard, that terrorists operating abroad 'should not enjoy immunity' and '[c]ounter force is the most obvious remedy [to terrorist attacks]; one uses fire to fight fire.'[274] Kaufman succinctly describes the arguments as follows:

> We find ourselves, it is widely claimed, in a new and unprecedented age of terrorism. The rules of the game, we are told, must change in order for us to respond to a new kind of threat from shadowy terrorist organizations not affiliated with any particular state, and with possible access to weapons of mass destruction.[275]

According to Bethlehem the 'reality of the threats, the consequences of inaction, and the challenges of both strategic appreciation and operational decision-making in the face of such threats frequently trump doctrinal debates' about the scope and limits of the right to self-defence.[276] It is important, he continues, that the legal 'principle is sensitive to the practical realities' on the ground 'even as it endeavours to prohibit the excess and egregious pursuit of national interest'.[277] These are, no doubt, important considerations

---

[273] See, e.g., Moir, *Reappraising the Resort to Force* 2010 (n. 14), 1, and Rosand, 'The UN Response to the Evolving Threat of Global Terrorism' 2010 (n. 14), 250.

[274] Schachter, 'The Extraterritorial Use of Force against Terrorist Bases' 1989 (n. 94), 316.

[275] Whitley Kaufman, 'What's Wrong with Preventative War? The Moral and Legal Basis for the Preventative Use of Force', *Ethics and International Affairs* 19 (2005), 23–38 (23). See also the address of the Secretary-General to the United Nations General Assembly, Mr Kofi Annan, on 23 September 2003: 'Now some say this [restricted interpretation of the right to self-defence] is no longer tenable, since "armed attack" with weapons of mass destruction could be launched at any time, without warning, or by a clandestine group.'

[276] Bethlehem, 'Principles Relevant to the Scope of a State's Right of Self-Defense against an Imminent or Actual Armed Attack by Nonstate Actors' 2012 (n. 99), 773. See also Wood, 'The Use of Force in 2015' 2016 (n. 144), 2.

[277] *Ibid.*

that should bear, at the very least, on the normative question of what the law ought to be in this area.

In assessing Bethlehem's views, it is useful to point out that there are policy considerations that pull in an altogether different direction. The broad interpretation of the right to use force against non-State actors on the territory of third States would, in the first place, bring us back the law of the jungle where might was right – if we are, as an empirical fact, already there, it would serve to legitimise that empirical fact. Militarily powerful States would be free to use force unilaterally in the territory of other States wherever they perceived, rightly or wrongly, that terrorist actors were operating. Corten warns that if this broad interpretation were allowed, in principle, 'every state would be allowed to launch a military campaign on another state's territory, under the sole pretext of the "inability" of this State' to put an end to the activities of the non-State actors.[278] This interpretation would counter the attempt identified by Bethlehem to 'prohibit the excess and egregious pursuit of national interest'. It risks bringing to fruition Franck's view of a world in which the UN architecture for peace and security had failed and wherein 'the national interest of the super-powers has usually won out over treaty obligations.'[279] Second, and more importantly, such a broad interpretation could undermine the very collective security system established by the UN Charter. A third State on whose territory force is being used against non-State actors in response to an attack from the non-State actors not imputable to that State could respond by forcible measures of its own against the State using force on its territory, with the potential for an all-out war.[280] Furthermore, consider that terrorists operate from potentially everywhere in the world. That means that potentially any State that has suffered an attack by a terrorist group may launch attacks against that group in any State if, in its view, that would prevent further attacks against it. It does not take an

---

[278] Corten, 'The "Unwilling or Unable Test"' 2016 (n. 201), 797.

[279] See Thomas M. Franck, 'Who Killed Article 2(4)? Or: Changing Norms Governing the Use of Force by States', *American Journal of International Law* 64 (1970), 809–37 (836). In a much later publication, Franck describes the world in which Article 2(4) has lost meaning and effect, by referring to Thucydides: 'the strong do what they can and the weak suffer what they must.' See Franck, 'What Happens Now?' 2003 (n. 16), 608.

[280] See, e.g., Banks and Criddle, 'Customary Constraints on the Use of Force' 2016 (n. 142), 71, explaining the views of what are termed 'conventional restrictivists': '[A]llowing military intervention without either the territorial state's consent or state responsibility for a prior attack would undermine international peace and security by increasing the likelihood of armed conflict between the two states. The state where dangerous non-state actors reside might view foreign intervention within its borders (rightly or wrongly) as "armed attack" justifying a military response.'

oracle to see that the slope to pre-twentieth-century international law, where the use of force was fully permitted under law, is a slippery one. These are all policy considerations that should be taken into account in determining, as a normative proposition, whether the law should shift towards a more expansive view of the right to use force in self-defence.

Much of the arguments in support of a broad right to use force often appeal to people's fears. This appeal to the fear of the citizenry, in fact, permits States with the power to use force to liberate themselves from the need to abide by international law.[281] The fear-inducing idea that not expanding the right to use force in self-defence against non-State actors on the territory of innocent States would place States at great peril is, as a matter of law, an overstatement. It ignores that the Charter architecture for peace and security is based, first and foremost, on collective security. In particular, that a State is rendered helpless, just because particular acts that threaten its security do not amount to an armed attack against it, ignores the primary role assigned to the UN Security Council. In such instances, the Security Council has both the right and responsibility to act. Indeed, even in cases that do amount to an armed attack as understood by the International Court of Justice, the right to use force in self-defence is meant to be temporary, in order to repel an attack until the Council has acted. The dangers of this expanded right to use force, which places the collective security architecture on the sidelines, is poignantly reflected on by the Secretary-General, responding to arguments for an attack against Iraq:

> According to this argument, States are not obliged to wait until there is agreement in the Security Council. Instead, they reserve the right to act unilaterally, or in ad hoc coalitions. The logic represents a fundamental challenge to the principles on which, however imperfectly, world peace and stability have rested for the last fifty-eight years. My concern is that, if it were to be adopted, it could set precedents that resulted in a proliferation of the unilateral and lawless use of force, with or without justification.[282]

Expanding on the need to adopt a strict interpretation of Article 51, the International Court of Justice has made the following observation:

> Article 51 of the Charter may justify a use of force in self-defence within the *strict confines* there laid down. It does not allow for the use of force by a State to protect perceived security interests beyond these parameters. Other means

[281] Anne-Charlotte Martineau, 'Concerning Violence: A Post-Colonial Reading of the Debate on the Use of Force', *Leiden Journal of International Law* 29 (2016), 95–112 (111).
[282] Kofi Annan, 23 September 2003 (n. 275).

are available to a concerned State, including in particular, recourse to the Security Council.[283]

It is true that often, due to political constraints, including the exercise of the veto by its permanent members, the Council does not act when it should. Proponents for the interpretation of the right to self-defence in international law to include the use of force on the territory of innocent third States point out that it would be unacceptable to subject the right of a State to protect itself to depend on an ineffective system. In addition to the general policy consideration already referred to – i.e. this broad interpretation would lead to legitimation of the 'might is right' phenomenon and would undermine the collective security system – this argument suffers from at least two flaws. First, the UN Security Council has, in fact, adopted measures against international terrorism.[284] The measures adopted by the Security Council need not necessarily be use of force measures. States might feel that the measures adopted are insufficient and that the Council may have, or even should have, done more, but that does not detract from the fact that the Council has acted. Second, it seems problematic, on the basis of any perceived ineffectiveness of the Security Council, to expand the rule relating to self-defence which, as suggested earlier, would significantly erode the prohibition on the use of force. The content of the law on self-defence should not be dependent on the effectiveness of the Security Council. If there is a problem with the collective security system, it is that problem that ought to be addressed.

Even if, as a policy requirement, current circumstances require some change to the law of self-defence as reflected in the jurisprudence of the International Court of Justice in order to allow affected States a greater possibility to respond to non-State actors, the question remains what those changes should be. As suggested above, the idea of removing the requirement for attribution is not only inconsistent with the law but it is also inappropriate from a policy perspective. One possibility, which would at least not offend the basic principles of fairness and equity, would be to lower the attribution standard of effective control stated in the *Nicaragua* case. From a policy perspective, permitting the use of force in self-defence in the territory of a State that harbours or aids non-State actors would seem acceptable. Importantly, this lowered standard retains the requirement of attribution

---

[283] ICJ, *Armed Activities in the Territory of the Congo* (n. 42), 148.
[284] See for discussion Trevor P. Chimimba, 'United Nations Security Council Resolution 1373 (2001) as a Tool for Criminal Law Enforcement', in Tiyanjana Maluwa, Max du Plessis and Dire Tladi (eds.), *The Pursuit of a Brave New World in International Law: Essays in Honour of John Dugard* (Dordrecht: Brill, 2017), 361–94.

and thus would not countenance the use of force in the territory of an innocent third State. This possibility has been considered and supported by, amongst others, Randelzhofer and Nolte and, it appears, Tams.[285] This approach is also consistent with some individual opinions of judges of the International Court of Justice.[286] At any rate, it appears the US attacks on Afghanistan, which did not meet with objection from third States, were based on this same standard. Whether that one single episode is sufficient to effect a change to the rules is less clear. Tams (p. 164) seems to suggest that events post-9/11 may have already resulted in a shift in the law to a point where the 'harbouring', 'aiding or abetting' or 'provision of assistance to' non-State actors involved in attacks in a State would allow the attacked State to use force in self-defence even in the absence of consent. As discussed above (section V.B.3), I have a different impression of the impact of that practice. Moreover, I am less certain that the law has *already* shifted, although I am prepared to accept that it *may* be shifting in that direction.

Murase, however, cautions that not any involvement by the territorial State can or should justify the use of force.[287] To the extent that such involvement constitutes the breach of an obligation under international law, then such a State can be held responsible for that assistance under the law of State responsibility.[288] He observes, correctly in my view, that not all cases of State responsibility permit recourse to the use of force in response.[289] The point here would be to emphasise the exceptional nature of the right to use force in self-defence. It is probably for this reason that the Court in the *Nicaragua* case set such a high threshold for attribution. Nonetheless, the law is not static and it does change. If it were to be developed in the direction of lowering the threshold for attribution from the strict 'sent by or on behalf of' test of *Nicarargua*, the key question would be to determine the *extent* of the third State's involvement necessary to attribute to the non-State actor's activities to the third State. It would require an assessment – well beyond the scope of this

[285] Randelzhofer and Nolte, 'Article 51' 2012 (n. 8), 1415 ('Taking the current forms of state disintegration and international terrorism into consideration, the original formulation of the ICJ in the *Nicaragua* judgment today appears too narrow and in need of further differentiation'). See also Tams, 'The Use of Force against Terrorists' 2009 (n. 10), 385.

[286] See ICJ, *Military and Paramilitary Activities* (n. 31), Dissenting Opinion of Judge Schwebel, 160–7; ICJ, *Armed Activities in the Territory of the Congo* (n. 42), Dissenting Opinion of Judge ad hoc Kateka, paras. 12–15; and ICJ, *Armed Activities in the Territory of the Congo* (n. 42), Declaration of Judge Koroma, para. 9.

[287] Shinya Murase, *International Law: An Integrative Perspective on Transboundary Issues* (Tokyo: Sophia University Press, 2011), 294.

[288] Ibid.

[289] Ibid.

contribution – of whether the involvement of the third State in the activities of the non-State actors was 'substantial'.[290]

For the purposes of this chapter, only two points need to be made. First, such a shift, even if desirable, cannot be achieved by separate and dissenting opinions of the judges of the International Court of Justice or the writings of commentators based on acts that either do not receive the acceptance of other States or that may be explained in terms of the *Nicaragua* test of attribution. To lead to a different interpretation of Article 51, there has to be practice of States establishing the agreement of the UN member States as a whole or general and widespread practice accepted as law to establish a rule of customary international law. The second important point for the purposes of this chapter is that, even if that shift has occurred, or does in the future occur, the requirement of attribution has (or would) remain intact because the lowering of the threshold does not detract from the requirement for attribution.

VII. SUMMARY AND CONCLUSIONS

The rules relating to the use of force and, in particular, self-defence are sensitive and complex. Yet these rules have a definite content and are not 'in the eye of the beholder'. Moreover, these rules have to be seen in the context of the broader collective security architecture underpinning the UN system. Under these rules, States are prohibited from using force against the territorial integrity or independence of another State. Any use of force *in* the territory of another State amounts to a use of force which is prohibited under international law. In the event of a threat to the State, including in the case of armed aggression, the Security Council has the primary responsibility to take measures on behalf of the international community as a whole. This mechanism for collective action is the primary tool through which threats to peace and security, including threats to individual States, are to be addressed. Recourse to self-defence, an important right recognised in the Charter, is meant to be exceptional, limited and temporary, ceasing to exist if and when the Council assumes its responsibility.

The exceptional right to self-defence applies in the case of an armed attack from a State. While the Charter does not stipulate that the armed attack must be by 'a State', this has, until recently, been the generally accepted interpretation of Article 51. Moreover, this interpretation is consistent with the context of the Charter provisions. Of course, where the acts of a non-State actor are

---

[290] See ICJ, *Military and Paramilitary Activities* (n. 31), Dissenting Opinion of Judge Schwebel, 167.

attributable to a State, the victim State is entitled, in order to repel the attack, to use force in the territory of the third State.

The arguments, based on 'practice', that international law does permit the unilateral use of force in self-defence against non-State actors on the territory of innocent third States are, at best, unconvincing and, at worst, dangerous. Very often the practice that is advanced has been objected to by other States such that it cannot contribute to the interpretation of Article 51 of the Charter or form the basis of a rule of customary international law. Where the acts have not been objected to, such as the post-9/11-related acts, these have not supported the proposition that international law permits the use of force in self-defence absent some form of attribution to the territorial State. It is true that the events in Syria, and in particular the use of force by the US-led coalition in Syria without the latter's consent, may suggest a turn of law in the direction of an expansive interpretation of the law on self-defence. However, even these acts by some States reveal sufficient inconsistencies to prevent an interpretative 180 degree turn of the law. At best they reveal the possibility that law *could*, with sufficient coordination by a group of States and the acquiescence of others, turn in that direction. This would be a dangerous turn, undermining the collective security architecture of the United Nations – a turn that may well lead to the unleashing of the 'scourge of war' on succeeding generations that the drafters of the Charter felt so inspired to prevent. Moreover, subsequent to the advent of operations in Syria, a large grouping of States, the NAM, reiterated its view that Article 51 does not permit the extraterritorial use of force against non-State actors.

The collective security system is imperfect. As a result, not all harm can be prevented. But the alternative, unilateralism, is much worse. It means that we are all in danger, at all times. Unilateralism means the militarily powerful are free to determine when and how to exercise force, and the weak are at the eternal mercy of the powerful.[291] However, any sense of security that comes with the power to unilaterally use force is a false sense of security. Unilateralism carries the risk of escalation that the authors of the Charter sought to avoid. States in a position to use their military power might not see the dangers now, but tomorrow other States will hold the military might to do the same and might point to the precedents of current actions to justify what might otherwise be generally understood as illegal acts under international law.[292]

[291] This is reminiscent of Franck's invocation of Thucydides: 'the strong do what they can and the weak suffer what they must', quoted above (n. 279).
[292] See generally Marxsen, 'International Law in Crisis' 2015 (n. 20), 13.

The law has not changed. It remains that the right of self-defence is an exceptional right, limited in scope, available only in the most urgent of cases to repel an attack. There are those arguing vociferously for an expansion of this right to such an extent that States would be free to use force in the territory of that State, without that State's consent or without attribution of the conduct of the non-State actors to that State. Terrorism, as heinous as it certainly is, does not offer sufficient reason to depart from the constraints placed by international law. What terrorism does do is offer an opportunity for us to enhance the cooperation necessary to make the collective security system more effective. The alternative, undermining the collective security system by promoting unilateralism and the law of the jungle, should be resisted. Indeed, this may be precisely what the terrorists want from us: to undermine the collective security system and the rule of law in favour of unilateralism, the law of the jungle and, ultimately, chaos and insecurity.

2

Self-Defence against Non-State Actors: Making Sense of the 'Armed Attack' Requirement

Christian J. Tams[*]

I. INTRODUCTION

A major debate: Whether States can act in self-defence against armed attacks carried out by non-State actors is one of the major debates of contemporary international law. It has *relevance*: the issues are significant and implicate a 'cornerstone rule' of the discipline, the prohibition against the use of force.[1] It has *drama*: 'two main camps'[2] are said to face each other in what is now frequently (if simplistically) portrayed as an epic argument opposing 'restrictivists' and 'expansionists'.[3] It has *focus*: positions are clearly articulated; academics take sides – where do you stand on the 'unwilling or unable' test;[4] what's your view on the 'Bethlehem Principles';[5] have you signed the 'Plea against the Abusive Invocation of Self-Defence'?[6] – and do

[*] The author is grateful to Claus Kress for long-standing and enriching debates on self-defence, to Olivier Corten for incisive comments on an early draft and to Eleni Methymaki for her competent research assistance.

[1] See ICJ, *Armed Activities in the Territory of the Congo* (Democratic Republic of the Congo v. Uganda), Judgment of 19 December 2005, ICJ Reports 2005, 168, para. 148.

[2] Raphaël van Steenberghe, 'The Law of Self-Defence and the New Argumentative Landscape on the Expansionists' Side', *Leiden Journal of International Law* 29 (2016), 43–65 (43).

[3] This binary optique has become dominant: see e.g. contributions to two recent symposia in the *Leiden Journal of International Law* 29 (2016), one convened by Jörg Kammerhofer (13 *et seq.*), the other by Théodore Christakis (737 *et seq.*).

[4] For detailed assessments, see e.g. Ashley Deeks, 'Unwilling or Unable: Toward a Normative Framework for Extra-Territorial Self-Defense', *Virginia Journal of International Law* 52 (2012), 483–500; Paulina Starski, 'Right to Self-Defense, Attribution and the Non-State Actor: Birth of the "Unable or Unwilling" Standard?', *Heidelberg Journal of International Law* 75 (2015), 455–501.

[5] Daniel Bethlehem, 'Self-Defense against an Imminent or Actual Armed Attack by Nonstate Actors', *American Journal of International Law* 106 (2012), 770–7.

[6] See 'A Plea against the Abusive Invocation of Self-Defence as a Response to Terrorism', 29 June 2016, available at http://cdi.ulb.ac.be/wp-content/uploads/2016/06/A-plea-against-the-abusive-invocation-of-self-defence.pdf.

not mince words.[7] And it has *topicality* and *momentum* – which most observers think is with the 'expansionists', as States assert a right to use force against non-State actors in Syria and elsewhere.[8]

A narrow debate: The major debate about self-defence against armed attacks by non-State actors is also (and this can get lost amidst the drama) rather narrow, or at least has a narrow kernel. Of course, disputes about particular uses of force turn on a range of issues: the lawfulness of a State's military response depends on questions of evidence and proof, the character and qualification of the attack, the timing, extent and locale of the response, etc. Yet to the extent that debates about particular incidents draw on these factors, they presuppose that self-defence can at all be invoked against armed attacks carried out by non-State actors – that it is not restricted to responses against armed attacks by States. This question is of a preliminary character; it is a *threshold question*. This threshold question is *narrow*. It depends on the proper construction of one rule of international law, and one element of that rule more particularly. The rule enshrines the right of self-defence, and the crucial element is the notion of 'armed attack'. That notion – 'armed attack' – certainly covers attacks by another State, and some commentators want to leave it at that. According to others, the notion covers all armed attacks, irrespective of their source; still others put forward a range of intermediary positions. Perhaps inevitably, the debate about this relatively narrow issue is replete with repetition and duplication: so much has been said before, and by so many.

A long-standing debate: In fact, so much has been said before by so many, *for so long*: self-defence against non-State actors has been discussed for centuries, and at least the practice of the Charter era remains significant. Since the beginning of the twenty-first century, the focus has firmly been on military responses against Islamic terrorism. But international terrorism did not begin on 9/11; and in the family of non-State actors, terrorists are but one tribe.[9] For decades, States have asserted a right to use force against insurgents, mercenaries and national liberation movements, and for decades, their claims have been

---

[7] *Pars pro toto*, see the exchange between Corten and d'Argent about the 'Plea' (n. 6), 14 July 2016, available at www.ejiltalk.org/a-plea-against-the-abusive-invocation-of-self-defenc e-as-a-response-to-terrorism.

[8] See van Steenberghe, 'The Law of Self-Defence and the New Argumentative Landscape on the Expansionists' Side' 2016 (n. 2), 43; Bethlehem, 'Self-Defense against an Imminent or Actual Armed Attack by Nonstate Actors' 2012 (n. 5), 775; Jörg Kammerhofer, 'Introduction: The Future of Restrictivist Scholarship on the Use of Force', *Leiden Journal of International Law* 29 (2016), 13–18 (15).

[9] In fact, the prominence of the label masks the fact that the family of non-State actors is incredibly heterogeneous: see further *infra*, II.A.2.

assessed within international fora. Greece's letter to the United Nations sent in
1946 – qualifying support to insurgents as a 'breach of the peace' – contains
much that sounds familiar.[10] Much that sounds familiar can also be found in
debates about French raids against FLN units operating from Tunisia during
the late 1950s,[11] about Israeli strikes against Palestinians of the Cold War era[12]
and in the discussions preceding the adoption of the 1974 General Assembly's
Definition of Aggression.[13] The threshold question, in short, has long been on
the agenda; attempts to find answers to it ought to reflect that fact. This is not to
exclude the possibility of normative change: even if the questions remain the
same, answers over time may well differ, as the law adapts. But it suggests that
change is likely to be gradual; and the popular terms suggesting decisive turn-
arounds – from 'tidal waves'[14] to 'paradigm shifts'[15] to the (seemingly inevitable)
'Grotian moments'[16] – ought to be viewed with caution.

A confused debate: If, despite decades of discussion, the question remains on
the agenda, it is because the issues are vexing, but also because much of the
debate is confused. There remains a surprising degree of uncertainty as to how the
question of self-defence against non-State actors should be approached. 'Method
is undoubtedly a weak point of the scholarship on the use of force', notes Jörg
Kammerhofer with refreshing frankness, and he may be right: there is just so
much uncertainty.[17] Some commentators discuss customary international law,
others the meaning of a treaty clause. While the 'threshold issue' remains central,
many recent contributions 'blend' it with discussions about the modalities of self-
defence, such as necessity.[18] As regards legal authorities, some authors emphasise
the role of the International Court of Justice (ICJ), others that of major States; still
others rely on UN resolutions. In the view of some, the law was shaped in 1945
(when the UN Charter was adopted); others point to clarifications in 1974 (GA

[10]   See SCOR, 2nd year, 147th and 148th meeting, 1118–29.
[11]   See *Annuaire Français de Droit International* 6 (1960), 1068–9, and 4 (1958), 809.
[12]   See, notably, debates prompted by the 1985 Israeli raid on the PLO Headquarters in Tunis
       (which the Security Council condemned in SC Res. 573 of 4 October 1985).
[13]   See GA Res. 3314 (XXIX) of 14 December 1974 ('Definition of Aggression').
[14]   André de Hoogh, 'Restrictivist Reasoning on the *Ratione Personae* Dimension of Armed
       Attacks in the Post 9/11 World', *Leiden Journal of International Law* 29 (2016), 19–42 (20).
[15]   James Green, *The International Court of Justice and Self-Defense in International Law*
       (Oxford: Hart Publishing, 2009), 157.
[16]   Michael P. Scharf, 'How the War against ISIS Changed International Law', *Case Western
       Reserve Journal of International Law* 48 (2016), 15–67 (19).
[17]   Kammerhofer, 'The Future of Restrictivist Scholarship on the Use of Force' 2016 (n. 8), 15, and
       (less trenchant) de Hoogh, 'Restrictivist Reasoning on the *Ratione Personae* Dimension of
       Armed Attacks in the Post 9/11 World' 2016 (n. 14), 23–5.
[18]   Notably in discussions of the unable and unwilling test; see Nicholas Tsagourias, 'Self-
       Defense against Non-State Actors', *Leiden Journal of International Law* 29 (2016), 801–25 (810).

Res. 3314), 1986 (*Nicaragua*) or 2001 (9/11). Still others refer back to legal views articulated in the aftermath of the 1837 *Caroline* affair, to which subsequent developments seem but a coda.[19] As a result, similar pieces of evidence are assessed within different argumentative frameworks. That 'agree[ment] on method could cure much of the current divergence of views'[20] (as has been suggested) may be overly optimistic: methods do not necessarily predetermine answers; they help explain how they are reached. But the surprising methodological confusion that besets the debate makes genuine engagement more difficult, to the point where much of it becomes a 'dialogue of the deaf'.[21]

***

All this forms the background to the present study, which is in the nature of a 'further take' on issues well-covered.[22] As a further take, it is unlikely to break radically new ground. And yet, the following analysis offers more than a rehash of well-worn arguments. Seeking to avoid the (often myopic) focus on recent crises, it engages with practice preceding the alleged 'paradigm shift' of 9/11 – which is diverse rather than uniform. Looking beyond the high-profile conflicts, it emphasises the breadth of self-defence practice – which includes well-covered military responses against ISIS and Al-Qaeda, but also uses of force outside the spotlight, by countries such as Tajikistan and Morocco. Whereas much of the literature dithers on the question of sources, the present study clarifies that the 'armed attack' requirement is a requirement of treaty law – whose meaning is ascertained in line with the accepted canons of treaty interpretation.

The fuller analysis thus offered does not necessarily lead to one obvious, 'natural' outcome: as with other vexing legal problems, responses have but 'varying degrees of legal merit',[23] and the subsequent analysis reflects as

---

19   Vaughan Lowe notes the 'near theological reverence for the formulation of the right [of self-defence] in the context of the 1837 *Caroline* episode': Vaughan Lowe, *International Law* (Oxford: Oxford University Press, 2007), 275.

20   Andrea Bianchi, 'The International Regulation of the Use of Force', *Leiden Journal of International Law* 22 (2009), 651–76 (652).

21   Olivier Corten, 'The Controversies over the Customary Prohibition on the Use of Force: A Methodological Debate', *European Journal of International Law* 16 (2005), 803–22 (822).

22   For the author's earlier 'takes', see Christian J. Tams, 'The Use of Force against Terrorists', *European Journal of International Law* 20 (2009), 359–97; Christian J. Tams, 'Swimming with the Tide, or Seeking to Stem It?', *Revue Québécoise de Droit International* 18 (2007), 275–90; Christian J. Tams, 'Light Treatment of a Complex Problem: The Law of Self-Defence in the Wall Case', *European Journal of International Law* 16 (2005), 963–78; Christian J. Tams and James G. Devaney, 'Applying Necessity and Proportionality to Anti-Terrorist Self-Defense', *Israel Law Review* 45 (2012), 91–106; Christian J. Tams, 'The Necessity and Proportionality of Anti-Terrorist Self-Defence', in Larissa van den Herik and Nico Schrijver (eds.), *Counter-Terrorism Strategies in a Fragmented International Legal Order* (Cambridge: Cambridge University Press, 2013), 373–422.

23   Cf. Hersch Lauterpacht, *The Development of International Law by the International Court* (London: Stevens, 1958), 398.

much – hopefully without too much sitting on fences. Given the firm opinions held on self-defence, it would be naïve to expect the views set out in the following to meet with general approval; the analysis is a 'best efforts' attempt to offer a 'legally meritorious'[24] construction. It identifies blind spots in the reasoning of expansionists, restrictivists and commentators resisting such labels. And it will hopefully be perceived, even by those who disagree with the proposed reading of self-defence, as a methodologically sound contribution that allows the debate to move beyond a dialogue of the deaf.

In order to rise to the methodological challenge, Section II of the subsequent analysis goes to some length to situate military responses against non-State actors within the framework of the contemporary *ius ad bellum*. Sections III, IV and V then set out the contemporary regime governing self-defence against armed attacks by non-State actors. Their focus is firmly on the notion of 'armed attack'. The meaning of this notion is ascertained through a doctrinal analysis that uses the 'tools' and arguments recognised in the sources regime of international law and that accepts the distinction between the law in force and the law as it should be.

This doctrinal approach shapes the subsequent analysis. It means that responses to the threshold question are sought through a relatively dense and technical argument. It also makes for a narrow analysis that, focused on the threshold question, leaves to one side important issues – among them the conditions governing the exercise of self-defence, but also considerations *de lege ferenda* about the desirability of the law[25] – and that, focused on one narrow problem, can yield but 'in principle' views on the availability of self-defence. Yet these limitations seem a price worth paying: they permit a focused engagement with a crucial question – a question that is specific to the major debate about self-defence against armed attacks by non-State actors and that continues to divide and confuse commentators.

II. SETTING THE STAGE

In important ways, the Introduction has presupposed too much. Asking whether military action against non-State armed attacks could be justified as self-defence, it has assumed that such action requires justification and that self-defence offers the most plausible basis. Neither of these assumptions is

---

[24] *Ibid.*

[25] This approach is narrower than that adopted by Mary Ellen O'Connell in her contribution: see in this volume e.g. 179–81 (offering details on the ban on force) and 228–44 (exploring the historical foundations of the ban on force and the influence of natural law thinking). Dire Tladi's contribution is situated mid-way in between: his focus (like here) is doctrinal and on self-defence, but (like Mary Ellen O'Connell) he offers detail on the ban on force and Chapter VII, at 22–36.

entirely accurate: not all military responses against armed attacks by non-State actors require justification, and self-defence is not always the most plausible basis. Yet a significant number of them do, and it typically is. In clarifying why this is so, sections II.A and II.B demarcate the scope of the inquiry and situate self-defence within its proper normative context. Following these preliminary clarifications, section II.C spells out methodological premises that guide the inquiry. It notably does so by emphasising that self-defence is *a rule of treaty law* and by outlining principles that structure its interpretation.

A. *A Problem of Force in International Relations*

1. The State-Centric Ban on Force

Justifications offer reasons for conduct; they clarify that conduct that *prima facie* violates a rule is lawful. Most discussions of self-defence against non-State actors are discussions about the scope of a justification. They assume that the conduct in question is *prima facie*, ostensibly, unlawful. More specifically, a State's self-defence against a non-State actor ostensibly seems to fall foul of the prohibition against the use of force in international relations, enshrined in Article 2(4) of the UN Charter and customary international law. This prohibition is the lynchpin of the contemporary *ius ad bellum*. It binds all States and is said to extend to State-like entities such as stabilised *de facto* regimes.[26] According to the dominant reading, it precludes the use of military force in a general and comprehensive manner, irrespective of its intensity or the motives underlying it,[27] and it does so as *ius cogens*, with peremptory force.[28]

---

[26] See e.g. Christian Henderson, 'Contested States and the Rights and Obligations of the Jus Ad Bellum', *Cardozo Journal of International and Comparative Law* 21 (2013), 367–408; Olivier Corten, *The Law against War: The Prohibition on the Use of Force in Contemporary International Law* (Oxford: Hart, 2010), 126.

[27] There have been regular attempts to identify loopholes in the text, notably with respect to uses of force that were said not to threaten another State's territorial integrity or political independence. Amongst other things, these attempts ignore the fact that force is prohibited if 'in any other manner inconsistent with the Purposes of the United Nations' and that the references to 'territorial integrity' and 'political independence' were included to strengthen the prohibition: see Thomas M. Franck, *Recourse to Force* (Cambridge: Cambridge University Press, 2002), 12; Oliver Dörr and Albrecht Randelzhofer, 'Article 2(4)', in Bruno Simma, Daniel-Erasmus Khan, Georg Nolte and Andreas Paulus (eds.), *The Charter of the United Nations: A Commentary* (Oxford: Oxford University Press, 3rd edn., 2012), vol. I, 200–34 (para. 37); Christine Gray, *International Law and the Use of Force* (Oxford: Oxford University Press, 3rd edn., 2008), 31–3; Yoram Dinstein, *War, Aggression and Self-Defense* (Cambridge: Cambridge University Press, 5th edn., 2012), 89–91.

[28] As a matter of principle, this is widely agreed – though there is debate about the reach of *ius cogens*, which according to some extends only to acts of aggression, while others are prepared

While general and comprehensive, the ban on force is purposefully limited: it prohibits the use of force by States 'in their international relations'. This was traditionally read to refer to 'the international relations *between States*',[29] notably the non-consented use of force on the territory (or within other recognised spheres of influence) of another State – as opposed to action 'within its own boundaries'.[30] It is today commonly extended to uses of force across internationally accepted armistice lines or against stabilised *de facto* regimes.[31] That is a modest extension, though, and the cornerstone rule against force has rightly been described as 'state-centric'.[32] This in turn affects the subsequent analysis in two crucial respects.

2. Wheat and Chaff

To begin with, the focus on the prohibition against force helps separate the wheat from the chaff, viz. distinguish military responses that require justification from those that do not. The starting point is straightforward: military responses require justification if – and only if – they ostensibly violate the prohibition against force. This is the case for uses of force that affect 'the international relations' in the State-centric sense described above. Military strikes targeting non-State actors based in another State are the obvious example in point. By contrast, other military responses do not need to be justified under the *ius ad bellum*. The most significant exclusion concerns military responses 'at home': in civil wars, against domestic terrorists, etc. Perhaps surprisingly (but indisputably), the prohibition against force, that 'cornerstone of the human effort to promote peace in a world torn by strife',[33] ignores the most significant forms of contemporary conflict.[34]

---

to treat Article 2(4) in its entirety as peremptory. For comment see O'Connell in this volume, 229–32; James Green, 'Questioning the Peremptory Status of the Prohibition of the Use of Force', *Michigan Journal of International Law* 32 (2011), 215–57. See also the views recorded in ICJ, *Military and Paramilitary Activities in and against Nicaragua* (Nicaragua v. United States), Merits, Judgment of 27 June 1986, ICJ Reports 1986, 14, para. 190. Implications of *ius cogens* are taken up *infra*, II.B.2 and II.B.3.

[29] Dörr and Randelzhofer, 'Article 2(4)' 2012 (n. 27), para. 32.

[30] See the ICJ's statement in *Legality of the Threat or Use of Nuclear Weapons*, Advisory Opinion of 6 January 1996, ICJ Reports 1996, 226, para. 50.

[31] See GA Res. 2625 (XXV) of 24 October 1970, Principle I, para. 5.

[32] Claus Kress, 'Major Post-Westphalian Shifts and Some Important Neo-Westphalian Hesitations in the State Practice on the International Law on the Use of Force', *Journal on the Use of Force and International Law* 1 (2014), 11–54 (40); Kimberley N. Trapp, 'Actor-Pluralism and the "Turn to Responsibility"', *Journal on the Use of Force and International Law* 2 (2015), 199–222 (201).

[33] ICJ, *Military and Paramilitary Activities* (n. 28), Separate Opinion of Judge Singh, 153.

[34] According to the International Committee of the Red Cross, 'about 80% of the victims of armed conflicts since 1945 have been victims of non-international conflicts': see 'Introduction to AP II', available at www.icrc.org/ihl/InTRO/475.

The other exclusion is more discrete; it illustrates that different non-State actors cannot always be treated alike. True enough, in a world carved up by States, a prohibition that precludes the use of force on the territory of another State covers most military strikes against non-State actors operating from outside the responding State's own boundaries. Much of the scholarship, especially on counter-terrorist responses, takes this for granted and seems to treat exceptions as oddities.[35] However, it is worth noting that one group of non-State actors has traditionally operated from outside State jurisdiction: namely pirates, who operate on the high seas or in a place outside the jurisdiction of any State.[36] Military action against pirates on the high seas is anything but an oddity. However, it is subject to a special set of rules: these impose restrictions,[37] but do not implicate general *ius contra bellum* provisions.[38] For reasons of convenience, they are left to a side here – but the brief reference suggests that the *ius ad bellum* does not necessarily treat different categories of non-State actors alike.

3. Asymmetry

Other than helping separate wheat from chaff, the focus on the ban on force draws attention to a complicating factor – in fact *the* major complicating factor that muddies discussions of self-defence against non-State actors and that can be described as a problem of 'asymmetry'.

Asymmetry is a consequence of the particular focus of the prohibition against force. State-centric as it is,[39] that prohibition addresses non-State actors only in an indirect manner. It requires a sequence of events involving one (attacking) non-State actor and one (responding) State to be appreciated on the basis of rules devised to apply between States. In that inter-State perspective, non-State actors hardly feature.[40] They do not feature as attackers, as their

---

[35]   Natalino Ronzitti, 'The Expanding Law of Self-Defence', *Journal of Conflict and Security Law* 11 (2006), 343–59 (349); Marko Milanovic, 'Self-Defense and Non-State Actors: Indeterminacy and the Jus ad Bellum', *EJIL Talk!*, 21 February 2010, available at www.ejiltalk.org/self-defen se-and-non-state-actors-indeterminacy-and-the-jus-ad-bellum.

[36]   See United Nations Convention on the Law of the Sea, 1833 UNTS 3, 10 December 1982 (UNCLOS), Article 101.

[37]   See notably Articles 100–7 UNCLOS.

[38]   For details see Alexander Proelss, 'Piracy and the Use of Force', in Panos Koutrakos and Achilles Skordas (eds.), *The Law and Practice of Piracy at Sea* (Oxford: Hart, 2014), 53–63 (53).

[39]   The subsequent passage, for reasons of simplicity, does not address 'state-like entities' and *de facto* regimes.

[40]   In her contribution to this volume, Mary Ellen O'Connell emphasises the link between the right to be free from unlawful force and the right to life (e.g., 178–9 and 203–4). There is no

initial attacks as such do not implicate the *ius ad bellum*.[41] And they do not feature as targets in their own right either: the responding State's military reaction violates the ban on force only if it is directed against targets on the territory (or in other spheres of influence) of another State.[42] If it does, it needs to be justified. And while this typically will be the case, the obligation remains State-centred: what needs to be justified is a breach of international law *vis-à-vis* another State. Military responses against non-State actors therefore cannot meaningfully be thought of as a bilateral relationship between responding State and targeted non-State actors.

Surprisingly often, this straightforward point is not made. Kimberley Trapp makes it when noting that any 'true exception to the prohibition on the use of force … must in some way excuse the violation of the host state's territorial integrity'.[43] In fact, as part of the State-centric *ius ad bellum*, this is all a 'true exception' needs to do.

On balance, State-centrism probably increases the scope for force to be used lawfully against non-State actors: host State consent in particular has become a convenient remedy, relied upon to ensure the legality of crossborder strikes. Yet absent such consent, responding States are 'caught' by the problem of asymmetry. What is motivated as a response against a non-State attack has to be justified within a set of rules operating between States. Between the logic of the response (State/non-State) and the rationale of the applicable legal rules (State/State), there is no equivalence: the two are asymmetrical. Much of what follows is an attempt to come to terms with this asymmetry.

B. *A Question of Self-Defence*

1. Self-Defence as the Justification of Choice

The analysis so far establishes that military responses against armed attacks by non-State actors usually require justification. So why should they be justified

doubt a common impetus to both. However, this impetus has been translated into different legal rules, with different rationales and limitations. The right to life does not assist in assessing whether the prohibition on the use of force has been violated in the first place – and it is on this question that the subsequent inquiry centres.

[41] See Dörr and Randelzhofer, 'Article 2(4)' 2012 (n. 27), para. 29.
[42] See Kimberley N. Trapp, 'Back to Basics: Necessity, Proportionality, and the Right of Self-Defense against Non-State Terrorist Actors', *International and Comparative Law Quarterly* 56 (2007), 141–56 (145–6); Jörg Kammerhofer, *Uncertainty in International Law: A Kelsenian Perspective* (Abingdon: Routledge, 2010), 38.
[43] Kimberley N. Trapp, 'The Use of Force against Terrorists: A Reply to Christian J. Tams', *European Journal of International Law* 20 (2010), 1049–55 (1049–50).

as self-defence? The short answer to this question is 'because States choose to rely on self-defence rather than on alternative justifications (other than host State consent and a Security Council authorisation)'.[44]

Self-defence emerged as the justification of choice for perfectly plausible reasons, but not over night. Nineteenth- and twentieth-century debates were characterised by much greater diversity. In the pre-Charter era, depending on type of attack and the timing and locus of the response, doctrines such as necessity,[45] armed reprisals and hot pursuit[46] were popular – at times in conjunction with self-defence. The adoption of the Charter, with its stricter system of prohibition and exceptions, initially did not affect this. The different explanations, recast as justifications for *prima facie* breaches of the ban on force, continued to be relied on; in fact, some doctrines such as 'hot pursuit on land' were only fully developed in the Charter era.[47]

Over time, though, the consolidation of the Charter regime led to a more streamlined discourse, in which self-defence became central.[48] This it became largely by default, as alternative justifications fell out of favour. The fate of necessity illustrates the process. During the twentieth century, necessity has come to be recognised as a circumstance precluding wrongfulness[49] and is now very much *en vogue* in other areas of international law.[50] Within the *ius ad bellum*, while significant as a limit on self-defence, it is no longer pleaded as a self-standing entitlement justifying recourse to force.[51]

---

[44]   As will be shown *infra*, IV.E.2, in some instances the lines between these claims are fine.

[45]   As famously, in the *Caroline* case: see Article 25 and commentary of the ILC's Articles on State Responsibility (ASR), *Yearbook of the International Law Commission* 2001, vol. II/2, 81 (para. 5).

[46]   See Ian Brownlie, 'International Law and the Activities of Armed Bands', *International and Comparative Law Quarterly* 7 (1958), 712–35 (733–4).

[47]   See e.g. Derek Bowett, 'Reprisals Involving Recourse to Armed Force', *American Journal of International Law* 66 (1972), 1–36 (17–21); Shane Darcy, 'Retaliation and Reprisals', in Marc Weller (ed.), *The Oxford Handbook of the Use of Force in International Law* (Oxford: Oxford University Press, 2015), 879–96.

[48]   For more on this see Tams, 'The Use of Force against Terrorists' 2009 (n. 22), 362–73.

[49]   Article 25 ASR completed the process: see *Yearbook of the International Law Commission* 2001, vol. II/2, 80.

[50]   For details, see the contributions to the *Netherlands Yearbook of International Law* 41 (2010) ('Necessity Across International Law').

[51]   Olivier Corten, 'Necessity', in Weller, *The Oxford Handbook of the Use of Force* 2015 (n. 47), 861–78 (863–7); Noam Lubell, *Extraterritorial Use of Force against Non-State Actors* (Oxford: Oxford University Press, 2010), 71–2.
        Gazzini and Dinstein, for different reasons, reach a different conclusion: Dinstein, *War, Aggression and Self-Defense* 2012 (n. 27), 271–2, considers necessity to be part of a flexible concept of 'extraterritorial law enforcement' that describes 'the phenomenon of recourse in self-defence to cross-border counter-force against terrorists and armed bands' (at 272) – but this

Claims based on hot pursuit have suffered a similar fate. Primarily espoused by South Africa and Southern Rhodesia during the 1970s and 1980s, they were always received coolly.[52] After the independence of Zimbabwe, and the end of South Africa's incursions into 'frontline States', they are no longer advanced.[53] Armed reprisals do not fare much better: declared illegal in prominent legal texts,[54] the concept has effectively been abandoned as a justification for the use of force.[55]

With alternative justifications losing ground, self-defence today seems to be the 'last claim standing'. Since the 1990s, it has become absolutely dominant: as Lubell notes, it is indeed the 'sole avenue for legitimizing unilateral forcible action by states against non-state actors in the territory of other states'.[56]

2. Reasons and Implications

Why self-defence should have become the justification of choice is not difficult to see. Unlike necessity, hot pursuit, and armed reprisals, the right to self-defence is expressly recognised as an exception to the ban on force, which is strong enough to justify conduct that ostensibly violates a peremptory norm.[57] Pursuant to Article 51 of the Charter and customary international law, the ban on force does not 'impair the inherent right of . . . self-defence if an armed attack occurs'. A State invoking self-defence can be criticised for over-stretching an exception; but it acts from within the accepted system. States

blurs the lines between separate legal concepts. Gazzini argues that measures directed against non-State actors ought to be treated as necessity. However, that ignores the conscious decision of States to rely on self-defence: see Tarcisio Gazzini, *The Changing Rules on the Use of Force in International Law* (Manchester: Manchester University Press, 2005), 204–10.

[52] See Edward Kwakwa, 'South Africa's May 1986 Military Incursions into Neighboring African States', *Yale Journal of International Law* 12 (1987), 421–43.

[53] See Dinstein, *War, Aggression and Self-Defense* 2012 (n. 27), 270–1; Tom Ruys, *'Armed Attack' and Article 51 of the UN Charter: Evolutions in Customary Law and Practice* (Cambridge: Cambridge University Press, 2010), 401 (fn. 174).

[54] See notably GA Res. 2625 (XXV) of 24 October 1970, Principle I, para. 6; Article 50(1)(a) ILC's Articles on State Responsibility (*Yearbook of the International Law Commission* 2001, vol. II/2, 31 *et seq.*); SC Res. 188 of 9 April 1964.

[55] See Darcy, 'Retaliation and Reprisals' 2015 (n. 47), 892 ('futile case for revival').

[56] Lubell, *Extraterritorial Use of Force against Non-State Actors* 2010 (n. 51), 74.

[57] This is accepted in principle, but gives rise to some conceptual 'muddling through': some commentators claim that, since self-defence justifies a *prima facie* breach of a peremptory rule, it must itself be peremptory: see e.g. Paulina Starski, 'Silence within the Process of Normative Change and the Evolution of the Prohibition on the Use of Force', *Journal on the Use of Force and International Law* 4 (2017), 14–65 (24). The more convincing approach suggests that only *illegal* uses of force are prohibited as *ius cogens*.

relying on it of course need to argue that self-defence is available against non-State actors. However, unlike States invoking necessity or hot pursuit, they do not have to make the broader claim that the contemporary *ius ad bellum* recognised exceptions not explicitly mentioned in the Charter. Reliance on self-defence to justify military responses against non-State actors thus is the 'safer option'.

Safety comes at a price though. The conscious choice of States to treat military responses against non-State actors as a question of self-defence means that claims are to be presented within the parameters of that particular exception. This has one obvious implication and a further one that is not so obvious. The obvious implication is that military responses against non-State actors have to meet the conditions and modalities of self-defence. Four of them stand out:

- The *first* concerns the triggering event: justified as self-defence, military responses can only be directed against attacks that qualify as 'armed attacks': the dominant view restricts this to qualified uses of force, or even the 'most grave forms of the use of force'.[58]
- The *second* concerns the timing of the response: particular care must be taken if action in self-defence is meant to avert future attacks; the right, after all, is recognised only 'if an armed attack occurs'.[59]
- The *third* concerns the scope of the right: reliance on self-defence implies acceptance of the twin conditions of necessity and proportionality – each of them offering some flexibility, but both in principle 'well settled'.[60]
- The *fourth*, and final, condition goes to the purpose of the response: a military response presented as self-defence needs to serve a defensive purpose. This functional element is by no means easy to apply in practice, but it can help to exclude action that is retaliatory or punitive.[61]

All this, one might say, comes with the terrain. It is the price States have to pay for relying on the 'safer option' of self-defence. In reality, things are more complicated. The four limitations cannot be seamlessly applied to military responses against non-State actors. But that is a question of operationalising a set of conditions – which is beyond the scope of the present study.

---

[58]   ICJ, *Military and Paramilitary Activities* (n. 28), para. 191.
[59]   On anticipatory self-defence, see e.g. Ruys, *'Armed Attack' and Article 51 of the UN Charter* 2010 (n. 53), chapter 4.
[60]   ICJ, *Oil Platforms* (Islamic Republic of Iran v. United States), Judgment of 6 November 2003, ICJ Reports 2003, 161, para. 76.
[61]   See Enzo Cannizzaro, 'Contextualizing Proportionality: Jus ad bellum and jus in bello in the Lebanese War', *International Review of the Red Cross* 88 (2006), 779–92.

3. More on Asymmetry

A) SELF-DEFENCE: BY DEFINITION SYMMETRICAL? Beyond the operational
implications, the decision to rely on self-defence shapes the discourse in
another manner. This second implication – hardly ever spelled out[62] – points
back to the problem of asymmetry.[63] In essence, in opting to rely on self-
defence to justify forcible acts against non-State actors, States have chosen to
address the problem under a justification that is often intuitively understood to
apply to symmetrical relationships only, in which the response targets the
author of the initial attack. This understanding informs many domestic law
concepts of self-defence as a response against an illegal attack *by the attacker*.
On the international plane, the exceptional nature of self-defence as one of the
few recognised exceptions to the ban on force has been said to support a
symmetrical reading. Roberto Ago's apodictic statement reflects this approach:
'the only international wrong which, exceptionally, makes it permissible for
the State to react ... by recourse to force ... is an offence which itself
constitutes a violation of the ban'[64] – in other words, a use of military force
by the State against which the response is directed.[65]

This 'symmetrical' view of self-defence can of course be contested. But the
point at this stage is that it enjoys support: this sets self-defence apart from
other justifications. Hot pursuit, for example, is by definition asymmetrical.
It is formulated as a right to interfere with non-State actors; the interference
with the territorial State's sovereignty and territorial integrity is incidental.[66]
Hot pursuit would be 'tailor-made' to fit the asymmetrical relationship of State
responses against a non-State actor. Necessity, too, offers significant room to
deal with asymmetry. Unlike self-defence, it is not a response against conduct
('armed attack'), but a way of dealing with a state of affairs ('grave and
imminent peril').[67] The response is not conditional upon the conduct of the

---

[62] But see Björn Schiffbauer, *Vorbeugende Selbstverteidigung im Völkerrecht* (Berlin: Duncker &
      Humblot, 2012), 82–8.
[63] See *supra*, II.A.3.
[64] Roberto Ago, 'Addendum to the 8th Report on State Responsibility', *Yearbook of the
      International Law Commission* 1980, vol. II/1, 54 (para. 89).
[65] For recent reprises see de Hoogh, 'Restrictivist Reasoning on the *Ratione Personae* Dimension
      of Armed Attacks in the Post 9/11 World' 2016 (n. 14), 22; Olivier Corten, 'The "Unwilling or
      Unable" Test: Has It Been, and Could It Be, Accepted?', *Leiden Journal of International Law*
      29 (2016), 777–99 (796–7).
[66] A nineteenth-century US statement illustrates this rationale: 'If Mexican Indians whom
      Mexico is bound to restrain are permitted to cross its border and commit depredations in
      the United States, they may be chased across the border and then punished' (cited in
      Brownlie, 'International Law and the Activities of Armed Bands' 1958 (n. 46), 733).
[67] Article 25 ASR.

targeted State; hence, the law of necessity can accommodate asymmetrical responses.[68] Within the law of self-defence, by contrast, it is by no means obvious that a State should be able to respond against conduct by an entity other than the targeted State: when it comes to dealing with asymmetry, self-defence is an 'away game'.

B) WAYS OF DEALING WITH ASYMMETRY While hardly spelled out, this problem is instinctively recognised. Over time, it has been addressed in two ways. One strategy has been to confront asymmetry head-on. The resulting argument is fairly straightforward. Self-defence, so the reasoning goes, is permissible against armed attacks irrespective of their source; the targeted State has to *tolerate* the response even though it has not committed an attack itself: the duty to endure is an implicit element of self-defence. The real task is to explain why and when targeted States are under a duty of toleration. Drawing on domestic debates about these matters, one might, for example, argue that it should derive from some form of involvement in the attack, or perhaps from a failure to suppress it.

The second strategy seeks to circumvent problems of asymmetry. This it does by postulating that a broad range of attacks can be treated as 'State attacks' – against which a response is permitted. More specifically, it claims that the circle of 'State attacks' is not restricted to attacks committed by the State's organs itself,[69] but extends to other acts for which the State has to answer. The task for this second approach is to explain why and when a State has to answer for acts that have not been committed by its organs. Again, one might query whether some form of participation in the attack, or a failure to prevent it, could offer arguments.

The existence of these two strategies is widely recognised, as is the fact that they are conceptually different: the latter approaches asymmetrical self-defence from within an inter-State framework; the former moves outside that framework to tackle asymmetry head on. Drawing on a popular (though controversial) trope of international legal discourse, Claus Kress pointedly distinguishes between 'Westphalian' and 'post-Westphalian avenues' towards recognising asymmetrical self-defence.[70]

---

[68] See Ian Johnstone, 'The Plea of Necessity in International Legal Discourse: Counter-Terrorism and Humanitarian Intervention', *Columbia Journal of Transnational Law* 43 (2005), 337–88 (368).

[69] Even this basic proposition – that the State has to answer for acts of its organs – is of course the result of a 'normative operation': see ILC, Introductory Commentary to Part One, Chapter II of the Articles on State Responsibility, *Yearbook of the International Law Commission* 2001, vol. II/2, 39.

[70] Kress, 'Major Post-Westphalian Shifts' 2014 (n. 32), 46.

This conceptual distinction is important – but more important still is another point. Insofar as the threshold question is concerned,[71] the Westphalian and post-Westphalian approaches raise essentially the same issue: they require the law to identify a sufficient link between the targeted State and the prior armed attack.[72] For want of a better term, this link is referred to in the following as the *State nexus*. Under the Westphalian approach, this State nexus determines which 'private attacks' can be treated as a 'State attack' for the purposes of self-defence. Under the post-Westphalian approach, the State nexus explains when the targeted State has to endure a military response. Crucially, both approaches have to address the very same set of questions. Does a State have to answer for (or tolerate a military response directed against) attacks whose commission it has facilitated? Does a State have to answer for (or tolerate a military response directed against) attacks that it has failed to suppress? Or, *in extremis*, does a State have to answer for (or tolerate a military response directed against) an attack simply because it emanates from its territory?

None of these questions needs to be addressed at this stage. They are raised to highlight that there is room for nuance in dealing with asymmetry – and to emphasise that the line between Westphalian and post-Westphalian approaches, at least for the purposes of the threshold question, is very fine indeed.[73] The choice for one over the other is a matter of predilection.

C. A Question of Treaty Law

1. The Continuing Appeal of Custom

Before pursuing arguments about asymmetrical self-defence, it is necessary to address a curious methodological problem that besets the debate. As indicated in the Introduction, there is considerable uncertainty about the proper source of self-defence, which is variably located in Article 51 of the UN Charter, custom or a blend of both.[74] Whether the different methodological choices

---

[71] When looking beyond the threshold question, there may well be differences between the Westphalian and post-Westphalian approaches, notably in defining against whom force in self-defence can be directed. These matters are beyond the scope of the present inquiry.

[72] Others see the two argumentative strategies as alternative: see e.g. Milanovic, 'Self-Defense and Non-State Actors' 2010 (n. 35) ; Trapp, 'Actor-Pluralism and the "Turn to Responsibility"' 2015 (n. 32), 201–3.

[73] As Claus Kress notes, once a tenuous State nexus is admitted, 'the Westphalian explanation . . . becomes indistinguishable, for all practical purposes, from its post-Westphalian competitor' (Kress, 'Major Post-Westphalian Shifts' 2014 (n. 32), 46).

[74] Separate considerations apply to States that remain outside the United Nations; this matter is left to one side.

actually affect outcomes is difficult to say with certainty;[75] but they make it more likely that debates turn into a dialogue of the deaf.

The source of the right of self-defence, to be sure, was a matter of dispute in the early days of the UN era. The wording of Article 51 of the Charter invited discussion: pursuant to its first sentence,

> Nothing in the present Charter shall impair the inherent right of individual or collective self-defence if an armed attack occurs against a Member of the United Nations, until the Security Council has taken measures necessary to maintain international peace and security.

As this is clearly a rather roundabout way of recognising an exception to the ban on force, it may not have been far-fetched to argue, in the early years of the United Nations, that a broad (customary) right of self-defence of the pre-Charter era would continue to exist ('un-impaired', as it were) alongside Article 51 – and that such a broader, customary right did not depend on a prior 'armed attack'.[76] But from early on, proponents of such a reading struggled to explain how their 'black hole' approach[77] could be squared with the Charter's desire to impose a strict set of rules regulating recourse to force.[78]

The debate about self-defence against non-State actors raises issues of a different character. It turns on the understanding of the term 'armed attack' (a term used in Article 51), not on the possibility of self-defence against other acts: in this sense, too, it is a debate that can be had 'within the system'.[79] And yet, uncertainties about the proper source of law persist; and if anything, the appeal of custom has increased over time. To illustrate by reference to prominent contributions: Daniel Bethlehem's widely discussed set of principles on self-defence is described by their author as an attempt 'to work with the grain of the UN Charter as well as *customary international law, in which resides the inherent right of self-defense*'.[80] Olivier Corten retraces 'Controversies Over the *Customary* Prohibition on the Use of Force'.[81] Others seek to have it both ways: hence Tom Ruys' book on *'Armed Attack' and Article 51 of the UN Charter* evaluates

---

[75] In his contribution to the volume, Dire Tladi suggests they do not: see Tladi in this volume, 48.

[76] See notably Derek Bowett, *Self-Defence in International Law* (Manchester: Manchester University Press, 1958), 187–8.

[77] See Kammerhofer, *Uncertainty in International Law* 2010 (n. 42), 7–11.

[78] *Ibid.*, 9.

[79] See *supra*, II.B.2.

[80] Bethlehem, 'Self-Defense against an Imminent or Actual Armed Attack by Nonstate Actors' 2012 (n. 5), 773 (emphasis added).

[81] Corten, 'The Controversies over the Customary Prohibition on the Use of Force' 2005 (n. 21), 803 (emphasis added).

'Evolutions in *Customary* International Law and Practice'.[82] According to André de Hoogh, 'most authors set forth their analysis or make arguments with a view to establishing the content of a rule of *customary* international law.'[83]

2. The Proper Focus: Treaty Law

The prominence of custom in discussion of self-defence against non-State actors is puzzling. To be sure, it would be perfectly understandable to locate the debate in custom if Article 51 of the UN Charter was merely a *renvoi* to extra-Charter law. But that view is not seriously maintained today. Self-defence is generally held to be 'regulated by both customary and conventional norms';[84] these two rules – even where 'they appear identical in content' – 'retain a separate existence'.[85] Of the two separate rules, the conventional one, Article 51, does not address all issues expressly; it needs to be applied in conjunction with concepts such as necessity and proportionality that it does not mention.[86] But its terms ('armed attack', 'occurs', etc.) do provide guidance on some issues, and they do so *as treaty law*.

The prominence of custom in debates about self-defence against non-State actors would also be understandable if the customary right of self-defence against armed attacks (however construed) could justify violations of the ban on force irrespective of their source. But such a view is difficult to square with general principles governing the interaction of treaty and custom. More specifically, it faces three significant objections. First, it presupposes a highly unusual view of co-existing rules of treaty and custom. Such co-existence, to be sure, is anything but exceptional. International law in many fields contains formally separate, but substantively similar, rules.[87] But such overlap is regularly dealt with by according primacy to treaty law rules. Custom (in the terms used by Dinstein and Thirlway, respectively) usually 'remains invisible': it 'is eclipsed' and 'reced[es] behind the treaty', waiting to 'reappear in its full vitality … whenever the treaty no longer blocks it from sight'[88] – e.g. when

---

[82]   Ruys, *'Armed Attack' and Article 51 of the UN Charter* 2010 (n. 53) (emphasis added).
[83]   De Hoogh, 'Restrictivist Reasoning on the *Ratione Personae* Dimension of Armed Attacks in the Post 9/11 World' 2016 (n. 14), 39.
[84]   Raphaël van Steenberghe, 'Self-Defence in Response to Attacks by Non-State Actors in the Light of Recent State Practice: A Step Forward?', *Leiden Journal of International Law* 23 (2010), 183–208 (185).
[85]   ICJ, *Military and Paramilitary Activities* (n. 28), para. 178.
[86]   See e.g ICJ, *Legality of the Threat or Use of Nuclear Weapons* (n. 30), para. 41.
[87]   Hugh Thirlway, *The Sources of International Law* (Oxford: Oxford University Press, 2014), 129.
[88]   Yoram Dinstein, 'The Interaction between Customary International Law and Treaties', *Recueil des Cours* 322 (2007), 243–427 (396); Thirlway, *The Sources of International Law* 2014 (n. 87), 139.

a treaty, on grounds of jurisdiction, cannot be applied (as in the *Nicaragua* case). Yet as debates about self-defence against non-State actors are not so jurisdictionally limited, one should expect customary self-defence to 'recede' behind the Charter rule.

Second, on a more practical level, it is by no means sure how the customary rule on self-defence should preserve its autonomy from the Charter rule. With the United Nations nearing universal membership, international practice can no longer easily be allocated to one particular source. Again, this problem is not specific to self-defence: custom and multilateral treaty norms, while retaining their separate identity, are becoming increasingly amalgamated in many fields. The doctrine of sources does not preclude this, but increasingly accepts 'Entangled Treaty and Custom'.[89] Treaty law, as will be discussed in section IV, can evolve; and treaty interpretation is to take account, in various ways, of subsequent practice in the application of the respective treaty.[90] Where the treaty in question, like the UN Charter, is widely ratified, the lines between 'subsequent treaty practice' (for the purposes of treaty interpretation) and 'international practice' (for the purposes of ascertaining custom) become blurred.[91] The acceptance of State conduct within the UN, and of UN resolutions themselves, as factors relevant to the ascertainment of custom reinforce this trend. In short, a customary right of self-defence (assuming it were not eclipsed) could hardly be insulated from developments in treaty law.

Third, and most significantly, even if it existed autonomously from its UN Charter equivalent, it is very difficult to see how a customary right of self-defence could provide an effective justification for military responses on foreign State territory.[92] Whatever the position under customary international law, it bears reminding that States using force against non-State actors operating in another State *prima facie* violate international law's prohibition against force, which is recognised in treaty law and in custom. If customary self-defence is to be an effective justification for such conduct, it would need to justify both violations. The customary rule on self-defence would not only need to apply alongside its treaty law equivalent, but it would need to 'trump' the Charter system. It is one thing to argue customary rules should continue to

---

[89] See Oscar Schachter, 'Entangled Treaty and Custom', in Yoram Dinstein (ed.), *International Law in a Time of Perplexity: Essays in Honour of Shabtai Rosenne* (Leiden: Nijhoff, 1989), 717–38 (717).

[90] For details see *infra*, IV.A.

[91] This point is often not made. But see van Steenberghe, 'Self-Defence in Response to Attacks by Non-State Actors' 2010 (n. 84), 186.

[92] See Jörg Kammerhofer, 'The Resilience of the Restrictive Rules on Self-Defence', in Weller, *The Oxford Handbook of the Use of Force in International Law* 2015 (n. 47), 627–48 (641).

exist, and to apply, alongside treaty-law rules governing the same ground. It is quite another to claim they should disapply the treaty law. This would turn the regular application of the *lex specialis* principle on its head.[93]

These three objections do not strictly rule out the possibility of an autonomous right of self-defence, recognised under customary international law, which would justify uses of force that are ostensibly illegal under custom and treaty. But they suggest it is a remote possibility, and one that – given the blurring of lines between customary law and treaty – would be very difficult to establish. Few contributors addressing questions of self-defence against non-State actors *as a question of customary international law* bother to engage with the three objections. Their preference for custom (as opposed to treaty law) may reflect a desire to focus on practice (undoubtedly a central element of custom, whose crucial role in treaty interpretation is not always appreciated) or an unwillingness to take the terms, context and *telos* of the Charter rules seriously. It may also simply show a *laissez faire* approach to the sources of international law, perhaps verifying Kammerhofer's charge of 'methodological weakness'.[94] Either way, it remains puzzling – and it ignores the main thrust of the preceding discussion: that self-defence, as regulated in Article 51, raises questions of treaty law. It is addressed as such in the following section.

3. Consequence: A Question of Treaty Interpretation

The focus on self-defence as a treaty-based right structures the inquiry. Whether States can invoke self-defence in response to armed attacks by non-State actors is a question of treaty interpretation, to be addressed on the basis of the principles codified in Articles 31 to 33 of the Vienna Convention on the Law of Treaties (VCLT), which reflect custom. In their customary guise, these apply to treaties predating the VCLT (such as the Charter).[95] They apply to a 'constituent instrument of an international organization', but are 'without prejudice to any relevant rules of the organization'.[96]

These considerations provide the framework for the subsequent analysis. This framework (unlike an inquiry based on custom) is capable of taking seriously the written treaty text, as read in light of its context and the Charter's

---

[93] Ago, 'Addendum to the 8th Report on State Responsibility' 1980 (n. 64), 63, considered it 'unconvincing ... that two really divergent notions of self-defence ... could co-exist'.
[94] Kammerhofer, 'The Future of Restrictivist Scholarship on the Use of Force' 2016 (n. 8), 15.
[95] Cf. Vienna Convention on the Law of Treaties, 23 May 1969, 1155 UNTS 331 (VCLT), Article 4.
[96] Article 5 VCLT.

object and purpose.[97] At the same time, it is flexible enough to accommodate the subsequent conduct of States, which can influence the interpretation of Article 51, either as an authentic or supplementary means of interpretation, as '[w]ords are given meaning by deeds.'[98]

Before approaching Article 51 on the basis of this flexible framework, two preliminary points need to be addressed. The first concerns the normative environment of Article 51, which is part of a treaty establishing an international organisation with an institutional structure. It is widely accepted that the interpretation needs to reflect this fact. This is typically achieved by broadening the range of actors whose conduct affects the interpretative process. More specifically, the 'deeds' that matter for the purposes of treaty interpretation are not only those of States; the subsequent practice relevant for the construction of self-defence encompasses the conduct of UN organs alongside that of member States.[99] In fact, to the extent that secondary acts of the UN are designed to concretise the meaning of Charter provisions, they are 'privileged sites' of treaty interpretation.[100]

If UN practice can, in principle, be easily integrated into the regular framework of treaty interpretation, the impact of judicial decisions poses a greater challenge. International courts – notably the ICJ – have pronounced on different aspects of the *ius ad bellum*.[101] Read properly, these decisions have limited binding force, but can carry considerable persuasive power.[102] Binding precedents they are certainly not: this is contradicted by Article 59 of the ICJ Statute and equivalent provisions.[103] Nevertheless, a judicial decision will often carry significant authority as a 'means for the determination of rules of law' as per Article 38(1)(d) of the ICJ Statute. In this respect, decisions of the ICJ have been described as 'persuasive precedents'[104] and as 'beacons, guides and orientation points'.[105] Those descriptions seem apt, as they highlight the

---

[97] Article 31(1) VCLT.

[98] Richard K. Gardiner, *Treaty Interpretation* (Oxford: Oxford University Press, 2nd edn., 2015), 225.

[99] See e.g. Stefan Kadelbach, 'The Interpretation of the Charter', in Simma, Khan, Nolte and Paulus (eds.), *The Charter of the United Nations* 2012 (n. 27), vol. I, 71–99 (para. 36).

[100] Raphaël van Steenberghe, *La légitime défense en droit international public* (Bruxelles: Larcier, 2012), 171.

[101] See further *infra*, IV.B.3.b and IV.D.3.b.

[102] For details see Christian J. Tams and James Sloan (eds.), *The Development of International Law by the International Court of Justice* (Oxford: Oxford University Press, 2013).

[103] These indeed make it 'clear . . . that the Court cannot legislate': see ICJ, *Legality of the Threat or Use of Nuclear Weapons* (n. 30), para. 18.

[104] See e.g. ICJ, *Continental Shelf* (Libyan Arab Jamahiriya v. Malta), Merits, Judgment of 3 June 1985, Dissenting Opinion of Judge Jennings, ICJ Reports 1984, 148, para. 27.

[105] Franklin Berman, 'The International Court of Justice as an "Agent" of Legal Development?', in Tams and Sloan, *The Development of International Law by the International Court of Justice* 2013 (n. 102), 7–21 (21).

authority of a judicial decision, but also clarify that such authority is not a given: a decision needs to 'persuade', and whether it does so has to be assessed. The judicial voice, then, is an important one, but the Court 'does not have the last word'[106] in questions of treaty interpretation.

The second preliminary consideration concerns the peremptory status of the ban on force. This status, in the view of some commentators, affects the principles of interpretation.[107] Mary Ellen O'Connell makes the point emphatically; according to her, '[g]iven the nature of peremptory prohibitions, ... valid interpretation must not result in a weaker norm. Logically, peremptory norms may expand, not contract. ... [D]iluting and contracting the prohibition on the use of force through interpretation is impermissible.'[108] This approach is informed by a desire to construe the ban against force effectively. However, it fails to appreciate that such effective interpretation ought to proceed from the general regime of interpretation codified in Articles 31 to 33 of the VCLT. As a plea for a special regime of interpretation, the approach faces two obstacles. For one, it seems to assume that the 'true meaning' of peremptory norms were certain and timeless.[109] But that is difficult to sustain. To illustrate by reference to matters not at issue here, the meaning of 'force' in Article 2(4), or of the 'special intent' requirement of the prohibition against genocide, is not God-given; it needs to be established – and in this process, the means of interpretation mentioned in Articles 31 to 33 of the VCLT have their place.[110]

---

[106] Alain Pellet, in Andreas Zimmermann *et al.* (eds.), *The Statute of the International Court of Justice* (Oxford: Oxford University Press, 2nd edn., 2012), Article 38, para. 334.

[107] The following assessment focuses on the argument set out by Mary Ellen O'Connell in her contribution to the present volume. For related arguments, see notably Alexander Orakhelashvili, 'Changing Jus Cogens Through State Practice?', in Weller, *The Oxford Handbook of the Use of Force in International Law* 2015 (n. 47), 157–75.

[108] O'Connell in this volume, 248 and 251.

[109] See O'Connell in this volume, 249: 'As *ius cogens*, however, meaning is stable'; hence 'contrary state practice is of little relevance.' It is worth noting that while, according to this approach, 'diluting and contracting the prohibition on the use of force through interpretation is impermissible, discerning a broader prohibition is not'; this is because '[i]nterpreting the meaning of peremptory norms logically follows the principle of progression' (251). The source of this 'principle' is not disclosed.

[110] As Oliver Dörr rightly notes, 'Interpretation is always required ... Whenever a subject of international law invokes, applies or goes about implementing a treaty, it can only do so on the basis of a certain understanding of its terms, ergo on the basis of an interpretation', in Oliver Dörr and Kirsten Schmalenbach (eds.), *Commentary on the Vienna Convention on the Law of Treaties* (Heidelberg: Springer, 2012), Article 31, para. 15. James Green notes that 'such a stifling restriction on the development of the jus ad bellum would not concord with the reality of the law on the use of force' (James Green, 'Questioning the Peremptory Status of the Prohibition of the Use of Force' 2011 (n. 28), 237).

But the plea for a special regime faces a more fundamental obstacle. It misconstrues the relationship between the ban on force, and the recognised exception of self-defence. '[B]uilt into the very nature of the UN system',[111] self-defence operates on the same hierarchical level as the ban on force.[112] Arguments about the peremptory status should reflect as much: what is peremptory is the rule against unlawful uses of force. Action in self-defence is simply not unlawful. Arguments about asymmetrical self-defence are advanced from 'within the system' of the UN Charter.[113] The rule is limited by the exception, which operates on the same level.

None of this is to criticise the quest for an effective construction of the ban against force. Nor should it be read as a plea for a *laissez-faire* approach to treaty interpretation. However, it suggests that if peremptory norms were subject to a special regime of interpretation, then this would have to apply to the ban on force *as limited by self-defence*. For the crucial question relevant here – is self-defence available against armed attack by non-State actors? – *ius cogens* offers fairly little.

***

On the basis of these clarifications, the threshold question can be approached in its proper normative setting: it requires the interpretation of a treaty clause, Article 51, that enshrines the right of self-defence against armed attacks as an exception to a State-centric ban on force. According to the International Law Commission's (ILC) much-quoted formula, this interpretation is 'a single combined operation', whereby different means of interpretation are 'thrown into the crucible', to allow for their 'interaction',[114] which accords each means of interpretation 'appropriate emphasis'.[115] For reasons of convenience, the subsequent discussion presents arguments relevant to this 'single, combined' process in two steps. The bulk of the analysis (section IV) looks at the approach of States and UN organs. Treaty interpretation, however, is more than a tracing of practice. It proceeds from the text ('armed attack'), presumed to reflect the parties' understanding of the proper scope of self-defence. Put differently, words are not only given meaning *by deeds*; they also have meaning *as words*, an ordinary meaning, which context, object and purpose help

---

[111] James Green, 'Questioning the Peremptory Status of the Prohibition of the Use of Force' 2011 (n. 28), 229.

[112] See n. 28 for brief comment on the scope of the peremptory ban on force.

[113] *Supra*, II.B.2.

[114] See *Yearbook of the International Law Commission* 1966, vol. II, 219, para. 8.

[115] See Draft Conclusion 3(5), adopted as part of the ILC's work on subsequent agreements and subsequent practice in relation to the interpretation of treaties, UN Doc. A/71/10 (2016), 120 *et seq.*

elucidate. A surprisingly large number of writers on self-defence fail to explore literal, contextual and teleological arguments, give short shrift to them, or use them uncritically.[116] Section III illustrates what they are missing: it takes Article 51 seriously as a rule of treaty law.

III. THE 'ARMED ATTACK' REQUIREMENT: MAKING SENSE OF THE TREATY TEXT

According to the general rule of interpretation reflected in Article 31(1) of the VCLT,

> [a] treaty shall be interpreted in good faith in accordance with the ordinary meaning to be given to the terms of the treaty in their context and in the light of its object and purpose.

This dense phrase offers a roadmap for the inquiry, which – in a process of 'progressive encirclement'[117] – moves from literal to contextual to purposive arguments before exploring the drafting history of Article 51.

A. '... the ordinary meaning to be given to the terms of the treaty ...'

The notion of 'armed attack' is at the heart of Article 51. Its ordinary meaning, reflecting the common use of the terms, is not easy to define with precision, but four basic points can be made on the basis of the English language version:

> (i) Self-defence is available against an '*attack*', i.e. an 'aggressive and violent act against a person or place'.[118]

---

[116] Of the detailed works, see e.g. Ruys, '*Armed Attack*' *and Article 51 of the UN Charter* 2010 (n. 53), 57–60 (brief discussion of the text of Article 51); Gray, *International Law and the Use of Force* 2008 (n. 27), 128 *et seq.* (approaching Article 51 via practice and jurisprudence); Gazzini, *The Changing Rules on the Use of Force in International Law* 2005 (n. 51), 132–3 (text and *travaux* 'scarcely ... conclusive'). Others mention the text of Article 51, but treat it *en passant*: van Steenberghe, *La légitime défense en droit international public* 2012 (n. 100), 270; Lindsay Moir, *Reappraising Resort to Force: International Law, Jus ad Bellum and the War on Terror* (Oxford: Hart, 2010), 22; Lubell, *Extraterritorial Use of Force against Non-State Actors* 2010 (n. 51), 31; Gregor Wettberg, *The International Legality of Self-Defense against Non-State Actors* (Bern: Peter Lang, 2007). Corten, *The Law against War* 2010 (n. 26) mentions text and purpose of self-defence, but focuses on UN practice (162 *et seq.* and 445–55).

[117] See *Aguas del Tunari v. Bolivia* (ICSID ARB/02/03), Objections to Jurisdiction, available at http://icsidfiles.worldbank.org/icsid/ICSIDBLOBS/OnlineAwards/C210/DC629_En.pdf, para. 91.

[118] *Oxford Dictionary of English* (Oxford: Oxford University Press, 2nd edn., 2005): *s.v.* 'attack' (noun), at no. 1.

(ii) In order to trigger self-defence, such attacks must be *'armed'*, i.e. involve the use of weaponry or firearms.[119]

(iii) Article 51 specifies the target of the attack, viz. 'a Member of the United Nations', i.e. a State.

(iv) Article 51 does not describe the identity of the attacker; the term 'armed attack' appears without qualifier. It is not expressly linked to conduct by 'a Member of the United Nations'.

The same four points apply to the (authentic) Spanish, Russian and Chinese versions.[120] Each of these mention a violent act, which is qualified by reference to weapons ('un ataque armado', 'вооруженное нападение' and 'gōngjí shi', respectively); and each qualifies the target of the required attack as a UN member State ('contra un Miembro de las Naciones Unidas'; 'против члена Организации Объединенных Наций'; etc.). By contrast, neither the Russian nor the Spanish or Chinese versions require the attack to be carried out *by* a State.

The French version differs, but not significantly. It, too, requires the violent act to be 'armed' (point (ii)) and clarifies that it must be directed against a State (point (iii)). As to point (i), the French text uses a different term, namely *'agression'*, which suggests a qualified attack, viz. an *'attaque non provoquée, injustifiée et brutale'*.[121] However, it does not affect point (iv) made above: *'agression'* does not qualify the identity of the attacker any more than the term 'attack'; it notably does not imply any State nexus.[122]

From this first glance at Article 51, it is clear that what matters, for present purposes, is what is *not* said: nothing, in any of the five languages, suggests that self-defence would necessarily be symmetrical; the provision 'fails to specify from whom or which entity such an attack should originate'.[123] This silence is widely noted,[124] but quite what it means is disputed. A narrow claim is that it

---

[119] *Ibid.*, *s.v.* 'armed' (adjective), at 1.1.

[120] The following draws on Schiffbauer, *Vorbeugende Selbstverteidigung im Völkerrecht* 2012 (n. 62), 294–306.

[121] Larousse, *Dictionnaire monolingue* (online), *s.v.* 'agression', available at www.larousse.fr/dictionnaires/francais/agression/1766.

[122] Claus Kress, *Gewaltverbot und Selbstverteidigungsrecht nach der Satzung der Vereinten Nationen* (Berlin: Duncker & Humblot, 1995), 208.

[123] de Hoogh, 'Restrictivist Reasoning on the *Ratione Personae* Dimension of Armed Attacks in the Post 9/11 World' 2016 (n. 14), 21.

[124] See e.g. van Steenberghe, *La légitime défense en droit international public* 2012 (n. 100), 270; Oscar Schachter, 'The Extraterritorial Use of Force against Terrorist Bases', *Houston Journal of International Law* 11 (1989), 309–16 (311); Carsten Stahn, 'Terrorist Acts as "Armed Attack": The Right to Self-Defense, Article 51(1/2) of the UN Charter, and International Terrorism', *Fletcher Forum of World Affairs* 27 (2003), 35–53 (42).

does not preclude asymmetrical self-defence: in Judge Higgins' phrase, 'nothing in the text of Article 51 . . . stipulates that self-defence is available only when an armed attack is made by a State.'[125]

That may be too cautious, though. While interpreters have only 'the words "armed attack" to go on',[126] these have a positive meaning: they require an 'aggressive and violent act', which is expressly qualified in terms of its modality ('armed') and direction ('against a Member of the United Nations'). It is simply incorrect to state that '[the] silence [of Article 51] makes a determination of the ordinary meaning of its terms impossible.'[127] While the provision does not expressly *include* attacks by non-State actors, its terms are clear: they require no State nexus, and absent indications to the contrary, that should be taken to mean that no unwritten qualifier is required. On a textual analysis, self-defence is available against armed attacks by non-State actors simply because '[a]rmed attacks by non-state actors are still armed attacks.'[128]

B. ' . . . in their context . . . '

Contextual arguments have more than the two 'words "armed attack" to go on';[129] they take into account the position of particular terms within the overall structure of the treaty, to ensure that an 'abstract ordinary meaning of a phrase [is not] divorced from the place which that phrase occupies in the [treaty as a whole]'.[130] To the extent that the terms of Article 51 are seriously interrogated, contextual arguments dominate. According to many commentators, they support a State-centric interpretation, which notably draws on the link between self-defence and the ban on force. The potential for contextual arguments is, however, rarely exhausted. The relationship between Articles 51 and 2(4) is relevant, but so is the immediate context of the term 'armed attack' and its relationship with provisions belonging to the same regulatory

---

[125] See ICJ, *Legal Consequences of the Construction of a Wall in the Occupied Palestinian Territory*, Advisory Opinion of 9 July 2004, Separate Opinion of Judge Higgins, ICJ Reports 2004, 136, 215, para. 33.

[126] Kammerhofer, *Uncertainty in International Law* 2010 (n. 42), 43.

[127] de Hoogh, 'Restrictivist Reasoning on the *Ratione Personae* Dimension of Armed Attacks in the Post 9/11 World' 2016 (n. 14), 24.

[128] As noted by Dinstein in earlier editions of his textbook: see Yoram Dinstein, *War, Aggression and Self-Defence* (Cambridge: Cambridge University Press, 3rd edn., 2001), 214.

[129] See Kammerhofer, *Uncertainty in International Law* 2010 (n. 42), 43.

[130] Oliver Dörr, in Dörr and Schmalenbach (eds.), *Commentary on the Vienna Convention on the Law of Treaties* 2012 (n. 110), Article 31, para. 44.

'scheme'.[131] The following four sub-sections explore well- and lesser-known contextual arguments.

1. The Immediate Context: The Terms of Article 51

A first contextual argument flows from the very phrase that contains the terms 'armed attack'.[132] As noted above (section III.A), Article 51 says nothing on the identity of the attacker, but specifies that it has to be directed against a 'Member of the United Nations', i.e. a State.[133] This is indicative; it makes it difficult to argue that Article 51, as a general matter, simply presupposes some form of State nexus. The argument can be put in the form of two questions. If such a nexus were assumed – why would the victim of an attack be expressly qualified as a UN member (State)? Conversely, if the provision expressly stipulates that only States can exercise self-defence under the Charter, does this not suggest that an armed attack, not so qualified, could emanate from a broader range of actors? This is not a necessary inference. But it is worth noting the contrast between the two sides of Article 51: the victim is expressly described as a State, the attacker not so, even though a qualifying term could easily have been added. This suggests that the silence in the text of Article 51 may have meaning.

2. Arguments Derived from Article 2(4) of the Charter: Conventional Wisdom

The most popular contextual argument suggesting that the silence should be ignored – and that self-defence is only available against a State attack – draws on the relationship between Articles 2(4) and 51.[134] Aspects of that relationship have been addressed already; the two most relevant ones for present purposes are that, first, Article 51 is an exception to the rule found in Article 2(4) and, second, that Article 2(4) in the main precludes the use of force directed against other States.[135] These starting points indeed favour a 'State-oriented' interpretation of the right of self-defence that construes the notion of 'armed

---

[131] Gardiner, *Treaty Interpretation* 2015 (n. 98), 205.

[132] This is, in Gardiner's phrase, the 'obvious initial contextual assessment that must be made' (*ibid.*, 197).

[133] See Articles 3 and 4 of the Charter, reserving membership to original members and 'peace-loving states'.

[134] This analysis largely draws on Kammerhofer, *Uncertainty in International Law* 2010 (n. 42), 37 *et seq.*

[135] *Supra*, sections II.A and II.B.

attack' like the ban on force.[136] As an exception justifying military conduct, self-defence can easily be construed as a 'responsive' right permitting symmetrical reactions against uses of force that violate Article 2(4). If it is the flip-side of the coin, then it should matter that the front side formulates a State-centric prohibition.[137]

Water-tight, or logically necessary, this conclusion is certainly not: perhaps self-defence is more than the flip-side of the ban. But it has considerable appeal, at least as long as the focus remains on unilateral uses of force.[138] Appeal, because prohibition and exception would follow the same (State-centric) rationale. Appeal, because it would reflect the close link between Articles 2(4) and 51, which are regularly presented as a 'package', the latter necessary to make the former palatable. Appeal, finally, because self-defence would operate in a straightforward manner: the exceptional response would only be available against States committing a qualified wrong.[139] The symmetric, State-centric construction of self-defence would, to put it bluntly, *make eminent sense* and *fit smoothly* within a Charter regime shaped by the State-centric ban on force.

3. Questioning the Conventional Wisdom

All of this, to be sure, is 'assailable',[140] and has been assailed. Three contextual counter-arguments could sever the link between prohibition and exception. Two of these can be dealt with relatively briefly; the third requires a fuller analysis.

The first counter-argument is an argument from the contrary. It, too, looks at the interplay of self-defence and the ban on force, but it emphasises differences. That Article 2(4) is State-centric only throws – so the argument runs – the openness of Article 51 into starker relief. The difference in wording, argues Andreas Zimmermann, 'seems to imply, by way of an *argumentum e contrario*, that Article 51 . . . does not require any inter-state

---

[136] For firm views to this effect see e.g. Ago, 'Addendum to the 8th Report on State Responsibility' 1980 (n. 64), para. 89; Corten, *The Law against War* 2010 (n. 26), 162; Michal Kowalski, 'Armed Attack, Non-State Actors and a Quest for the Attribution Standard', *Polish Yearbook of International Law* 30 (2010), 101–30 (122).

[137] Ago, 'Addendum to the 8th Report on State Responsibility' 1980 (n. 64), para. 89.

[138] But see section III.B.4 that looks beyond unilateral responses.

[139] See de Hoogh, 'Restrictivist Reasoning on the *Ratione Personae* Dimension of Armed Attacks in the Post 9/11 World' 2016 (n. 14), 22–3; Kammerhofer, *Uncertainty in International Law* 2010 (n. 42), 38–9; Robert Kolb, *Ius Contra Bellum* (Basel: Helbing Lichtenhahn, 2nd edn., 2009), 293.

[140] Kammerhofer, *Uncertainty in International Law* 2010 (n. 42), 39.

situation'.[141] But this only goes so far. Every argument by analogy can in theory be turned into an *argumentum e contrario*. The question is whether the *ratio legis* warrants a 'contrarian' construction.[142] The close link between Articles 2(4) and 51 would rather seem to support a concordant reading.[143]

The second counter-argument questions the idea of symmetry between Articles 2(4) and 51. If these two provisions were truly symmetrical, every breach of Article 2(4) should trigger the right of self-defence. However, that is not the case: according to the dominant view, there is a 'gap' between the two, as self-defence is available only against qualified uses of force.[144] Perhaps, then, other forms of asymmetry should not be ruled out? But that, too, only goes so far. The accepted case of asymmetry between Articles 2(4) and 51 concerns the intensity of force, not the actors. As the two asymmetries are different, the move from the accepted (intensity) to the disputed one (actors) requires a leap of faith.

4. In Particular: Chapter VII of the Charter

More powerful is a third contextual counter-argument, which is rarely made.[145] It derives from a comparison between Article 51 on the one hand and Articles 39 and 42 on the other. Articles 39 and 42 – like Articles 2(4) and 51 – form part of the Charter's *ius ad bellum*. As read today, they permit the use of force by States with a Security Council mandate.[146] While that institutional setting is particular, from the perspective of the responding State, Articles 39 and 42 operate in much the same way as Article 51: they justify conduct that ostensibly violates the ban on force.[147] What is more, Article 51 reinforces the link between unilateral and institutionalised reactions by precluding self-

---

[141] Andreas Zimmermann, 'The Second Lebanon War', *Max Planck Yearbook of United Nations Law* 11 (2007), 99–141 (117); and further Christiane Wandscher, *Internationaler Terrorismus und Selbstverteidigungsrecht* (Berlin: Duncker & Humblot, 2006), 134.

[142] See Karl Larenz, *Methodenlehre der Rechtswissenschaften* (Heidelberg: Springer, 2nd edn., 1991), 279.

[143] Wandscher, *Internationaler Terrorismus und Selbstverteidigungsrecht* 2006 (n. 141), 234–5.

[144] *Supra*, section II.B.2.

[145] The point is hinted at in Trapp, 'Actor-Pluralism and the "Turn to Responsibility"' 2015 (n. 32), 203–4, and Constantine Antonopoulos, 'Force by Armed Groups as Armed Attack and the Broadening of Self-Defence', *Netherlands International Law Review* 55 (2008), 159–80 (163).

[146] See Franck, *Recourse to Force* 2002 (n. 27), 24 *et seq.*; Gazzini, *The Changing Rules on the Use of Force in International Law* 2005 (n. 51), 43 *et seq.*

[147] See Green, 'Questioning the Peremptory Status of the Prohibition of the Use of Force' 2011 (n. 28), 229: 'In either case – self-defense or collective security – the *prima facie* unlawfulness of the use of force is precluded.'

defence when the UN's collective security mechanism is activated. All this suggests that Articles 39 and 42 can inform the contextual interpretation of the 'armed attack' requirement.

Article 39 clarifies that by adopting collective security measures. The Security Council can respond to acts of aggression, breaches of the peace or threats to the peace. Just as Article 51 is worded openly, so is Article 39: nothing in the text suggests that Security Council responses are dependent on some form of unlawful inter-State conduct, let alone the use of force.[148] Yet for some time, such an inter-State, symmetrical reading enjoyed considerable support. Article 39 was read to presuppose an unlawful use (or threat) of force in the international relations between States.[149] Lacking a foothold in the wording of Article 39, this interpretation was supported by contextual arguments, notably the close link with Article 2(4).[150]

Twenty-five years after *Desert Storm*, such readings are but a remote echo from a distant past. It is beyond doubt today that the Security Council may authorise military measures in situations *not* involving an inter-State force.[151] In fact, the Council has hardly ever responded to breaches of Article 2(4).[152] Perhaps more importantly, it has also authorised military measures against non-State actors.[153] On the face of it, States implementing such mandates would have violated the prohibition against the use of force. Yet covered by Articles 39 and 42, their conduct did not violate Article 2(4) and had to be endured by the host State.

This development is part of a new, robust construction of Chapter VII of the Charter that accommodates what Kimberley Trapp calls 'actor pluralism'.[154] And while some of the Council's other arrogations of competence are viewed sceptically, its decision to overcome an inter-State

[148] As noted by Nico Krisch, 'Article 39', in Simma, Khan, Nolte and Paulus, *The Charter of the United Nations* 2012 (n. 27), vol. I, 1273–96 (para. 7): 'The concept of "peace" ... can take on many meanings.'

[149] See e.g. Wilhelm Wengler, *Das völkerrechtliche Gewaltverbot* (Berlin: de Gruyter, 1967), 23–4; Joachim Arntz, *Der Begriff der Friedensbedrohung in Satzung und Praxis der Vereinten Nationen* (Berlin: Duncker & Humblot, 1975), 21 *et seq*. According to Kress ('Major Post-Westphalian Shifts' 2014 (n. 32), 14), '[t]he meaning originally given ... to the term "international" [in Article 39] was "inter-state".'

[150] Arntz, *Der Begriff der Friedensbedrohung* 1975 (n. 149), 44.

[151] As Krisch notes, the Security Council, from early on, engaged with conflicts not involving a threat or use of force: see Krisch, 'Article 39' 2012 (n. 148), para. 19.

[152] *Ibid.*, paras. 16–29.

[153] For details see Pieter H. Koojimans, 'The Security Council and Non-State Entities', in Karel Wellens (ed.), *International Law: Theory And Practice – Essays in Honour of Eric Suy* (The Hague/Boston, MA/London: Martinus Nijhoff, 1998), 333–46.

[154] Trapp, 'Actor-Pluralism and the "Turn to Responsibility"' 2015 (n. 32), 204–5.

construction of Chapter VII has met with general approval. For the debate on self-defence, this development is instructive in two respects. First, it shows that inter-State readings of another openly worded Charter provision (Article 39) at some point enjoyed support – and were abandoned subsequently. Perhaps the law of self-defence could have undergone a similar transformation. And, second, a quick glance at the development of Chapter VII undermines the claim that, under the Charter's *ius ad bellum* regime, military force could *only ever* be lawfully used in response to prior breaches of Article 2(4):[155] uses of force authorised under Chapter VII can clearly be asymmetrical.[156]

***

Contextual arguments point in different directions. The immediate context of the term 'armed attack' supports a broad construction of Article 51: the provision qualifies the victim of an armed attack (which must be a State) but not the attacker. By contrast, the close relationship between Articles 51 and 2(4) seems to support a State-centric construction. However, the popular argument derived from Article 2(4) rests on a narrow comparison that ignores the Charter's other exception to the ban on force, viz. force authorised by the Security Council. Once Articles 39 and 42 are appreciated (which they hardly ever are), the argument derived from Article 2(4) loses much of its force. The Charter's *ius ad bellum* scheme, if looked at as a whole, is significantly more diverse than commentators exploring the relationship between Articles 2(4) and 51 recognise. This suggests that, contrary to a commonly held view, contextual arguments do not support a State-centric construction of self-defence. On balance, they would seem to offer support for a reading that accepts the possibility of asymmetrical self-defence.

---

[155] Even Kammerhofer in his otherwise excellent analysis ignores this: cf. *Uncertainty in International Law* 2010 (n. 42), at 43: 'the Charter in all other respects relevant to its *ius contra bellum* ... is directed exclusively towards inter-state action.'

[156] Dire Tladi, in this volume, 64, disagrees: he notes that '[t]he expansive reading of Article 39 and 42 has been facilitated in part by the special powers of the Council and its primary mandate for the maintenance of international peace and security, powers and a mandate that States, acting unilaterally, simply do not have. To suggest, as this contextual interpretation [set out here, CJT] might imply, that the scope of the rights of an individual State under Article 51 is the same as or even comparable to the scope of the powers of the Security Council in Chapter VII is wrong and dangerous.' This is correct, but misses the narrower point advanced here: no equivalence between self-defence and collective security is asserted. What is argued is that a look at the evolution of Chapter VII weakens the claim that the Charter's *ius ad bellum* scheme was necessarily State-centric.

C. '... and in the light of its object and purpose'

This finding can be tested by taking into account the Charter's object and purpose, which, under the general principles of interpretation, can help elucidate the ordinary meaning of the terms of the treaty.[157] Conventional wisdom directs interpreters to the preamble and introductory clauses of a treaty. The Charter seems to facilitate such an approach, since it expressly sets out the UN's 'Purposes and Principles'.[158] However, as with many other treaties of broad substantive scope, these comprise 'a variety of different, and possibly conflicting, objects and purposes'.[159] This in turn affects the impact of a teleological interpretation, which yields relatively few weighty arguments.

1. Ensuring the Maintenance of Peace and Security

The main teleological argument supporting a State-centric construction proceeds from what has been referred to as the UN's 'purpose of all purposes',[160] the maintenance of international peace and security. Under the Charter scheme – so the argument runs – the UN is to maintain peace and security primarily through measures of collective security, while unilateral military action is strictly limited by Article 2(4). Reinforced by the preamble's emphatic statement against the 'scourge of war', this purposive reading is said to mandate a narrow reading of entitlements to use military force unilaterally: 'as a product of the horrors of the Second World War inspired by the desire to end the "scourge of war", the whole object of the Charter was precisely to limit the scope for unilateral use of force as much as possible and to subject it to the control of the Security Council.'[161] In the present context, unilateral force in self-defence is most effectively limited if the trigger event is narrowly construed; and this is best achieved by limiting it to (armed) State attacks.[162]

---

[157] Gardiner, *Treaty Interpretation* 2015 (n. 98), 211.
[158] Kadelbach, 'The Interpretation of the Charter' 2012 (n. 99), para. 31.
[159] WTO Appellate Body, *US Import of Certain Shrimp and Shrimp Products*, WT/DS58/AB/R (1998), para. 17.
[160] Rüdiger Wolfrum, 'Article 1', in Simma, Khan, Nolte and Paulus, *The Charter of the United Nations* 2012 (n. 27), vol. I, 107–20 (para. 5).
[161] Ruys, *'Armed Attack' and Article 51 of the UN Charter* 2010 (n. 53), 59–60.
[162] See e.g. Tladi in this volume, 64: 'The object and purpose of the Charter, simply put, are the prevention of wars and conflict. Interpreting Article 51 to permit the use of inter-State force in the territory of another State – thereby violating the third State's territorial integrity – is contrary to this purpose.' See also Kowalski, 'Armed Attack, Non-State Actors and a Quest for the Attribution Standard' 2010 (n. 136), 123; Ruys, *'Armed Attack' and Article 51 of the UN Charter* 2010 (n. 53), 59; Starski, 'Right to Self-Defense, Attribution and the Non-State Actor' 2015 (n. 4), 498.

If all of this sounds a bit too good to be true, then that is because it is. More specifically, the purposive argument just summarised suffers from two problems. First, it proceeds from a traditional understanding of the Charter's peace and security scheme, which emphasises the absence of military conflict between States. This traditional understanding remains prominent, but is no longer dominant.[163] A brief passage from the UN Secretary-General's Report *In Larger Freedom* outlines a twenty-first century view of the institution's 'purpose of purposes':

> The threats to peace and security in the twenty-first century include not just international war and conflict but civil violence, organized crime, terrorism and weapons of mass destruction. They also include poverty, deadly infectious disease and environmental degradation since these can have equally catastrophic consequences.[164]

The move from one (inter-State) to another (broader) understanding of peace and security is a gradual process. But that it is well under way seems difficult to dispute.[165] And this is sufficient to weaken arguments premised on an equation of peace and security on the one hand and 'international war and conflict' on the other: for in the new, 'multidimensional',[166] understanding, non-State actors are certainly capable of threatening international peace and security. Action against them could well be portrayed as an attempt to *maintain* peace.

The point need not be explored, as the purposive reading faces a second, more serious, problem:[167] it is premised on a selective view of the Charter's peace and security design. No doubt the two aspects mentioned by its proponents, viz. collective security and the ban on force, are central. However, so is the right of self-defence, which the purposive argument just sketched out conveniently ignores: an 'un-impaired' part of the Charter regime, self-defence operates as a limitation on the general ban on force, and is itself limited by collective security action. Read properly, the Charter's object is to maintain peace and security by banning military force, but only to the extent that force is *not used in self-defence*. In other words, the maintenance of peace and security as the Charter's primary

---

163 For general accounts see Nadine Susani, 'United Nations, Purposes and Principles', in *Max Planck Encyclopedia of Public International Law* (online edn), March 2009; and Rüdiger Wolfrum's discussion of 'Article 1' 2012 (n. 160).

164 In Report of the Secretary-General, *In Larger Freedom: Towards Development, Security and Human Rights for All*, UN Doc. A/59/2005 (21 March 2005), para. 78.

165 See Susani, 'United Nations, Purposes and Principles' 2009 (n. 163), para. 25: '[T]he notion of "international peace and security" ... has certainly become much more multidimensional.'

166 *Ibid.*

167 The following draws on Schiffbauer, *Vorbeugende Selbstverteidigung im Völkerrecht* 2012 (n. 62), 317–18.

purpose is operationalised through particular Charter provisions, of which Article 51 is one. These provisions concretise the Charter's object of maintaining peace and security; and a solution to problems of interpretation ought to be sought through them, not by reference to the abstract notion of peace and security.[168] Adapting the terms used by the ICJ in response to a broad, purposive construction of a jurisdictional treaty, one could say that '[a]lthough … States had expressed in general terms in the [Charter's Chapter I] their desire to [maintain peace and security], their consent thereto had only been given in the terms laid down in [the specific provisions operationalising that purpose].'[169] Once this is accepted, the purposive argument collapses: it depends on a selective analysis that simply bypasses Article 51.

2. Facilitating Effective Responses

Whereas purposive arguments favouring a State-centric construction may appear lofty, considerations in support of an asymmetrical understanding of self-defence seem a little prosaic. They are quite rare. Some commentators suggest that Article 51 sought to permit effective responses against real threats or real attacks – which is taken to favour a broad construction of the armed attack requirement.[170] Similarly, others claim that the Charter's peace and security design looked to substantive factors (such as the intensity of an attack) and should not depend on the status of the attacker.[171] But neither prong of the argument is really convincing. The purpose of self-defence (as opposed to that *of the Charter*) is not as such a relevant teleological consideration. Moreover, the Charter is incredibly 'status-conscious' in some fields (including in formulating a State-centric ban on force). And self-defence could still be effective if it applied only to State attacks.

***

[168] Dire Tladi takes issue with this argument, noting that 'self-defence is a provision in the Charter' whose overall aim is to prevent war and conflict through collective action (Tladi in this volume, 65). This is correct; but it fails to appreciate that the preference for collective action is built into Article 51: self-defence becomes unavailable once collective security measures are taken. Precisely because 'self-defence is a provision in the Charter' (*ibid.*), attempts to construe treaty clauses by reference to the Charter's object and purpose should not ignore it.

[169] See ICJ, *Arbitral Award of 31 July 1989* (Guinea-Bissau v. Senegal), Merits, Judgment of 12 November 1991, ICJ Reports 1991, 53, para. 56.

[170] See e.g. Zimmermann, 'The Second Lebanon War' 2007 (n. 141), 117; Kress, *Gewaltverbot und Selbstverteidigungsrecht nach der Satzung der Vereinten Nationen* 1995 (n. 122), 214–15.

[171] Wandscher, *Internationaler Terrorismus und Selbstverteidigungsrecht* 2006 (n. 141), 134–5; Kolb, *Ius Contra Bellum* 2009 (n. 139), 276; Christopher Greenwood, 'International Law and the "War against Terrorism"', *International Affairs* 78(2) (2002), 301–17 (307).

All things considered, it may be understandable that commentators accord 'relatively little weight'[172] to teleological considerations. These simply do not offer compelling arguments either way. None of this should come as a real surprise. The Charter seeks to integrate competing goals into one overarching framework. While the UN's main purposes may 'have proved timeless and universal',[173] the Charter regime has been adapted and can no longer be reduced to 'one single, undiluted object and purpose'.[174] It is perhaps no wonder teleological considerations lack focus.

D. *The Preparatory Work of the Treaty and the Circumstances of its Conclusion*

Finally, a brief glance at the *travaux préparatoires* and the circumstances of the Charter's conclusion can help understand the meaning of the treaty text. Pursuant to the general principles of treaty interpretation, historical considerations are treated as 'supplementary means' with a more limited role than the 'primary means' of interpretation discussed so far.[175] That said, recourse to them is envisaged where (as here) the primary means 'leav[e] the meaning [of a treaty clause] ambiguous or obscure'.[176]

And yet, the *travaux* and the circumstances of the Charter's conclusion do not dispel lingering doubts.[177] In fact, they yield little. Article 51 was a late addition to the Charter text and discussed only briefly.[178] What is a major concern today then simply did not seem to merit debate. It is sometimes asserted that the Charter's drafters, perhaps intuitively, thought only of armed attacks by States, as the historical context was one of an inter-State war.[179] That may be true or not. (More likely, it is not: States after all did respond militarily to 'private' armed attacks prior to 1945.)[180] However, if it

---

[172] De Hoogh, 'Restrictivist Reasoning on the *Ratione Personae* Dimension of Armed Attacks in the Post 9/11 World' 2016 (n. 14), 24.

[173] See GA Res. 55/2 of 18 September 2000, para. 3.

[174] See WTO Appellate Body, *US Import of Certain Shrimp and Shrimp Products* 1998 (n. 159), para. 17.

[175] Hence 'supplementary means' are referred to in a separate provision, Article 32 VCLT.

[176] Article 32(a) VCLT.

[177] The discussion draws on Kimberley N. Trapp, 'Can Non-State Actors Mount an Armed Attack?', in Weller, *The Oxford Handbook of the Use of Force in International Law* 2015 (n. 47), 679–96 (683–5).

[178] No reference to self-defence could be found in the Dumbarton Oaks proposals.

[179] Jochen A. Frowein, 'Der Terrorismus als Herausforderung für das Völkerrecht', *Heidelberg Journal of International Law* 62 (2002), 879–905 (887); van Steenberghe, *La légitime défense en droit international public* 2012 (n. 100), 270.

[180] See Kress, *Gewaltverbot und Selbstverteidigungsrecht nach der Satzung der Vereinten Nationen* 1995 (n. 122), 217–31.

were true, the drafters left precious little written trace of their intuition. An early American proposal did refer to 'an attack by any State'.[181] However, as Kimberley Trapp notes, other proposed texts did not mention a State nexus: 'A UK proposal relied on "a breach of the peace" as the trigger for the right of self-defence ..., while a French proposal had member states reserving a "right to act as they may consider necessary in the interest of peace, right and justice" in the event of Security Council deadlock."[182]

The subsequent debates about what was to become Article 51 were based on two proposals, one jointly submitted by the United States and the United Kingdom, the other by the Soviet Union.[183] Both of these permitted self-defence (only) if the Security Council had not acted; both viewed it as a response against an 'armed attack' – but neither of them required a State attack. As the deliberations were not minuted, the drafters' motives are difficult to re-establish. One could speculate that the reference to another State (found in the early US proposal) had been dropped deliberately; alternatively, the requirement of a State nexus may have simply been taken for granted. Whatever the correct view, the *travaux* themselves are so obscure that they do not help much.

E. The Text of Article 51: Where Do We Stand?

The preceding considerations illustrate the benefit of taking the text of Article 51 seriously. The drafters did not discuss the term 'armed attack' in any detail. However, textual and contextual – as well as (to a lesser extent) teleological – considerations offer important pointers. The existing scholarship fails fully to reflect this, and often rehearses arguments that do not withstand scrutiny.

The preceding sections have analysed literal, contextual, purposive and historical arguments in deliberate detail. They suggest that the text of Article 51, on balance, supports a broad construction of self-defence that permits responses against armed attacks by non-State actors. The wording of Article 51 is the clearest indicator of such a broad understanding, which – contrary to conventional wisdom – is not contradicted by contextual arguments. Purposive and historical considerations, in turn, do not offer firm guidance either way. All things considered, the analysis nudges interpreters towards a broad understanding of Article 51.

---

[181] *Foreign Relations of the United States*, Diplomatic Papers (1945), vol. I, 659. See also *United Nations Conference on International Organization* (UNCIO) III, 483 (statement by Turkey); and UNCIO XII, 687 (Colombia).

[182] Trapp, 'Can Non-State Actors Mount an Armed Attack?' 2015 (n. 177), 685 (fn. 32).

[183] See *Foreign Relations of the United States*, Diplomatic Papers (1945), vol. I, at 705 and 813.

This finding seems to run counter to what has been described earlier as the intuitive symmetrical construction of self-defence as a response against illegal uses of force by another State. That the drafters simply presumed such an intuitive construction is often asserted – and cannot be ruled out. But an analysis of the text, context, purpose and *travaux* reveals little evidence supporting it. If anything, experience suggests that symmetrical readings can be overcome: the evolution of the UN's collective security system illustrates as much.

None of this, to reiterate, settles the threshold question. Perhaps UN members and organs (to adapt Gardiner's phrase again[184]), through their deeds, have given a State-centric meaning to the words 'armed attack'. The text itself, when interrogated, however, does not mandate, or encourage, such a construction. The subsequent practice of UN member States and organs is to be assessed against this background.

IV. 'MEANING THROUGH DEEDS': SUBSEQUENT PRACTICE IN APPLICATION OF THE 'ARMED ATTACK' REQUIREMENT

A. Subsequent Practice in Treaty Interpretation

Since 1945, the right of self-defence has been applied and discussed by States and UN organs. Their practice is rich and diverse. It comprises the conduct of States asserting self-defence, as well as international reactions to such claims. It also includes general statements from which the intended scope of self-defence can be inferred, and decisions of international courts. The following analysis cannot do justice to this rich practice. Instead of assessing developments comprehensively,[185] it offers a (long) synthesis that seeks to retrace key trends in the application of Article 51.

This synthesis provides a 'reality check'. Yet it also does more than that: under the general principles outlined above, it can be an element in the process of treaty interpretation if it reflects the understanding of Article 51. As a matter of principle, this much is undisputed; in fact, the drafters of the Vienna Convention considered '[t]he importance of [...] subsequent practice ... as an element of interpretation' to be 'obvious'.[186] Quite how subsequent practice should be operationalised is, however, not obvious.

---

[184] Gardiner, *Treaty Interpretation* 2015 (n. 98), 225 ('Words are given meaning by deeds').

[185] For fuller accounts see Ruys, *'Armed Attack' and Article 51 of the UN Charter* 2010 (n. 53); and Kress, *Gewaltverbot und Selbstverteidigungsrecht nach der Satzung der Vereinten Nationen* 1995 (n. 122).

[186] *Yearbook of the International Law Commission* 1966, vol. II, 221.

The following synthesis takes its cue from the ILC's work on 'Subsequent agreements and subsequent practice in relation to interpretation of treaties'.[187] More specifically, it proceeds from the Commission's set of 'Draft Conclusions' adopted on second reading in 2018, which (building on the first reading text adopted in 2016) 'situate subsequent agreements and subsequent practice within the framework of the rules of the Vienna Convention on interpretation'.[188] For the purposes of the present study, three aspects of that framework, as construed by the ILC, are significant.

First, treaty interpretation can draw on a diverse range of subsequent practices.[189] The Vienna Convention in Article 31(3) mentions two instances expressly, viz. 'subsequent agreements' and 'subsequent practice in the application of the treaty which establishes the agreement of the parties regarding its interpretation'. These two instances describe different modalities of establishing the meaning of a treaty provision, which can find expression 'in a common act or undertaking', or in 'separate acts that in combination demonstrate a common position'.[190] That said, Articles 31(3)(a) and Article 31(3)(b) both require an agreement of *all* treaty parties. Under multilateral treaties with near-universal membership, such all-party agreement will often be difficult to establish.[191] Against that background, it is significant to note that the subsequent practice of *some parties* can also affect the interpretation of a treaty.[192] In the ILC's work, this was initially referred as 'other subsequent practice'; in the Draft Conclusions as adopted in 2018, this shorthand term is dropped, but the key aspect maintained: subsequent practice by *some parties* can be relevant

---

[187] Details and documents (including four Reports by the Commission's Special Rapporteur, Georg Nolte) are reproduced on the ILC's website at http://legal.un.org/ilc/guide/1_11.shtml.

[188] See ILC, 'Subsequent Practice: Text of the Draft Conclusions and Commentaries Thereto', reproduced in UN Doc. A/73/10 (2018), 16 *et seq.*, para. 2 of the commentary to Draft Conclusion 1. For the 2016 version, see ILC, 'Subsequent Practice: Text of the Draft Conclusions and Commentaries Adopted on First Reading' in UN Doc. A/71/10 (2016), 120 *et seq.*

[189] Terminology on this point is not entirely satisfactory: in line with the jurisprudence of the International Court of Justice (see IJC, *Pulp Mills on the River Uruguay* (Argentina v. Uruguay), Provisional Measures, Order of 13 July 2006, *Pulp Mills*, Provisional Measures, ICJ Reports 2006, 113, para. 53), the following discussion uses the term 'subsequent practice' to describe the manifold forms of subsequent conduct, including agreements.

[190] See ILC, 'Subsequent Practice' 2018 (n. 188), commentary to Draft Conclusion 4, at para. 10.

[191] With respect to the WTO, it has, e.g., been held that '[b]ecause of the large number of WTO Parties, there in fact appears to be only limited scope for evidence of "subsequent practice", since ... the practice is intended to be the practice of ... the Parties to the Agreement *as a whole*': Michael Lennard, 'Navigating by the Stars: Interpreting the WTO Agreements', *Journal of International Economic Law* 5 (2002), 17–89 (34).

[192] This was recognised in the ILC's earlier work on the law of treaties: see e.g. *Yearbook of the International Law Commission* 1964, vol. II, 203–4.

as a supplementary means of interpretation in the sense of Article 32 of the Vienna Convention.[193] This 'other practice' 'consists of conduct by one or more parties in the application of the treaty':[194] while not reflecting 'the agreement of [all] the parties', it 'can contribute to the clarification of the meaning of a treaty',[195] e.g. if that meaning is otherwise 'ambiguous or obscure'.[196] In light of the difficulties of establishing a common understanding of all UN members, this 'other subsequent practice' is significant. It means that the analysis needs to take into account the conduct of States and UN organs even where it does not reflect an 'agreement of *the parties* regarding [the Charter's] interpretation' in the sense of Article 31(3)(a) or (b).

Second, the general regime of treaty interpretation, as reflected in the ILC's work, helps determine the interpretative weight to be accorded to the different forms of subsequent practice. At the outset, it is worth emphasising that subsequent practice is but one element, which needs to be 'taken into account' alongside other (textual, contextual, purposive, etc.) considerations: not binding-ness, but its relative weight, is at stake.[197] As regards their weight, a distinction is often drawn between the forms of 'authentic interpretation' reflecting the agreement of all treaty parties on the one hand, and the 'other subsequent practice' of some parties on the other. This distinction is no doubt relevant, as an authentic interpretation offers 'objective evidence' of the 'common will of the parties' and carries 'specific authority'.[198] Overall, though, interpretative weight is not a question of categorisation, but requires a case-by-case assessment. Common sense suggests (and the ILC's work confirms) that 'clarity' and 'specificity' should be relevant factors.[199] Where the understanding is not reached in a single act, it will be relevant also 'whether and how [a practice] is repeated',[200] while the interpretative weight of 'other subsequent practice' also depends on 'the number of affected states that engage in [it]'.[201] These are no doubt malleable criteria, but they contain helpful pointers.

---

[193]   ILC, 'Subsequent Practice' 2018 (n. 188), Draft Conclusion 4(3); and the earlier version in ILC, 'Subsequent Practice' 2016 (n. 188), Draft Conclusion 4(3).
[194]   ILC, 'Subsequent Practice' 2018 (n. 188), Draft Conclusion 4(3).
[195]   *Ibid.*, Draft Conclusion 7(2).
[196]   Article 32(a) VCLT.
[197]   See ILC, 'Subsequent Practice' 2018 (n. 188), para. 4 of the commentary to Draft Conclusion 3.
[198]   *Ibid.*, Draft Conclusion 3 and para. 3 of the Commentary thereto.
[199]   *Ibid.*, Draft Conclusion 9(1).
[200]   *Ibid.*, Draft Conclusion 9(2).
[201]   *Ibid.*, Commentary to Draft Conclusion 9, para. 15. In Draft Conclusion 9(3), the ILC notes that '[t]he weight of subsequent practice as a supplementary means of interpretation ... *may* depend on the criteria referred to in paragraphs 1 and 2.' It offers no alternative criteria, though.

Third, the general regime as reflected in the ILC's work provides guidance as to the possible effects of subsequent practice on the interpretation of a treaty. Subsequent practice in all its forms can 'contribute ... to the clarification of the meaning of a treaty'.[202] Whether it can do more is disputed: there have been long-standing debates on whether subsequent practice could tacitly modify or amend a treaty,[203] and move (in Kelsen's terminology[204]) outside the 'normative frame' of plausible meanings. The Commission recognises the controversy,[205] but rightly notes that the question is typically avoided: 'States and courts prefer to make every effort to conceive of an agreed subsequent practice of the parties as an effort to interpret the treaty in a particular way'[206] – and not as an amendment or modification. Hence subsequent practice is 'presumed ... to interpret the treaty, not to amend or to modify it'.[207]

As is clear from the foregoing, the general regime as reflected in the ILC's work leaves room for finetuning. However, the Commission's Draft Conclusions offer a helpful framework within which subsequent practice in the application of Article 51 can be assessed. This framework is drawn upon in the following, which reflects the breadth of subsequent practice, evaluates its weight in light of factors such as 'clarity', 'specificity' and 'repetition', and accepts the preference for interpretation over treaty modification.

As noted above, the assessment is in the form of a (long) synthesis that identifies the main lines of development. More specifically, three main lines are retraced:

- *first*, the acceptance of an inter-State reading of self-defence, which would remain dominant during the Cold War era;
- *second*, the flexible application of these general rules to concrete instances of asymmetrical self-defence during the same period; and
- *third*, the gradual and palpable rise of asymmetrical self-defence over the past twenty-five years, i.e. broadly since the end of the Cold War.

---

[202] For authentic means of interpretation, the ILC specifies that such clarification 'may result in narrowing, widening, or otherwise determining the range of possible interpretations'; see ILC, 'Subsequent Practice' 2018 (n. 188), Draft Conclusion 7(1).

[203] For a detailed analysis see ILC, 'Subsequent Practice' 2018 (n. 188), Commentary to Draft Conclusion 7, paras. 21–38.

[204] See Hans Kelsen, *Pure Theory of Law* (Berkeley, CA: University of California Press, 1967), 348 *et seq.*

[205] ILC, 'Subsequent Practice' 2018 (n. 188), Draft Conclusion 7(3).

[206] *Ibid.*, Commentary to Draft Conclusion 7, at para. 38.

[207] *Ibid.*, Draft Conclusion 7(3).

B. The General Framework: An Inter-State Reading of Self-Defence

The first trend set in soon after the adoption of the UN Charter; it would provide a framework for the application of Article 51 for decades. As an exception to the State-centric ban on force, self-defence was construed as a defence between States, and viewed as a response against armed attacks for which another State was answerable. In practice, a State nexus – absent from the text of Article 51 – was read into the provision. This first trend is frequently noted. Missing from many accounts are the twists and turns that accompanied it: that the State nexus was never seriously debated; that it was construed very flexibly for a time and only gained contours from the late 1960s onwards; and that the more 'stratified' regime emerging then was not applied strictly to particular disputes. The subsequent sections outline the general trend and its twists and turns.

1. Sleepwalking into an Inter-State Reading

Looked at from a contemporary perspective, the most significant feature of the debates during the first decades of the UN era is that the inter-State framework was accepted without serious discussion. There was no equivalent, in the early years of the United Nations, to today's protracted debates between 'restrictivists' and 'expansionists'.[208] States (and UN organs) seemed simply to take for granted that an armed attack had to be one with some level of State involvement: they *sleepwalked* into an inter-State construction. As a result, straightforward statements explicitly rejecting the possibility of self-defence against non-State actors are rare.[209] The contemporary evidence supporting an inter-State construction is essentially indirect. It is a by-product of debates about the *level* of State involvement required to turn an attack into an 'armed attack'. As will

---

[208]　See Kammerhofer, *Uncertainty in International Law* 2010 (n. 42), 37 (fn. 165): 'there is a marked absence of argument [in support of State-centric constructions].'

[209]　For rare exceptions, see e.g. Josef L. Kunz, 'Individual and Collective Self-Defense in Article 51 of the Charter', *American Journal of International Law* 41 (1947), 872–9 (878); and a Report of the US Committee on Foreign Relations, quoted in Ian Brownlie, *International Law and the Use of Force by States* (Oxford: Clarendon, 1963), 278 ('an attack by one State upon another'). Both statements recognise private attacks can be 'elevated' to the level of State attacks; eg 'if a revolution were aided and abetted by an outside power' (*ibid.*). The same seems true for a statement by Hans Kelsen referred to in Dire Tladi's contribution (Tladi in this volume, 37): Kelsen refers to an armed attack 'made by one state against another' ('Collective Security and Collective Self-Defence under the Charter of the United Nations', *American Journal of International Law* 42 (1948), 783–96 (791)) – but notes this could cover instances in which 'another state has interfered in a civil war taking place within another state by arming or otherwise assisting the revolutionary group' (792).

be discussed more fully below,[210] this level remained disputed for a while. Crucially, though, even States that took a broad view of self-defence argued on the basis of an inter-State framework.

Greece's complaint to the United Nations, one of the earliest invocations of self-defence in the Charter era, in many ways set the tone. The debates of 1946/ 7 were prompted by 'private attacks', but centred on the role of sponsoring States: Yugoslavia and Albania had allegedly supported armed bands or tolerated their activities – and thereby had 'breached the peace' and committed an 'aggression' against Greece.[211] From 1946 until around the late 1980s, in debates about attacks by non-State actors and possible responses thereto – from Burma/China (1953)[212] to the French raids on Tunisia in the late 1950s and the manifold Israeli strikes against Palestinian targets in Jordan, Lebanon and elsewhere[213] – the focus was squarely on the respective host States. The problem of armed attacks by non-State actors was treated, in Brownlie's words, as one of 'State complicity in, or toleration of, the activities of armed bands directed against other States'.[214] It was a problem of determining the required degree of State involvement: that there had to be some State nexus was generally assumed – asymmetrical self-defence was to be approached via the 'Westphalian avenue'.[215]

2. The State Nexus: Initial Flexibility

If the inter-State framework was taken for granted, it was anything but rigid, but initially understood flexibly. To some extent, this flexibility resulted from the fact that States did not proceed from any preconceived general regime of attribution defining for which acts a State would have to bear responsibility; quite to the contrary, the matter was treated as a question of the (primary) rules governing recourse to force.[216] Different views as to the required State nexus came to the fore during the long-standing debates about the proper legal

---

[210] See *infra*, IV.B.3 and IV.C.
[211] SCOR, 2nd year, 147th and 148th meeting, 1118–29.
[212] See GAOR, 7th session, 1st Committee, 605th meeting, at 665–6. For details see Kress, *Gewaltverbot und Selbstverteidigungsrecht nach der Satzung der Vereinten Nationen* 1995 (n. 122), 48–9.
[213] On which *infra*, IV.C.1.
[214] Brownlie, 'International Law and the Activities of Armed Bands' 1958 (n. 46), 733, 784.
[215] See Kress, 'Major Post-Westphalian Shifts' 2014 (n. 32), 46.
[216] Partly, this was a question of timing: the debates about indirect aggression preceded the ILC's focused work on State responsibility, which would consolidate rules governing attribution: see *infra*, IV.B.3.c.

qualification of instances of 'indirect aggression', notably held within the UN General Assembly.

Indirect aggression was recognised as a pressing problem in the 1950s and 1960s. In a number of consensus resolutions, UN member States seemed ready to equate indirect and direct forms of force (and thereby to dilute the State-centric character of the prohibition).[217] The Friendly Relations Declaration, adopted in 1970, consolidated the process: it expressly qualified a broad range of ancillary acts as self-standing violations of the ban on force, among them a State's 'acquiesc[ence] in organized activities within its territory directed towards the commission of [acts of civil strife or terrorist acts]'.[218]

Quite how this should affect the understanding of the right of self-defence proved controversial. Should a State's 'participation in the use of force by unofficial bands',[219] or perhaps even its acquiescence, qualify as an armed attack? The practice of the 1950s and 1960s, reflected in the Friendly Relations Declaration, left the matter open. For a significant period of time, the inter-State framework was applied flexibly. In the words of Olivier Corten: 'In the first two decades after the Charter's entry into force, no decisive precedent can . . . be invoked [for or against the permissibility of self-defence against acts of indirect aggression].'[220]

3. GA Res. 3314 and Beyond: A Stratified General Framework

In the course of the 1970s and 1980s, the initially flexible framework came under pressure. While concrete disputes about self-defence continued to be handled pragmatically,[221] the general framework was stratified, and the required State nexus construed restrictively. This was a gradual development, but with the benefit of hindsight, one can identify three important catalysts: a) the General Assembly's Definition of Aggression; b) the interpretation given to that resolution in the ICJ's *Nicaragua* judgment; and c) the agreement, in the course of the ILC's work on State responsibility, on a set of narrow rules of attribution.

A) A DEFINITION OF AGGRESSION The General Assembly's Definition of Aggression annexed to GA Res. 3314 marked the culmination of 'toilsome

---

[217] See e.g. GA Res. 380 (V)of 17 November 1950; GA Res. 2131 (XX) of 21 December 1965.
[218] GA Res. 2625 (XXV) of 24 October 1970, Principle I, paras. 8, 9.
[219] See Dörr and Randelzhofer, 'Article 2(4)' 2012 (n. 27), para. 23.
[220] Corten, *The Law against War* 2010 (n. 26), 456.
[221] See *infra*, IV.C.

discussion[s]'[222] about indirect aggression. Belittled at the time,[223] the resolution's understanding of the term 'aggression' has become an important reference point.[224] Debate proceeded from two competing (irreconcilable) draft texts: one proposal, submitted by thirteen (mostly non-aligned) States, ruled out the possibility of self-defence against indirect aggression;[225] another, submitted by six (Western) powers, equated direct and indirect acts of aggression and expressly qualified three forms of active State involvement ('organizing, supporting or directing') as self-standing acts of aggression.[226]

GA Res. 3314 as eventually adopted reflected a compromise between these positions. It maintained an inter-State understanding of 'aggression', defined as the 'use of armed force by a State against ... another State'.[227] In line with this approach, all but one of the 'acts of aggression' listed in the Declaration presupposed conduct by a State's 'armed forces'.[228] The one exception, Article 3(g), singled out two forms of 'indirect force', namely (i) '[t]he sending by or on behalf of a State of armed bands, groups, irregulars or mercenaries, which carry out acts of armed force against another State of such gravity as to amount to the acts listed above [describing acts of aggression by regular armed forces]', and (ii) a State's 'substantial involvement therein'.[229] All this, to be sure, was not meant to be 'construed as in any way enlarging or diminishing the scope of the Charter, including its provisions concerning cases in which the use of force is lawful',[230] but it gave meaning to an important Charter rule.

As is clear, GA Res. 3314 required both sides to make significant concessions. It did not rule out the possibility of self-defence against attacks by non-State actors; quite to the contrary, Article 3(g) expressly recognised certain exceptions, one of which (requiring no more than a State's 'substantial involvement') was of 'potentially broad scope'.[231] At the same time, Article 3, if read as a whole, reflected a gradual shift. Indirect and direct forms of aggression were clearly not placed on an equal footing: action by the armed forces

---

[222] Ruys, *'Armed Attack' and Article 51 of the UN Charter* 2010 (n. 53), 389.
[223] See e.g. Julius Stone, 'Hopes and Loopholes in the 1974 Definition of Aggression', *American Journal of International Law* 73 (1977), 224–46.
[224] That a text defining 'aggression' should affect the interpretation of 'armed attack' is not obvious but it has generally been accepted, as 'many States ... thought of aggression as a constituent part of self-defence'; see Corten, *The Law against War* 2010 (n. 26), 404.
[225] UN Doc. A/AC.134/L.16 (and Corr. 1), 24 March 1969.
[226] UN Doc. A/AC.134/L.17 (and Corr. 1), 25 March 1969.
[227] GA Res. 3314 (n. 13), Article 1.
[228] *Ibid.*, Article 3(a)–(f).
[229] *Ibid.*, Article 3(g).
[230] *Ibid.*, Article 6.
[231] Corten, *The Law against War* 2010 (n. 26), 446.

remained the paradigm case; forms of proxy warfare were the exception. What is more, unlike in the Friendly Relations Declaration, a State's acquiescence in the activities of armed groups was clearly not sufficient to amount to an aggression: some *active* role ('sending', 'substantial involvement') seemed required.[232] GA Res. 3314 thus not only consolidated the inter-State framework, but pointed towards a more restrictive construction. Thirty years after the founding of the United Nations, that restrictive construction reflected a 'subsequent agreement' of the parties.

b) *NICARAGUA* AND THE TURN TO ATTRIBUTION In the aftermath of GA Res. 3314, the restrictive approach informing Article 3(g) soon came to be embraced and further tightened. Rather than making use of the flexibility preserved in Article 3(g), the dominant approach construed the provision to fit a State-centric understanding of the terms 'aggression' and, by implication, 'armed attack'. The ICJ's majority judgment in the *Nicaragua* case was of particular significance. The Court's reliance on Article 3(g) as a reflection of the customary international law on self-defence[233] ensured the provision's rise to prominence. What rose to prominence, though – via *Nicaragua* – was a narrowly construed version of Article 3(g).

In the circumstances of the case, the Court had to assess whether Nicaragua's supply of weapons to, and other support for, rebels amounted to an armed attack. The majority of the Court rejected this on the basis of a robust argument, holding that 'assistance to rebels in the form of the provision of weapons or logistical or other support' could not qualify as a 'substantial involvement' in the sense of Article 3(g).[234] This interpretation was not implausible. However, it was on the restrictive end of the plausibility spectrum and caused a 'deep rift between the ... Hague judges'.[235] As Judge Jennings noted, the fact that the majority did not specify what level of involvement (beyond supplying weapons) would be 'substantial' made it 'difficult to understand what it is, short of direct attack by a State's own forces, that may not be done apparently without a lawful response in the form of ... self-defence'.[236] In essence, the restrictive approach of the *Nicaragua* judgment 'exorcised' the flexibility from the 'substantial involvement' test and thereby narrowed down the 'Westphalian avenue'[237]

---

[232] Ruys, *'Armed Attack' and Article 51 of the UN Charter* 2010 (n. 53), 390.
[233] ICJ, *Military and Paramilitary Activities* (n. 28), para. 195.
[234] *Ibid.*
[235] Ruys, *'Armed Attack' and Article 51 of the UN Charter* 2010 (n. 53), 415.
[236] ICJ, *Military and Paramilitary Activities* (n. 28), Separate Opinion of Judge Sir Robert Jennings, 543.
[237] Cf. *supra*, II.B.3.b.

towards asymmetrical self-defence. Under the *Nicaragua* logic, self-defence effectively became a right to respond to armed attacks that could be attributed to another State.

c) STATE RESPONSIBILITY: ENTRENCHING THE PUBLIC–PRIVATE DIVIDE This narrow reading of a potentially flexible clause, Article 3(g), was facilitated by the clarification of the law of State responsibility. The late 1970s and early 1980s saw significant development of this area of law, which was consolidated as a body of *secondary rules* laying down 'general conditions under international law for the State to be considered responsible'.[238] These secondary rules drew a clear distinction between responsibility for conduct, and responsibility for complicity in the conduct of others. What is more, they included a small set of seemingly technical principles of attribution, stipulating conditions under which conduct is allocated to a State for the purposes of responsibility.[239]

Part of a general regime, these rules of attribution were residual: the law in special fields could of course opt for narrower or broader approaches.[240] However, the general regime shaped the discourse and set the standard. That standard entrenched the divide between public and private acts, which was to be drawn primarily by reference to the status of the actor within the State's structure. More specifically, a State had to answer 'at the international level [for] ... the acts of its "organs" or "agents"'[241] but not for '[t]he conduct of a ... group of persons not acting on behalf of the State'.[242] Exceptions to this principle were admitted only cautiously: they included provisions attributing to a State the conduct of 'completely dependent' *de facto* organs,[243] of private actors over whose specific acts the State exercised effective control,[244] and of acts carried out 'in the absence or default of the official authorities'.[245] But

[238] See para. 1 of the ILC's Introductory Commentary to the Articles on State Responsibility (*Yearbook of the International Law Commission* 2001, vol. II/2, 31–143).
[239] ILC, Commentary to Art. 2 ASR, para. 12 (*ibid.*, 36).
[240] Article 55 ASR (*ibid.*, 140).
[241] Para. 3 of the introductory commentary to Chapter II of the ILC's first reading text, *Yearbook of the International Law Commission* 1973, vol. II, 189.
[242] See Draft Article 11(1) of the ILC's first reading text, *Yearbook of the International Law Commission* 1975, vol. II, 70.
[243] See Article 5 ASR, as construed in ICJ, *Application of the Convention on the Prevention and Punishment of the Crime of Genocide* (Bosnia and Herzegovina v. Serbia and Montenegro), Judgment of 26 February 2007, ICJ Reports 2007, 43, para. 392.
[244] Enunciated in *Nicaragua* (in relation to the use of force), this proposition would later be formulated as a general rule and be reaffirmed in the *Genocide* judgment: see ICJ, *Military and Paramilitary Activities* (n. 28), para. 115; Article 8 ASR (*Yearbook of the International Law Commission* 2001, vol. II/2, 47); and ICJ, *Genocide Convention Case* (n. 243), paras. 398–406.
[245] Article 9 ASR.

these were narrow exceptions that 'offer[ed] little prospect in dealing with indirect aggression'.[246]

None of this, to reiterate, directly affected the regime of self-defence or the concept of 'armed attack'. But it resulted in a general regime that demarcated acts of the State from other forms of conduct, one that required far more than a mere (flexibly construed) 'substantial involvement'[247] for an act to qualify as an act of the State, and that treated responsibility for complicity as a conceptually separate category. As that general regime came to 'encode the way [international lawyers] think about responsibility',[248] alternative approaches to attribution looked increasingly unusual. A more tenuous State nexus had to be based (as the ICJ noted) on a 'clearly expressed *lex specialis*'.[249] Just as the Court's *Nicaragua* case, so the consolidation of the law of responsibility during the 1970s and 1980s pointed towards a more properly State-centric framework of international law. In Tal Becker's words, '[t]he pull of the public/private distinction was too strong.'[250]

***

The preceding sections offer a broad-brush account of the development of legal thinking about the 'armed attack' requirement over the course of the first four decades of the UN's existence. They highlight that, from early on, self-defence was viewed as an inter-State defence permitting responses against armed attacks with some level of State involvement. The required level of involvement was initially understood flexibly, but over time States came to embrace a stricter approach that informed the General Assembly's Definition of Aggression. Self-defence against attacks by non-State actors was of course not entirely excluded, but preserved in Article 3(g). Yet the ICJ's construction of Article 3(g) in the *Nicaragua* case, and the gradual elaboration of the ILC's regime of responsibility, saw the room for flexible approaches shrinking. If GA Res. 3314 had reflected a shift towards a stratified general framework, the combined effect of the *Nicaragua* judgment and the ILC's work on State responsibility made that stratified framework look like a straightjacket.

---

[246] Ruys, *'Armed Attack' and Article 51 of the UN Charter* 2010 (n. 53), 414.
[247] Cf. Article 3(g) GA Res. 3314 (n. 13).
[248] James Crawford, 'The International Court of Justice and the Law of State Responsibility', in Tams and Sloan, *The Development of International Law by the International Court of Justice* 2013 (n. 102), 71–86 (81).
[249] ICJ, *Genocide Convention Case* (n. 243), para. 401.
[250] Tal Becker, *Terrorism and the State* (Oxford: Hart, 2006), 361.

C. Particular Instances of Self-Defence (1946–Late 1980s): A Plea for Nuance

Developments described so far suggest a relatively clear picture, or at least a clear trend, towards a State-centric reading of self-defence. This trend dominates much of the discussion. According to a popular narrative, until the 1990s (or indeed until 2001), the law of self-defence was 'sufficiently clear' and only permitted action in self-defence against armed attacks that could be attributed to other States.[251] This popular narrative is charmingly straightforward, but lacks nuance. It fails to appreciate that the actual self-defence practice was diverse – and remained so notwithstanding the move towards a stratified *general* framework. A significant number of States, over time, claimed a right to respond militarily to armed attacks that were clearly not carried out by another State nor came within the scope of Article 3(g), as narrowly construed in *Nicaragua*. What is more, their claims met with mixed responses: they remained controversial, but were not rejected consistently. In other words, while embracing a more rigorous approach in general debates, States throughout the Cold War era preferred to retain flexibility when discussing particular disputes about asymmetrical self-defence.

Against that background, the subsequent analysis makes a case for nuance. That case is a modest one. It is not suggested that broad readings of self-defence were generally endorsed. However, such readings, even during the Cold War era, enjoyed support. Practice was significant, responses mixed; and a number of statements made outside the self-defence context reflected the continuing appeal of construing the terms of 'armed attack' and 'aggression' broadly.

1. Significant Practice

To begin with practice, a significant number of States – during the entire period of the Cold War – responded to 'private' armed attacks by using force on the territory of another State, or clearly asserted a right to do so.[252] They did so even though the other State concerned was neither responsible for sending the

---

[251] Antonio Cassese, 'Terrorism is also Disrupting Some Crucial Legal Categories of International Law', *European Journal of International Law* 12 (2001), 993–1001 (995); and further Tladi in this volume, 65; ICJ, *Construction of a Wall* (n. 125), Separate Opinion of Judge Kooijmans, para. 35 (arguing that 'it has been the generally accepted interpretation for more than 50 years' that an 'armed attack must come from another State'); Pierre Klein, 'Le droit international à l'épreuve du terrorisme', *Recueil des Cours* 321 (2006), 203–484 (375).

[252] The following analysis draws on Kress, *Gewaltverbot und Selbstverteidigungsrecht nach der Satzung der Vereinten Nationen* 1995 (n. 122), 42–92.

irregular bands nor 'substantially involved' in their activities in the sense of Article 3(g), narrowly construed. In line with the dominant understanding, responding States regularly justified their conduct from within an inter-State framework, but construed this framework flexibly. In the typical setting, responding States asserted that host States had supported armed attacks, or at least offered armed groups a safe haven. In some instances, host States were also said to bear responsibility for attacks they had failed to suppress; in still others, 'support' and 'harbouring' rationales were combined. Whatever the details, a more tenuous State nexus was considered sufficient to trigger a right to respond.

France's raids into Tunisia during the Algerian War of Independence are illustrative.[253] They were considered necessary to 'assurer [France's] légitime défense'[254] against FLN attacks from Tunisia: Tunisia, argued France, had to endure them, as it had permitted the FLN to use its territory and failed to suppress its activities.[255] France's assessment echoed Greece's above-mentioned claims[256] as well as views expressed by India during the early stages of the Kashmir conflict.[257] In India's view, Pakistan's support for armed bands crossing into Jammu and Kashmir amounted to an 'act of aggression against India'; in response, India claimed to be 'entitled, under international law, to send [its] armed forces across Pakistan territory'.[258]

From the late 1950s onwards, variations of this broader understanding of self-defence would be embraced by a number of countries embroiled in national liberation conflicts. Portugal (in the 1960s and 1970s),[259] South Africa (during the 1970s and 1980s, once 'hot pursuit' claims had lost appeal)[260] and Rhodesia (during the 1970s)[261] invoked self-defence to justify military action against neighbouring States that provided support and sanctuary to armed groups.[262]

---

[253] See Jean Charpentier, 'Pratique française du droit international', *Annuaire Français de Droit International* 4 (1958), 791–826 (809) and 6 (1961), 1068–9.

[254] See *ibid.*, 1069.

[255] *Ibid.*

[256] *Supra*, III.B.1.

[257] See Kress, *Gewaltverbot und Selbstverteidigungsrecht nach der Satzung der Vereinten Nationen* 1995 (n. 122), 44–5.

[258] SCOR, 3rd year, Nov. 1948 (Suppl.), 139, 143.

[259] See Kress, *Gewaltverbot und Selbstverteidigungsrecht nach der Satzung der Vereinten Nationen* 1995 (n. 122), 63–4; Becker, *Terrorism and the State* 2006 (n. 250), 189.

[260] For details, see Kwakwa, 'South Africa's May 1986 Military Incursions into Neighboring African States' 1987 (n. 52); and *supra*, II.B.

[261] See the references in A. J. Luttig, 'The Legality of the Rhodesian Military Operation Inside Mozambique; The Problem of Hot Pursuit on Land', *South African Yearbook of International Law* 3 (1977), 136–49.

[262] For clear examples see e.g. SCOR, 24th year, 1520th meeting, 2 (Portugal); *United Nations Yearbook* 1979, 221 (South Africa); and further *South African Yearbook of International Law* 12 (1986/7), 221–7.

Lesser known is Morocco's reliance on essentially the same argument in the West Sahara conflict during the late 1970s.[263] Following repeated attacks by Polisario forces operating from within Algeria, Morocco claimed a right to 'poursuivr[e] ses agresseurs sur et hors son territoire', i.e. into Algeria, which was accused of having armed, trained, financed and sheltered Polisario fighters.[264] From the early 1980s, Turkey began to advance similar claims.[265] In 1983/4, foreshadowing subsequent operations on a much larger scale,[266] it mounted armed incursions against PKK bases in northern Iraq, which was accused of serving as a sanctuary.

While Turkey's justification remained elusive, other countries offered greater specificity. Israel did so frequently. From 1948, it regularly invoked self-defence to justify its military actions against Palestinian fedayeen based in Arab countries.[267] Having initially pointed to the close operational ties, or the willing cooperation, between Palestinian fighters and host States,[268] from 'the 1970s, Israel gradually adopted a broader version of the "harbouring" rationale' pursuant to which self-defence could be exercised against a host State that 'was either unwilling *or unable* to prevent cross-border attacks from taking place'.[269] In the 1980s, the United States moved towards the same position. The so-called 'Shultz doctrine' asserted a right to respond forcibly against armed attacks by terrorists and guerrillas, and to do so by using force against foreign countries that 'support, train, or harbour [them]'.[270]

All this suggests that decades before 9/11, the argument for asymmetrical self-defence had been clearly articulated by a considerable number of States, and acted upon with some regularity. In the debates of the day, the problem of asymmetry was typically not addressed 'head on', but from within an inter-State framework in which some State nexus was sufficient. As regards the

---

[263] Kress, *Gewaltverbot und Selbstverteidigungsrecht nach der Satzung der Vereinten Nationen* 1995 (n. 122), 44–5, 65–6, provides further references.

[264] See UN Doc. S/13394, 13 June 1979, and statements in SCOR, 34th year, 2151st meeting, 3.

[265] See Charles Rousseau, 'Chronique des faits internationaux', *Revue Générale de Droit International Public* 87 (1983), 884–5 and 89 (1985), 455–6; and further Gray, *International Law and the Use of Force* 2008 (n. 27), 140–1.

[266] See *infra*, IV.D.1 and IV.D.2.

[267] For references see Kress, *Gewaltverbot und Selbstverteidigungsrecht nach der Satzung der Vereinten Nationen* 1995 (n. 122), 82–8.

[268] See e.g. *United Nations Yearbook* 1968, 228–9.

[269] See e.g. *United Nations Yearbook* 1972, 158 ('as long as Lebanon was unwilling or unable to prevent armed attacks from its territory against Israel, it could not complain against actions taken in self-defence'), and references in Ruys, *'Armed Attack' and Article 51 of the UN Charter* 2010 (n. 53), 401. Emphasis added.

[270] See George Shultz, 'Low-Intensity Warfare: The Challenge of Ambiguity', *International Legal Materials* 25 (1986), 204–6.

character of this nexus, much of the practice – echoing views put during the preparation of GA Res. 3314 – concerned instances in which a host State had allegedly actively supported armed groups. However, the lines between support, the provision of safe havens, and mere toleration were blurred, and at least Israel began to claim that self-defence could be used against States *unable* to suppress armed groups.

2. Inconsistent Responses

Unsurprisingly, these assertions of a broadly construed right of self-defence prompted debate: express responses were rarely supportive, and often hostile. And yet, a careful analysis reveals a nuanced picture. Broad claims of self-defence were by no means consistently rejected, and when they were, disputes about the scope of Article 51 played a limited role.

To begin with the latter aspect, the conduct of South Africa, Rhodesia, Portugal and Israel met with widespread criticism, often expressed in strongly worded UN resolutions.[271] To give just two examples, the Security Council in 1985 'condemn[ed] vigorously' Israel's raid on the PLO Headquarters, which it qualified as an 'act of armed aggression . . . in flagrant violation of the Charter of the United Nations';[272] three years earlier, it had '[s]trongly condemn[ed] the apartheid regime of South Africa for its premeditated aggressive act against the Kingdom of Lesotho'.[273] Below the surface, things were not quite as clear. The debates about these and other incidents indicate that the conduct of States such as South Africa, Southern Rhodesia, Portugal and Israel 'was condemned on many different grounds'.[274] Facts and evidence often were crucial. (Had the responding States been able to make out their allegation of State support for armed bands? Had there been cross-border raids at all?)[275] As to the law, many military actions were considered to be disproportionate, or punitive and thus outside the scope of self-defence.[276] Most importantly, overarching perspectives were hardly conducive to a positive assessment.[277]

---

[271] The list of Security Council resolutions is lengthy. Ruys, *'Armed Attack' and Article 51 of the UN Charter* 2010 (n. 53) lists them comprehensively (at 402, in his note 178).

[272] SC Res. 573 of 4 October 1985.

[273] SC Res. 527 of 15 December 1982.

[274] Gray, *International Law and the Use of Force* 2008 (n. 27), 139.

[275] See e.g. the statements by Ireland and Sierra Leone in UN Doc. S/PV.2407, 15 December 1982, para. 89; UN Doc. S/PV.2408, 16 December 1982, para. 77.

[276] See e.g. UN Doc. S/PV.1650, 26 June 1972, paras. 9–11; *United Nations Yearbook* 1965, 135, *United Nations Yearbook* 1968, 193–8; *United Nations Yearbook* 1970, 231–3, 236.

[277] For clear statements to this effect see e.g. Becker, *Terrorism and the State* 2006 (n. 250), 189–90; Gray, *International Law and the Use of Force* 2008 (n. 27), 138.

During the 1960s and 1970s, broad understandings of self-defence were prominently espoused by States defending deeply unpopular causes (and losing ones at that), viz. colonialism, apartheid and military occupation. With friends like these, asymmetrical self-defence really needed no enemies. In fact, claims of South Africa, Southern Rhodesia, Portugal and also Israel were typically rejected *a limine*: as Christine Gray observes, they 'were undermined by the fact that the states invoking self-defence were regarded as being in illegal occupation of the territory they were purporting to defend'.[278] 'The right of self-defence could not be invoked to perpetuate colonialism and to flout the right of self-determination and independence'[279] – statements like these were common, and overshadowed finer normative arguments about the required degree of State involvement. In fact, so dominant were these 'different grounds'[280] that the minutes of Security Council debates yield 'virtually no statements directly dealing with the applicability of Article 51 to cross-border attacks by non-State actors'.[281] To reiterate: none of this suggests the broader view of self-defence adopted by Israel, South Africa and others was widely endorsed. But it was hardly ever rejected *specifically*.

The international response to claims of asymmetrical self-defence by States other than Israel, South Africa, Portugal and Southern Rhodesia points in the same direction. Outside the colonial or apartheid context, broad claims to self-defence attracted far less opprobrium. India's assertion of a right to 'send . . . armed forces across Pakistan territory'[282] in response to that country's support of cross-border raids was not rejected.[283] When the Security Council engaged with Morocco's similar claim in 1979, a number of States mentioned Polisario's struggle for national liberation, but Morocco's view of self-defence went unchallenged.[284] The legality of Turkey's incursions into northern Iraq in the early 1980s was hardly discussed; and even France's cross-border

---

[278] Gray, *International Law and the Use of Force* 2008 (n. 27).

[279] See *United Nations Yearbook* 1969, 142.

[280] Gray, *International Law and the Use of Force* 2008 (n. 27), 139.

[281] Ruys, *'Armed Attack' and Article 51 of the UN Charter* 2010 (n. 53), 404, and further Jean Combacau, 'The Exception of Self-Defence in UN Practice', in Antonio Cassese (ed.), *The Current Legal Regulation of the Use of Force* (Dordrecht/Boston, MA: Nijhoff, 1986), 9–38 (23).

[282] SCOR, 3rd year, November 1948 (Suppl.), at 139, 143.

[283] See Kress, *Gewaltverbot und Selbstverteidigungsrecht nach der Satzung der Vereinten Nationen* 1995 (n. 122), 44–5.

[284] See statements in UN Doc. S/PV.2151, 20 June 1979; UN Doc. S/PV.2152, 21 June 1979; UN Doc. S/PV.2153, 22 June 1979.

ripostes into Tunisia, which did target a national liberation movement, were not firmly censured.[285]

3. Circumstantial Evidence and Interim Assessment

A careful scrutiny of international practice thus suggests that the international community seemed prepared to live with the occasional instance of self-defence even where it did not meet the criteria of Article 3(g), narrowly construed. The international response often seems to have turned on questions of facts and evidence, or on overarching views of the rightfulness of a particular struggle. Some host State involvement in an armed attack seemed indispensable, but even during the 1970s and 1980s, well-founded claims of support (or even harbouring) could be sufficient to expose a host State to responses on its territory.

When looking beyond disputes in which a right to self-defence was exercised or clearly asserted, the picture becomes fuzzier still. Attacks by armed bands were often described as acts of aggression or armed attacks, irrespective of whether they could be traced back to a foreign State. The Security Council on occasion condemned as 'aggression' or 'armed attack' the conduct of mercenaries on foreign soil.[286] In his detailed analysis, Claus Kress identifies a significant number of further disputes, in which States considered private armed attacks within a framework of self-defence, or referred to them as 'aggression' in a legal sense. His analysis includes protests by Guatemala against cross-border attacks by rebel forces,[287] for which (according to Guatemala) Honduras and Nicaragua bore responsibility.[288] It also comprises a curious dispute, in which two States – Portugal and Zaire – agreed that support for mercenaries could amount to an armed attack.[289]

---

[285] See Kress, *Gewaltverbot und Selbstverteidigungsrecht nach der Satzung der Vereinten Nationen* 1995 (n. 122), 90; Combacau, 'The Exception of Self-Defence in UN Practice' 1986 (n. 281), 21.

[286] See SC Res. 405 of 14 April 1977; SC Res. 419 of 24 November 1977; SC Res. 496 of 15 December 1981; SC Res. 507 of 18 May 1982.

[287] Kress, *Gewaltverbot und Selbstverteidigungsrecht nach der Satzung der Vereinten Nationen* 1995 (n. 122), 50–1; and further J. E. S. Fawcett, 'Intervention in International Law: A Study of Some Recent Cases', *Recueil des Cours* 103 (1961), 343–421 (372 *et seq.*).

[288] SCOR, 9th year, 675th meeting, at 5.

[289] Zaire had accused Portugal of allowing mercenary attacks to be carried out from Angola. Portugal disputed this claim on the facts, but 'indicated it would welcome an official United Nations investigation of alleged mercenary bases in Angola, if the Congo would allow similar inspections of known anti-Portuguese bases in Congolese territory'; see Carl A. Anderson, 'Portuguese Africa: A Brief History of United Nations Involvement', *Denver Journal of International Law and Policy* 4 (1974), 133–51 (142).

The value of this evidence varies, and some of it may not amount to much.[290] States typically responded within their boundaries (so that the *ius ad bellum* was not implicated[291]), or stopped short of expressly claiming a right of self-defence. However, the statements form part of the broader normative discourse about the scope of the *ius ad bellum*. Perhaps they are best qualified as 'circumstantial evidence': of lesser weight, but a further indication that terms such as 'aggression' and 'armed attack' could be construed broadly.

Viewed in this perspective, the circumstantial evidence supports the modest argument advanced here: that in its treatment of particular disputes, the international community could be prepared to accept a tenuous State nexus. In a relevant number of instances, States advanced broad constructions of self-defence. Their views never remotely reflected the views of 'all UN members' and hence could never 'establish the agreement of the parties regarding the interpretation of [Article 51]'.[292] But, of course, the practice of Israel, South Africa, Turkey, France etc. could be relevant as 'other subsequent practice' in the sense of the ILC's Draft Conclusions. As such, it could help clarify the meaning of the terms 'armed attack' and indicate that the trend towards a stratified general framework was not fully 'grounded' in treaty practice.[293] As regards the weight of this 'other practice', it is worth reiterating that instances of asymmetrical self-defence were not rare, and that the views of responding States often were set out clearly. The largely negative, or at best indifferent, response to such claims is of course significant; it reduces their probative value significantly. But contrary to common perceptions, claims of asymmetrical self-defence were not systematically rejected. Subsequent practice suggests that they could in principle (though exceptionally) be accepted; there was room for nuance in the Cold War era.

D. Post-Cold War Practice: Gradual, Palpable Change

Since the late 1980s, in statistical terms, the exception seems to have become the rule: over the past twenty-five years, self-defence has been invoked regularly against non-State attacks, most likely more often than in the traditional, inter-State setting. Many of the no-longer-exceptional claims have remained controversial, and the all-too-ready reliance on self-defence has prompted

---

[290] But cf. Dinstein, *War, Aggression and Self-Defense* 2012 (n. 27), 227.
[291] Cf. *supra*, II.A.2.
[292] Cf. Article 31(3)(b) VCLT.
[293] Cf. ILC, 'Subsequent Practice' 2018 (n. 188), para. 5 of the commentary to Draft Conclusion 6.

concerns about 'normative drift'.[294] But there has been a palpable change, and no more than a quick glance at the treatment of the issue in successive editions of standard works such as Charter commentaries and textbooks is required to reveal it.[295]

This change, it must be reiterated (since it is frequently ignored), has been gradual, not sudden. High-profile disputes have been catalysts, and dramatic crises particularly powerful agents of change. But not everything can be explained by reference to 9/11, or the more recent struggle against Daesh/ISIS. The gradual change that has taken place is both more profound and less drastic: more profound because it goes beyond high-profile campaigns; less drastic because it builds on claims that were espoused during the Cold War era.[296] In essence, minority positions articulated then enjoy widespread support today. At the same time, the new practice remains heterogeneous, and there has been a concern to avoid perceptions of rupture, especially in documents of a general nature and in court decisions. In the following, these developments are traced in three steps that summarise the rise and diversification of self-defence against non-State actors, the more positive reception of this new practice, and the relevance of documents and decisions emphasising normative continuity.

1. Regular, Heterogeneous Practice

The practice of States invoking self-defence against non-State actors is the most obvious indicator of change. Over the course of the past twenty-five years, self-defence claims have become significantly more common and more diverse.

A) A SHARP INCREASE IN PRACTICE More specifically, broad self-defence claims that at some point might have been dismissed have been espoused by States on all continents, of different ideological leanings and different levels of

---

[294]   The term is Daniel Bethlehem's: see 'International Law and the Use of Force' (Select Committee on Foreign Affairs, 8 June 2004), available at www.publications.parliament.uk/pa/cm200304/cmselect/cmfaff/441/4060808.htm, para. 21.

[295]   In van Steenberghe's words, 'expansionists no longer struggle to demonstrate that a right to act in self-defence in response to armed attacks by non-state actors exists'; van Steenberghe, 'The Law of Self-Defence and the New Argumentative Landscape on the Expansionists' Side' 2016 (n. 2), 46.

[296]   Hence 9/11 has been described 'as a powerful crystallizing moment [rather] than ... a dramatic departure from prior state practice': Kress, 'Major Post-Westphalian Shifts' 2014 (n. 32), 43.

development. The subsequent summary of instances (which is unlikely to be exhaustive) suggests that around twenty-five States[297] have themselves exercised, or firmly asserted, a right to react militarily against attacks by non-State actors even where these could not be attributed to another State under the traditional criteria. For reasons of convenience, four groups of supporters of such a right can be distinguished.

(i) **Traditional supporters of a broadly construed right:** Perhaps unsurprisingly, States that had put forward broad readings of self-defence during the Cold War era have clung to their view. Israel and Turkey are examples in point. The former has continued to invoke self-defence to justify repeated military strikes against Lebanon and Syria as a response to armed attacks by terrorist groups (notably Hezbollah).[298] Turkey has been less outspoken,[299] but if anything more active on the ground: from the 1990s, with Iraqi central authority waning, it has repeatedly attacked PKK bases in northern Iraq,[300] including, in 2008, in a large-scale ground operation ('Operation Sun') involving several thousand troops.[301]

(ii) **The United States in particular:** A relative latecomer among the States endorsing a broad understanding of self-defence against terrorists, the United States has emerged as its most vocal advocate. From the 1990s onwards, it has regularly employed force against terrorists operating from foreign States. The 1998 strikes against Sudan and Afghanistan, much discussed at the time,[302] in retrospect seem to have been no more than a prelude. Among twenty-first century practice, two large-scale events stand out: the armed invasion of Afghanistan begun in late 2001 and the current military campaign against Daesh in Syria, both justified on the basis of self-

---

[297] This figure does not include the conduct of States endorsing claims to self-defence *by other States*. The line between the two is fine, though.

[298] UN Doc. S/2006/51, 21 January 2006.

[299] Turkey has not invoked Article 51, but acted on the basis of a 'self-defence rationale'; see e.g. UN Doc. S/1996/605, 30 July 1996 (claiming to react against 'blatant cross-border attacks of a terrorist organization based and operating from a neighbouring country, if that country is unable to put an end to such attacks').

[300] According to Kress, Turkey also asserted a right to pursue Kurdish fighters into Iran and Syria: Kress, *Gewaltverbot und Selbstverteidigungsrecht nach der Satzung der Vereinten Nationen* 1995 (n. 122), 90 (fn. 373).

[301] See Tom Ruys, '*Quo Vadit Jus Ad Bellum?* A Legal Analysis of Turkey's Military Operations against the PKK in Northern Iraq', *Melbourne Journal of International Law* 9 (2008), 334–64.

[302] See Jules Lobel, 'The Use of Force to Respond to Terrorist Attacks: The Bombing of Sudan and Afghanistan', *Yale Journal of International Law* 24 (1999), 537–57.

defence.[303] In addition to letters to the Security Council, the US practice has been accompanied by a sequence of official documents setting out a broad understanding of that right.[304]

(iii) **States joining US-led campaigns on the basis of broad readings:** While Israel and Turkey have typically acted alone, the US-led campaigns in Afghanistan and Syria were joined by a significant number of other States. A considerable number of these States has invoked Article 51 to justify their own involvement, and expressly endorsed broad constructions of the right to collective or individual self-defence.[305] In 2001, the United Kingdom, Canada, France, Australia, Germany, the Netherlands, New Zealand and Poland sent letters to this effect to the Security Council.[306] Fifteen years later, most of these States,[307] as well as Norway,[308] Denmark[309] and Belgium,[310] would again expressly invoke Article 51 to justify their involvement in the fight against ISIS in Syria. A significant number of these States has clarified its view of the law (endorsing asymmetrical forms of self-defence) in general statements.[311]

(iv) **Other States – self-defence outside the limelight:** At least thirteen other States have exercised, or clearly asserted, a right of self-defence against non-State actors. They have often done so in conflicts that did not necessarily reach the headlines; perhaps as a result, their conduct has not always been scrutinised in depth. But their practice exists: it notably comprises cross-border raids in pursuit of rebels, at times

---

[303] See UN Doc. S/2001/946, 7 October 2001; UN Doc. S/2014/695, 23 September 2014.

[304] See e.g. Speech of Attorney General Eric Holder at Northwestern University School of Law, Chicago, IL, United States, Monday 5 March 2012, available at www.justice.gov/opa/speech/attorney-general-eric-holder-speaks-northwestern-university-school-law.

[305] The line between States that joined US-led efforts, and those that endorsed US self-defence, is fine. In both instances, the respective States' conduct remains relevant as subsequent practice.

[306] See UN Doc. S/2001/1005, 24 October 2001 (Canada); UN Doc. S/2001/1103, 23 November 2001 (France); UN Doc. S/2001/1104, 23 November 2001 (Australia); UN Doc. S/2001/1127, 29 November 2001 (Germany); UN Doc. S/2001/1171, 6 December 2001 (Netherlands); UN Doc. S/2001/1193, 17 December 2001 (New Zealand); UN Doc. S/2002/275, 15 March 2002 (Poland).

[307] See e.g. letters of the United Kingdom (UN Docs. S/2014/851, 25 November 2014, S/2015/688, 7 September 2015, and S/2015/928, 3 December 2015); Canada (UN Doc. S/2015/221, 31 March 2015); Australia (UN Doc. S/2015/693, 9 September 2015); France (UN Doc. S/2015/745, 8 September 2015); Germany (UN Doc. S/2015/946, 10 December 2015). The reasoning is not identical, but all letters refer to self-defence.

[308] UN Doc. S/2016/513, 3 June 2016.

[309] UN Doc. S/2016/34, 11 January 2016.

[310] UN Doc. S/2016/523, 9 June 2016.

[311] *Pars pro toto*, see the German government's statement to Parliament, *Bundestags-Drucksache* 18/6866, 1 December 2015, available at http://dipbt.bundestag.de/doc/btd/18/068/1806866.pdf.

conveniently labelled terrorists. Such raids (or airstrikes) have been undertaken by at least eight States, namely Iran (against Iraq),[312] Tajikistan (against Afghanistan),[313] Russia (against Georgia),[314] Rwanda (against the DRC),[315] Colombia (against Ecuador)[316] and Uganda (against the DRC),[317] as well as Senegal (against Guinea Bissau) and Thailand (against Myanmar).[318] Of these eight States, three – Iran, Tajikistan and Russia – expressly relied on Article 51 in their correspondence with the Security Council,[319] while Uganda described its self-defence action in the General Assembly.[320] The arguments of other States, such as Colombia or Rwanda, were not as clearly put, but upon analysis seem to have been based on a self-defence rationale.[321] The same is true for statements by India,[322]

---

[312]   See e.g. UN Doc. S/25843, 26 May 1993; UN Doc. S/1994/1273, 10 November 1994; UN Doc. S/1996/602, 29 July 1996; UN Doc. S/1999/781, 12 July 1999; UN Doc. S/2000/216, 14 March 2000; UN Doc. S/2001/271, 26 March 2001; UN Doc. S/2001/381, 14 April 2001.

[313]   See UN Doc. S/26091, 14 July 1993; UN Doc. S/26092, 15 July 1993; UN Doc. S/1994/992, 24 August 1994; and further van Steenberghe, *La légitime défense en droit international public* 2012 (n. 100), 301.

[314]   See e.g. UN Doc. S/2002/1012, 12 September 2002; Ruys, *'Armed Attack' and Article 51 of the UN Charter* 2010 (n. 53), 464–5; Wettberg, *The International Legality of Self-Defense against Non-State Actors* 2007 (n. 116).

[315]   During the Second Congo War, Rwandan troops repeatedly moved into Congolese territory to fight militias. Amongst other things, Rwanda accused the DRC of failing to disarm militias; this 'failure . . . may force Rwanda to take appropriate measures in self-defence'; see UN Doc. S/2004/652, 16 August 2004.

[316]   In 2008, Colombia invoked self-defence to justify an attack on a FARC camp in Ecuador: see Comunicado No. 081 del Ministeria de Relaciones Exteriores de Colombia, Bogotá, 2 March 2008, available at http://historico.presidencia.gov.co/comunicados/2008/marzo/81 .html; Tatiana Waisberg, 'Colombia's Use of Force in Ecuador', American Society of International Law Insights 12 (2008), available at https://www.asil.org/insights/volume/12/issue/ 17/colombias-use-force-ecuador-against-terrorist-organization-international.

[317]   See UN Doc. A/53/PV.95 (23 March 1999), 14.

[318]   During the 1990s, Thai and Senegalese forces crossed into neighbouring States (Myanmar and Guinea-Bissau respectively) in pursuit of armed rebels: see *Keesing's Record of World Events* 38 (1992), 39228; *Keesing's Record of World Events* 41 (1995), 40396; *Keesing's Record of World Events* 41 (1995), 40554; and further van Steenberghe, *La légitime défense en droit international public* 2012 (n. 100), 300 (fn. 1127).

[319]   See e.g. UN Doc. S/1996/602, 29 July 1996, S/2001/381, 18 April 2001 (both Iran); UN Doc. S/ 2002/1012, 12 September 2002 (Russia); UN Doc. S/26091, 14 July 1993; UN Doc. S/26092, 15 July 1993 (Tajikistan).

[320]   UN Doc. A/53/PV.95 (23 March 1999), 14.

[321]   See UN Doc. S/2004/652, 16 August 2004 (Rwanda); Comunicado No. 081 del Ministeria de Relaciones Exteriores de Colombia, Bogotá, 2 March 2008, available at http://historico .presidencia.gov.co/comunicados/2008/marzo/81.html (Colombia).

[322]   See statements in Louis Balmond, 'Chronique du faits internationaux', Revue Générale de Droit International Public 106 (2002), 389 and 107 (2003), 138.

Liberia,[323] Chad and Sudan,[324] all of which have asserted a right to respond in self-defence against armed attacks by terrorists. Finally, Ethiopia relied on self-defence to justify a significant military operation in support of the beleaguered government of Somalia: its conduct may have looked like an intervention upon invitation, but was presented as a 'self-defensive measure' aimed at 'counter-attacking the aggressive extremist forces of the Islamic Courts and foreign terrorist groups'.[325]

B) GREATER DIVERSITY Claims of asymmetrical self-defence have not just become more common, they have also become more diverse. Whereas the Cold War debate centred on problems of State support, more recent practice has embraced new rationales. While no case is exactly the same, the instances summarised in the preceding paragraphs can be broadly grouped into three categories.[326]

> Active support: Active support (comprising e.g. forms of training, financing, arming and logistic support) is the first of these patterns; while no longer dominant, it has remained popular. In a number of the more recent instances, States have justified their forcible reactions by claiming that host States had actively supported non-State actors carrying out attacks – and thus had to answer for these acts and endure the use of responsive force on their territory. The claims of Senegal, Tajikistan, Chad and Sudan are illustrative of this pattern.[327] This body of practice remains within the boundaries of the Cold War era debates.

> Harbouring: Whilst State complicity has remained relevant, the focus has clearly shifted towards a State nexus of a different sort. There are two aspects to this. For a start, variations of the 'harbouring doctrine' have

---

[323] UN Doc. S/2001/474, 11 May 2001.

[324] See UN Doc. S/2008/325, 14 May 2008 (Sudan), and I. M. Lobo de Souza, 'Revisiting the Right of Self-Defence', *Canadian Yearbook of International Law* 53 (2016), 202–43 (232).

[325] Statement by Prime Minister Zenawi, quoted in UN Doc. S/PV.5614, 26 December 2006, 3; and further Zeray W. Yihdego, 'Ethiopia's Military Actions against the Union of Islamic Courts and Others in Somalia: Some Legal Implications', *International and Comparative Law Quarterly* 56 (2007), 666–76; Olivier Corten, 'La licéité douteuse de l'action militaire de l'Ethiopie en Somalie', *Revue Générale de Droit International Public* 111 (2007), 513–37.

[326] The following distinction draws on Brownlie's categorisation (Brownlie, 'International Law and the Activities of Armed Bands' 1958 (n. 46)), but in the spirit of a synthesis, does not take up Brownlie's finer distinctions.

[327] See *supra*, references in notes 313, 318, 319, 324.

become much more popular: responding States have claimed a right to target safe havens of terrorist and irredentist groups abroad.[328] *Operation Enduring Freedom,* for the most part, was justified as a response against a regime accused of offering Al-Qaeda terrorists an operational base.[329] Harbouring also seems to have been the dominant theme in the self-defence claims of Colombia, Russia and Turkey,[330] and played a role in Tajikistan's argument.[331]

Loss of effective control: Significantly, in their more recent practice, reacting States have moved beyond the 'harbouring' doctrine. A number of the disputes just discussed involved the use of force against armed groups that had established areas of influence beyond the effective control of the host State. In this third setting, self-defence is exercised on the territory of the host State even though that host State is not accused of connivance with non-State actors; instead, it has to endure a response because it fails to control its territory. Barely hinted at in the Cold War era,[332] this 'idea of [self-defence within] an ungoverned space'[333] is now put more firmly, and regularly: by States relying on self-defence against ISIS in 'part of Syrian territory over which the Government of the Syrian Arab Republic does not, at this time, exercise effective control';[334] by Iran and Turkey justifying their respective incursions into northern Iraq;[335] and by Israel to support its strikes against Hezbollah targets in Lebanon.[336]

While the lines between the three categories can be blurred – where does 'harbouring' turn into 'support'?; when does a 'safe haven' become an 'ungoverned space'? – the overall trend seems clear: in addition to being more regular, the more recent practice has stretched the concept of asymmetrical self-defence and embraced arguments based on a more tenuous nexus – to the

---

[328]   As noted *supra* (IV.D), this reasoning is not entirely novel, but it has gained considerable traction.

[329]   See the US letter to the Security Council, UN Doc. S/2001/946, 7 October 2001 (9/11 had been 'made possible by the decision of the Taleban regime to allow the parts of Afghanistan that it controls to be used by this organization as a base of operation'); and references in Ruys, *'Armed Attack' and Article 51 of the UN Charter* 2010 (n. 53), 439–43.

[330]   See references in notes 299–300, 314, 316.

[331]   See references in notes 313.

[332]   See the brief reference to Israel's practice in section IV.D.1.

[333]   Starski, 'Silence within the Process of Normative Change' 2017 (n. 57), 32.

[334]   As noted in the Belgian letter to the Security Council: UN Doc. S/2016/523, 7 June 2016. For further examples, see the references in notes 307–11.

[335]   See references in notes 299–301.

[336]   See reference in note 298.

point where a State's failure to exercise effective control over its territory is said to have become sufficient. The newly popular formula of self-defence against 'unable or unwilling' States reflects the greater diversity of contemporary self-defence claims strands.[337]

Notwithstanding these changes, as in the Cold War era, reacting States have often gone to some lengths to justify why their response could not only target the attackers, but also violate the host State's territorial integrity. Responsibility has remained central in this respect: in nearly all instances self-defence claims have been accompanied by an assertion that the host State bore some form of responsibility, even though the armed attack itself could not be attributed to it under the general standards set out in the ILC's Articles on State Responsibility. What has changed is the character of responsibility incurred by the targeted State: in addition to claims based on responsibility for support (which dominated the Cold War practice), reacting States have frequently justified their conduct by claiming that host States bore responsibility for unlawfully shielding terrorists or failing to suppress their activities. The gradual recognition on positive duties to prevent and suppress terrorists has facilitated such arguments.[338]

2. A Greater Willingness to Accept Claims of Self-Defence

As was the case during the Cold War era, many of the more recent self-defence claims have been discussed internationally, including in the United Nations. As before, the international community's response has not been uniform. It has not always clearly focused on the proper construction of the armed attack criterion either: States have often preferred to address proportionality or been guided by overarching perspectives on the conflict.[339] Yet these caveats notwithstanding, international reactions confirm a changing attitude: gradual, no doubt, but palpable. The following four considerations illustrate this change.

---

[337] For detailed discussions see e.g. Deeks, 'Unwilling or Unable' 2012 (n. 4); Starski, 'Right to Self-Defense, Attribution and the Non-State Actor' 2015 (n. 4). Tsagourias' warning is worth reiterating: 'the "unable or unwilling" test [should not be] projected as if it were the only ground for using defensive force against non-state attacks': 'Self-Defense against Non-State Actors' 2016 (n. 18).

[338] For a telling example, see Israel's assertion (n. 298) that the Lebanese government bore responsibility because its 'ineptitude and inaction' had allowed Hezbollah to control parts of Lebanon.

[339] For similar trends in the Cold War practice see *supra*, IV.C.

A) OUTRIGHT CONDEMNATIONS HAVE BECOME RARE *First*, outright condemnations have become rare. Action in self-defence has continued to prompt protests. However, States have only rarely been censured in the way South Africa, Portugal or Israel were during the 1970s and 1980s. In fact, in only two of the instances referred to above was the conduct of States firmly rejected in widely endorsed international resolutions: the OAS and the Rio Group denounced Colombia's 2008 raid on FARC camps in Ecuador and required Colombia to give an assurance of non-repetition;[340] the Security Council 'strongly condemn[ed]' Rwanda's military action in the DRC.[341] None of these resolutions specifically rejected broad constructions of self-defence.

B) SOME SELF-DEFENCE CLAIMS HAVE MET WITH EXPLICIT SUPPORT: *Second*, certain instances of asymmetrical self-defence have met with broad approval. Unlike in the Cold War era, the international community has, in some recent instances, firmly supported the use of force in self-defence against non-State actors. In particular, UN organs have begun to endorse or encourage forcible responses against particular armed groups. In late 2001, the Security Council, recognised that the attacks of 9/11 implicated Article 51; hence its recognition and reaffirmation, in the preambles of Security Council Resolutions 1368 and 1373 (adopted when 'much [still] remained unknown as to the source of the attacks'[342]) of 'the inherent right of individual or collective self-defence in accordance with the Charter'.[343] In 2015, the Security Council called upon member States to 'eradicate the safe haven that [ISIS and others] have established over significant parts of Iraq and Syria'[344] (while stopping short of authorising military action under Chapter VII).[345] Both responses have been described as exercises in constructive ambiguity;[346] and no doubt they are: in neither case did the Council authorise forcible action.[347] But there is

---

[340] OAS Doc. OEA/Ser.G, CP.RES.930 (1632/08), 5 March 2008; OAS, Resolution of the Twenty-Fifth Meeting of Consultation of Ministers of Foreign Affairs, 17 March 2008, Doc. OEA/Ser.F/II.25, RC.25/RES.1/08 rev.1.
[341] See UN Doc. S/PRST/2004/45, 7 December 2004; UN Doc. S/2004/966, 13 December 2004; UN Doc. S/2004/385, 13 May 2004.
[342] Ruys, *'Armed Attack' and Article 51 of the UN Charter* 2010 (n. 53), 434.
[343] SC Res. 1368 of 12 September 2001.
[344] See SC Res. 2249 of 20 November 2015, para. 5.
[345] For details see Starski, 'Silence within the Process of Normative Change' 2017 (n. 57), 35 *et seq.*
[346] See Dapo Akande and Marko Milanovic, 'The Constructive Ambiguity of the Security Council's ISIS Resolution', *EJIL Talk!*, 21 November 2015, available at www.ejiltalk.org/th e-constructive-ambiguity-of-the-security-councils-isis-resolution.
[347] In fact, in SC Res. 2249 of 20 November 2015, the Security Council encouraged only measures taken 'in compliance with international law, in particular with the United Nations Charter' (para. 5).

a risk of missing the forest amidst the trees: Security Council Resolutions 1368, 1373, 2249 and 2254 were passed in full awareness of the argument on self-defence; they lent international authority to forcible responses contemplated by States.[348] Importantly, they did so in scenarios that reflect the new diversity of self-defence claims: responses targeted host States accused of harbouring terrorists (Afghanistan) and lacking effective control over parts of their territory (Syria).

Outside the UN, forcible responses against Al-Qaeda and Daesh/ISIS have been significant, too. For the former instance, it is well documented. Michael Byers refers to supportive 'statements of more than 100 countries, and acquiescence on the part of all but two others';[349] others see practice after 9/11 as an 'implicit general endorsement of a broad interpretation of Art. 51'.[350] Responses to the use of force against ISIS in Syria are more difficult to evaluate, as the situation continues to evolve and as different explanations are put forward, including self-defence, intervention upon invitation (Russia, Iran) and an alleged right to defend peoples rising against authorities (Islamic Military Alliance). Specific support for a particular understanding of self-defence is not as widespread as in the wake of 9/11. However, the use of force against Daesh seems to meet with general (unspecific) approval. Reversing Christine Gray's assessment of the fate of South Africa's or Israel's claims during the Cold War era, one might perhaps say that it is endorsed 'on many different grounds'[351] – not specifically supporting the intervening States' self-defence claim, but accepting the outcome of their conduct.

C) A TREND TOWARDS ACCEPTANCE AMIDST CONTROVERSY *Third*, typically, forcible responses have met with a more equivocal response. Trends can nevertheless be made out, and they, too, suggest a changing attitude. It is, for example, reflected in a number of regional treaties that define core concepts in relatively broad terms. The 2005 African Union Non-Aggression and Common Defence Pact is illustrative: it considers certain uses of armed force to amount to aggression irrespective of whether they have been committed by

---

[348] Paulina Starski speaks of 'legitimized self-defence': '"Legitimized Self-Defense" – Quo Vadis Security Council?', *EJIL Talk!*, 10 December 2015, available at www.ejiltalk.org/legitimized-self-defense-quo-vadis-security-council.

[349] Michael Byers, 'The Intervention in Afghanistan (2001–)', in Olivier Corten and Tom Ruys (eds.), *The Use of Force in International Law – A Case-Based Approach* (Oxford: Oxford University Press, 2018), 625–38 (634).

[350] Olivier Corten, 'Has Practice Led to an "Agreement Between the Parties" Regarding the Interpretation of Article 51 of the UN Charter?', *Heidelberg Journal of International Law* 77 (2017), 15–17.

[351] Gray, *International Law and the Use of Force* 2008 (n. 27), 139.

'a State, a group of States, an organization of States or non-State actor(s)', and in this respect mentions the 'encouragement, support, harbouring or provision of any assistance for the commission of terrorist acts and other violent transnational organized crimes against a Member State'.[352] No provision of the Pact explicitly recognises a right to self-defence against aggression.[353] And while that is of course also true for other important definitions,[354] the safer reading might be to see the Pact, in the terminology used above, as a piece of circumstantial evidence. The fact that this circumstantial evidence is found in the definitional provisions of an important agreement is perhaps indicative.

The response to particular self-defence claims is a further indicator of change. Many recent instances of self-defence against non-State actors simply did not prompt significant debate. For operations of a limited scale (such as Senegal's and Thailand's incursions into neighbouring countries) this seems entirely understandable, especially if the countries involved did not raise the matter in international fora. More significant is the international community's willingness to accept larger-scale operations that were reported, such as Iran's incursions into Iraq or Tajikistan's significant operations in Afghanistan (expressly justified as an exercise of self-defence).[355] The silence with which these claims met need not amount to acquiescence.[356] However, the least that can be said is that the repeated reliance on a broad concept of self-defence did not seem problematic enough to warrant responses.

Where matters were taken up, the scales seem to have tipped in favour of States invoking self-defence. The US strikes against Afghanistan and Sudan in 1998,[357] Ethiopia's intervention in Somalia,[358] Turkey's incursions and

---

[352]   See Article 1(c) chapeau and lit. xi. of the African Union Non-Aggression and Common Defence Pact (Abuja Pact), 31 January 2005, available at https://au.int/sites/default/files/trea ties/7788-treaty-0031_-_african_union_non-aggression_and_common_defence_pact_e.pdf.

[353]   A point emphasised by Corten, *The Law against War* 2010 (n. 26), 167–8. Unlike Corten, van Steenberghe views the Pact as 'une application du droit de légitime défense' (*La légitime défense en droit international public* 2012 (n. 100), 338).

[354]   Notably GA Res. 3314 (n. 13), whose text explicitly safeguards the right of States under 'the Charter, including its provisions concerning cases in which the use of force is lawful' (Article 6).

[355]   See e.g. UN Doc. S/1996/602, 27 July 1996, S/2001/381, 18 April 2001 (both Iran); UN Doc. S/ 26091, 14 July 1993; UN Doc. S/26092, 15 July 1993 (Tajikistan).

[356]   For attempts to apply the rationale of acquiescence see Starski, 'Silence within the Process of Normative Change' 2017 (n. 57), 8 *et seq.*

[357]   See the references in Sean D. Murphy, 'Contemporary Practice of the United States Relating to International Law', *American Journal of International Law* 93 (1999), 161–94 (164–5); Franck, *Recourse to Force* 2002 (n. 27), 94–6.

[358]   The African Union endorsed Ethiopia's intervention, and the UN quickly authorised the deployment of a regional force to consolidate the situation following the withdrawal of Ethiopian troops. While these actions approved the outcome, they need not be construed as an

'Operation Sun' in Iraq[359] – all of these met with a mixed response, but criticism was 'decidedly muted'.[360] As in previous decades, engagement with the specifics of self-defence has remained rare; instead, reactions focused on questions of fact or the scope of the response. Where States could claim to make out a credible case (US–Afghanistan 1998), or were considered to have avoided excesses ('Turkey–'Operation Sun'),[361] they could expect a significant level of under-standing. As with operations against Al-Qaeda and ISIS, such understanding did not seem to depend on proof of host State *support* for non-State actors. It was also shown where self-defence was directed against States accused of harbouring terrorists, or targeted areas beyond the host State's effective control (as in the disputes involving Russia/Georgia, Iran/Iraq and Turkey/Iraq).[362]

D) AN ILLUSTRATION – ISRAEL'S USE OF FORCE IN LEBANON (2006) The gradual, yet palpable shift in opinion is illustrated by the international response to Israel's use of force in Lebanon during 2006.[363] Israel asserted a right of self-defence against Lebanon, whose government had responded to Hezbollah attacks with a mix of 'ineptitude and inaction' and 'not exercised jurisdiction over its own territory for many years'.[364] Israel's intervention raised many of the questions that had beset earlier strikes against targets in Arab countries.[365] The Security Council debates on the issue reflected entrenched views on the Israeli–Arab conflict. Many States preferred to discuss proportionality and warned against excessive force – warnings that Israel, in the view of most (including supportive) States, ignored.[366] And yet, unlike in previous debates,

---

acceptance of Ethiopia's self-defence claim: see Gray, *International Law and the Use of Force* 2008 (n. 27), 244.

[359] For references see Tams, 'The Necessity and Proportionality of Anti-Terrorist Self-Defence' 2013 (n. 22), 395–6.

[360] As noted by Murphy in relation to the 1998 strikes: see Murphy, 'Terrorism and the Concept of "Armed Attack"' 2002 (n. 90), 50.

[361] See Franck, *Recourse to Force* 2002 (n. 27), 96; Ruys, '*Quo Vadit Jus Ad Bellum?*' 2008 (n. 301), 334; but contrast Tladi in this volume, 70–1.

[362] See the references in notes 314, 312, and 299–301.

[363] The following draws on Christian J. Tams and Wenke Brückner, 'The Israeli Intervention in Lebanon (July 2006)', in Corten and Ruys (eds.), *The Use of Force in International Law* 2018 (n. 349), 673–88. For a different assessment of the intervention see Tladi in this volume, at 71–2.

[364] UN Doc. S/2006/515, 12 July 2006.

[365] See *supra*, IV.D.1 and IV.D.2.

[366] By way of illustration, having affirmed Hezbollah's attacks, France 'condemn[ed] the dispro-portionate response by Israel, whose military operations are holding the Lebanese people hostage, killing large numbers of civilians and causing substantial material damage in Lebanon': UN Doc. S/PV.5493, 21 (Resumption), 21 June 2006, 11.

Israel's claim was widely endorsed as a matter of principle. 'Being attacked, as Israel was, grants the right to self-defence', observed Denmark in the Security Council, without mentioning a State nexus.[367] According to Tom Ruys, in two debates in the Security Council, '[n]otwithstanding deep concern at or outright condemnation of the excessive use of force, a majority of participants agreed as a matter of principle that Israel had the right to defend itself against the attacks by Hezbollah':[368] alongside the 'usual suspects', this majority included Russia, Turkey, Argentina, Brazil, Ghana, Iceland, Japan, Ukraine, Guatemala and Peru, and their view was shared by the UN Secretary-General.[369]

Outside the Security Council, the picture was more mixed: the Non-Aligned Movement condemned Israel's 'relentless ... aggression', and while it singled out the 'indiscriminate and massive' nature of Israel's attacks (perhaps suggesting a focus on the conduct of operations), nothing in its statement implies any in-principle acceptance.[370] That said, as in the Cold War era, the criticism remained unspecific, and not one State claimed that self-defence could only be exercised against State attacks.

***

These references illustrate the controversies prompted by self-defence claims in 2006. Still, stepping back from the details, the tone of the debate seemed to have changed. This was, to recall, Israel – whose reliance on self-defence had regularly been condemned in the Cold War era.[371] In 2006, a new voice had joined the chorus of opinion: the voice of States that in principle, explicitly, accepted Israel's reliance on self-defence. That voice was prominent even though Israel could not conceivably accuse Lebanon of having supported Hezbollah's attacks; and at least in the open Security Council debates, it was the voice of a majority. If viewed in this perspective, the international response to the 2006 conflict indeed 'is very remarkable'.[372]

---

[367] *Ibid.*, 7.
[368] Ruys, '*Armed Attack*' *and Article 51 of the UN Charter* 2010 (n. 53), 452.
[369] See the statements in UN Docs. S/PV.5492, 20 July 2006, S/PV.5493 and S/PV.5493 (resumption), 21 July 2006, S/PV.5498, 30 July 2006; and the references in Tams and Brückner, 'The Israeli Intervention in Lebanon' 2018 (n. 363), 4–6, 8.
[370] See Final Document of the Fourteenth Conference of Heads of State or Government of Non-Aligned Movement (Havana, 11–16 September 2006), UN Doc. A/61/472, S/2006/780, 29 September 2006, at paras. 142–5.
[371] See the references *supra*, IV.D.2.
[372] But see van Steenberghe, 'Self-Defence in Response to Attacks by Non-State Actors' 2010 (n. 84), 193.

3. The Appeal of Normative Continuity

Whilst the preceding discussion emphasises elements of change, this change has been accompanied by affirmations of continuity. As in many other disputes about the proper interpretation of the *ius ad bellum*, there has been a tendency to protect the normative *acquis* against rupture. This is particularly obvious from assessments removed from the 'heat' of a particular dispute.

A) FRAMEWORK DOCUMENTS AFFIRMING THE SUFFICIENCY OF THE EXISTING LAW   Framework documents emanating from international organisations reflect the considerable appeal of normative continuity; many of them affirm the sufficiency of the existing law.

The Non-Aligned Movement has been particularly vocal. It has emphasised that 'consistent with the practice of the UN and international law, as pronounced by the ICJ, Article 51 . . . is restrictive and should not be rewritten or re-interpreted.'[373] This – now regular – formula has remained general and does not mention specific controversies about the scope of self-defence.[374] But its general message is clear.

As regards the UN, the world organisation has in recent years restated fundamental principles of friendly relations, including those governing recourse to force. In documents such as the World Summit Outcome Document of 2005,[375] the High Level Panel Report and Kofi Annan's *In Larger Freedom*,[376] the post-Cold War practice is not even hinted at. All documents affirm the primacy of the Charter regime, which the Outcome Document considers 'sufficient to address the full range of threats to international peace and security'.[377]

Six years after Kosovo and two years after Iraq, this statement probably mainly illustrated the UN's capacity to imagine order amidst chaos. But can it be taken as an affirmation of a State-centric construction of self-defence?[378] The argument seems rather strained, if only because it is circular: it

---

373   See e.g. Iran's statement on behalf of the Non-Aligned Movement, UN Doc. S/PV.7621, 15 February 2016, 34.

374   Contrast e.g. the G77's specific 'reject[ion] [of] the so-called right of humanitarian intervention' in the wake of the Kosovo crisis: Declaration of the South Summit, Havana, 10–14 April 2000, para. 54, available at www.g77.org/summit/Declaration_G77Summit.htm.

375   GA Res. 60/1 of 24 October 2005.

376   See UN Doc. A/59/565 (2 September 2004) and UN Doc. A/59/2005 (26 May 2005) respectively.

377   GA Res. 60/1 of 24 October 2005, para. 79.

378   For variations of this argument see Corten, *The Law against War* 2010 (n. 26), 164–5; Olivier Corten, 'Regulating Resort to Force: A Response to Matthew Waxman from a "Bright-Liner"', *European Journal of International Law* 24 (2013), 191–7 (195).

presupposes what it seeks to prove – viz. that the Charter regime excludes asymmetrical self-defence, and that the regime *thus interpreted* is sufficient. Yet four years after 9/11, State-centric readings were no longer unchallenged. Moreover, as is clear from the debates, States did not seriously discuss the question of non-State attacks.[379] Against that background, the more plausible view is that the Outcome Document sought to 'paper over' controversies concerning the scope of self-defence: an affirmation of the Charter's significance served that purpose, yet it did not settle long-standing debate about symmetrical or asymmetrical readings.

B) RECENT ICJ DECISIONS The more recent jurisprudence of the International Court of Justice equally reflects the appeal of normative continuity. Unlike the UN's general documents, this jurisprudence is relevant, but it lacks the certainty of the Court's earlier pronouncements.

To recall, the Court's *Nicaragua* judgment had approached self-defence firmly from within an inter-State framework and set a high threshold for attacks to qualify as State attacks.[380] Two more recent decisions – the *Israeli Wall* opinion (2004) and the *Armed Activities* judgment (2005) – provided the Court with an opportunity to assess the impact of recent practice. On the face of it, they send a message of continuity. Both majority decisions seem firmly based on an inter-State understanding of self-defence. In the *Wall* case, the Court explicitly rejected Israel's argument that the construction of a wall was in line with Article 51, which 'recognizes the existence of an inherent right of self-defence in the case of armed attack by one State against another'.[381] In *Armed Activities*, the Court was faced with arguments about the proper reading of Article 3(g) of the General Assembly's Definition of Aggression, which Uganda considered to encompass cases of aid and assistance. However, as in the *Wall* opinion, the Court rejected claims of self-defence: Uganda had not established a sufficient State nexus; cross-border attacks 'remained non-attributable to the DRC';[382] and 'the legal and factual circumstances for the exercise of a right of self-defence by Uganda against the DRC were not present.'[383] All this reads like a succinct restatement of the Cold War orthodoxy: it is difficult to avoid the impression that, in the view of the Court's

---

[379] By contrast, they did discuss questions of anticipatory self-defence, and decided not to include a passage recognising such a right: see Corten, 'Regulating Resort to Force' 2013 (n. 378), 195.

[380] *Supra*, IV.B.3.b.

[381] ICJ, *Construction of a Wall* (n. 125), para. 139.

[382] ICJ, *Armed Activities in the Territory of the Congo* (n. 1), para. 146.

[383] *Ibid.*, para. 147.

majority, more recent trends in practice (at least as of 2004/5) could be ignored.[384]

When probing further, the picture becomes rather more blurred. For one, other passages of the *Wall* and *Armed Activities* decisions raise doubts. In the former, the Court noted that Israel's situation was different from that 'contemplated by Security Council resolutions 1368 (2001) and 1373 (2001)', adopted after 9/11.[385] In *Armed Activities*, the Court felt it could leave open 'whether and under what conditions contemporary international law provides for a right of self-defence against large-scale attacks by irregular forces'.[386] Both statements are curious. In the *Wall*, if self-defence required an 'armed attack by one State against another',[387] why did Security Council Resolutions 1368 and 1373 need to be distinguished? The majority's disclaimer in the *Armed Activities* case takes this confusion to a higher level. Benevolent commentators have suggested that Uganda had not expressly relied on a right of self-defence against non-State attacks.[388] But that ignores the fact that, according to Uganda, host States tolerating armed rebel bands on their territory 'were under a super-added standard of responsibility'.[389] The majority's decision not to respond to this contention is indeed 'not altogether clear'.[390] Problems of internal consistency notwithstanding, it is perhaps best taken at face value: as an express recognition that the question of non-State attacks is an open one.

A number of judges went further; they explicitly accepted that self-defence was available against armed attacks by non-State actors. The majority decisions just summarised were, in other words, reached over pronounced opposition. In the *Wall* case, Judges Higgins and Kooijmans expressed disappointment at the majority's apodictic approach, but stopped short of saying it was wrong as a matter of law.[391] Judge Buergenthal thought it was, and said so,[392] as did – one year later – Judges Kooijmans and Simma in the *Armed Activities* case. All three accepted that an attacked State could not be

---

[384] See, in this sense, Klein, 'Le droit international à l'épreuve du terrorisme' 2006 (n. 251), 407; Corten, *The Law against War* 2010 (n. 26), 467–70.

[385] ICJ, *Construction of a Wall* (n. 125), para. 139.

[386] ICJ, *Armed Activities in the Territory of the Congo* (n. 1), para. 147.

[387] ICJ, *Construction of a Wall* (n. 125), para. 139.

[388] Ruys, *'Armed Attack' and Article 51 of the UN Charter* 2010 (n. 53), 483; Zimmermann, 'The Second Lebanon War' 2007 (n. 141), 116.

[389] *Armed Activities* case, Oral Hearings, CR 2005/7, 30, para. 80 (Brownlie).

[390] See ICJ, *Armed Activities in the Territory of the Congo* (n. 1), Separate Opinion of Judge Kooijmans, 306, para. 20.

[391] ICJ, *Construction of a Wall* (n. 125), Separate Opinion of Judge Higgins, 207, para. 33; Separate Opinion of Judge Kooijmans, 219, para. 35.

[392] ICJ, *Construction of a Wall* (n. 125), Declaration of Judge Buergenthal, 240, para. 6.

'den[ied] ... the right to self-defence merely because there is no attacker State'.[393] Judge Tomka, too, seemed to accept that where a territorial State no longer exercised governmental control in parts of its territory, a 'neighbouring State, victim of attack, [could] step in and put an end to the attacks'.[394]

The Court's recent jurisprudence, then, seems to reflect a considerable degree of uncertainty about the proper understanding of self-defence. The majority decisions have given short shrift to post-Cold War practice. Individual judges have gone further, but the fact that they felt the need to do so, especially in *Armed Activities*, suggests that despite the disclaimer, the majority may not have succeeded in leaving matters open.[395] However one looks at it, the recent ICJ jurisprudence is fairly difficult to make sense of. As in Michelangelo Antonioni's *Blow Up*, the closer one looks, the more blurred the picture appears. This is, to be sure, of the Court's own making: its recent jurisprudence 'combin[es] an ostensible reaffirmation of the *Nicaragua* threshold with a smoke screen of ambiguity'.[396] Perhaps, indeed, the central message is one of indecision.

E. Subsequent Practice: Where Do We Stand?

1. General Considerations

Since 1945, States and UN organs have sought to give meaning to the 'armed attack' requirement, in their assessment of particular self-defence claims, and in the course of attempts at clarifying the law in general terms. Their subsequent practice is rich and diverse. For the most part, it has been a debate about nuances – about exploring under what circumstances a State would have to answer for armed attacks carried out by non-State actors. The preceding synthesis of practice highlights that over time, States' views on this question have changed considerably. And yet, contrary to a popular narrative, this is not a story of radical breaks, let alone of one clear trajectory. If anything, there have been *two* main trends: *first*, the move towards a stratified framework in the course of debates about GA Res. 3314, amplified by the *Nicaragua* judgment

---

[393] ICJ, *Armed Activities in the Territory of the Congo* (n. 1), Separate Opinion of Judge Kooijmans, 306, para. 30; similarly Separate Opinion of Judge Simma, 334, para. 12.

[394] ICJ, *Armed Activities in the Territory of the Congo* (n. 1), Declaration of Judge Tomka, 351, para. 4.

[395] See ICJ, *Armed Activities in the Territory of the Congo* (n. 1), Separate Opinion of Judge Kooijmans, 306, para. 22.

[396] Ruys, *'Armed Attack' and Article 51 of the UN Charter* 2010 (n. 53), 487.

and the ILC's work on State responsibility; and *second*, the rise of asymmetrical self-defence since the end of the Cold War. This analysis contradicts the popular assumption that practice had been State-centric for decades before the 'tidal changes'[397] of early twenty-first-century practice swept aside restrictive approaches: the pendulum has swung back and forth.

What is more, throughout these pendulum swings, the law has remained contested. Even during the heyday of a restrictive analysis, the international community could tolerate the odd instance of asymmetrical self-defence. Conversely, the broad reading of self-defence of the post-Cold War era is primarily 'driven' by claim and contestation in concrete disputes, but has not trickled down to the level of multilateral documents; these – just as the ICJ – emphasise continuity. This is, in short, not a simple story of 'things are different now. Practice, law and/or its interpretation were radically transformed by "9/11" and its aftermath.'[398] What has changed is the *relative* support for the different positions.

2. The Significance of the Two Main Trends

The significance of subsequent practice for the interpretation of Article 51 to some extent depends on these preliminary considerations. More importantly, though, it depends on a detailed assessment of the two main trends just identified. This assessment needs to reflect the general rules governing the role of subsequent practice in treaty interpretation, as reflected in the ILC's recent work.

Looked at from that perspective, the first of the two main trends – the stratification of the regime during the Cold War era – at the time undoubtedly was significant. GA Res. 3314 reflected a 'subsequent agreement' of UN members to view self-defence primarily as an inter-State defence. This agreement was recorded in an important document, through which the parties purported to clarify the meaning of aggression, and by extension, self-defence. The key provision of that agreement, Article 3(g), was debated at length; this suggests that it should have significant weight.

For the purposes of treaty interpretation, Article 3(g) offered three main messages: (i) there was *some* room for asymmetrical self-defence; (ii) such asymmetrical self-defence was to be exceptional – as a minimum, it

---

[397] De Hoogh, 'Restrictivist Reasoning on the *Ratione Personae* Dimension of Armed Attacks in the Post 9/11 World' 2016 (n. 14), 20.

[398] But contrast Kammerhofer, 'The Future of Restrictivist Scholarship on the Use of Force' 2016 (n. 8), 13.

presupposed a State's 'substantial involvement'; and (iii) this by implication seemed to exclude asymmetrical self-defence on the basis of the harbouring (and similar) doctrines. Beyond that, however, the precise contours of the 'substantial involvement' test remained unspecific – which, in line with the general regime, would affect its weight.[399]

The *Nicaragua* judgment and the ILC's work on State responsibility 'fine-tuned' these messages. *Nicaragua* suggested that State support would be insufficient – and was taken to suggest that attribution was required, which the ILC construed narrowly. Yet these subsequent 'specifications' had to be seen against the backdrop of an inconsistent practice, which could raise doubts about whether the very narrow construction of Article 3(g) was firmly established.[400]

The significance of the second pendulum swing – the move towards a broader understanding of self-defence in the post-Cold War era – is more difficult to assess. While the analysis has revealed a palpable change in practice, it needs to be asked whether this change could neutralise the earlier move towards State-centrism. The question is pertinent as the broader construction of self-defence in recent practice is not reflected in general documents of the calibre of GA Res. 3314; in the ILC's terminology, it is relevant only as 'other subsequent practice'.[401] Some commentators suggest that this 'lesser' practice could not modify the earlier position.[402]

At least for the purposes of treaty interpretation, such an approach seems too hierarchical and formal. Subsequent practice is only one factor to be 'taken into account' in processes of treaty interpretation; and its weight depends on material criteria (specificity, clarity, repetition). Commentators requiring something akin to an *actus contrarius* for changes to take effect fail to appreciate the character of interpretation as a 'single combined operation'.[403] They also ignore the terms of GA Res. 3314, which – far from purporting to 'freeze' the law – was not meant to 'diminish[] the scope ... [of the] Charter ... provisions concerning cases in which the use of force is lawful'.[404] All this

---

[399] ILC, 'Subsequent Practice' 2018 (n. 188), Draft Conclusion 9(1).

[400] Cf. *ibid.*, para. 5 of the commentary to Draft Conclusion 6, noting that 'the way in which a treaty is applied' was indicative of 'the degree to which the interpretation that the States parties have assumed is "grounded" and thus more or less firmly established'.

[401] The near-unanimous response to the attacks of 9/11 is the exception that proves the rule: see Corten, 'Has Practice Led to an "Agreement Between the Parties"?' 2017 (n. 350), 15.

[402] See *ibid.*, 16 ('difficult to understand how a clear "agreement between the parties" (Art. 31.3 a) could be challenged by an erratic and ambiguous practice, particularly as far as it has not led to any new "agreement of the parties" (Art. 31.3 b)').

[403] *Yearbook of the International Law Commission* 1966, vol. II, 219, para. 8.

[404] GA Res. 3314 (n. 13), Article 6.

suggests that the impact of the more recent 'other subsequent practice' cannot be dismissed *a limine*, but needs to be carefully assessed.

3. In Particular: The Impact of the Post-Cold War Practice

A careful assessment needs to inquire whether developments since the end of the Cold War are significant enough to challenge the impact of the State-centric trend of the 1970s and 1980s. This question eschews a clear-cut answer. The preceding analysis suggests a nuanced response that distinguishes between the different 'messages' identified above and approaches the problem in engaging with three questions.

A) DOES SUBSEQUENT PRACTICE AT ALL LEAVE ROOM FOR ASYMMETRICAL SELF-DEFENCE AGAINST ATTACKS THAT CANNOT BE ATTRIBUTED TO ANOTHER STATE? It is convenient to begin by asking whether the recent practice affects the most restrictive aspect of the State-centric approach, viz. the highly restrictive reading of GA Res. 3314 brought about by the ICJ's *Nicaragua* judgment, which effectively viewed self-defence as a response against State attacks. This first inquiry is a modest one, no doubt: all that is assessed is whether the recent practice can be taken to have freed the 'substantial involvement' test from the '*Nicaragua* straightjacket'. The preceding analysis suggests that it has: this first, modest, proposition is supported by a body of widespread and sustained subsequent practice that is clear and specific.[405] Practice since the end of the Cold War is no doubt in many ways heterogeneous, reflecting different rationales ('support', 'harbouring', 'loss of effective control'); but these different rationales share a common denominator: they all assume that (contrary to what *Nicaragua* has been read to suggest) there is scope for self-defence outside the ILC's general categories of attribution. The practice in support of this view is common and long-standing: around twenty-five States from different regions of the world have asserted a right of self-defence outside the '*Nicaragua* setting'; many more have supported it. Adapting terms endorsed by the ILC,[406] one can certainly speak of 'a discernible pattern' of practice. This pattern extends over a significant period of time. Claims of asymmetrical self-defence have been on the rise for roughly twenty-five years. They are not a 'one-off',[407] but exceed the period between

---

[405] Cf. the criteria identified in ILC, 'Subsequent Practice' 2018 (n. 188), Draft Conclusion 9 and commentary.

[406] *Ibid.*, para. 7 of the commentary to Draft Conclusion 9.

[407] Cf. *ibid.*, para. 11 of the commentary to Draft Conclusion 9.

GA Res. 3314 and the end of the Cold War, the heyday of a restrictive analysis of the *ius ad bellum*. Finally, while some States have preferred to muddle through, a greater number has been straightforward in setting out their view of the law, including in letters to the Security Council: the debate about asymmetrical self-defence, for the most part, is conducted openly, and arguments are clearly articulated.

Perhaps most importantly, the first, modest, proposition meets with relatively little resistance. It does not, to reiterate, leave the 'safe ground' of GA Res. 3314, but merely suggests that its State-centric yet flexible terms should be taken seriously. As such it can be reconciled with statements emphasising the need for normative continuity, such as the Non-Aligned Movement's insistence to construe self-defence 'consistent with UN practice'.[408] All this suggests that the subsequent practice bears out a first, modest proposition: there is room for self-defence beyond instances of attribution.

B) DOES SUBSEQUENT PRACTICE RECOGNISE THE POSSIBILITY OF ASYMMETRICAL SELF-DEFENCE AGAINST STATES SUPPORTING ARMED ATTACKS?

Whether the subsequent practice of the post-Cold War era has consolidated sufficiently to go beyond this is more difficult to state with certainty. As in many other fields of law, it is easier to describe trends than to identify the contours of an emerging regime with precision. The fact that the lines between the different rationales of asymmetrical self-defence that have emerged – support, harbouring, loss of effective control – are not sharply delineated, adds to this.

Notwithstanding these caveats, differences of degree exist. Of the different rationales, the case for self-defence against States that had actively supported 'private' armed attacks is the strongest. 'Support' has not been a dominant feature of recent practice, but it has remained prominent. What is more, it seems reasonable to assume that the significant number of States that have come out in support of asymmetrical self-defence on the basis of broader doctrines (harbouring, loss of effective control, 'unable and unwilling') by implication endorsed self-defence against supporting States. Perhaps more importantly, of the different patterns of asymmetrical self-defence that have risen to prominence since the end of the Cold War, 'State support' presents the least risk of rupture. The practice of old may not have endorsed it, but the matter was debated: during the debates about indirect aggression, and in the assessment of particular self-defence claims, 'support' was the obvious

[408] See 17th Summit of Heads of State and Government of the Non-Aligned Movement, Island of Margarita, 17–18 September 2016, Doc. NAM2016/CoB/DOC.1, para. 25.2.

'candidate'. Finally, State support of a certain intensity seemed the obvious candidate, too, for inclusion in the category of 'substantial involvement' recognised in GA Res. 3314. These considerations would seem to point towards a second proposition: that the subsequent practice of States and UN organs in the application of Article 51 on balance accepts the possibility of self-defence against States complicit in the commission of armed attacks.

C) DOES SUBSEQUENT PRACTICE RECOGNISE THE POSSIBILITY OF ASYMMETRICAL SELF-DEFENCE ON THE BASIS OF BROADER DOCTRINES? Asymmetrical self-defence beyond complicity gives rise to greater problems. States have frequently invoked self-defence on the basis of broader doctrines (harbouring, loss of effective control), but these claims pose greater challenges than instances of 'State support' and prompt significant resistance. The possibility of self-defence in 'ungoverned spaces' was not seriously entertained in the Cold War era, while 'harbouring' (which has a longer pedigree) was generally considered to fall below the 'substantial involvement' test of GA Res. 3314. As regards the more recent practice, extensive self-defence claims seem the main cause for concern about 'normative drift'.[409]

A closer look at the treatment of particular instances of self-defence yields a different picture though. Since the end of the Cold War, the harbouring doctrine has become the most common basis for asymmetrical self-defence claims. In assessing self-defence claims, States seem not to draw any principled distinction between instances of complicity on the one hand and broader doctrines on the other: in fact, prominent conflicts illustrating the trend towards asymmetry have involved self-defence in 'ungoverned spaces'; by the same token, the United States' reliance on the harbouring doctrine to justify *Operation Enduring Freedom* met with near-universal support. In other words, judging from its assessment to individual cases, the international community certainly seems prepared to accept (and has in the aftermath of 9/11 near-unanimously accepted) self-defence on the basis of broader doctrines in exceptional cases. This suggests that a more tenuous State nexus (below the level of active support) is not in principle excluded.

The real question, then, is how such exceptional cases can be identified. Practice so far yields very few insights: as noted above, States seem to have been influenced by a broad range of contextual factors – from the credibility of the evidence to the magnitude of the threat – and the contours of the exception remain fuzzy. In light of these considerations, the current situation is perhaps best described as follows. In the recent practice of States, the

---

[409] See Bethlehem, 'International Law and the Use of Force' 2004 (n. 294).

possibility of self-defence on the basis of the 'harbouring' and 'loss of effective control' doctrines has not been generally admitted, but self-defence claims based on these doctrines have been tolerated or widely endorsed in a relevant number of individual instances.

V. ASSESSMENT AND CONCLUDING THOUGHTS

The preceding analysis illustrates how much is at stake in the major, narrow, long-standing and often confused debate about self-defence against non-State actors. Answers to the threshold question proceed from 'no more than the words "armed attack"',[410] but these two words are an integral part of the contemporary *ius ad bellum*, which is at the heart of the Charter and of the contemporary regime of international law. The analysis needs to reflect this; so it is perhaps no wonder that contributions to it (including this one) tend to be heavy and dense.

Long-standing, major debates rarely yield obvious answers. This one does not either. It takes more than a fair share of chuzpe to assert that one's preferred 'position [on the matter] cannot be seriously doubted'.[411] Of course it can, and of course it is: for decades, States, UN organs, courts and commentators have taken different views on whether (and under which conditions) self-defence could be invoked against attacks by non-State actors. Few of the answers given are obviously right or obviously wrong. There is room for disagreement; different views have no more than 'varying degrees of legal merit'.[412]

To admit as much should not be read as a 'post-truthian' suggestion that all things were equal: degrees of legal merit vary after all. The preceding analysis points towards a more convincing view. It suggests that under contemporary international law, self-defence is more than a right to respond to State attacks by another State. It can in principle be invoked against armed attacks by non-State actors, even though this possibility will often be subject to stringent conditions. The remainder of this concluding section summarises why this is so (A), and what it implies (B).

A. The Case for Asymmetrical Self-Defence

The 'case' for recognising asymmetrical self-defence against armed attacks by non-State actors draws on the preceding exercise in treaty interpretation.

---

[410]   Kammerhofer, *Uncertainty in International Law* 2010 (n. 42), 43.
[411]   Lowe, *International Law* 2007 (n. 19), 278.
[412]   Cf. Lauterpacht, *The Development of International Law by the International Court* 1958 (n. 23), 398.

As noted above, according to the drafters of the Vienna Convention regime, the different means of interpretation are to be 'thrown into the crucible'[413] where each is accorded 'appropriate emphasis'.[414] In this process 'law-applying agents [no doubt enjoy] a certain scope of discretion',[415] but the regime of treaty interpretation does 'nudge treaty interpreters towards the 'correct' [approach]',[416] and it does so notably by focusing attention on 'the elucidation of the meaning of the text'.[417]

1. The Meaning of the Text: Reprise

Given ongoing uncertainties about the proper source of self-defence, section III of the present study has engaged with a range of textual, contextual, teleological and historical arguments. Contrary to a popular understanding, these arguments on balance point towards a broad understanding of the 'armed attack' requirement that leaves room for asymmetrical self-defence. The terms of Article 51 are particularly significant in this respect: the provision refers to 'armed attacks' without specifying the character of the attacker. This is to be taken at face value, not only because the text is 'presumed to be the authentic expression of the intentions of the parties',[418] but also because Article 51 explicitly qualifies the character of the victim (which must be a State): 'what matters' is indeed 'the armed attack, not the attacker'.[419]

Contextual arguments on balance reinforce this understanding. Notably, over time, the Charter's other recognised exception to the ban on force – the use of force with Security Council authorisation – has come to be read asymmetrically: under the Charter's collective security system, States can clearly be authorised to use force on the territory of another State even where that other State has not committed any wrong (let alone violated Article 2(4)); the State-centric approaches of the early Charter era have been

---

[413] See *Yearbook of the International Law Commission* 1966, vol. II, 219, para. 8.

[414] See ILC, 'Subsequent Practice' 2018 (n. 188), Draft Conclusion 2(5).

[415] Ulf Linderfalk, 'Is Treaty Interpretation an Art or a Science?', *European Journal of International Law* 26 (2015), 169–89 (189).

[416] Michael Waibel, 'Uniformity Versus Specialization', in Christian J. Tams, Antonios Tzanakopoulos and Andreas Zimmermann (eds.), *Research Handbook on the Law of Treaties* (Cheltenham: Edward Elgar, 2014), 375–411 (381).

[417] *Yearbook of the International Law Commission* 1966, vol. II, para. 11; and see further Gardiner, *Treaty Interpretation* 2015 (n. 98), 144; Waibel, 'Uniformity Versus Specialization' 2014 (n. 416), 380 ('qualified textualism').

[418] *Yearbook of the International Law Commission* 1966, vol. II, 220, para. 11.

[419] Karin Oellers-Frahm, 'What Matters is the Armed Attack, not the Attacker!', *Heidelberg Journal of International Law* 77 (2017), 44–51.

overcome. Self-defence could be construed in much the same way. Contrary to a prominent view, it need not be read as the 'flip-side' of the State-centric ban on force. All this suggests that, when construed in light of the general rule of treaty interpretation, Article 51 is open to, and actually encourages, a reading that permits self-defence against armed attacks by non-State actors.

2. Subsequent Practice: Reprise

This finding crucially affects the role of subsequent practice in the process of treaty interpretation. Embedded in a broader inquiry, subsequent practice is one among a range of elements of interpretation, which 'in [its] interaction with other means of interpretation, [contributes] to the clarification of the meaning of a treaty'.[420] The assessment of subsequent practice, in other words, does not take place in a legal vacuum, and nor does it start from scratch. Part of the 'single, combined operation', subsequent practice is assessed with a view to determining whether the parties' conduct in the application of a treaty 'confirms or modifies the result arrived at by the initial interpretation of the ordinary meaning (or by other means of interpretation)'.[421] Applied to the present case, it is thus to be asked whether the subsequent practice of States and UN organs in the application of Article 51 'confirms or modifies [the potentially "open" construction of self-defence] arrived at by the initial interpretation'.[422]

Looked at from this vantage-point, the long synthesis of subsequent practice conducted in section IV can be distilled into five main points:

(i) During the UN's early practice, States and UN organs seemed prepared to make some use of Article 51's potential for openness: in debates about indirect aggression, the possibility of self-defence against 'private' armed attacks that another State had supported or allowed to be conducted from its territory was discussed.

(ii) The General Assembly's Definition of Aggression constrained options for such flexibility: in it, all States agreed on a more State-centric approach that permitted asymmetrical self-defence only in exceptional settings. The flexible formulation of the exception ('substantial involvement') seemed to leave some leeway, though.

(iii) In its *Nicaragua* judgment, the International Court of Justice interpreted the 'substantial involvement' test very narrowly and

---

[420] As noted by the ILC: see 'Subsequent Practice' (n. 188), Draft Conclusion 7(1).
[421] *Ibid.*, para. 3 of the commentary to Draft Conclusion 7.
[422] *Ibid.*

largely deprived it of meaning. The *Nicaragua* approach effectively construed self-defence as a right to respond against armed attacks by another State. This approach – corroborated by the agreement on a narrow concept of attribution in the ILC's work on State responsibility – excluded the possibility of asymmetrical self-defence and therefore, at the time, pointed towards a modification of the results of the 'initial interpretation' of Article 51. It was, however, not strictly followed in the actual practice of States, which tolerated the odd instance of asymmetrical self-defence.

(iv) In the post-Cold War practice, the potential for asymmetrical self-defence is being reclaimed. The palpable change in practice is not so far recorded in framework texts or international jurisprudence of the calibre of the Definition of Aggression or the *Nicaragua* judgment. However, it is reflected in a rich body of subsequent practice that gives expression to the views of a large number of States. Insofar as these States, as a basic proposition, claim that there must be *some* room for asymmetrical self-defence outside cases of attribution, their views meet with little resistance. The more specific claim that asymmetrical self-defence should be available against States that had actively supported private armed attacks also has relatively broad support. In both respects, the recent subsequent practice neutralises the earlier, more restrictive approaches – and returns to the result of the 'initial interpretation'.

(v) Insofar as the recent practice supports a right of self-defence on the basis of broader doctrines (harbouring, loss of effective control), it meets with greater resistance. This does not mean that self-defence has been categorically excluded. Quite to the contrary, self-defence claims based on these doctrines have been tolerated or widely endorsed in a relevant number of individual instances. However, there is as yet no clear pattern suggesting under which circumstances they would be tolerated or endorsed. In the absence of clear guidance, all that can be tentatively said is that States relying on self-defence have to be particularly careful to establish the necessity of their action and in particular set out why the armed attack cannot be repelled or averted by the host State.

***

This summary suggests that over seven decades of subsequent practice under the Charter, States and UN organs have given meaning to the 'armed attack' requirement. Notwithstanding its trends, twists and turns, the subsequent practice in a number of ways helps concretise the scope of Article 51. It does so by specifying the nexus required to make a State answerable for (or requiring it to tolerate responses directed against) armed attacks by private individuals.

In two respects, the subsequent practice confirms the findings of the initial interpretation of Article 51. It recognises that there is in principle room for self-defence against non-State actors: this has been the position during most of the Charter's history, overshadowed only during the dominance of the *Nicaragua* judgment; and it clarifies that States supporting 'private' armed attacks can be targets in self-defence.

Beyond instances of State support, matters are more complex. The subsequent practice provides conflicting guidance. While there is much resistance against explicitly recognising self-defence against States harbouring non-State actors, or against States that fail to exercise control over non-State actors operating on their territory, in practice such a right is gradually being accepted in individual instances. Practice certainly no longer excludes self-defence based on a more tenuous State nexus categorically; but it offers as yet neither strong support nor clear guidance.

There are different ways of describing the resulting uncertainty. With Tom Ruys, one can fall back on a trusted formula developed in British government parlance and describe self-defence on the basis of the 'harbouring' and 'loss of effective control' doctrines as 'not unambiguously illegal'.[423] A more cautious reading would require change to be consolidated before it produces legal effects: during the 'interregnum',[424] the old law would then govern by default.[425]

A more convincing approach ought to proceed from the result of the initial inquiry, which after all points towards an asymmetric reading. In that perspective, one might view in the handling of individual cases since the end of the Cold War a willingness to 'activate' an option that was there from the beginning. This shift of perspective results in a slightly different verdict: The 'harbouring' and 'loss of effective control' doctrines no longer appear merely 'not unambiguously unlawful' – but have been accepted in individual

---

[423]   Ruys, *'Armed Attack' and Article 51 of the UN Charter* 2010 (n. 53), 531.

[424]   In Antonio Gramsci's much-quoted phrase, an interregnum marks a period when 'the old is dying and the new cannot be born': see *Selections from the Prison Notebooks of Antonio Gramsci* (New York: International Publishers, 1971). (Gramsci continues with: 'in this interregnum a great variety of morbid symptoms appear').

[425]   Corten is very clear in this respect: Corten, 'Has Practice Led to an "Agreement Between the Parties"?' 2017 (n. 350), 16.

cases and thus are no longer excluded in principle. And they have been so accepted, not as 'novel rights',[426] but on the basis of a treaty clause that has, since its entry into force, permitted, and indeed encouraged, asymmetrical readings of self-defence.

***

This final consideration yields a broader lesson and permits us to return to a point made at the outset. As noted in the Introduction, the preceding analysis is a narrow one; its exclusive focus has been on the threshold question, viz. can self-defence be invoked against attacks by non-State actors? Responses to this question are always 'in principle' responses: they clarify against which types of attacks the right of self-defence can be invoked, but do not imply that in a particular instance all the conditions for the lawful exercise of self-defence had been met. Whether such exercise has been lawful not only depends on the intensity of the prior attacks (for they have to qualify as 'armed attacks', which according to the dominant reading presupposes a certain gravity[427]), it also depends on a host of contextual factors, among them the strength of the reacting State's factual case and the persuasiveness of its claim that military action is necessary as a measure of last resort and that it be exercised on the territory of the targeted State. These contextual factors have not been the focus of the present inquiry. Yet the preceding analysis of subsequent State practice suggests that they determine whether self-defence can exceptionally be invoked on the basis of doctrines beyond complicity. It indicates that the line between lawful and unlawful exercises of self-defence can not, or no longer, be drawn on the basis of a pre-defined State nexus ('harbouring', 'support' etc.), but requires a more comprehensive assessment of the situation. The State nexus certainly forms part of this overall assessment. However, it forms a part only.

B. Implications

The case for asymmetrical self-defence, as set out in the preceding section, is of course open to challenge. It is based, as has been stated in the Introduction, on a 'best efforts' attempt to deal with one particular ('threshold') question and to ascertain the meaning of the 'armed attack' requirement. This best efforts attempt reflects the author's 'discretion'[428] in evaluating arguments pointing in

---

[426] Cf. ICJ, *Military and Paramilitary Activities* (n. 28), para. 207.
[427] See II.B.2 for brief comment.
[428] Linderfalk, 'Is Treaty Interpretation an Art or a Science?' 2015 (n. 415), 189.

different directions as much as the methodological starting-points from which the threshold question is approached.

The response offered here – even if only an 'in principle' response, which requires many further factors to be considered – of course has implications. As options for asymmetrical self-defence are being activated, a universally accepted right can be exercised on the territory of a foreign State even though that State has not committed any armed attack itself. It is no wonder that this prompts concerns about risks of abuse.

In the case of self-defence, that risk is significant because other limiting factors, and the conditions governing the exercise of the right, do not seem fully effective. The gravity requirement distinguishing the 'most grave forms of the use of force' qualifying as armed attacks[429] from 'lesser' uses of force is not easy to apply. The twin limitations of necessity and proportionality are highly dependent on the characterisation of threats and on the ready availability of evidence. International control over self-defence claims in practice remains limited: once the genie of self-defence is out of the bottle, it is not easily put back in again. All of these, to be sure, are problems that arise is relation to all self-defence claims. But the 'in principle' recognition of asymmetrical self-defence means they are to be confronted more regularly. Though non-specific, the risk of abuse is very real.

To argue that this is a risk consciously taken – by States and UN organs that, over the past decades, have activated Article 51's asymmetrical potential, fully aware of its implications – is to state the obvious, but helps little. Of equally little use are counter-factual thought experiments: of course some of the alternative legal claims discussed until the 1970s (hot pursuit, necessity) might have offered a 'safer' path towards admitting certain military responses on foreign soil, and would have been less open to abuse. As in many other controversies, the international community's strong stance against unwritten exceptions to the use of force has preserved the Charter regime with its ban on force and two recognised exceptions relatively intact[430] – but it has had the effect that assertions of a right to use force unilaterally are almost inevitably presented as self-defence claims: the 'sole avenue for legitimizing unilateral forcible action' is widely used precisely because it is the only 'safe' argumentative option.[431]

---

[429] ICJ, *Military and Paramilitary Activities* (n. 28), para. 191; and cf. *supra*, II.B.2.
[430] See Tams, 'The Use of Force against Terrorists' 2009 (n. 22), 383.
[431] See Lubell, *Extraterritorial Use of Force against Non-State Actors* 2010 (n. 51), 74; and *supra*, II.B.

What, then, can be done to mitigate the risk of abuse? Multilateral approaches are the obvious cure. The time may not be conducive to 'grand designs', but there is no lack of options. A General Assembly-sponsored attempt to produce authoritative guidance in the form '*Definition of Armed Attack*', mooted in the literature,[432] could well end in polarised debates and acrimony – but then again, the same was said about GA Res. 3314, which seems to have outlived expectations. A Security Council resolution authorising future forcible reactions against terrorists (and defining general conditions governing their lawfulness) would meet with serious concerns about executive law-making – but might offer the most obvious 'way out' of the current debate.

Below the level of 'grand designs', a number of less ambitious but nevertheless useful initiatives would be worth exploring. A more active, and more robust, debate about the necessity and proportionality of self-defence could help define the limits of forcible responses more clearly.[433] Insistence on credible evidence supporting self-defence claims could force reacting States into a public dialogue.[434] Finally, drawing on experience with targeted sanctions, institutional options could be explored. '[A] space for formal self-defence discourse [could indeed] encourag[e] States, including third States, to be explicit in their position on the scope of self-defence.'[435] None of this promises quick returns – but all of this could help curb the risk of abuse. A more robust, and more rigorous discourse among States and other stakeholders offers the best chance of curbing abuse.

***

Academic debate has been robust for decades, and frequently rigorous. As noted in the Introduction, self-defence against non-State actors is (and has been, and likely will be) one of the discipline's most prominent sites of contestation. The present study reflects that fact; significant parts of it have been in the form of an engagement with earlier writings. This engagement confirms many points made elsewhere, but it also identifies a number of blind spots and a worrying degree of methodological uncertainty. Quite apart from offering a ('best effort') response to the threshold question, the present inquiry has been an attempt to contribute to greater methodological clarity.

---

[432] Ruys, '*Armed Attack' and Article 51 of the UN Charter* 2010 (n. 53), 535 *et seq.*

[433] For proposals to this effect see Tams, 'The Necessity and Proportionality of Anti-Terrorist Self-Defence' 2013 (n. 22), 419 *et seq.*

[434] See in this respect the 'Leiden Policy Recommendations on Counter-Terrorism and International Law', *Netherlands International Law Review* 17 (2010), 531–50 (para. 44).

[435] Larissa van den Herik, '"Proceduralising" Article 51', *Heidelberg Journal of International Law* 77 (2017), 65–7 (58).

In concluding, its main findings in this respect can be summarised in six propositions:

(i) The problem of self-defence against non-State actors operating from a foreign (host) State must be addressed on the basis of the UN Charter regime governing recourse to force. As that regime is State-centric, the host State under regular circumstances cannot be ignored: self-defence against non-State actors is problematic because (and if and when) it ostensibly violates the Charter's ban against force in relation to the host State.

(ii) The challenge of appreciating armed attacks by non-State actors from within the State-centric *ius ad bellum* is essentially a problem of asymmetry. This problem can be addressed from different ('Westphalian' and 'post-Westphalian') perspectives: one assessing under which conditions a host State has to answer for private armed attacks emanating from its territory (and thus is exposed to self-defence); the other accepting that self-defence can be exercised against private attacks and inquiring under which conditions the host State would have to tolerate such exercise on self-defence on its territory. Both perspectives raise essentially the same question: they are debates about the required State nexus.

(iii) Answers to this question depend on an assessment of Article 51 of the Charter as a rule of treaty law, whose meaning is to be ascertained in a process of treaty interpretation, guided by the general principles of interpretation.

(iv) This interpretation is more than a tracing of practice. Textual, contextual, purposive and historical considerations offer a rich array of arguments that help establish the meaning of the 'armed attack' requirement. These arguments do not point in one direction and of course need to be evaluated – but they deserve careful scrutiny.

(v) Under the general principles of treaty interpretation, the subsequent practice of States and UN organs can help clarify the meaning of the 'armed attack' requirement, notably by confirming or modifying the results of the initial interpretation. Subsequent practice comprises conduct that reflects a 'common understanding' of all UN members, as well as (as a supplementary means) conduct reflecting the understanding of a more limited number of parties.

(vi) Subsequent practice over time has not followed one direction and has rarely been fully consistent. For most of the UN's history, debates about the required State nexus have explored nuances and degrees. Informed scholarship ought to reflect this; it needs to move beyond the binary logic that draws lines between the 'two main camps' of 'expansionists' and 'restrictivists', and that suggests sharp, sudden shifts from 'old' to 'new' understandings, such as 'pre-9/11' versus 'post 9/11'.

In a field as contentious as this, 'agree[ment] on method' may perhaps not really 'cure much of the current divergence of views'.[436] But it could at least render the major and long-standing debate about self-defence against non-State actors a little less confused – and perhaps make it a bit more likely for the law to affect and inform the shaping of policy. It is hoped that even those readers who disagree with the substantive findings of this study will see in it some contribution towards greater methodological clarity.

---

[436] Bianchi, 'The International Regulation of the Use of Force' 2009 (n. 20), 652.

3

Self-Defence, Pernicious Doctrines, Peremptory Norms

Mary Ellen O'Connell

I. INTRODUCTION

On 21 August 2015, British Prime Minister David Cameron authorised the killing with military force of a British national, twenty-one-year-old Reyaad Khan. Khan and two other men riding in a vehicle with him were blown to shreds by Hellfire missiles launched from a remotely piloted drone. The attack occurred in Syria, despite the fact that the United Kingdom Parliament had voted to restrict UK involvement in the Syrian Civil War. The Prime Minister declared the killings a lawful exercise of Britain's 'inherent right to self-defence'[1] against a 'very real threat'.[2] The British suspected Khan of recruiting individuals to ISIS[3] and of plotting terrorist attacks to be carried out in the UK.[4] A few days later, the United

[1]   Stephen Castle, 'Britain Says First Drone Strike in Syria Hit ISIS Suspects', *The New York Times* (8 September 2015) (A4).

[2]   Spencer Ackerman, 'Drone Strikes by UK and Pakistan Point to Obama's Counter-Terror Legacy', *The Guardian*, 9 September 2015, available at www.theguardian.com/us-news/2015/sep/09/obama-drone-strikes-counterterror-uk-pakistan. See also UK House of Lords, House of Commons, Joint Committee on Human Rights, 'The Government's Policy on the Use of Drones for Targeted Killing', Second Report of Session 2015–16, HL Paper 141, HC 574, available at www.publications.parliament.uk/pa/jt201516/jtselect/jtrights/574/574.pdf and perspectives on the Joint Committee report in the *Journal of International Law on the Use of Force* 3 (2016), 194–233. In April 2017, members of Parliament announced that the UK government had not provided key documents to an investigating committee. 'Drone Strike that Killed Reyaad Kahn, "Not Transparent"', *Al Jazeera*, 26 April 2017, available at www.aljazeera.com/news/2017/04/drone-strike-killed-reyaad-khan-transparent-170426195532654.html.

[3]   'ISIS' is an acronym for the Islamic State of Iraq and Syria, a group also known by the acronym 'ISIL', the Islamic State in Iraq and the Levant. Increasingly, the group is known as "Daesh", the Arabic form of the acronym. ISIS broke with Al-Qaeda in Iraq and has subsequently been denounced by the main Al-Qaeda organisation. Ali Soufan, *Anatomy of Terror, From the Death of Bin Laden to the Rise of the Islamic State* (New York: W. W. Norton & Co., 2017).

[4]   Less than two years after these killings, terrorists in the UK with links to ISIS succeeded in carrying out a series of attacks, killing about thirty-three people. UK authorities reportedly foiled hundreds of additional plots. Rukmini Callimachi and Laure Fourquet, 'Shrinking Turf,

States also conducted a drone attack in Syria and announced with a 'high level of confidence' that it had succeeded in killing another twenty-one-year-old British national, Junaid Hussain.[5] Hussain was also a member of ISIS, as well as a convicted computer hacker and suspected plotter.[6]

ISIS, the group to which Khan and Hussain belonged, is part of a long line of non-State organisations that have used terrorist tactics and armed force to achieve political ends. ISIS emerged after a break with another such group, Al-Qaeda,[7] and bears comparison with earlier Middle East groups such as the Palestine Liberation Organization (PLO). The PLO formed to oppose the establishment of Israel in the former British Mandate of Palestine. Israel itself came into being in part through the efforts of organisations such as the Irgun and the Stern Gang.[8] The African National Congress (ANC) formed in the 1950s to oppose white minority rule in South Africa. The ANC employed violence until its leader, Nelson Mandela, famously embraced non-violent resistance.[9] The list of examples could continue back to Antiquity.

Governments have responded to these groups in different ways. The United Kingdom and United States long took the position that lawful and effective counter-terrorism involves law enforcement measures, not military force. Their position began to shift as the Cold War ended and new weapons technology emerged. First the US and then the UK put forward new legal arguments aimed at justifying the use of military force.[10] The UK's earlier commitment to law enforcement is seen in its response to the 'Troubles' in Northern Ireland. The UK tended to treat the Irish Republican Army (IRA) and its offshoots as criminal organisations, not as insurgencies. When the UK joined Additional

---

Bigger Reach: The ISIS Plan, Britain and Iran Fixed in Group's Sights', *The New York Times* (11 June 2017) (A1).

[5] 'UK Jihadist Junaid Hussain Killed in Syria Drone Strike, Says US', *BBC*, 27 August 2015, available at www.bbc.com/news/uk-34078900. Published reports do not indicate if anyone is thought to have died alongside Hussain. Less is known about the strike than the one that killed Khan because the United States keeps such details secret. It is known that he was on the Pentagon's 'kill list' for his computer hacking ability. He posted Prime Minister Cameron's private contact information online, among other crimes. Lucy Clarke-Billings, 'British Hacker for Islamic State "Killed in Syria Drone Strike"', *Telegraph* (UK), 27 August 2015, available at www.telegraph.co.uk/news/worldnews/islamic-state/11827214/British-hacker-for-Islamic-State-Junaid-Hussain-killed-in-Syria-drone-attack.html.

[6] See previous note.

[7] Graeme Wood, 'What ISIS Really Wants', *The Atlantic*, March 2015, available at www.theatlantic.com/magazine/archive/2015/03/what-isis-really-wants/384980.

[8] Ian Black, 'Long Shadow Over Palestine Killing', *The Guardian*, 23 April 2014, available at www.theguardian.com/world/on-the-middle-east/2014/apr/23/israel-palestinian-territories.

[9] Nelson Mandela, *Long Walk to Freedom* (Austin, TX: Holt, Rinehart, Winston, 2000).

[10] The US position as of 2017 is detailed *infra*, III.C. The UK position is seen in III.B.

Protocol I to the 1949 Geneva Conventions on the protection of victims in armed conflict, it appended this understanding:

> [T]he term "armed conflict" of itself and in its context denotes a situation of a kind which is not constituted by the commission of ordinary crimes including acts of terrorism whether concerted or in isolation.[11]

The United States took a similar position, refusing to join Additional Protocol I out of concern that the Protocol treats individuals using terrorist tactics in liberation struggles as combatants.

Like the UK, the United States policy applied national criminal law to terrorist suspects and organisations. President Ronald Reagan explained that terrorists have and should have the status of criminals, not combatants or irregular fighters in armed conflict.[12] He said that to 'grant combatant status to irregular forces even if they do not satisfy the traditional requirements ... would endanger civilians among whom terrorists and other irregulars attempt to conceal themselves'.[13] Reagan took the first significant step away from this policy in 1986, however, when he ordered an air attack on Libyan military sites following violent incidents linked to the Libyan government under Muammar Gaddafi. In 1998, US President Bill Clinton extended Reagan's tactic to non-State actors, bombing Sudan and Afghanistan where Al-Qaeda, known to lack State sponsorship, had camps.[14]

In 2000, Clinton modified a presidential executive order banning assassination that had been in place since the 1970s. By doing so he removed a domestic legal obstacle to the CIA deploying the newly weaponised Predator drone to hunt for and assassinate Bin Laden.[15] The CIA failed in that attempt, and 9/11 followed. By 7 October 2001, the US and UK were at war in Afghanistan.[16] The US then began drone-launched missile attacks targeting individuals in Yemen, Pakistan, and Somalia.[17] In 2008, the CIA joined Israeli intelligence in using a car bomb to

---

[11] Reservation by the United Kingdom to Article 1, para. 4 and Article 96, para. 3 of Protocol I, available at www.icrc.org/ihl.nsf/e29be9b3462f48b8c12563110050c790/0a9e03f0f2ee757c c1256402003fb6d2?.

[12] Ronald Reagan, Letter of Transmittal, The White House (29 January 1987), reprinted in *American Journal of International Law* 81 (1987), 910–12 (911). But see Hans Peter Gasser, 'An Appeal for Ratification by the United States', *American Journal of International Law* 81 (1987), 912–25.

[13] Ronald Reagan, Letter of Transmittal (n. 12).

[14] See Jules Lobel, 'The Use of Force to Respond to Terrorist Attacks: The Bombing of Sudan and Afghanistan', *Yale Journal of International Law* 24 (1999), 537–57.

[15] Chris Woods, *Sudden Justice: America's Secret Drone Wars* (Oxford: Oxford University Press, 2015), 37.

[16] UN Doc. S/2001/946, 7 October 2001 (USA).

[17] For data on US drone attacks outside combat zones, see Jack Surle and Jessica Purkiss, 'Drone Wars: The Full Data', *The Bureau of Investigative Journalism*, 1 January 2017, available at www .thebureauinvestigates.com/stories/2017-01-01/drone-wars-the-full-data.

assassinate a member of Hezbollah in Damascus, Syria.[18] The United States has continued to expand the list of non-State actors, locations attacked, and weapons used in targeted killing operations.[19]

In 2015, the United Kingdom also abandoned its approach of treating terrorism as a law enforcement matter with its drone attack in Syria. Cameron's invocation of Article 51 in his justification fits a scholarly trend which began in the 1950s, arguing the Charter should be interpreted to allow States to use armed force in more situations than its terms allow.[20] The first proposals for such 'flexible' interpretation relied on policy arguments.[21] Over time the proposals evolved to incorporate examples of State practice, asserting that practice subsequent to the Charter's adoption is capable of altering the meaning of its terms.[22] The underlying assumption appears to be that desiderata such as security from terrorism or the advancement of democracy have a higher moral status than the prohibition on force and that the violation of an inferior principle in the pursuit of a superior one should be permitted or excused.[23]

[18] Adam Goldman and Ellen Nakashima, 'CIA and Mossad Kill a Hezbollah Figure with a Car Bomb', *The Washington Post*, 30 January 2015, available at www.washingtonpost.com/world/national-security/cia-and-mossad-killed-senior-hezbollah-figure-in-car-bombing/2015/01/30/eb b88682-968a-11e4-8005-1924ede3e54a_story.html?utm_term=.19904722f9a4.

[19] 'Targeted killing' is a term used euphemistically to replace the word 'assassination'. Nehal Bhuta, 'States of Exception: Regulating Targeted Killing in a "Global Civil War"', in Philip Alston and Euan MacDonald (eds.), *Human Rights, Intervention, and the Use of Force* (Oxford: Oxford University Press, 2008), 243–74 (246 (fn. 20)). See also Christine Gray, 'Targeted Killings: Recent US Attempts to Create a Legal Framework', *Current Legal Problems* 66 (2013), 75–106 and Nils Melzer, *Targeted Killing in International Law* (Oxford: Oxford University Press, 2008), 5.

[20] Recent references to this trend use the terms 'abusive' and 'openly instrumental', e.g., Olivier Corten, 'A Plea against the Abusive Invocation of Self-Defence as a Response to Terrorism', *EJIL Talk!*, 14 July 2016, available at www.ejiltalk.org/a-plea-against-the-abusive-invocation-of-self-defence-as-a-response-to-terrorism, and Jochen von Bernstorff, 'Drone Strikes, Terrorism and the Zombie: On the Construction of an Administrative Law of Transnational Executions', *ESIL Reflection* 5(7) (2016), available at www.esil-sedi.eu/node/1368.

[21] Christian Tams uses the term 'flexible' for this approach to interpretation. Other terms are 'broad' or 'expansionist'. For two of the original proponents of flexible interpretation from the policy perspective, see Derek Bowett, *Self-Defence in International Law* (New York: Frederick A. Praeger, 1958) and Julius Stone, *Aggression and World Order: A Critique of United Nations Theories of Aggression* (Clark, NJ: The Lawbook Exchange, 1958).

[22] For an example of this approach, see Tams in this volume, 142–3 and 90 n. 2. Tams relies for his methodology on Raphaël van Steenberghe, 'State Practice and the Evolution of the Law of Self-Defence: Clarifying the Methodological Debate', *Journal on International Law and the Use of Force* 2 (2015), 81–96. See also Michael P. Scharf, 'How the War against ISIS Changed International Law', *Case Western Reserve Journal of International Law* 48 (2016), 15–63.

[23] For several of these arguments, see Harold Koh, 'The War Powers and Humanitarian Intervention', *Houston Law Review* 53 (2016), 971–1033 (1004–15). See also Harold Koh, 'Not Illegal: But Now the Hard Part Begins', *Just Security*, 7 April 2017, available at www

This chapter examines these lines of argument. It finds each inadequate to justify a State's use of military force against non-State actors on the territory of another State, when the force is used without the territorial State's express consent. The situations under consideration are comparable to the UK and US attacks in Syria targeting ISIS members in August 2015. Section II presents a solidly evidence-based understanding of the law on the use of force against non-State actors. This reading of the law relies on UN Charter provisions and related general principles of international law. It also includes the negotiating history of the Charter, as well as resolutions and decisions of UN organs since 1945. The law prohibiting the use of force is shown to be *ius cogens*, from which no derogation is permitted. *Ius cogens* and the general principles relevant to the use of force do not emerge from the positive law sources of international law – treaty and custom – but are rather discerned, as will be discussed briefly in this section and in greater detail in section IV.

Before reaching that discussion, section III presents three prominent scholarly challenges to the understanding of the law set out in section II. These 'pernicious doctrines' rely on policy, State practice and a reassessment of international law's normative hierarchy to claim a far broader and more flexible right of States to resort to armed force against non-State actors than the analysis in section II reveals the law permits.

Section IV responds to these challenges to the law on various grounds, including, most significantly, by explaining how the methodology used by advocates of flexibility is inappropriate for analysing peremptory norms and the general principles that govern the use of force. The section will emphasize that peremptory norms are non-derogable. They are derived from ancient and universal moral principles. They are superior to contrary policies and principles of a lesser status. Each peremptory norm is equal to the other peremptory norms. They are not subject to change through the operation of standard treaty and customary international law processes for creation and modification, nor may derogation occur through reinterpretation. Peremptory norms reflect the international community's highest ethical values, expressed as legal principles. No superior laws exist to excuse or justify the breach of a peremptory norm.

Arguments to expand the right to resort to force not only conflict with the peremptory prohibition on the use of force, they also conflict with the human right to life. The International Covenant on Civil and Political Rights affirms:

.justsecurity.org/39695/illegal-hard-part-begins; Daniel Bethlehem, 'Self-Defense against an Imminent or Actual Armed Attack by Nonstate Actors', *American Journal of International Law* 106 (2012), 770–7. For an analysis of how war came to be seen as 'ethical' in the West, see Maja Zehfuss, *War and the Politics of Ethics* (Oxford: Oxford University Press, 2018).

Every human being has the inherent right to life. This right shall be protected by law. No one shall be arbitrarily deprived of his right to life.[24]

Any killing that does not conform to the law governing resort to force, the law governing the conduct of armed conflict, or peacetime criminal law, violates the right to life. It is a right so fundamental to all of law that some scholars have discerned that it, too, is *ius cogens*.[25]

The analysis in section IV also shows that even ignoring the special status of *ius cogens* and general principles, expansionist challenges to the prohibition on the use of force are unpersuasive. Under standard principles of treaty interpretation, the case for broader, more flexible rights to use force is weak at best. This should come as no disappointment, however, given the data showing that military force is a poor means of ending non-State actor violence. The confidence in military solutions reflected in the expansionist approach is misguided. The far better approach lies in promoting political engagement and respect for the rule of law.

II. EVIDENCE OF THE DURABLE MEANING OF SELF-DEFENCE

In 1945, the United Nations was founded for the express purpose of preventing war. The UN Charter preamble begins by affirming that the peoples of the United Nations desire to save 'succeeding generations from the scourge of war.' In Article 2(4) of the Charter, member States promise to 'refrain in their international relations from the threat or use of force against the territorial integrity or political independence of any State, or in any other manner inconsistent with the Purposes of the United Nations'. Chapter VII sets out the only two exceptions to the Article 2(4) prohibition. States may use force in self-defence under the restrictive terms of Article 51 or when they have UN Security Council authorisation, per Articles 39, 41 and 42.[26] Much of the rest of the Charter addresses the underlying causes of armed conflict by promoting respect for human rights, the peaceful resolution of disputes, and economic development. Beyond the Charter, principles of State responsibility as well as

---

[24]   International Covenant on Civil and Political Rights, 16 December 1966, 999 UNTS 171.

[25]   For evidence of a peremptory norm on the right to life, see Christof Heyns and Thomas Probert, 'Securing the Right to Life: A Cornerstone of the Human Rights System', *EJIL Talk!*, 11 May 2016, available at www.ejiltalk.org/securing-the-right-to-life-a-cornerstone-of-the-human-rights-system.

[26]   See Bert V. A. Röling, 'The Ban on the Use of Force and the UN Charter', in Antonio Cassese (ed.), *The Current Legal Regulation of the Use of Force* (Dordrecht: Martinus Nijhoff, 1986), 3–8 (4–5), and Jean Combacau, 'The Exception of Self-Defence in U.N. Practice', in *ibid.*, 9–38.

the general principles of necessity and proportionality constitute main aspects of the *ius ad bellum*. The meaning of relevant Charter terms and related principles are found by analysing the text of the Charter, the drafting history of the Charter, and decisions of the UN General Assembly, International Court of Justice (ICJ) and Security Council. The approach is different from that of Christian Tams who relies on these sources but also believes State practice can modify the meaning of the Charter's terms to permit more force.[27] Yet, permitting more force conflicts with the *ius cogens* status of the prohibition. *Ius cogens* and general principles are not modifiable through the impact of State practice. The law of self-defence may change over time but only in the direction of greater restrictions on the right to resort to force.[28]

A. *The Terms of the Charter*

1. The Prohibition in Article 2(4)

Article 2(4) forms the primary international legal rule with respect to the use of force. Any lawful resort to force is an exception to the Article 2(4) prohibition. The accurate approach to arguing whether a use of force is lawful begins with Article 2(4), then identifies the exception to it that makes the use justified.[29] This structural aspect of international law on the use of force is significant for several reasons. Exceptions to a general rule tend to be narrow.[30] In case of doubt as to whether an exception applies, standard legal interpretation

---

[27] Tams in this volume, 142–3.
[28] See *infra*, section IV.C.
[29] '[M]ost commentators begin the process of exegesis with Art. 2(4), in deference to the paramount concern of the Charter with the maintenance of "international peace and security". It then becomes desirable to interpret the word "force" in Art. 2(4) at least widely enough to ensure that any significant use of military force is banned; and to give the acknowledged exception created by Art. 51 a correspondingly narrow meaning.' Röling, 'The Ban on the Use of Force and the UN Charter' 1986 (n. 26), 4–5.
[30] Cf. the General Agreement on Tariffs and Trade, 15 April 1994, 1867 UNTS 187, Article XX, which provides exceptions to the general principles supporting free trade. The WTO's Dispute Settlement Body consistently holds that Article XX is to be construed narrowly. See e.g. the explanation of how to interpret exceptions to general treaty rules in WTO Appellate Body, 'Import Prohibition of Certain Shrimp and Shrimp Products', Appellate Body Report of 12 October 1998, WT/DS58/AB/R. The Dispute Settlement Body's holding is consistent with common legal maxims derived from Roman Law, such as *singularia non sunt extendenda*, which can be translated as exceptions should not be applied extensively, and *quae communi legi derogant stricte interpretantur*, derogations from the common law should be interpreted narrowly. See Aleksander Peczenik, 'Analogia Legis. Analogy from Statutes in Continental Law', *Logique & Analyse* 14 (1971), 329–36 (333–4) and Ward E. Lattin, 'Legal Maxims, and Their Use in Statutory Interpretations', *Georgetown Law Journal* 26 (1938), 1–16 (7–8).

supports the primary rule in distinction to the exception. Also, exceptions are interpreted in light of the object and purpose of the primary rule.

Despite this understanding of Article 2(4), within a few years of 1945, several international law scholars began offering arguments aimed at limiting Article 2(4)'s scope. Perhaps the best-known early scholar advocating a broader right to resort to force was the University of Sydney's Julius Stone. He was a harsh critic of the UN, writing an opinion piece in 1950 about the new organisation titled, 'A Mad Hatter's World Tea Party'.[31] Soon after the op-ed, he put forward an interpretation of Article 2(4) that functionally eliminated its restrictions on a State's right to use force.[32] In 1958, Stone published a book defending Israel's attack on Egypt during the Suez Crisis, asserting that Article 2(4) only restricted a State's use of force aimed at interfering with the territorial integrity or political independence of the State being attacked.[33] Stone did not take Article 2(4) as his starting place, but Article 51, casting it as a permissive right, a tool to seek justice, rather than as an exception to a general prohibition.[34]

Stone plainly wanted to expand the right for some States to use more military force irrespective of the Charter's terms. He took no account of the objects and purposes of the Charter, of the negotiating history,[35] or of the status of Article 2(4) as *ius cogens*. He attempted to undermine the legitimacy of the Charter restrictions on the use of force by tainting them as mere concessions to great power demands.[36] As will be discussed next, Article 51 was a concession, but to Latin American States, not to Stone's great powers.

> Several prominent American cases interpreting international law provide additional examples. In *Parsons & Whittemore Overseas Co. v. Société Générale De L'Industrie Du Papier (RATKA)*, 508 F.2d 969, 973-4 (US 2d Cir. Ct. of Appeal 1974), the Court narrowly applied the public policy exception in the United Nations Convention on the Recognition and Enforcement of Foreign Arbital Awards. In *Siderman de Blake v. Republic Argentina*, 965 F.2d 699, 720 (US 9th Cir. Ct. of Appeal 1992), the Court interpreted the waiver of sovereign immunity narrowly, which 'conforms to the general rule of a narrow construction of the exception'.

31   Julius Stone, 'A Mad Hatter's World Tea Party', *The Argus* (7 December 1950), 2, available at www.trove.nla.gov.au/newspaper/article/23032557.

32   Julius Stone, 'Force and the Charter in the Seventies', *Syracuse Journal of International Law and Commerce* 2 (1974), 1–17. Stone comments on page 6 of this article that he developed his interpretation in the early 1950s. See also Julius Stone, *Quest for Survival: The Role of Law and Foreign Policy* (Cambridge, MA: Harvard University Press, 1961), 40–56.

33   Stone, *Aggression and World Order* 1958 (n. 21), 100–3. See also a perspective that the Charter instituted a permissive regime respecting force, not a restrictive one. Ian Hurd, 'The Permissive Power of the Ban on War', *European Journal of International Security* 2 (2017), 1–18.

34   Stone, *Aggression and World Order* 1958 (n. 21), 43, 95, 181–3. See also Röling, 'The Ban on the Use of Force and the UN Charter' 1986 (n. 26), 4–5.

35   Vienna Convention on the Law of Treaties (VCLT), 23 May 1969, 1155 UNTS 331, Articles 31 and 32.

36   Stone, 'Force and the Charter' 1974 (n. 32), 13.

2. The Exception in Article 51

Article 51 was a late addition to the Charter and was drafted not just as an exception to Article 2(4), but in deference to the Security Council's power to authorise the use of force. States may use force in individual or collective self-defence if an armed attack occurs until the Security Council acts. It is worth setting out the entirety of Article 51 to underscore the restricted and contingent nature of the exception for self-defence:

> Nothing in the present Charter shall impair the inherent right of individual or collective self-defence if an armed attack occurs against a member of the United Nations, until the Security Council has taken measures necessary to maintain international peace and security. Measures taken by members in the exercise of this right of self-defence shall be immediately reported to the Security Council and shall not in any way affect the authority and responsibility of the Security Council under the present Charter to take at any time such action as it deems necessary in order to maintain or restore international peace and security.

'Self-defence' is a term of art in international law and a term that was well known to the drafters of Article 51. In an exercise of lawful self-defence, a State that is a victim of an armed attack may counter-attack using significant offensive military force on the territory of the State legally responsible for the initial, triggering attack.[37]

Article 51 is understandably restrictive in light of Article 2(4) and the role created for the Security Council. Article 51 qualifies self-defence as an 'inherent right', or '*droit naturel*' in the French version of the Charter, but one that is severely limited. In the same sentence in which self-defence is referred to as an 'inherent right', Article 51 restricts the exercise of that inherent right to cases where an 'armed attack occurs'. The armed attack requirement is an objective and restrictive condition on the use of force. It is a critical feature of the practical design of the Charter. The French version of Article 51 indicates an even higher threshold. Force may be used in self-defence not just upon an armed attack but after '*agression armée*' (armed aggression – more than a single attack). Article 51 provides further restrictions by requiring States to immediately report their actions to the Security Council. The use of force in self-defence is envisaged as a short-term emergency measure until the Security Council can act.

---

[37] Mary Ellen O'Connell, 'Lawful Self-Defense to Terrorism', *University of Pittsburgh Law Review* 63 (2002), 889–908 (889–90).

B. The Drafting History of the Charter

Given the early arguments by Stone in favour of interpreting the Charter so as to expand the right to use force, it is helpful to return briefly to the drafting history to indicate the intentions behind the words actually chosen. In 1938, United States President Franklin Roosevelt assigned a US State Department official the job of drafting a new treaty for a new world organisation to replace the League of Nations, which had failed to prevent the Second World War.[38] Article 51 was added in 1945 during the final negotiating session in San Francisco.[39] The drafters did not intend to provide a permissive basis for resorting to force as Stone and others have contended. The purpose was to allow the creation of an organisation prepared to act in collective self-defence should the need arise.

Article 51 was a late addition, not part of the plans for the Charter from the outset, in contrast to Article 2(4). The new organisation charter was to have a more straightforward and direct prohibition on the use of force than the Covenant of the League of Nations.[40] The new prohibition was inspired by a renewed global commitment to ending war, as well as the major US diplomatic initiative in the inter-war period, the Kellogg–Briand Pact. The Kellogg–Briand Pact or Pact of Paris was concluded and came into force in 1928 with just two substantive paragraphs:

> Article I. The High Contracting Parties solemnly declare in the names of their respective peoples that they condemn recourse to war for the solution of international controversies, and renounce it, as an instrument of national policy in their relations with one another.
>
> Article II. The High Contracting Parties agree that the settlement or solution of all disputes or conflicts of whatever nature or of whatever origin they may be, which may arise among them, shall never be sought except by pacific means.[41]

---

[38] Stephen C. Schlesinger, *Act of Creation: The Founding of the United Nations: A Story of Superpowers, Secret Agents, Wartime Allies and Enemies, and Their Quest for a Peaceful World* (Boulder, CO: Westview Press, 2003).

[39] *The United Nations Conference on International Organization, San Francisco, California, 25 April to 26 June 1945 – selected documents* (Washington: US Government Printing Office, 1946), 334–5.

[40] See League of Nations, Covenant of the League of Nations, 28 April 1919, Article X: 'The Members of the League undertake to respect and preserve as against external aggression the territorial integrity and existing political independence of all Members of the League. In case of any such aggression or in case of any threat or danger of such aggression the Council shall advise upon the means by which this obligation shall be fulfilled.'

[41] Treaty for the Renunciation of War as an Instrument of National Policy, 27 August 1928 (United States Department of State, Treaty Series, No. 796) [Kellogg–Briand Pact]. The US State Department's Office of the Historian offers this interpretation of the Pact: 'After the severe losses of the First World War, the idea of declaring war to be illegal was immensely

The Kellogg–Briand Pact says nothing about self-defence, but scholars have commented they assumed the Pact did not interfere with the customary international law right of self-defence.[42] Like the Pact, the early drafts of the Charter had no reference to self-defence, which is why the Latin American States requested that it be added. The main Charter innovation over the League was the introduction of a powerful Security Council authorised to take measures to respond to breaches of international peace and security.[43] It would be the new council's job to respond to any violations of Article 2(4).

The US not only drafted the Charter, it organised and led the negotiating conference in 1945 at San Francisco to reach agreement on the final version. The records from San Francisco clearly indicate the understanding that Article 2(4) was intended to cover the use of armed force in distinction to more general forceful or coercive measures not involving the use of force, such as economic sanctions or minimal uses of force involved in law enforcement.[44] The States involved expressed their interest in banning the first use of military force beyond any *de minimis* use.[45] The United States had carefully chosen the terms of Article 2(4). The references to 'territorial integrity', 'political independence' and, especially, 'in any other manner inconsistent with the Purposes of the United Nations' were meant to generate a broad prohibition. A member of the US delegation, in responding to a question by the Brazilian delegation on Article 2(4)'s scope, said that 'the authors of the original text intended an absolute all-inclusive prohibition; the phrase "or in any other manner" was designed to insure that there should be no loopholes.'[46]

---

popular in international public opinion. Because the language of the pact established the important point that only wars of aggression – not military acts of self-defence – would be covered under the pact, many nations had no objections to signing it'; available at https://history.state.gov/milestones/1921-1936/kellogg.

[42] See, e.g., Hans Kelsen, 'Collective Security and Collective Self-Defence under the Charter of the United Nations', *American Journal of International Law* 42 (1948), 783–96.

[43] Charter of the United Nations, 24 October 1945, 1 UNTS XVI, Articles 39, 41 and 42.

[44] *The United Nations Conference on International Organization, San Francisco, California, 1945* (n. 39), 334 (discussing the rejection of a proposal by Brazil to extend the prohibition on force to economic coercion).

[45] A *de minimis* use of force for law enforcement might involve a government vessel firing shots across the bow of a trespassing fishing vessel. See Mary Ellen O'Connell, 'The Prohibition of Force', in Nigel D. White and Christian Henderson (eds.), *The Research Handbook on International Conflict and Security Law* (Cheltenham: Edward Elgar, 2013), 89–119. But see Tom Ruys, 'The Meaning of Force and the Boundaries of the *Jus Ad Bellum*: Are Minimal Uses of Force Excluded from UN Charter Article 2(4)?', *American Journal of International Law* 108 (2014), 159–210 (159).

[46] *The United Nations Conference on International Organization, San Francisco, California 1945* (n. 39), 334–5.

When the Latin American States arrived in San Francisco, they were in the midst of organising a new collective security system for the Americas. They became concerned during the conference that the terms of Article 2(4) would restrict the right of a State to come to the assistance of a State attacked in violation of the new prohibition. They then requested an additional provision making it clear that members of the Rio Treaty Organization would be permitted to treat an attack on one of them as an attack on all.[47] Article 2(4) could be construed as requiring a State to get Security Council authorisation prior to assisting another State fighting in self-defence. Thus, for the purposes of allowing the Rio collective self-defence arrangement to proceed upon an armed attack, Article 51 was added to the Charter permitting assistance pending Security Council action.[48]

The US delegation provided the draft of Article 51, placing it in Chapter VII of the Charter, which otherwise sets out the Security Council's power to respond to breaches of international peace. The formulation has been criticised as clumsy,[49] but it accomplished three objectives: it preserved the far-reaching general prohibition on the use of force in Article 2(4) by limiting the right to a response to an armed attack; it clarified the right of other States to join in collective self-defence, and it maintained the Security Council's supremacy in all matters related to the use of force.

The US delegation discussed the possibility of allowing resort to self-defence in anticipation of an armed attack. This, however, was rejected. One member of the delegation, Senator Harold Stassen, explained: 'We did not want exercised the right of self-defence before an armed attack.'[50] Indeed, only a narrow right of self-defence would be consistent with other provisions of the Charter. In addition to the general prohibition on force in Article 2(4), the provisions of Chapters VII and VIII giving the Security Council principal authority over peace and security made sense only in the case of a narrow

---

[47] Two years later, in 1947, parties to the Rio Treaty provided in Article 3: 'The High Contracting Parties agree that an armed attack by any State against an American State shall be considered as an attack against all the American States and, consequently, each one of the said Contracting Parties undertakes to assist in meeting the attack in the exercise of the inherent right of individual or collective self-defence recognised by Article 51 of the Charter of the United Nations'; Inter-American Treaty of Reciprocal Assistance, 2 September 1947, 21 UNTS 77, 324.

[48] The United Nations Conference on International Organization, San Francisco, California, 25 April to 26 June 1945, Commission III: Security Council, Summary Report of Fourth Meeting of Committee III/4 (23 May 1945), Volume 12, 680–2.

[49] See generally, Stone, *Aggression and World Order* 1958 (n. 21).

[50] See Minutes from the 48th Meeting of the US Delegation of 20 May 1945, *Foreign Relations of the United States* 1 (1945), 813–23 (818).

exception for the use of force by States acting independently of the Security Council. The terms of Article 51 reflect the Security Council's central role, as does Chapter VIII's Article 53 requiring prior Security Council authorisation for all uses of force by an organisation other than one responding in collective self-defence as provided for in Article 51.[51]

The UN Charter's drafters were well aware of the justification Axis States had used for violating the League Covenant and Kellogg–Briand Pact during World War II. They used arguments developed by their lawyers based on self-defence. The German Reich strived for 'Lebensraum' in order to ensure – so they claimed – survival.[52] Germany invaded Norway and the Low Countries citing a right of self-defence to pre-empt any future attacks by those States.[53] Imperial Japan made similar arguments for its territorial aggression in Asia aimed at securing vital natural resources, especially oil.[54] The new United Nations would permit unilateral self-defence only in cases where objective evidence of an emergency existed for the entire world to see, namely an armed attack. Other, less tangible or immediate threats required the collective scrutiny of the Security Council before the use of force would be permitted. The collective deliberation of the Council replaced the unilateral judgment of the potential victim.

C. The Understanding in UN Organs

Three UN organs have regularly taken up consideration of the Charter principles on the use of force. Their deliberations, resolutions, and decisions are the most relevant sources for understanding the terms of the Charter on

[51] Article 53 UN Charter: 'The Security Council shall, where appropriate, utilise such regional arrangements or agencies for enforcement action under its authority. But no enforcement action shall be taken under regional arrangements or by regional agencies without the authorisation of the Security Council, with the exception of measures against any enemy state, as defined in paragraph 2 of this Article, provided for pursuant to Article 107 or in regional arrangements directed against renewal of aggressive policy on the part of any such state, until such time as the Organisation may, on request of the Governments concerned, be charged with the responsibility for preventing further aggression by such a state.'

[52] See Gerhard L. Weinberg, The Foreign Policy of Hitler's Germany; Diplomatic Revolution in Europe, 1933–36 (Chicago, IL: University of Chicago Press, 1970), 26–7.

[53] Joachim von Ribbentrop, a foreign minister in the Third Reich, was indicted for, among other crimes, providing a legal justification of pre-emptive self-defence for the invasions of Norway and the Low Countries. International Military Tribunal, Trial of the Major War Criminals Before the International Military Tribunal, 14 November 1945–1 October 1946, vol. X, 68–70.

[54] See Michael A. Barnhart, Japan Prepares for Total War: The Search for Economic Security, 1919–1941 (Ithaca, NY: Cornell University Press, 1987), 144–5.

self-defence against non-State actors. Various efforts of the Secretary-General have been relevant and will be mentioned as well. Again, the discussion below seeks to show how these important bodies have understood the Charter, not how their activities purport to modify it.

1. The General Assembly

In 1970, on the twenty-fifth anniversary of the adoption of the UN Charter, the General Assembly adopted its Declaration on the Principles of International Law Concerning Friendly Relations and Cooperation Among States in Accordance with the Charter of the United Nations.[55] The first three principles in the Declaration relate to the use of force and generally follow the basic understanding outlined above. These include:

(a) The principle that States shall refrain in their international relations from the threat or use of force against the territorial integrity or political independence of any State, or in any other manner inconsistent with the purposes of the United Nations,

(b) The principle that States shall settle their international disputes by peaceful means in such a manner that international peace and security and justice are not endangered,

(c) The duty not to intervene in matters within the domestic jurisdiction of any State, in accordance with the Charter.[56]

The elaboration of Principle (a) in the Declaration includes the statement:

Nothing in the foregoing paragraphs shall be construed as enlarging or diminishing in any way the scope of the provisions of the Charter concerning cases in which the use of force is lawful.[57]

Principle (b)'s further elaboration emphasises that

armed intervention and all other forms of interference or attempted threats against the personality of the State or against its political, economic and cultural elements, are in violation of international law.[58]

---

[55] Declaration on Principles of International Law concerning Friendly Relations and Co-operation among States in accordance with the Charter of the United Nations, GA Res. 2625 (XXV) of 24 October 1970.

[56] *Ibid.*

[57] *Ibid.*

[58] *Ibid.*

The comment to Principle (c) includes the duty on all States 'to refrain from organizing, instigating, assisting or participating in acts of civil strife or terrorist acts in another State'.[59] At the end, the Declaration reaffirms that States have a duty to fulfil their Charter obligations in good faith together with their general obligations under international law.

While the Declaration generally supports the Charter as adopted, it also affirms the right of self-determination in a way some scholars see as supporting a right to intervene on behalf of non-State actors fighting for regime change or secession. If the analysis of the prohibition offered here is accurate, if such intervention involves military force it violates Article 2(4). As will be discussed in the final section of the chapter, section V, support for self-determination should not involve military force.

Four years later, the General Assembly adopted the Definition of Aggression. In the preamble to the Definition, the General Assembly expressed the view that 'aggression is the most serious and dangerous form of the illegal use of force.'[60] During the preparatory discussions of the Definition, delegates recalled that the Nuremberg Tribunal referred to aggression as the 'supreme international crime'.[61] The Versailles Treaty of 1919 had provided for a special tribunal to try the German Kaiser for 'a supreme offense against international morality and the sanctity of treaties' in waging the First World War.[62] These references to 'supreme' and 'international morality' reflect an understanding by member States of the peremptory character of the prohibition on force.

In defining this most dangerous form of illegal force, the General Assembly incorporated two approaches. It provided both a general purpose description in Article 1 as well as an illustrative set of examples in Article 3. The Article 1 description is based on Article 2(4). It describes aggression as 'the use of armed force by a State against the sovereignty, territorial integrity, or political independence of another State, or in any other manner inconsistent with the Charter of the United Nations . . . '. Article 2 then provides that any first use of force in violation of the UN Charter is *prima facie* evidence of an act of aggression. The acts listed in Article 3 'are not exhaustive and the Security Council may determine that other acts constitute aggression under the provisions of the Charter'. Thus, the General Assembly foresaw the expansion of the

---

[59] *Ibid.*
[60] Definition of Aggression, GA Res. 3314 (XXIX) of 14 December 1974, preamble.
[61] International Military Tribunal (Nuremberg), Judgment and Sentences, 1 October 1946, reprinted in *American Journal of International Law* 41 (1947), 172–333 (186).
[62] The Treaty of Versailles, 28 June 1919, relevant provisions reprinted in Mary O'Connell, *International Law and the Use of Force* (New York: Foundation Press, 2nd edn., 2009), 142.

list in the future. There is no hint of the possibility of moving in the other direction.

Acts constituting aggression trigger the right of self-defence when the act is on a significant scale, such as invasion of territory, bombardment of territory, blockade of ports, attack on air, sea or land forces, and the 'sending ... of armed bands, groups, irregulars or mercenaries, which carry out acts of armed force against another State of such gravity as to amount to the acts listed above, or its substantial involvement therein'.[63] The last example is perhaps most relevant respecting non-State actors. The term 'sending' is critical. It refers to a sovereign State sending a group to fight, which implicates a sovereign State's responsibility. The Definition does not support self-defence against a State bearing no legal responsibility for a non-State actor's conduct. The Definition also introduces some conceptual and normative confusion. It uses language similar to the Declaration on Friendly Relations respecting assistance to non-State actors, confirming their right to 'struggle' and to 'seek and receive support'.[64] To be consistent with the Charter, outside assistance to groups seeking to expel colonial or occupying powers would have to be non-military. The Definition of Aggression provides little solid evidence in support of arguments seeking to expand the right to use force. It is another intentionally vague provision that can hardly alter a treaty term, even one open to change.[65]

In 2003, following the invasion of Iraq by the United States, United Kingdom, Poland, and Australia, the then UN Secretary-General undertook a review of UN principles and institutional processes related to the use of force. The Secretary-General's High Level Panel on United Nations Reform, reporting in December 2004,[66] and the Secretary-General's own report of March 2005,[67] both discussed some of the expansionist proposals but reaffirmed that any lawful

---

[63] Definition of Aggression 1974 (n. 60).

[64] *Ibid.*, Article 7.

[65] The Definition of Aggression has remained an important topic as the UN moved forward over the years toward a permanent international criminal court to succeed the Nuremberg and Tokyo Tribunals. Several scholars and government officials have sought to restrict future prosecutions of the crime of aggression consistently with their advocacy for expanding the right to use force. E.g. Harold Hongju Koh and Todd F. Buchwald, 'The Crime of Aggression: The United States Perspective', *American Journal of International Law* 109 (2015), 257–323; John Bellinger, 'USG Concerns with the ICC Aggression Amendments', *Lawfare*, 5 January 2016, available at www.lawfareblog.com/usg-concerns-icc-aggression-amendments; Claus Kress and Leonie von Holtzendorff, 'The Kampala Compromise on the Crime of Aggression', *Journal of International Criminal Justice* 8 (2010), 1179–217.

[66] See Secretary-General's High-Level Panel on Threats, Challenges and Change, *A More Secure World: Our Shared Responsibility*, UN Doc. A/59/565, 2 December 2004.

[67] Report of the Secretary-General, *In Larger Freedom: Towards Development, Security and Human Rights for All*, UN Doc. A/59/2005, 21 March 2005.

use of force outside the terms of Article 51 required Security Council authorisation. These restatements of the Charter were fully accepted at the 2005 United
Nations World Summit:

> 78. We reiterate the importance of promoting and strengthening the multi-
> lateral process and of addressing international challenges and problems by
> strictly abiding by the Charter and the principles of international law, and
> further stress our commitment to multilateralism.
>
> 79. We reaffirm that the relevant provisions of the Charter are sufficient to
> address the full range of threats to international peace and security.
> We further reaffirm the authority of the Security Council to mandate coer-
> cive action to maintain and restore international peace and security.
> We stress the importance of acting in accordance with the purposes and
> principles of the Charter.[68]

The only relaxation of the Charter's express terms to be found in the Outcome
Document links the Security Council's existing authority to act to restore
'international peace and security' to a broader understanding of what disturbs
international peace:

> 139. The international community, through the United Nations, also has the
> responsibility to use appropriate diplomatic, humanitarian and other peace-
> ful means, in accordance with Chapters VI and VIII of the Charter, to help to
> protect populations from genocide, war crimes, ethnic cleansing and crimes
> against humanity. In this context, we are prepared to take collective action, in
> a timely and decisive manner, through the Security Council, in accordance
> with the Charter, including Chapter VII, on a case-by-case basis and in
> cooperation with relevant regional organizations as appropriate, should
> peaceful means be inadequate and national authorities are manifestly failing
> to protect their populations.

The Security Council has long acted with the understanding that its mandate
to take measures to restore international peace and security covers humanitarian crises. The Outcome Document confirms this in Paragraph 139.[69]

Otherwise, the Outcome Document generally supports the terms of the
Charter as adopted. Four years later, however, in 2009, the Secretary-General

---

[68] 2005 World Summit Outcome, UN Doc. A/RES/60/1, 24 October 2005.

[69] See section II. The Council is limited by the general principles of necessity, proportionality,
and attribution as obligations restricting the use of force regardless of the actor carrying out
or authorising the force. For a discussion of the Security Council's obligations to comply
with relevant international law outside the Charter, see Anne Peters, 'Article 25', in
Bruno Simma, Daniel-Erasmus Khan, Andreas Paulus and Georg Nolte (eds.),
The Charter of the United Nations: A Commentary (Oxford: Oxford University Press, 3rd
edn., 2012), vol. I, 787–854 (826–7).

introduced some uncertainty respecting the scope of Member State rights to use force without Security Council authorisation. In his Report on implementing aspects of the World Summit Outcome, Ban Ki-Moon asserted:

> When a State refuses to accept international prevention and protection assistance, commits egregious crimes and violations relating to the responsibility to protect and fails to respond to less coercive measures, it is, in effect, challenging the international community to live up to its own responsibilities under paragraph 139 of the Summit Outcome. Such collective measures could be authorized by the Security Council under Articles 41 or 42 of the Charter, by the General Assembly under the 'Uniting for peace' procedure ... or by regional or subregional arrangements under Article 53, with the prior authorization of the Security Council.[70]

This formulation suggests the General Assembly may authorise the use of force under the terms of its Uniting for Peace Resolution.[71] The Secretary-General does not clearly support this position, nor could he do so consistently with the terms of the Charter. Under the Charter, the Security Council alone authorises the use of military force. The General Assembly may recommend action that is already lawful in the area of the use of force, such as coordinating certain types of economic sanctions or organising peacekeeping missions that have been authorised by the Security Council or have the consent of all parties to a conflict. The Charter does not support any wider authority. The Report's vague reference stands in contrast to the World Summit Outcome Document's clear confirmation of UN members' understanding of what the Charter means respecting the use of force. In the years since the Report, the General Assembly has not attempted to authorise force.

More specifically with respect to terrorism and terrorist non-State actors, the General Assembly has consistently reiterated that terrorism is a form of crime, not armed conflict. The General Assembly has had primary responsibility for action against terrorism because of this classification. In a 1 July 2016 resolution adopted in connection with a review of the UN's counter-terrorism efforts, the only reference to the use of military force is this provision, in which the General Assembly,

> 21. *Urges* Member States to ensure that any measures taken or means employed to counter terrorism, including the use of remotely piloted aircraft, comply with their obligations under international law, including the Charter,

---

[70] Report of the Secretary-General, *Implementing the Responsibility to Protect*, UN Doc. A/63/ 677, 12 January 2009.

[71] GA Res. 377 (V) of 3 November 1950.

human rights law and international humanitarian law, in particular the principles of distinction and proportionality.[72]

The focus of the General Assembly has been on law enforcement efforts, cooperation among States, education, and ending the financing of terrorist groups. The attempt to adopt a comprehensive treaty against terrorism along these lines has not yet succeeded owing to disagreement over the definition of terrorism, not on the effective ways of countering it.[73] Some member States do not want violent acts of national liberation groups to count as terrorism. Despite this persistent disagreement, the approach to terrorism has a high level of consensus. The 2016 resolution stresses 'that a national criminal justice system based on respect for human rights and the rule of law, due process and fair trial guarantees is one of the best means for effectively countering terrorism and ensuring accountability'.[74]

2. The International Court of Justice

The UN General Assembly's most important resolutions relevant to the use of force, the Declaration on Friendly Relations and the Definition of Aggression, support the Charter's terms based on the meaning intended in 1945. During the committee and plenary debates to draft the resolutions, member States tended to stress the original understanding of the Charter as drafted, not examples of State practice or other arguments to justify new meanings for terms. The ICJ has taken the same approach in use of force cases with one apparent exception. In the *Nicaragua* case, the ICJ did delve into what it called State practice.[75] Yet, the important examples of practice it relied upon turned out to be the same General Assembly resolutions that sought an authentic understanding of terms rather than reviewing the practice of States following the adoption of

---

[72] UN Global Counter-Terrorism Strategy Review, GA Res A/70/291 of 1 July 2016.

[73] The UN General Assembly established an *ad hoc* committee tasked with finally ending the impasse with this mandate: 'In its resolution 71/151 of 13 December 2016, the General Assembly decided to recommend that the Sixth Committee, at the seventy-second session of the General Assembly, establish a working group with a view to finalizing the process on the draft comprehensive convention on international terrorism as well as discussions on the item included in its agenda by Assembly resolution 54/110 concerning the question of convening a high-level conference under the auspices of the United Nations (para. 24)'; Ad Hoc Committee Established by UN GA Res. 51/210 of 17 December 2016, legal.un.org/committees/terrorism/.

[74] UN Global Counter-Terrorism Strategy Review 2016 (n. 72).

[75] ICJ, *Military and Paramilitary Activities in and against Nicaragua* (Nicaragua v. United States), Merits, Judgment of 27 June 1986, ICJ Reports 1986, 14, paras. 184–6.

the Charter in 1945. Beyond the resolutions, the Court looked to condemnation of violations of the Charter, an approach consistent with the
Charter prohibition on the use of force having a status beyond customary
international law. It also restated the view of the International Law
Commission as well as the two parties to the case that Article 2(4) is
a peremptory norm.[76]

The ICJ's first judgment involving the use of force by States was *Corfu
Channel*, decided in 1948.[77] Albanian shore batteries had fired on British
naval vessels navigating through the channel formed by the Island of
Corfu and the Greek and Albanian coasts. When the British navigated
through the channel again to assert its right to do so, its ships struck
marine mines. The British then sent minesweepers to collect evidence
for the case it brought against Albania at the ICJ. The Court found that
both Albania and the UK violated international law in the incident.
The Court found no violation of Article 2(4). The forceful actions involved
were presumably below the Article 2(4) threshold. Albania violated the UK
right, which existed in 1948, to traverse the channel. Albania also owed the
UK a duty under principles of humanity to warn of the marine mines.
The UK, on the other hand, had violated Albania's sovereignty by sweep-
ing for mines, regardless of the purpose, without Albania's consent.
'Between independent States, respect for territorial sovereignty is an essential foundation of international relations. ... [T]he Court must declare
that the action of the British Navy constituted a violation of Albanian
sovereignty.'[78]

In 1986, the Court delivered its judgment in the *Nicaragua* case, which was
its first involving a violation of Article 2(4) and a claim to self-defence.[79]
The judgment affirmed that self-defence is an inherent or natural right of
States,[80] but also one to 'be regarded as limited and legitimated by law', in
particular by the terms of Article 51 itself.[81] The Court has subsequently

---

[76]   *Ibid.*, para. 190.
[77]   ICJ, *Corfu Channel* (United Kingdom v. Albania), Merits, Judgment of 9 April 1949, ICJ
       Reports 1949, 4.
[78]   *Ibid.*, 35. The Court said regarding the British claim of a right to enter Albanian waters to
       collect evidence: '[T]he alleged right of intervention [w]as the manifestation of a policy of
       force, such as has, in the past, given rise to most serious abuses and such as cannot, whatever be
       the present defects in international organization, find a place in international law.'
[79]   ICJ, *Military and Paramilitary Activities* (n. 75), 14.
[80]   *Ibid.*, para. 176.
[81]   Oscar Schachter, 'Self-Defense and the Rule of Law', *American Journal of International Law*
       83 (1989), 259–77 (266, 277).

confirmed these statements in *Nuclear Weapons*,[82] *Oil Platforms*,[83] *The Wall*[84] and *Congo*.[85]

A) THE CLASSIFICATION OF SELF-DEFENCE In *Nicaragua*, the Court could not apply the Charter directly because the US had made a reservation to the ICJ's jurisdiction that restricted consideration of certain treaties. The Court undertook to find the law of self-defence in customary international law but in a way that was compatible with discerning it to also be a peremptory norm. It observed:

> Article 2, paragraph 4, of the Charter of the United Nations ... is frequently referred to in statements by State representatives as being not only a principle of customary international law but also a fundamental or cardinal principle of such law. The International Law Commission, ... expressed the view that 'the law of the Charter concerning the prohibition of the use of force in itself constitutes a conspicuous example of a rule in international law having the character of *jus cogens*' ... The United States, in its Counter-Memorial on the questions of jurisdiction and admissibility, found it material to quote the views of scholars that this principle is a 'universal norm', a 'universal international law', a 'universally recognized principle of international law', and a 'principle of *jus cogens*'.[86]

The Court did not explain the method to be used with respect to identifying peremptory norms. The Court's methodological focus was rather on the development of customary international law.[87] Alexander Orakhelashvili suggests that the method for finding a peremptory norm is basically the same as that used to find a rule of custom, but that the evidence of practice must be stronger and the *opinio iuris* must relate to the status of *ius cogens*.[88] The *Nicaragua* judgment is in his view compatible with the finding that

---

82 ICJ, *Legality of the Threat or Use of Nuclear Weapons*, Advisory Opinion of 6 January 1996, ICJ Reports 1996, 226.
83 ICJ, *Oil Platforms* (Islamic Republic of Iran v. United States), Judgment of 6 November 2003, ICJ Reports 2003, 161.
84 ICJ, *Legal Consequences of the Construction of a Wall in the Occupied Palestinian Territory*, Advisory Opinion of 9 July 2004, ICJ Reports 2004, 136.
85 ICJ, *Armed Activities in the Territory of the Congo* (Democratic Republic of the Congo v. Uganda), Judgment of 19 December 2005, ICJ Reports 2005, 168.
86 ICJ, *Military and Paramilitary Activities* (n. 75), para. 190.
87 *Ibid.*, paras. 172–86.
88 Orakhelashvili cites the provision of Article 53 VCLT that *ius cogens* reflect 'acceptance and recognition by the international community as a whole'; Alexander Orakhelashvili, 'Changing *Jus Cogens* Through State Practice? – The Case of the Prohibition of the Use of Force and Its Exceptions', in Marc Weller (ed.), *The Oxford Handbook of the Use of Force in International Law* (Oxford: Oxford University Press, 2015), 157–78 (165).

Articles 2(4) and 51 form a rule that is both *ius cogens* and customary international law.[89] Section III will discuss the methodology indicated in international law for identifying *ius cogens*. For present purposes, suffice it to say that
peremptory norms are distinctive from rules of customary international law.
They are not a category of 'super' custom. Some *ius cogens* norms may have
insufficient affirmative State practice to qualify as customary international
law, and, yet, they are still binding. The ICJ found plenty of evidence that
Articles 2(4) and 51 fit the definition of customary international law in addition
to being *ius cogens*. The Court could have also made clear that while customary rules may change with changing State practice, peremptory norms do not.
The US reservation, however, only required the Court to apply customary
international law. That is all it had to do in *Nicaragua*, and all it did do.[90]

What the Court did not do was set out a method for undermining the Charter
prohibition on the use of force by finding State practice and *opinio iuris* contrary
to Articles 2(4) and 51. Yet, ever since the *Nicaragua* decision, those who want
a weaker prohibition on the use of force have sought to show that contrary
practice has modified the Charter. Perhaps the most popular such claim is that,
owing to State practice, certain conditions found in or associated with Article 51
are no longer required.[91] This approach reflects a fundamental misunderstanding of the *Nicaragua* decision, which the Court could have prevented by
clarifying the nature of *ius cogens* in the text of the decision.

B) THE CONDITIONS OF LAWFUL SELF-DEFENCE: SIGNIFICANT ARMED
ATTACK; NECESSITY, PROPORTIONALITY AND ATTRIBUTION The Court
did, however, affirm the armed attack requirement as the *sine qua non* of self-
defence. It clarified that the armed attack of Article 51 must be significant to
trigger the right of a defending State to counter-attack on the territory of
another State. Minor uses of force, including minor armed attacks, will not
give rise to the right of self-defence.[92] In the jurisdictional phase of the case,

---

[89]   *Ibid.*
[90]   As will be discussed in section IV, the ICJ has yet to say anything in a majority opinion about
       how *ius cogens* norms are discerned. In *Jurisdictional Immunities of the State*, the Court again
       acknowledged the existence of *ius cogens* but limited its decision to the narrowest conclusion
       possible. Peremptory norms invalidate rules that directly contradict the norm, not ones that
       are permissible but might have a tendency, for example, to make enforcement of *ius cogens*
       more difficult. ICJ, *Jurisdictional Immunities of the State* (Germany v. Italy, Greece interven-
       ing), Merits, Judgment of 3 February 2012, ICJ Reports 2012, 99, para. 93.
[91]   See, e.g., Theresa Reinold, 'State Weakness, Irregular Warfare, and the Right to Self-Defense
       Post 9/11', *American Journal of International Law* 105 (2011), 244–86 (284), on the requirement
       of attribution.
[92]   ICJ, *Military and Paramilitary Activities* (n. 75), para. 195.

the United States argued that Nicaragua had attacked El Salvador by supplying weapons to rebels fighting El Salvador's government. The US argued it
had joined in collective self-defence with El Salvador in defending against
these shipments, which the US characterised as constituting armed attacks.
The ICJ found that to constitute an armed attack in the legal sense the conduct
in question must be more serious than a 'mere frontier incident', and that the
delivery of weapons would not constitute an armed attack:

> The Court sees no reason to deny that, in customary law, the prohibition of
> armed attacks may apply to the sending by a State of armed bands to the
> territory of another State, if such an operation, because of its scale and effects,
> would have been classified as an armed attack rather than as a mere frontier
> incident had it been carried out by regular armed forces. But the Court does
> not believe that the concept of 'armed attack' includes not only acts by armed
> bands where such acts occur on a significant scale but also assistance to rebels
> in the form of the provision of weapons or logistical or other support. Such
> assistance may be regarded as a threat or use of force, or amount to interven-
> tion in the internal or external affairs of other States.[93]

In a later passage, the Court states more directly that it excludes weapons
shipments and the provision of supplies from the armed attack category: '[T]he
Court has indicated that while the concept of an armed attack includes the
despatch by one State of armed bands into the territory of another State, the
supply of arms and other support to such bands cannot be equated with armed
attack.'[94]

In the absence of a significant armed attack (when a use of force is minor),
a State may respond with counter-measures but not armed force in self-
defence. Countermeasures are otherwise unlawful coercive measures short
of armed force.[95] The ICJ devoted only two of fifteen separate findings in the
Nicaragua case to US violations of the prohibition on the use of armed force.
These findings cited action that resulted in material damage, injury and death.
The Court characterised US interference with Nicaragua's airspace by over-
flight of military planes to have been a violation of Nicaraguan sovereignty, but
not a violation of the prohibition on the use of force.[96] Nicaragua's supply of
weapons to armed groups fighting to overthrow the government of El Salvador
were also examples of unlawful intervention, not armed attack. These findings
support the conclusion that economic, cyber and other types of coercive

93 *Ibid.*
94 *Ibid.*, para. 247.
95 *Ibid.*, paras. 201, 210, 248, 257.
96 *Ibid.*, para. 292.

measures that do not have direct kinetic effects are unlikely to constitute the use of armed force as prohibited in Article 2(4). States may respond to attacks in the non-kinetic category with counter-measures, not military force, per *Nicaragua*.[97]

The ICJ also inquired in *Nicaragua* into the meaning of the term 'inherent right' in Article 51. The Court explained that the 'inherent right' of self-defence is referring to the set of rules and principles both within and beyond the Charter. Articles 2(4) and 51 provide the lawful bases for resort to force as well as certain procedural rules, such as the Article 51 requirement that States using force in self-defence must report to the Security Council. The principles of State responsibility such as attribution, as well as the principles of necessity and proportionality and other conditions on the lawful resort to force, make up the 'inherent right'. In the jurisdiction phase of the case, the ICJ referenced 'principles of customary and general international law' that exist alongside treaties. The ICJ provided the examples of non-intervention and respect for the independence and territorial integrity of States.[98] In the merits phase, the Court went on to say,

> On one essential point, this treaty [the Charter] itself refers to pre-existing customary international law; this reference to customary law is contained in the actual text of Article 51, which mentions the 'inherent right' (in the French text the 'droit naturel') of individual or collective self-defence, which 'nothing in the present Charter shall impair' and which applies in the event of an armed attack. The Court therefore finds that Article 51 of the Charter is only meaningful on the basis that there is a 'natural' or 'inherent' right of self-defence ... Moreover the Charter, having itself recognized the existence of this right, does not go on to regulate directly all aspects of its content. For example, it does not contain any specific rule whereby self-defence would warrant only measures which are proportional to the armed attack and necessary to respond to it.[99]

Necessity and proportionality are best categorised as part of general international law, rather than customary international law.[100] As general law or

---

97   For more on why cyber attacks do not amount to armed attacks applying the ICJ's analysis in the *Nicaragua* case, see Mary Ellen O'Connell, 'Cyber Security Without Cyber War', *Journal of International Conflict & Security Law* 17 (2012), 187–209. For a different view see International Group of Experts, *Tallinn Manual on the International Law Applicable to Cyber Warfare* (Cambridge: Cambridge University Press, 2013).

98   ICJ, *Military and Paramilitary Activities* (n. 75), Jurisdiction and Admissibility, Judgment of 26 November 1984, ICJ Reports 1984, 392, para. 73.

99   ICJ, *Military and Paramilitary Activities* (n. 75), para. 176.

100 Bin Cheng, *General Principles of Law as Applied by International Courts and Tribunals* (London: Stevens and Sons, 1953), 69–77 (71, 74) (citing 'The Neptune' (Jefferies, master:

general principles, they have much in common with peremptory norms. They do not change in the same manner as treaties or customary international law rules. They have a stable and timeless quality that is at odds with arguments to permit greater resort to lawful force. The nature of these principles and their importance to the functioning of any legal system will be discussed further in Section III.

The ICJ did not need to reach issues of necessity, proportionality or attribution with respect to the US use of military force against Nicaragua because no significant use of force and hence no armed attack was proven:

> Since the Court has found that the condition *sine qua non* [armed attack] required for the exercise of the right of collective self-defence by the United States is not fulfilled in this case, the appraisal of the United States activities in relation to the criteria of necessity and proportionality takes on a different significance. As a result of this conclusion of the Court, even if the United States activities in question had been carried on in strict compliance with the canons of necessity and proportionality, they would not thereby become lawful.[101]

The Court did not comment on the history or nature of the requirement of attribution, but found the US not responsible for the human rights violations of a non-State actor armed group, the Contras, because the US did not control them.[102]

The US did violate the principle of non-intervention in some of its actions against Nicaragua, including financing and advising the Contras. The ICJ also referred to the Declaration on Friendly Relations comment on the principle of non-intervention and its example that State-sponsored terrorist attacks on the territory of another State violate non-intervention.[103] This passage in the judgment is a reminder that States need not stretch Article 51 to fit cases beyond those involving significant armed attack. International law also has such principles as non-intervention to govern inter-State conduct.

In the 1996 *Nuclear Weapons* advisory opinion, the ICJ returned to the general principles of necessity and proportionality again in the context of self-defence: '[T]here is a specific rule whereby self-defence would warrant only measures which are proportional to the armed attack and necessary to respond

---

provisional case) in John Basset Moore (ed.), *International Adjudication Ancient and Modern, History and Documents: Modern Series Vol. IV* (New York: Oxford University Press, 1931), 372–443); Judith Gardam, *Necessity, Proportionality and the Use of Military Force by States* (Cambridge: Cambridge University Press, 2004), 4–5.

[101] ICJ, *Military and Paramilitary Activities* (n. 75), para. 237.
[102] Ibid., para. 116.
[103] Ibid., para. 192.

to it, a rule well established in customary international law."[104] The Court referred to necessity and proportionality as customary international law but with no reasoning to support that categorisation. As with peremptory norms, the ICJ has been hesitant about the category of general principles. In the *Nuclear Weapons* opinion, the Court seemed to default to customary rules simply because necessity and proportionality are not treaty rules.

Regardless of this methodological weakness in reference to necessity and proportionality, the ICJ was right to emphasise that the principles are critical to the law of self-defence. Necessity and proportionality provide additional support for the conclusion that the Article 51 conditions cannot as a practical matter be read out of the Charter. Unless an actual attack is in evidence, the State planning to respond will be unable to accurately calculate whether force in self-defence is needed, whether it will succeed or whether it will be proportionate. In such a situation, the defending State is engaging in lethal action based on mere guesses respecting the actual use of force. In the killing of Khan and Hussain (the ISIS members mentioned at the beginning of this chapter), their future plots were hypothetical and as such inadequate to assess the requirements of necessity and proportionality. Equally, a hypothetical attack cannot meet the additional requirement that an initial attack must be sufficiently grave or significant to trigger the right of self-defence. The requirement of gravity hinges on the attack being significant *in reality*. It is not enough to guess that an attack will occur and to further guess that it will be sufficiently serious.

In two subsequent cases, the ICJ again emphasised both the need for the triggering attack to be significant and attributable to the State against which force in self-defence is being exercised. In the 2003 *Oil Platforms* case, the Court held:

> [I]n order to establish that it was legally justified in attacking the Iranian platforms in exercise of the right of individual self-defence, the United States has to show that attacks had been made upon it for which Iran was responsible; and that those attacks were of such a nature as to be qualified as 'armed attacks' within the meaning of that expression in Article 51 of the United Nations Charter, and as understood in customary law on the use of force. As the Court observed in the case concerning *Military and Paramilitary Activities in and against Nicaragua*, it is necessary to distinguish 'the most grave forms of the use of force (those constituting an armed attack) from other less grave forms.' . . . 'In the case of individual self-defence, the exercise of this

---

[104] See ICJ, *Legality of the Threat or Use of Nuclear Weapons* (n. 82), para. 41 (quoting ICJ, *Military and Paramilitary Activities* (n. 75), para. 176, and ICJ, *Oil Platforms* (n. 83), para. 76).

right is subject to the State concerned having been the victim of an armed attack'.[105]

The ICJ also relied on the principle of attribution in *The Wall* advisory opinion.[106] The case arose from a General Assembly request for an opinion on the legality and consequences of illegality of the security barrier or wall that Israel has constructed at some points within the Occupied Palestinian Territories (OPT). Israel took the position that the structure within the OPT is justified as an exercise of its right of self-defence under Article 51.[107] The Court, however, said Article 51 was not relevant to the case. Israel, as the occupying power, exercises control over the OPT.[108] Invoking Article 51 in such a case would be analogous to a government invoking Article 51 in responding to a high level of violence by a non-State actor on its own territory. Only when the violence reached a level of armed conflict and Israel no longer exercised the control necessary to qualify as an occupier would there be a reasonable case for invoking Article 51.

In her often-cited separate opinion in the case, Judge Rosalyn Higgins argued that Article 51 makes no mention that the armed attack requirement means an armed attack by a sovereign State.[109] While this statement is correct, Higgins did not disagree with the conclusion of the majority that Israel is the occupying power in the OPT.[110] Her separate opinion, therefore, includes an implicit contradiction. An occupier is in control of territory. It is a situation analogous to a government's relation to its own territory. When a State uses force against an uprising, it does not invoke Article 51. For Article 51 to be relevant, Israel must have lost control of the OPT, which Higgins acknowledges was not the case.

The ICJ discussed loss of control in the 2005 *Congo* case. There the Court said that attacks on Uganda by non-State actors located in Congo but outside the control of Congo did not trigger Article 51 self-defence by Uganda against its neighbour. The Court added that this was not a case where a 'large-scale attack' on Uganda emanated from Congolese territory.[111] The Court's comment is brief but implies that where a State is not responsible for a non-State actor, that actor must itself control enough territory to have the capacity to

---

[105]   ICJ, *Oil Platforms* (n. 83), para. 51.
[106]   ICJ, *Construction of a Wall* (n. 84), para. 138 (the Court uses the term 'imputable' to a State).
[107]   Ibid.
[108]   Ibid., para. 139.
[109]   ICJ, *Construction of a Wall* (n. 84), Separate Opinion of Judge Higgins, 207, para. 33.
[110]   Ibid.
[111]   ICJ, *Armed Activities in the Territory of the Congo* (n. 85), para. 147.

launch a large-scale attack. In such a situation Article 51 may be relevant to self-defence against a non-State actor.

In occupation law and the law of self-defence, the relevant concept is 'control', as the ICJ held in the *Nicaragua* case and *Bosnia v. Serbia*, and implied in *Congo*. Where a State wishes to use force in self-defence following an attack by a non-State actor, the defending State must establish that the State where the counter-attack will occur controlled the non-State actor,[112] or had lost control of territory so that the non-State actor could mount 'large-scale' attacks. The ICJ underscored this point in the *Congo* case. The Court rejected Uganda's argument that attacks by irregular forces not attributable to Congo triggered Uganda's right to use force on Congolese territory.[113]

Judges Simma and Kooijmans disagreed. They argued that a State acting in self-defence may carry out an attack on the territory of a State regardless of the host State's responsibility for a non-State actor.[114] Their position, however, fails to account for the rights of the host State where a defending State inflicts death, destruction and injury. The ICJ majority made it clear in *Congo* and *Oil Platforms* that self-defence is lawful only against a State proven to bear responsibility for an unlawful armed attack.[115] The territorial State may have failed to exercise due diligence with respect to controlling non-State actors, but failure of due diligence does not in itself give rise to another State's right to use force in self-defence. This is a point of law that the ICJ has emphasised in most of its cases on the use of force.[116]

[112] ICJ, *Military and Paramilitary Activities* (n. 75), para. 277; ICJ, *Armed Activities in the Territory of the Congo* (n. 85), paras. 146–7. See also ICJ, *Application of the Convention on the Prevention and Punishment of the Crime of Genocide* (Bosnia and Herzegovina v. Serbia and Montenegro), Judgment of 26 February 2007, ICJ Reports 2007, 43, para. 391.

[113] One ambiguous passage by the ICJ is cited by a few expansionists: '[T]he Court finds that the legal and factual circumstances for the exercise of a right of self-defence by Uganda against the DRC were not present. Accordingly, the Court has no need to respond to the contentions of the Parties as to whether and under what conditions contemporary international law provides for a right of self-defence against large-scale attacks by irregular forces'; ICJ, *Armed Activities in the Territory of the Congo* (n. 85), para. 147. See Jordan Paust, 'Self-Defense Targeting of Non-State Actors and Permissibility of US Use of Drones in Pakistan', *Journal of Transnational Law & Policy* 19 (2010), 237–80 (fn. 36).

[114] ICJ, *Armed Activities in the Territory of the Congo* (n. 85), Separate Opinion of Judge Kooijmans, 306, para. 30, and Separate Opinion of Judge Simma, 334, para. 12. See also Tom Ruys and Sten Verhoeven, 'Attacks by Private Actors and the Right to Self-Defence', *Journal of Conflict and Security Law* 10 (2005), 289–320.

[115] ICJ, *Armed Activities in the Territory of the Congo* (n. 85), paras. 146, 301; ICJ, *Oil Platforms* (n. 83), paras. 43 and 76; and ICJ, *Legality of the Threat or Use of Nuclear Weapons* (n. 82), para. 41. See also James Gathii, 'Irregular Forces and Self-Defence Under the UN Charter', in Mary Ellen O'Connell (ed.), *What is War? An Investigation in the Wake of 9/11* (Leiden: Martinus Nijhof, 2012), 97–108 (98).

[116] Gathii, 'Irregular Forces and Self-Defence Under the UN Charter' 2012 (n. 115), 100–1.

C) INTERVENTION BY INVITATION These conclusions on the importance of attribution are further supported in judgments respecting intervention by invitation. The ICJ has discussed invitation as a distinctive basis for justifying the use of force on another State's territory when strict conditions are met. In the *Congo* case, the DRC government issued invitations to neighbouring States to assist it in defeating insurgent forces. The Charter says nothing about the legality of participation in internal armed conflict. Article 51 permits joining in collective self-defence at the invitation of a State. If invitation to civil war is permissible under international law, then some of the restrictions on a State joining in collective self-defence may apply directly or indirectly. One restriction that likely applies is that an invitation must be public and express. The ICJ indicated the importance of proof of invitations in the *Nicaragua* case where the US lacked evidence of an invitation by El Salvador to join in self-defence against Nicaragua.[117]

Without consent, military activities on the territory of another State will violate the principle of non-intervention or the prohibition on the use of force. Consent precludes such wrongfulness, to use the language of the International Law Commission in the Articles on State Responsibility. Consent is not so much customary international law as a general principle of law. As such, the particulars are not necessarily found in State practice and *opinio iuris* but in logic and the necessity of the legal system. According to the commentary on the Articles on State Responsibility, consent to forego a right as a general matter must 'be freely given and clearly established. It must be actually expressed by the State rather than merely presumed on the basis that the State would have consented if it had been asked.'[118] Consent must be given by the 'legitimate' government,[119] signalled by effective exercise of governmental authority[120] or control 'through internal processes'.[121] Where a government that has been exercising effective control is fighting a civil war, it retains its position as the legitimate government so long as it has a chance of winning.[122]

---

[117] ICJ, *Military and Paramilitary Activities* (n. 75), paras. 200, 235–6.
[118] ILC Articles on the Responsibility of States for Internationally Wrongful Acts, GAOR, 56th Sess., Suppl. 10, 73 (commentary to Article 20, para. 6).
[119] Louise Doswald-Beck, 'The Legal Validity of Military Intervention by Invitation of the Government', *British Yearbook of International Law* 56 (1985), 189–252 (191).
[120] See *Tinoco Case* (Great Britain v. Costa Rica), Case no. 10 (18 October 1923), 1 RIAA 369, 381–2.
[121] Brad R. Roth, 'The Virtues of Bright Lines: Self-Determination, Secession, and External Intervention', *German Law Journal* 16 (2015), 384–415 (388–9).
[122] As Roth acknowledges, it is a complex judgment when a non-State actor reaches the status traditionally known as 'belligerency' in a civil war. He restates the better-known part of the

In *Congo*, the ICJ found that consent must be 'unequivocally implied from the conduct of the State'.[123] Withdrawing consent requires no formal, express evidence. Indirect evidence suffices. This finding is consistent with the position that a high bar exists to the lawful exercise of armed force on a foreign State's territory under a justification of invitation or consent. Indirect and even ambiguous evidence of withdrawal of consent is sufficient to end it. Decades ago, Louise Doswald-Beck pointed to the concerns of many States that intervention on either side of a civil war interferes with self-determination.[124] In most cases, such intervention also leads to escalation in violence. If international law develops in the direction of further restrictions on the use of force, intervention by invitation could come to be understood as a violation of the Charter. At present, the weight of opinion, including the ICJ's implied view in *Congo* and the *Nicaragua* case, is that invitation is a lawful basis for the use of force abroad but only when issued by a government generally in control.[125] When a non-State actor seeks to replace a government in all or part of a State's territory, the existing government remains the government until the non-State actor reaches the point at which it will likely succeed in taking control.[126]

Intervention by the invitation of either side in a civil war conflicts with self-determination. It also conflicts with the right to life, a norm some consider to be *ius cogens*.[127] The United Nations International Covenant on Civil and Political Rights, drafted through the General Assembly, declares in Article 6:

rule, which says that if an insurgent reaches belligerent status, meaning it has sufficient organisation, resources, and success in hostilities to predict it has a good chance of defeating the government, all other States must remain neutral or risk becoming a party to the conflict; Roth, 'The Virtues of Bright Lines' (n. 121), 412 (fn. 101). The belligerency rule implies that the government retains its position as the government to the extent practicable until its chances of defeating the insurgent force are clearly lost. Aiding insurgents in any way until they become the government by taking general control of the State violates the principle of non-intervention. ICJ, *Military and Paramilitary Activities* (n. 75), para. 192.

[123]   ICJ, *Armed Activities in the Territory of the Congo* (n. 85), para. 239.

[124]   Doswald-Beck, 'The Legal Validity of Military Intervention by Invitation of the Government' (n. 119), 189. See also Christian Marxsen, 'The Crimea Crisis: An International Law Perspective', *Heidelberg Journal of International Law* 74 (2014), 367–91 (374–9) and Brad R. Roth, *Governmental Illegitimacy in International Law* (Oxford: Oxford University Press, 1999), 185–99. The right to issue an invitation to join in collective self-defence to an armed attack by another State is expressly provided for in UN Charter Article 51.

[125]   The ICJ discusses only the conditions of withdrawing consent in the *Congo* case, not issuing it. In *Nicaragua*, however, the ICJ does indicate limits on invitations. They must be reported to the Security Council and related to the use of force in collective self-defence. Invitations do not give rise to a right to take 'collective counter-measures'. ICJ, *Armed Activities in the Territory of the Congo* (n. 85), paras. 92–105; ICJ, *Military and Paramilitary Activities* (n. 75), paras. 126, 200, 249.

[126]   Roth, 'The Virtues of Bright Lines' 2015 (n. 121), 412 (fn. 101).

[127]   See Heyns and Probert, 'Securing the Right to Life' 2016 (n. 25).

> Every human being has the inherent right to life. This right shall be protected by law. No one shall be arbitrarily deprived of his right to life.[128]

Article 6 renders every first use of military force lacking a Security Council authorisation unlawful. The initiator of military force will almost inevitably violate the human right to life. Non-State actor group members who initiate killing are committing murder. Government authorities have the right to use force to protect a life immediately. Force used in excess of that limit will also constitute murder.[129] Despite these principles, governments and non-State actors may engage in fighting that escalates beyond crime to armed conflict. At that point, international humanitarian law (IHL) becomes relevant to protecting the right to life. Parties to an armed conflict will violate Article 6 if they do not comply with relevant IHL.[130]

Outside of armed conflict, the United Nations Basic Principles for the Use of Force and Firearms by Law Enforcement Officials (*UN Basic Principles*), which are widely adopted by police throughout the world, provide in Article 9:

> Law enforcement officials shall not use firearms against persons except in self-defence or defence of others against the imminent threat of death or serious injury, to prevent the perpetration of a particularly serious crime involving grave threat to life, to arrest a person presenting such a danger and resisting their authority, or to prevent his or her escape, and only when less extreme means are insufficient to achieve these objectives. In any event, intentional lethal use of firearms may only be made when strictly unavoidable in order to protect life.[131]

In considering the legality of using force in self-defence, the ICJ relies generally on the terms of the Charter, the general principles of law, and its own past decisions. The *Nicaragua* case may seem to be an outlier because of

---

[128] International Covenant on Civil and Political Rights (n. 24), Article 6.
[129] ILA Committee on the Use of Force, *Final Report on the Meaning of Armed Conflict under International Law* (2010), available at https://ila.vettoreweb.com/Storage/Download.aspx?D bStorageId=1266&StorageFileGuid=84ac02f3-e51a-4308-adf0-e94256758f38. For an application of the definition of armed conflict as set out in the ILA Report, see 'Syria in a Civil War, Red Cross Says', BBC, 15 July 2012, available at www.bbc.com/news/world-middle-east-18849362.
[130] See, e.g., ECtHR, *Isayeva, Yusupova and Bazayeva v. Russia*, Judgment of 24 February 2005, Application Nos 57947/00, 57948/00 and 57949/00; ECtHR, *Isayeva v. Russia*, Judgment of 24 February 2005, Application No. 57950/00; ECtHR, *Khashiyev & Akayeva v. Russia*, Judgment of 24 February 2005, Application Nos 57942/00 and 57945/00. Similarly, in ECtHR, *Ergi v. Turkey*, Judgment of 28 July 1998, Application No. 66/1997/850/1057.
[131] Adopted by the Eighth United Nations Congress on the Prevention of Crime and the Treatment of Offenders, Havana, Cuba, 27 August to 7 September 1990, available at www .ohchr.org/EN/ProfessionalInterest/Pages/UseOfForceAndFirearms.aspx.

the reliance on customary international law. Even in *Nicaragua*, however, the Court used resolutions and declarations of the United Nations and condemnations of State practice involving the use of force to confirm that customary international law and even *ius cogens* mirrored the Charter as drafted in 1945.

3. Security Council

As with the other UN organs, the over seventy-year history of Security Council action indicates a consistent understanding that the right of self-defence is highly restricted. The right reflects Article 51's plain terms. During the Cold War, the Security Council paid scant attention to the problem of terrorism. Since 9/11, however, the Council has played a larger role. That role will be discussed briefly here, but several non-terrorism related incidents will also be considered. These incidents are worth considering as several have figured prominently in arguments to expand the right to use force. The Security Council, unlike the expansionists, has generally remained close to the Charter's terms in carrying out its mandate as the debates and resolutions concerning Korea (1950), Suez (1956), Cuba (1962), Osirak (1981), Kuwait (1990–1), Kosovo (1999), 9/11 (2001), Iraq (2003), Libya (2011), Syria (2012–) and terrorist attacks in Europe, the Middle East and North Africa indicate.

While leaving terrorism to the General Assembly for most of its history, the Security Council did adopt a resolution in its first years condemning the assassination of the UN mediator in the Arab–Israeli conflict, Count Folke Bernadotte by 'a criminal group of terrorists' – the Lehi, a pro-Israel, non-State actor armed group.[132] The Council did not pass another resolution on terrorism until 1970.[133] This record is further confirmation that at the UN terrorism has, since the founding, been categorised as an issue of crime, not military force.

An early crisis involved the Korean peninsula. At the end of the Second World War in the Pacific, the United States and the Soviet Union competed to replace Japan as it withdrew from conquered territory following its sudden, unconditional surrender. American military staff believed the US was in a position to hold Korea on behalf of the United Nations but only south of the thirty-eighth parallel. The Soviet Union brought its influence to bear on the north. This situation prevailed until June 1950, when the Soviet Union,

---

[132] SC Res. 57 of 18 September 1948. See also Jane Boulden, 'The Security Council and Terrorism', in Vaughan Lowe, Adam Roberts, Jennifer Welsh and Dominik Zaum (eds.), *The United Nations Security Council and War, The Evolution of Thought and Practice since 1945* (Oxford: Oxford University Press, 2008), 608–23 (609).

[133] SC Res. 286 of 9 September 1970 called on member States to prevent aeroplane hijacking.

enlisting the help of the new Chinese communist leadership, induced North Korea to attack the South in a bid to reunite the country.[134] On news of the attack, the United States requested that the Security Council allow it to lead a United Nations counter-attack. The Soviet Union was boycotting Security Council deliberations at the time to protest the refusal to transfer China's seat from the government on Taiwan to the new communist government. The Korea resolutions passed.[135] The war that ensued continued until 1953 when an armistice re-established the *de facto* border at the thirty-eighth parallel. For the international law on the use of force, the Korean War is important as confirming the role of the Security Council in responding to uses of force beyond Article 51 self-defence. The Korean War was not an inter-State war of self-defence.[136] The Soviet Union and subsequently Russia never boycotted Security Council meetings again, helping to solidify the Council's central role in peace and security.

Once the Soviet Union returned to the Council, the United States tried to open an alternative avenue for authorising the use of force outside the Security Council by sponsoring the Uniting for Peace Resolution in the UN General Assembly.[137] The Uniting for Peace Resolution has been invoked several times, including in the Suez Crisis. As already mentioned, the General Assembly has no authority to authorise force.[138]

The Suez Crisis raised the issue of self-defence under the Charter front and centre. Tensions in the Middle East erupted into armed conflict following Egypt's nationalisation of the Suez Canal on 26 July 1956. The Canal had been owned by a British–French consortium. After attempts to get the UN involved on their behalf, France, Israel and the United Kingdom developed an extraordinary plan for retaking the Canal in which Israel would attack Egypt, then France and the UK would intervene between the two warring States to restore order.[139] During the intervention, French and British forces would wrest control of the Canal away from Egypt. Israel duly attacked on the night of 29 October. On 30 October, the US called an emergency session of the Security Council. During the session, France and the UK issued an

---

[134] See the US government's documents on this incident in John P. Glennon (ed.), 'Korea', *Foreign Relations of the United States* 7 (1950), 291–329. See also Chang-Il Ohn, 'The Causes of the Korean War (1950–1953)', *International Journal of Korean Studies* 14 (2010), 19–44.
[135] SC Res. 83 of 27 June 1950; SC Res. 84 of 7 July 1950; and SC Res. 85 of 31 July 1950.
[136] SC Res. 82 of 25 June 1950 refers to Korea as one country with a legitimate government located south of the thirty-eighth parallel. SC Res. 83 of 27 June 1950 is more equivocal, finding South Korea has suffered an armed attack.
[137] GA Res. 377A(V) of 3 November 1950.
[138] Report of the Secretary-General, *Implementing the Responsibility to Protect* 2009 (n. 70).
[139] See Sèvres Protocol of 25 October 1956, CAB/128/30.

ultimatum to Egypt and Israel to cease fire and withdraw ten miles from the Canal area. France and the UK vetoed other proposals for a ceasefire. On 31 October, after announcing that Egypt had rejected their ultimatum, France and the UK intervened. A meeting of the General Assembly under the Uniting for Peace Resolution was convened and organised the United Nations Emergency Force to enforce a ceasefire.[140] France and the UK withdrew their troops by the end of December 1956. Israel withdrew by the end of March 1957.

Israel put forward three arguments based on self-defence to justify its use of force against Egypt. The Israeli representative began by arguing in the Security Council that Israel had taken protective action against the Egyptian Fedayeen, a group that formed to oppose British encroachments on Egyptian sovereignty.[141] He added that Israel was exercising its 'inherent right of self-defence'.[142] In the Emergency Special Session of the General Assembly, Israel's delegation asserted that while no single attack from Egypt triggered Israel's right of self-defence, an accumulation of 'encroachments' did.[143] In other words, 'Israel relied on a broad interpretation of Article 51.'[144] It was certainly a flexible reading of the attribution requirement. The interpretation was clearly rejected in a General Assembly resolution disapproving of Israel's use of force by sixty-four votes to five with six abstentions out of a total UN membership at the time of seventy-six.[145] In addition, various representatives criticised the lack of necessity for the use of force and for its disproportion. Alexandra Hofer observes that the most consistent critique among UN member States was of Israel's methods, which 'exceeded what the situation required'.[146] The US Secretary of State, John Foster Dulles, speaking to the General Assembly, said of the Fedayeen encroachments that 'these provocations – serious as they were – cannot justify the resort to armed force which has occurred during these last two or three days and which is continuing tonight.'[147]

---

[140]   GA Res. 1000 (ES-I) of 5 November 1956 and GA Res. 1001 (ES-I) of 7 November 1956.
[141]   SC Verbatim Record of 30 October 1956, UN Doc. S/PV.748, para. 71.
[142]   SC Verbatim Record of 30 October 1956, UN Doc. S/PV.749, paras. 33, 36.
[143]   GA Verbatim Record of 1 November 1956, UN Doc. A/PV.562, paras. 105, 146.
[144]   Alexandra Hofer, 'The Suez Canal Crisis – 1956', in Olivier Corten and Tom Ruys (eds.), *The Use of Force in International law – A Case-Based Approach* (Oxford: Oxford University Press, 2018), 36–47 (38).
[145]   GA Res. 997 (ES-I) of 2 November 1956.
[146]   Hofer, 'The Suez Canal Crisis' 2018 (n. 144), 45.
[147]   GAOR, 11th Session, Plenary Meetings and Annexes, First Emergency Special Session, Plenary Meetings 561 of 1 November 1956 (10), cited in Robert R. Bowie, *Suez 1956, International Crisis and the Role of Law* (Oxford: Oxford University Press, 1974), 70.

The British and French made a series of arguments of their own to try to justify their counter-intervention: they claimed they were enforcing the Armistice Agreement between Egypt and Israel; they wanted to guarantee freedom of navigation in the canal; they were acting because the Security Council had proven itself unable to do so; their action was a mere 'police action' outside the scope of the Charter;[148] and they were protecting their nationals abroad.[149] During confidential cabinet discussions British Prime Minister Anthony Eden also expressed the view that it was justifiable to use force to secure vital national interests.[150] He had, however, been advised by the head of the British Foreign Office Legal Department, Gerald Fitzmaurice, that attacking Egypt to re-take the Canal would be 'a clear illegality and breach of the United Nations Charter'.[151] The United States and the Soviet Union took the same position.

It was a brief moment of superpower unity. In 1962 the US discovered a Soviet plan to locate missiles on Cuba with the capacity to reach the United States. Some Kennedy administration officials strongly urged bombing the missile sites and the ships delivering rockets.[152] Such a first use of force would clearly violate Article 2(4). President Kennedy's brother, Robert, compared such an attack with Japan's attack on Pearl Harbor, Hawaii.[153] The Soviet Ambassador to the United States, Anatoly Dobrynin, would later write that '[t]hose days revealed the mortal danger of a direct armed confrontation of the two great powers, a confrontation headed off on the brink of war thanks to both sides.'[154]

Instead of attacking, the US sought to interdict the ships by imposing a naval blockade, which it called a 'quarantine' since a 'blockade' had long been

[148] See Suzanne Bastid, 'L'action militaire franco-britannique en Égypte et le Droit des Nations Unies', in Gilbert Gidel (ed.), *Mélanges en l'honneur de Gilbert Gidel* (Paris: Sirey, 1961), 49–78 (65).
[149] Rosalyn Higgins, 'The Legal Limits to the Use of Force by Sovereign States, United Nations Practice', *British Yearbook of International Law* 37 (1961), 269–319 (317).
[150] Ibid., 315.
[151] Fitzmaurice to Sir George Coldstream, Top Secret, 6 September 1956, LCO 2/5760.
[152] See Abram Chayes, *The Cuban Missile Crisis: International Crisis and the Role of Law* (Oxford: Oxford University Press, 1974), 62–6.
[153] Robert F. Kennedy, *Thirteen Days: A Memoir of the Cuban Missile Crisis* (New York: W.W. Norton & Company, 1969); Rick Klein, 'Kennedy Book Blasts Bush, "Preventive War"', *Boston Globe*, 5 April 2006, available at http://archive.boston.com/ae/books/articles/2006/04/05/kennedy_book_blasts_bush_preventive_war.
[154] Bart M. J. Szewczyk, 'Pre-emption, Deterrence, and Self-Defence: A Legal and Historical Assessment', *Cambridge Review of International Affairs* 18 (2005), 119–35 (121, fn. 6), quoting Anatoly Dobrynin, *In Confidence: Moscow's Ambassador to America's Six Cold War Presidents (1962–1986)* (New York: Times Books Division of Random House, 1995), 93.

considered a *casus belli*.[155] Regardless of the label, State Department lawyers advised that it would violate the Charter unless authorised by the Security Council, which was a non-starter due to the guaranteed Soviet veto. The US went instead to the Organisation of American States (OAS).[156] The OAS had no authority to authorise a use of force in the absence of an armed attack,[157] but US officials believed the move gave some recognition of restraint in using force out of respect for the law.[158] The only other idea was to argue that the placement of weapons in Cuba constituted an armed attack for purposes of Article 51.[159] Apparently, there was real concern about establishing an expansive interpretation of the phrase 'if an armed attack occurs'.[160] In the end, the US quarantine did not materialise into a use of force because Khrushchev ordered Soviet ships to reverse course rather than confront the US ships. The crisis was resolved when the Soviet Union agreed not to place missiles on Cuba in exchange for a secret promise by the US to withdraw its missiles from Turkey.

The Security Council's most important debate on self-defence was likely the multi-day session held following Israel's 7 June 1981 attack on a nuclear reactor under construction at Osirak, Iraq. Israeli Prime Minister Menachem Begin justified the raid citing Israeli intelligence reports that the reactor could go into operation as early as 1 July 1981.[161] The International Atomic Energy Agency (IAEA), however, intended, once the reactor became operational, to place full-time inspectors in Iraq 'which would have made *any* plutonium production impossible'.[162] Iraq was a State party to the Nuclear Non-Proliferation Treaty and its nuclear installations were inspected on a regular

---

[155]   See generally Quincy Wright, 'The Cuban Quarantine', *American Journal of International Law* 57 (1963), 546–65 (553–6).

[156]   *Ibid.*, 557–8.

[157]   *Ibid.*, 557–9.

[158]   *Ibid.*, 557. 'The main argument put forward by the United States to justify the quarantine was that it was permitted by Articles 6 and 8 of the Rio Treaty of 1947, implemented by the Consultative Organ of the Organization of American States . . . '

[159]   *Ibid.*, 557, 560–1.

[160]   Thomas Ehrlich and Mary Ellen O'Connell, *International Law and the Use of Force* (Boston, MA: Little, Brown & Co., 1993), 342–3, reproducing a memo written by Ehrlich while a State Department lawyer setting out a legal argument attempting to justify the quarantine.

[161]   UN Doc. S/PV.2280, 12 June 1981, paras. 57–9, 97; Trudy Rubin, 'That Israeli Raid on the Iraqi Reactor: The Facts – and Deeper Issues', *Christian Science Monitor*, 24 June 1981, available at https://www.csmonitor.com/1981/0624/062461.html. After the reactor entered operation, 'it would be impossible to bomb it without threatening Baghdad's population with radiation.'

[162]   Richard Wilson, 'Incorrect, Incomplete, or Unreliable Information Can Lead to Tragically Incorrect Decisions', available at http://users.physics.harvard.edu/~wilson/publications/OSI RAK(2) (emphasis in original). The Osirak 'was a light water cooled reactor explicitly designed to be unsuited for making plutonium'; *ibid.*

basis by the IAEA.[163] Israel was determined to thwart any nuclear activity in Iraq, but its air attack was almost universally condemned as an act of aggression.[164] At the Security Council, Israel argued it was justified in attacking Iraqi nuclear facilities to halt a potentially 'fatal process before it reaches completion'.[165] The Security Council in Resolution 487 nevertheless condemned the Israeli action as a pre-emptive attack on the Osirak 'in clear violation of ... the norms of international conduct' and 'a serious threat to the entire safeguards regime of the [IAEA and of the NPT]'.[166] Even the US voted against Israel. Resolution 487 passed unanimously. The US Permanent Representative to the UN, Jeane Kirkpatrick, observed that 'the means Israel chose to quiet its fears about the purposes of Iraq's nuclear programme have hurt, and not helped, the peace and security of the area ... Israeli action has damaged the regional confidence that is essential for the peace process to go forward.'[167]

Despite this rejection of Israel's expansive claim to a right of self-defence to pre-empt a hypothetical future attack, Israel continued to assert broad claims of lawful self-defence, especially against non-State actor attacks from Lebanon, Jordan and Tunisia. In 1982, Israel invaded Lebanon, advancing as far as the capital, Beirut – well beyond the area where attacks on Israel originated. Israel remained in Lebanon for three-and-a-half months. The United States supported Israel's right of self-defence in these incidents, but criticised the actual use of force as disproportionate.[168]

In 1985, Israel attacked the PLO headquarters in Tunis in response to attacks by PLO members in Israel. Israel again raised as justification its right of self-defence and Tunisia's failure to control terrorists on its territory. The Security Council was not persuaded that Tunisia was legally responsible for the PLO's violence against Israel or that Israel's response was proportionate. The Council condemned 'vigorously the act of armed aggression perpetrated by Israel against Tunisian territory' by a vote of fourteen to zero, with the

---

[163] UN Doc. S/PV.2280 (n. 161), paras. 37, 44.
[164] See W. Thomas Mallison and Sally V. Mallison, 'The Israeli Aerial Attack of June 7, 1981, Upon the Iraqi Nuclear Reactor: Aggression or Self Defence?', *Vanderbilt Journal of Transnational Law* 15 (1982), 417–48 (437–41).
[165] UN Doc. S/PV.2280 (n. 161), para. 101.
[166] SC Res. 487 of 19 June 1981, paras. 1, 3.
[167] UN Doc. S/PV.2288, 19 June 1981, para. 30.
[168] D. Brian Hufford and Robert Malley, 'The War in Lebanon: The Waxing and Waning of International Norms', in W. Michael Reisman and Andrew Willard (eds.), *International Incidents: The Law that Counts in World Politics* (Princeton, NJ: Princeton University Press, 1988), 144–80 (155–77).

US abstaining.[169] The Council also condemned the PLO for violence in its struggle with Israel, finding no justification for the PLO's methods in the right of self-determination.

Throughout the 1980s and 1990s, the Security Council became more involved in terrorism suppression. In 1999, after imposing sanctions on Afghanistan to pressure it to hand over Al-Qaeda's leader, Osama bin Laden, the Council adopted Resolution 1269 condemning 'all acts, methods and practices of terrorism as criminal and unjustifiable, regardless of their motivation'.[170] The attacks of 9/11 did mark a departure, however. The Security Council cited the terms of Article 51 ('inherent right of self-defence') in its immediate post-9/11 resolutions, although only in the non-operative parts.[171] The Council did not authorise the use of force or make findings with respect to any of the other conditions of lawful self-defence. Critically, the Council said nothing about attribution, necessity or proportionality. In a subsequent comprehensive resolution (Resolution 2249) in the aftermath of attacks in five cities during 2015, the Council used its typical formulation for authorising the use of force ('all necessary means') but linked those terms to ISIS control of Iraqi and Syrian territory. The Council did not cite Chapter VII as the legal basis of the resolution but referred more generally to member States' obligations to act in compliance with international law. Most of Resolution 2249 emphasises the need for solidarity against terrorism.[172] No reference is made to Article 51. Nevertheless, expansionists have tried to use resolutions like 1368, 1373 and 2249 to support their arguments for the legality of using military force against terrorist suspects regardless of the responsibility of the State where they are found.[173]

The Security Council pattern is remarkably consistent with that of the General Assembly and ICJ. Each UN organ has reflected an understanding of the Charter principles on use of force aligned with the plain terms of the text

---

[169] SC Res. 573 of 4 October 1985. See also Christine Gray, *International Law and the Use of Force* (Oxford: Oxford University Press, 3rd edn., 2008), 116.

[170] SC Res. 1269 of 19 October 1999.

[171] SC Res. 1368 of 12 September 2001; SC Res. 1373 of 28 September 2001. The most concrete obligation of Resolution 1373 concerned controls on financing of terrorist organisations.

[172] SC Res. 2249 of 20 November 2015 mentions terrorist attacks in Sousse, Ankara, Sinaï, Beirut and Paris, but does not cite Article 51. Since 2015, additional attacks have been carried out in Nice (2016), Brussels (2016), Istanbul (2016), Berlin (2016), Manchester (2017), London (2017) and Tehran (2017). See also notes 253–55 and accompanying text.

[173] For an expansionist perspective, see Marc Weller, 'Permanent Imminence of Armed Attacks: Resolution 2249 (2015) and the Right to Self-Defence against Designated Terrorist Groups', *EJIL Talk!*, 25 November 2015, available at www.ejiltalk.org/permanent-imminence-of-arm ed-attacks-resolution-2249-2015-and-the-right-to-self-defence-against-designated-terrorist-groups.

and the drafters' intentions. The often-cited exception is Security Council Resolution 1368, which mentions Article 51 in the aftermath of a non-State actor attack.[174] Such an example would not alter even legal principles subject to change through subsequent practice.

III. THREE PERNICIOUS DOCTRINES OF EXPANSIVE SELF-DEFENCE

The law's durability is linked to the normative underpinnings of the prohibition on the use of force. Despite them, scholars have persisted in challenging the prohibition. Three prominent challenges are discussed in this section. They are presented chronologically. Each was introduced as a *post hoc* justification for a government's policy of force. All three have been influential, but they also conflict with the peremptory status of the prohibition on the use of force. The conflict with *ius cogens* is the most significant issue, but the doctrines suffer from other flaws as well.

The doctrines consist of, first, the assertion of a right to use force in self-defence against imminent or threatened attacks based on the term 'inherent right' in Article 51. The second characterises crimes committed by terrorists as the equivalent of armed attacks or armed conflict. It also asserts that many small incidents can be accumulated to reach the significance threshold for the armed attack requirement of Article 51. The third asserts that where a State is 'unable or unwilling' to control terrorism, the legal requirements of attribution or consent no longer apply.

Bowett presented the first idea in 1958 in the aftermath of the Suez Crisis. He drew liberally on the *Caroline* incident to assert that the 'inherent right of self-defence' of States includes a right to use force in the face of necessity and not only 'if an armed attack occurs'.[175] His argument has heavily influenced the debate around self-defence. Jeremy Wright, UK Attorney General, for example, re-stated the Bowett thesis in January 2017, as constituting the UK understanding of the 'modern' law on self-defence.[176] The second perspective is associated with Judge Sir Christopher Greenwood's support of a United States claim that terrorist crime can amount to armed attack under Article 51.[177] Sir Daniel

---

[174]   Resolution 2249 is sometimes invoked as well. See discussion at notes 253–55.

[175]   See Bowett, *Self-Defence in International Law* 1958 (n. 21) and Stone, *Aggression and World Order* (n. 21).

[176]   Jeremy Wright, 'The Modern Law of Self-Defence', *International Institute for Strategic Studies*, 11 January 2017, available at https://www.ejiltalk.org/the-modern-law-of-self-defence/.

[177]   Christopher Greenwood, 'International Law and the United States' Air Operation against Libya', *West Virginia Law Review* 89 (1986–7), 933–60.

Bethlehem, a former legal adviser to the British Foreign and Commonwealth Office, made the third proposal following a decade of US targeted killing operations against non-State actors using military force outside armed conflict zones and without a showing that acts of the non-State actor could be attributed to the host State.[178] These attempts to broaden the scope of the right to self-defence are – to borrow Henkin's label for Bowett's argument – 'pernicious doctrines' of self-defence. By 'pernicious' Henkin meant the proposition has had a persistent, negative influence on the prohibition on the use of force. Why these doctrines persist despite their legal defects would require a sociological enquiry. They do reflect a contemporary faith in the utility of military force and take as a given that politicians will ignore the law unless it supports their policies.[179] These power-related factors should not, in principle, influence legal analysis. Regardless of formal doctrine, diluting rules to please politicians only destroys the law in the attempt to save it.

Henkin firmly rejected attempts to dilute the Charter. He did so out of personal knowledge and experience. He had been a lawyer for the United States government dealing with international law issues. He had also been a soldier. Henkin won the Silver Star for valour on the battlefield during the Second World War. Nevertheless, he staunchly repudiated inflated views of the utility of military force and attempts to weaken the legal prohibition against it. He was also a man of faith and deep moral conviction. He said of efforts to expand the right to use military force:

> It is not in the interest of the United States to re-construe the law of the Charter so as to dilute and confuse its normative prohibitions … [I]t is important that Charter norms – which go to the heart of international order and implicate war and peace in the nuclear age – be clear, sharp, and comprehensive; as independent as possible of judgments of degree and of issues of fact; as invulnerable as can be to self-serving interpretations and to temptations to conceal, distort, or mischaracterize events.[180]

---

[178] Bethlehem, 'Self-Defence against an Imminent or Actual Armed Attack by Nonstate Actors' 2012 (n. 23), 770.

[179] Bethlehem constructed his proposals to appeal to 'those within governments and the military who are required to make decisions in the face of significant terrorist threats emanating from abroad'; *ibid.* See also views of lawyers from the administrations of Presidents George W. Bush and George H. W. Bush: Matthew Waxman, 'Regulating Resort to Force: Form and Substance of the UN Charter Regime', *European Journal of International Law* 24 (2013), 151–90, and Abraham D. Sofaer, 'On the Necessity of Pre-Emption', *European Journal of International Law* 14 (2003), 209–26.

[180] Louis Henkin, 'The Use of Force: Law and US Policy', in Louis Henkin *et al.* (eds.), *Right v. Might: International Law and the Use of Force* (New York: Council on Foreign Relations Press, 1991), 37–70 (60).

A. Inherent/Imminent

Bowett introduced his idea that the 'inherent right' of self-defence permits a State to attack in the absence of an armed attack occurring just fourteen years after the adoption of the Charter. More relevantly, he introduced it just two years after the ill-fated attempt by Britain and France to regain control of the Suez Canal. Bowett wrote in the preface to his 1958 book, *Self-Defence in International Law*, that Suez had a 'considerable impact' on his writing of the book.[181] When the truth emerged of the pre-arranged plan to have Israel attack Egypt to create a pretence for British and French intervention, France and Britain fell back on claims of self-defence. Standing in the way of these claims was the UN Charter's Article 51 with its requirement of an armed attack. Bowett, however, supported his government's self-defence claims by attacking the terms of Article 51, saying, 'there is no explanation of this curious proviso "if an armed attack occurs".'[182] States, he asserted, retained a right to act in self-defence consistent with the customary international law in place prior to the adoption of the Charter in 1945, as signalled by the reference in Article 51 to an 'inherent right' of self-defence. Essentially, in Bowett's view, States could simply overlook the Article 51 requirement of an armed attack occurring. Bowett also ignored the relationship of Article 51 to the Charter as a whole, the Charter's drafting history, and discussions to that point in the UN, including on Suez. Bowett moved directly from the words 'inherent right of self-defence' back to 1841 and correspondence between British and American officials about the scuttling of the ship *Caroline* over Niagara Falls.[183] He contended that customary international law permits the use of armed force in situations of 'necessity'.[184] The subsequent impact of Bowett's use of the *Caroline* episode is noteworthy. While he failed to reverse the consensus that the UK acted unlawfully in the Suez, he succeeded in raising considerable doubt about the armed attack requirement of Article 51. Since 1958, the *Caroline* incident has been invoked repeatedly to try to justify uses of force as self-defence that plainly conflict with Article 51.

Ian Brownlie, another British academic, provided a point-by-point refutation of Bowett's thesis in his own 1963 book, *International Law and the Use of Force by States*. Brownlie warned against the tendency of writers to claim

---

[181] Bowett, *Self-Defence in International Law* 1958 (n. 21).

[182] Ibid., 3, 184.

[183] Louis Henkin confirms that scholars have invoked the *Caroline* incident to open-up Article 51 to interpretations permitting more expansive use of force; Henkin, 'The Use of Force' 1991 (n. 180), 45.

[184] Bowett, *Self-Defence in International Law* 1958 (n. 21), 3, 184–5.

justifications for the use of force found in customary law prior to the 1920s. He singled out for particular criticism attempts to base rights of self-defence on the correspondence over the *Caroline* incident. Brownlie took a strict position on interpreting Article 51, finding no room for anticipatory self-defence or self-defence under Article 51 to respond to actions not involving armed force. He defended his strict stance, saying, '[T]he dominant policy of the law and of the United Nations is to maintain international peace and to avoid creating possibilities of breaches of the peace, in the form of vague and extensive justifications for resort to force . . .'[185]

Despite Brownlie's persuasive analysis, certain American legal analysts kept Bowett's *Caroline* thesis alive in the 1980s and 1990s. They cited it to justify the use of force in a variety of situations, such as using force in anticipation of a future attack.[186] *Caroline* is today being cited most often to justify using force long after a terrorist attack has occurred or in anticipation of a future terrorist attack as a preventive or pre-emptive measure.[187] In 2004, UK Attorney General Lord Goldsmith spoke in Parliament about his understanding of Article 51:

> It is clear that the language of Article 51 was not intended to create a new right of self-defence. Article 51 recognises the inherent right of self-defence that States enjoy under international law. That can be traced back to the 'Caroline' incident in 1837 . . . The Government's position is supported by the records of the international conference at which the UN Charter was drawn up and by State practice since 1945. It is therefore the Government's view that international law permits the use of force in self-defence against an imminent attack but does not authorise the use of force to mount a pre-emptive strike against a threat that is more remote. However, those rules must be applied in the context of the particular facts of each case. That is important.
>
> The concept of what constitutes an 'imminent' armed attack will develop to meet new circumstances and new threats. For example, the resolutions passed by the Security Council in the wake of 11 September 2001 recognised both that large-scale terrorist action could constitute an armed attack that will give rise to the right of self-defence and that force might, in certain circumstances, be used in self-defence against those who plan and perpetrate such

---

[185] Ian Brownlie, *International Law and the Use of Force by States* (Oxford: Clarendon Press, 1963), 428–36. See also Henkin, 'The Use of Force' 1991 (n. 180), 60.

[186] Anthony Clark Arend and Robert J. Beck, *International Law and the Use of Force: Beyond the UN Charter Paradigm* (London: Routledge, 1993), 186.

[187] W. Michael Reisman, 'International Legal Responses to Terrorism', *Houston Journal of International Law* 22 (1999), 3–61 (42–9).

acts and against those harbouring them, if that is necessary to avert further such terrorist acts.[188]

Goldsmith is in error respecting the drafting history of the UN Charter.[189] As for his reference to the UK government's long policy, no actual case involving the use of force relying on Bowett's 'inherent right' doctrine is evident between Suez in 1956 and Syria in 2015. One example scholars often cite is the UN Security Council's failure to clearly condemn Israel for attacking Egypt in the 1967 Six-Day War. The UK was not involved in the Six-Day War. Moreover, it is an equivocal case at best given that Israel argued before the Security Council in 1967 that it had actually been attacked by Egypt *prior* to responding with the use of force.[190] Israel did not claim to be anticipating an Egyptian attack. Despite this, the UK Parliamentary joint committee implies, in its report on the UK's policy with respect to the use of drones in targeted killing, issued following the August 2015 attacks, that international law permits using force in self-defence when an opponent's attack is 'imminent'.[191] Goldsmith's successor, Jeremy Wright, cited the *Caroline* incident for legal support of a right to use force in the absence of an armed attack in his January 2017 speech.[192]

Goldsmith and Wright go to some trouble to try to limit the potentially open-ended nature of the concept of 'imminence' in the 'inherent right' doctrine. Goldsmith attempts to show UK policy to be different from the US Bush administration's asserted right of 'pre-emptive' self-defence. Later, Wright tried to distinguish the UK position from that outlined by the Obama administration in which US government lawyers re-defined 'imminent' to mean not immediate.[193] Neither attempt at containing the potential expansion is persuasive. They both conflict with the plain terms of Article 51. Perhaps the UK's positions are more defensible as a matter of law than those of the US under Bush and Obama. They nevertheless conflict with the prohibition on the use of force.

---

[188] House of Lords Debate, *Lords Hansard*, vol. 660, 21 April 2004, column 370, available at www.publications.parliament.uk/pa/ld200304/ldhansrd/vo040421/text/40421-07.htm.
[189] See *supra*, II.B.
[190] Eric Rouleau, 'Le general Rabin ne pense pas que Nasser voulait la guerre', *Le Monde* (29 February 1968).
[191] UK House of Lords, House of Commons, Joint Committee on Human Rights, 'The Government's Policy on the Use of Drones for Targeted Killing' (n. 2), 45–7.
[192] Wright, 'The Modern Law of Self-Defence' 2017 (n. 176).
[193] United States Department of Justice, 'White Paper on Lawfulness of a Lethal Operation Directed against a US Citizen who is a Senior Operational Leader of Al-Qaida or Associated Force' (2010), 7–8, available at https://www.globalsecurity.org/security/library/policy/national/doj-wp-imminent-threat.htm.

President George W. Bush first revealed a new US understanding of Article 51 in a speech at the West Point Military Academy in June 2002. He indicated 'that not only will the United States impose pre-emptive, unilateral military force when and where it chooses, but the nation will also punish those who engage in terror and aggression and will work to impose a universal moral clarity between good and evil'.[194] Similar statements appeared subsequently in the Secretary of Defence's 2002 Annual Report to the President and the Congress[195] and the National Security Strategies of 2002 and 2006.[196] The 2006 National Security Strategy also stated a claim for the right to use force to pre-empt future attacks.[197] The terminology may not appeal to UK lawyers, but there is little difference between launching an attack when fearing an attack is imminent, launching an attack in anticipation of an attack, and launching an attack to pre-empt one. In all cases, the attack is launched based on the subjective belief of a future attack, rather than the evidence of an attack occurring.

In 2010, lawyers in the Obama administration provided legal advice generally supporting the Bush administration. In lengthy memos focused on the legality of using military force to target and kill US citizens abroad and outside armed conflict zones, the lawyers concluded 'imminent' need not mean 'immediate'. An individual's propensities and potential were enough to justify using military force on the territory of another State.[198] Again, the decision to use force is based on a guess about a future attack. The UK's Wright recognises the problem of 'imminent' having no objective meaning: 'So one of the real-world legal questions we face today is not so much who threatens an armed attack, but the standards by which we judge whether such an attack is imminent, allowing a lawful response by way of self-defence.'[199] He adopts Bethlehem's proposals to supply the needed 'standards'.[200] These are the

[194] Mike Allen and Karen DeYoung, 'Bush: US Will Strike First at Enemies; In West Point Speech, President Lays Out Broader US Policy', *Washington Post* (2 June 2002), A01. The speech did not go on to differentiate between 'pre-emptive, unilateral military force' and 'aggression'; *ibid.*

[195] Donald H. Rumsfeld, 'Annual Report to the President and the Congress', 16 August 2002, available at www.hsdl.org/?view&did=851.

[196] 'The National Security Strategy of the United States of America', 17 September 2002, available at www.state.gov/documents/organization/63562.pdf.

[197] 'The National Security Strategy of the United States of America', 16 March 2006, available at https://www.state.gov/documents/organization/64884.pdf.

[198] US Department of Justice, 'Lawfulness of a Lethal Operation Directed against a US Citizen' 2010 (n. 193), 6.

[199] Wright, 'The Modern Law of Self-Defence' 2017 (n. 176).

[200] For the full set of proposals, see Bethlehem, 'Self-Defence against an Imminent or Actual Armed Attack by Nonstate Actors' 2012 (n. 23).

nature and immediacy of the threat; the probability of an attack; whether the
anticipated attack is part of a concerted pattern of continuing armed activity;
the likely scale of the attack and the injury, loss or damage likely to result
therefrom in the absence of mitigating action; and the likelihood that there
will be other opportunities to undertake effective action in self-defence that
may be expected to cause less serious collateral injury, loss or damage.[201]

These standards are as subjective as the term 'imminent'. They do not
provide meaningful limits on the use of force, even if they were the law.
They do not even supply much restraint on the position that 'imminent' need
not mean 'immediate'.

Despite the inherent weaknesses of Bowett's *Caroline* thesis from a legal and
practical perspective, its influence continues to spread. A UN Special
Rapporteur on extrajudicial killing, Christof Heyns, characterised Article 51
as recognising 'the right to self-defence where an armed attack occurs, but also
refer[ring] to self-defence as an inherent right of States. This has given rise to
arguments that the right to self-defence under customary law is not displaced
by the Charter.'[202] As Heyn's comment shows, Bowett's attempt to defend the
UK decades ago has evolved to be a persistent and pernicious pattern in Article
51 interpretation. Instead of basing the right to use force on a response to an
initial armed attack, the view has been growing that States may use military
force to target and kill terrorist suspects who possess the material capacity to
perpetrate violence and who have given some indication of willingness to
do so.

Pakistani scholar Sikander Ahmed Shah rejects the Bowett view. He, like
Brownlie, points out that the *Caroline* correspondence contains no basis for
a right of self-defence that survived the adoption of the UN Charter: '[T]he test
the US Government is relying on arises out of pre-UN Charter customary
international law norms that have long since been refined and restrained by
the application of the UN regime ...'[203]

B. Terrorism/War

In 1986, the United States justified an attack on Libya that killed over 100
people citing the right of self-defence. The US claimed that Libya was
responsible for a series of violent incidents, the most serious of which was

---

[201] *Ibid.*, 775.
[202] Report to the UN General Assembly on Extrajudicial, Summary, or Arbitrary Executions
        (Christof Heyns), UN Doc. A/68/382, 13 September 2013, para. 87.
[203] Sikander Ahmed Shah, *International Law and Drone Strikes in Pakistan: The Legal and
        Socio-Political Aspects* (New York: Routledge, 2015), 41.

the bombing of a disco in Berlin frequented by US armed service personnel, in which two US servicemen and a civilian woman were killed.[204] The US claimed it also had evidence proving the same attackers were planning more attacks.[205] US President Ronald Reagan ordered air strikes on military sites in Libya. Ghaddafi, the Libyan leader, had a home at one of the sites. His young daughter was among the people killed in the attack.

Greenwood defended the US attacks under Article 51 of the UN Charter, citing Bowett's theory of 'inherent right'. Greenwood expanded Bowett's position to include the right to respond in self-defence to low level criminal acts that have occurred in the past as evidence they might occur again in the future. Greenwood concluded his analysis as follows:

> [T]he air strike against Libya would be justifiable as an exercise of the right of self-defence if, but only if, it satisfied the following conditions:
> 1. that the air strike was carried out in order to prevent a Libyan campaign of terrorist attacks against United States nationals and targets, which there was good reason to believe was imminent, in the sense that the campaign was to be launched in the immediate future;
> 2. that no other effective means of preventing this terrorist campaign were available to the United States in the necessarily very short period before the terrorist attacks took place; and
> 3. that the air strike represented a use of force reasonably proportionate to the threat which it was designed to meet.[206]

During the several years following the Tripoli attack, US legal analysts sought to further expand Greenwood's broad reading of Article 51 to reach beyond State actors. Several suggested that if terrorists conducted a series of attacks and planned future ones, and their identities and whereabouts were known to the defending State, the conditions of lawful self-defence might be met, so long as the use of force was necessary and proportional.[207]

In 1989 Judge Abraham Sofaer, Legal Adviser to the US State Department, argued that military force in self-defence targeting a single individual could be justified on the basis of Article 51 if that individual was suspected of terrorism. Sofaer went even further, arguing that the 'inherent right of self-defence

---

[204] Lobel, 'The Use of Force to Respond to Terrorist Attacks' 1999 (n. 14), 548–9.
[205] Greenwood, 'International Law and the United States' Air Operation against Libya' 1987 (n. 177), 933.
[206] *Ibid.*, 946–7.
[207] Louis Henkin, 'International Law: Politics, Values and Functions', *Recueil des Cours* 216 (1989), 9–416 (159–62).

potentially applies against any illegal use of force, and that it extends to any group or State that can properly be regarded as responsible for [. . . terrorist] activities'.[208]

The first major terrorist attack on the US planned from abroad and occurring after Sofaer's argument was the 1993 truck bomb at New York City's World Trade Center. Six people were killed in the blast and more than 1,000 were injured. The US employed law enforcement techniques to discover that the plot had been perpetrated by Al-Qaeda members. Six were arrested, successfully prosecuted, and sentenced to life in prison.[209]

By 1998, however, the Clinton administration changed tactics. Al-Qaeda rigged more truck bombs and detonated them outside the US embassies in Nairobi and Dar-es-Salaam, killing and wounding hundreds, including twelve Americans. Clinton responded with air strikes on Sudan and Afghanistan.[210] The bombings had no detectable deterrent effect. In 2000, Al-Qaeda members attacked a US Navy ship docked in the port of Aden. Seventeen sailors died. The US again used law enforcement measures, working with Yemeni counterparts, to identify, detain and prosecute those who had carried out the attack, with considerable success.[211] Then, on 11 September 2001, Al-Qaeda members attacked again in the US, hijacking passenger planes and flying them into the World Trade Center, the Pentagon and a farm field. Within hours President George W. Bush declared a 'war on terrorism'. On 7 October, the US, joined by the UK, attacked Afghanistan. Both States sent letters to the UN Security Council providing the Council with the required notice under Article 51.[212] The US letter cited the 9/11 attacks only and the Taliban government's support for Al-Qaeda in Afghanistan:

> In accordance with Article 51 of the Charter of the United Nations, I wish, on behalf of my Government, to report that the United States of America, together with other States, has initiated actions in the exercise of its inherent

---

[208] Abraham D. Sofaer, 'Sixth Annual Waldemar A. Solf Lecture in International Law: Terrorism, the Law, and the National Defense', *Military Law Review* 126 (1989), 89–123 (93). For an earlier version of this argument, see, Yehuda Z. Blum, 'State Response to Acts of Terrorism', *German Yearbook of International Law* 19 (1976), 223–37 (233).

[209] CNN, '1993 World Trade Center Bombing, Fast Facts', 2 February 2017, available at www .cnn.com/2013/11/05/us/1993-world-trade-center-bombing-fast-facts/index.html.

[210] CNN, 'US Missiles Pound Targets in Afghanistan/Sudan', 20 August 1998, available at http:// edition.cnn.com/US/9808/20/us.strikes.01; Tim Weiner and Steven Lee Myers, 'After the Attacks: The Overview; Flaws in US Account Raise Questions on Strike in Sudan', *The New York Times* (29 August 1998), A1, A4.

[211] Ali H. Soufan, 'Scenes from the War on Terrorism in Yemen', *The New York Times*, 2 January 2010, available at www.nytimes.com/2010/01/03/opinion/03soufan.html.

[212] UN Doc. S/2001/946, 7 October 2001 (USA) and UN Doc. S/2001/947, 7 October 2001 (UK).

right of individual and collective self-defence following the armed attacks that were carried out against the United States on 11 September 2001 . . .

Since 11 September, my Government has obtained clear and compelling information that the Al-Qaeda organization, which is supported by the Taliban regime in Afghanistan, had a central role in the attacks. There is still much we do not know. Our inquiry is in its early stages. We may find that our self-defence requires further actions with respect to other organizations and other States. The attacks on 11 September 2001 and the ongoing threat to the United States and its nationals posed by the Al-Qaeda organization have been made possible by the decision of the Taliban regime to allow the parts of Afghanistan that it controls to be used by this organization as a base of operation.[213]

The US did attack other States but did so covertly for the remainder of the Bush administration. No detailed legal memorandum was apparently prepared to justify military force against terrorists beyond Afghanistan, but the legal position can be deduced from public statements and conduct. The *Los Angeles Times*, for example, published a detailed account of a CIA drone attack in Yemen in November 2002 that left six men dead in a country not at war. The article stated that the US Air Force would not carry out the attack because of legal concerns.[214] The CIA continued to carry out such attacks in Pakistan and Somalia throughout Bush's presidency.[215] The CIA also used a car bomb to assassinate a terrorism suspect in Syria in 2008.[216]

Bush declared the United States to be involved in a 'global war on terrorism'[217] and terrorists to be 'enemy combatants'[218] who would be fought 'until every terrorist group of global reach has been found, stopped and defeated'.[219]

---

[213] UN Doc. S/2001/946, 7 October 2001 (USA).

[214] Doyle McManus, 'A US License To Kill', *Los Angeles Times* (11 January 2003), A1.

[215] Surle and Purkiss, 'Drone Wars: The Full Data' 2017 (n. 17).

[216] Goldman and Nakashima, 'CIA and Mossad Kill a Hezbollah Figure with a Car Bomb' 2015 (n. 18).

[217] See George W. Bush, 'Statement by the President in His Address to the Nation', 11 September 2001, available at https://georgewbush-whitehouse.archives.gov/news/releases/2001/09/20010 911-16.html; George W. Bush, 'Address to a Joint Session of Congress and the American People', 20 September 2001, available at https://georgewbush-whitehouse.archives.gov/news/ releases/2001/09/20010920-8.html; George W. Bush, 'Presidential Address to the Nation', 7 October 2001, available at https://georgewbush-whitehouse.archives.gov/news/releases/200 1/10/20011007-8.html; George W. Bush, 'President Delivers "State of the Union"', 28 January 2003, available at https://georgewbush-whitehouse.archives.gov/news/releases/2003/01/20030 128-19.html.

[218] William J. Haynes, 'Enemy Combatants', *Council on Foreign Relations*, 12 December 2002, available at https://web.archive.org/web/20110304173206/www.cfr.org/international-law/ene my-combatants/p5312 (Haynes was the General Counsel of the US Department of Defence).

[219] See Bush, 'Statement by the President' 11 September 2001 (n. 217); Bush, 'Address to a Joint Session of Congress' 20 September 2001 (n. 217).

US National Security Adviser Condoleeza Rice explained the global war on terror was a 'new kind of war' to be fought on 'different battlefields'.[220] Apparently, US officials believed being in a global war gave the legal right to target and kill Al-Qaeda suspects anywhere, including on the streets of Hamburg, Germany.[221]

US Justice Department lawyers argued in Federal court that the US was in a worldwide war justified as self-defence.[222] Military operations were occurring far from Afghanistan. The November 2002 CIA attack in Yemen, mentioned above, targeted Abu Ali Al Harithi.[223] Harithi played no role in 9/11. He was killed in the attack along with a twenty-three-year-old American and four others.[224] In 2003, the US began military operations in Somalia.[225] In 2004, it began drone strikes in Pakistan.[226]

When Barack Obama took office in 2009, he increased drone strikes. In March 2010, administration lawyers presented a modified version of the 'global war on terror' argument that began with 9/11.[227] The new claim blended both the 'inherent right' doctrine and the 'terror attack/armed attack' argument. The analysis rested on reading the *Caroline* incident as permitting attacks prior to an armed attack occurring. Obama's lawyers moved beyond the Bush administration in re-defining 'imminent' to mean 'not immediate' and by arguing that crude bombs carried by a single individual are sufficient to count as an armed attack.[228]

The legal advice cleared the way for the US to hunt for a reputed Al-Qaeda propagandist, Anwar al-Awlaki. After a failed attempt that killed two, Awlaki

---

[220] 'Transcript: Condoleezza Rice on Fox News Sunday', *Fox News*, 10 November 2002, available at www.foxnews.com/story/2002/11/11/transcript-condoleezza-rice-on-fox-news-sunday.html?refresh=true.

[221] Anthony Dworkin, 'Law and the Campaign against Terrorism', *Global Policy Forum*, 16 December 2002, available at www.globalpolicy.org/component/content/article/163/28224.html. This account is consistent with the administration's position as to who is subject to indefinite detention. See Haynes, 'Enemy Combatants' 2002 (n. 218) and also, Adam Liptak, 'In Terror Cases, Administration Sets Own Rules', *New York Times*, 27 November 2005, available at www.nytimes.com/2005/11/27/us/nationalspecial3/in-terror-cases-administration-sets-own-rules.html?_r=0&pagewanted=all.

[222] Liptak, 'In Terror Cases, Administration Sets Own Rules' 2005 (n. 221).

[223] McManus, 'A US License to Kill' 2003 (n. 214).

[224] *Ibid.*; Jack Kelly, 'US Kills Al-Qaeda Suspects in Yemen', *USA Today*, 5 November 2002, usatoday30.usatoday.com/news/world/2002-11-04-yemen-explosion_x.htm.

[225] International Security, 'Drone Wars Somalia: Analysis, US Air and Ground Strikes in Somalia', available at http://securitydata.newamerica.net/drones/somalia-analysis.html.

[226] Mark Mazzetti, 'A Secret Deal on Drones, Sealed in Blood', *New York Times*, 6 April 2013, available at www.nytimes.com/2013/04/07/world/asia/origins-of-cias-not-so-secret-drone-war-in-pakistan.html?pagewanted=all.

[227] Harold Hongju Koh, 'The Obama Administration and International Law', *US Department of State*, 25 March 2010, available at https://2009-2017.state.gov/s/l/releases/remarks/139119.htm.

[228] US Department of Justice, 'Lawfulness of a Lethal Operation Directed against a US Citizen' 2010 (n. 193).

and several bystanders were killed in September 2011.[229] Less than two weeks later, the US attacked in Yemen again, killing Awlaki's teenage son, also a US citizen, among others.[230]

Greenwood, who had equated a series of terrorist attacks with the significant armed attack of Article 51, restricted his argument to State-sponsored terrorism. With 9/11, the US was following Sofaer's extension to non-State actors. Greenwood objected:

> In the language of international law there is no basis for speaking of a war on Al-Qaeda or any other terrorist group, for such a group cannot be a belligerent, it is merely a band of criminals, and to treat it as anything else risks distorting the law while giving that group a status which to some implies a degree of legitimacy.[231]

Awlaki is not even known to have participated in a violent attack on a single American, let alone perpetrated anything like the sort of armed attack that could trigger self-defence under Article 51. He was a propagandist and lives on through his recorded sermons. He may now be more influential as a martyr than he was in life.[232]

State-sponsored or not, terrorist attacks are rarely comparable to the type of attack envisioned in Article 51. Terrorist attacks require police work to gather evidence of responsibility. This can require days, weeks or even years to uncover sufficient evidence to foil future plots and bring suspects to justice. Article 51 sets the legal conditions to respond to an armed attack occurring when there is a need to defend. Terrorist attacks are usually brief and isolated. Swedish scholar Ingrid Detter writes, 'International terrorism implies the intermittent use or threat of force against person(s) to obtain certain political objectives of international relevance from a third party. [T]he intermittent factor, which is a hallmark of terrorism, excludes it from constituting war *per se.*'[233] Responding weeks or months later becomes an unlawful reprisal, not an act of self-defence.[234]

---

[229] Margaret Coker, Adam Entous and Julian E. Barnes, 'Drone Targets Yemeni Cleric', *The Wall Street Journal*, 7 May 2011, available at http://online.wsj.com/article/S B10001424052748703992704576307594129219756.html.

[230] On the Awlaki killing, see Jeremy Scahill, *Dirty Wars: The World is a Battlefield* (New York: Nation Books, 2014); Scott Shane, *Objective Troy: A Terrorist, a President, and the Rise of the Drone* (New York: Crown/Archetype, 2015).

[231] Christopher Greenwood, 'War, Terrorism and International Law', *Current Legal Problems* 56 (2003), 505–30 (529).

[232] Shane, *Objective Troy* (n. 230), 302.

[233] Ingrid Detter, *The Law of War* (Cambridge: Cambridge University Press, 2nd edn., 2000), 25.

[234] The Declaration on Friendly Relations 1970 (n. 55) states explicitly that 'States have a duty to refrain from acts of reprisal involving the use of force.' See also ICJ, *Corfu Channel* (n. 77), 108–9.

The armed attack/terrorist attack doctrine began with an attempt to replace the significant armed attack requirement of Article 51 with an accumulation of less significant, intermittent terrorist crimes. The doctrine was silent as to the duty of the defending State to target only a State bearing responsibility under principles of attribution. After 9/11, US administrations attempted to justify military force against States with no link of responsibility to attacks on the US. They then moved on to assert a right to use force against non-State actors with the potential and the propensity to use terrorism.

C. Unable/Unwilling

In 2006, Bethlehem joined an effort to draft 'The Chatham House Principles of International Law on the Use of Force in Self-Defence'.[235] The document was sponsored by the foreign affairs think tank Chatham House (the Royal Institute of International Affairs).[236] One of the proposed principles, which Bethlehem has promoted since the publication of 'The Chatham House Principles', would allow States to attack non-State actors when those groups are located in another State that is 'unable or unwilling' to control them.[237]

Presumably the point of this vague idea is that it frees the attacking State from the need to show a link of legal responsibility between the State being attacked and the non-State actors. Bethlehem may also consider the unable/unwilling idea to obviate the need for an invitation from a government to participate in a civil war. This second aspect of unable/unwilling is indicated by his expansion of what counts as consent in international law: 'Consent may be strategic or operational, generic or *ad hoc*, express or implied.'[238] Where his flexible consent standards are not met, States could still exercise military force, under his unable/unwilling concept. Bethlehem's proposal leaves it wholly to the State claiming a right of self-defence to determine what the terms 'unable' and 'unwilling' mean.[239]

---

[235] Elizabeth Wilmshurst, 'The Chatham House Principles of International Law on the Use of Force in Self-Defence', *The International and Comparative Law Quarterly* 55 (2006), 963–72 (969–70).
[236] *Ibid.*, 963, and comments to the author by Wilmshurst.
[237] Chatham House, 'Principles of International Law on the Use of Force by States in Self-Defence' (1 October 2005), Principle 6, available at www.chathamhouse.org/publications/papers/view/108106; and Bethlehem, 'Self-Defence against an Imminent or Actual Armed Attack' 2012 (n. 23), 776 (principle 11).
[238] Bethlehem, 'Self-Defence against an Imminent or Actual Armed Attack' 2012 (n. 23), 777 (principle 13).
[239] Wilmshurst, 'The Chatham House Principles' (n. 235), 963, 969–70.

The terms are not used in the UN Charter, the drafts of the Charter, nor decisions of the ICJ on the use of force. Yet the UK Attorney General has used them and they appear in letters to the Security Council respecting the use of force in Syria by Australia, Canada, Turkey and the United States.[240] In a question to the US State Department Legal Adviser Brian Egan about the legal basis of 'unable/unwilling' by the author at a meeting of the American Society of International Law, he replied only that there are 'some cases' in support.[241] Shah believes Bethlehem developed the concept from *Caroline*.[242] The first use of the expression appears to have been in 1976 by the US representative to the UN when he spoke in support of Israel's rescue operation at Entebbe, Uganda, saying, '[T]here is a well-established right to use limited force for the protection of one's own nationals from an imminent threat of injury or death in a situation where the state in whose territory they are located either is *unwilling or unable* to protect them.'[243] Oscar Schachter believed the formula was drawn from Waldock's Hague Lectures.[244] Waldock, drawing on *Caroline*, says something similar about rescue: 'There must be (1) an imminent threat of injury to nationals, (2) a *failure or inability* on the part of the territorial sovereign to protect them and (3) measures of protection strictly confined to the object of protecting them against injury.'[245] Rescue of nationals is, of course, something quite different from the offensive use of force against non-State actors. 'Failure or inability' to rescue is a definite standard in the context of a hostage situation – either the victim has been liberated or not. Rescue could not contrast more starkly with the scenarios Bethlehem had in mind. The origin of 'unable/unwilling' in this very different context speaks against its use in regard to non-State actors.

Ashley Deeks, a long-time US State Department lawyer, has offered a different justification for 'unable/unwilling' – linking it to the venerable law of neutrality. She admits that 'neutrality law does not directly govern uses of force between States and non-state actors', but sees an analogy between

---

[240] See UN Doc. S/2015/693, 9 September 2015 (Australia); UN Doc. S/2015/221, 31 March 2015 (Canada); UN Doc. S/2015/563, 24 July 2015 (Turkey); UN Doc. S/2014/695, 23 September 2014 (USA).
[241] Brian Egan, State Department, 'International Law, Legal Diplomacy, and the Counter-ISIL Campaign', Address at the American Society of International Law, *Lawfare*, 1 April 2016, available at www.lawfareblog.com/state-department-legal-adviser-brian-egans-speech-asil.
[242] Shah, *International Law and Drone Strikes in Pakistan* 2015 (n. 203), 16, 45–51.
[243] Oscar Schachter, 'In Defense of Rules on the Use of Force', *University of Chicago Law Review* 53 (1986), 113–146 (139) (emphasis added).
[244] *Ibid.*, 139, fn. 107.
[245] C. H. M. Waldock, 'The Regulation of the Use of Force by Individual States in International Law', *Recueil des Cours*, 81(2) (1952-II), 451–571 (467) (emphasis added).

States attacked by non-State actors and the territorial State where non-State actors are found and an 'offended' belligerent State *vis-à-vis* a neutral State.[246] The need for such an analogy seems unwarranted, however, given that international law has directly applicable rules and principles to govern State uses of force against non-State actors. Deeks discloses that her aim is to bolster the 'unable/unwilling' exception by linking it to existing law.[247]

The article also supported the efforts of her former boss, US Legal Adviser to the State Department John Bellinger, to promote 'unable/unwilling' as customary international law.[248] Diplomatic cables obtained by Wikileaks describe steps to obtain expressions of *opinio iuris* from European governments that also involved Sir Daniel Bethlehem.[249] It is beyond the scope of this chapter to discuss whether such an effort, typical for treaty-making, can effect customary international law. Suffice it to say that the effort could not succeed in inserting 'unable/unwilling' into international law for several reasons. First, 'unable/unwilling' attempts to create a new exception to a peremptory norm, which cannot be done. Second, the attempt uses customary international law methodology to alter general principles of State responsibility and consent. Customary law methodology does not affect general principles. Finally, even if customary international law methodology did apply to these principles, the officials focused their confidential efforts mostly on Europe. They did not seek to establish a general State practice.[250] At the time of writing only five States have attempted to justify a use of force by invoking 'unable/unwilling' and those States have invoked other justifications in addition to 'unable/unwilling'.[251] The case for *opinio iuris* is almost non-existent.[252]

---

[246] Ashley Deeks, '"Unwilling or Unable": Toward a Normative Framework for Extraterritorial Self-Defense', *Virginia Journal of International Law* 52 (2011–12), 483–550 (497).

[247] *Ibid.*

[248] Victor Kattan, 'Furthering the "War on Terrorism" through International Law: How the United States and the United Kingdom Resurrected the Bush Doctrine on Using Preventive Military Force to Combat Terrorism', *Journal on the Use of Force and International Law* 23 (2017), 1–48 (24–6, fn. 110).

[249] *Ibid.*, 26–8.

[250] *Ibid.*, 24. See also Jutta Brunnée and Stephen J. Toope, 'Self-Defence against Non-State Actors: Are Powerful States Willing but Unable to Change International Law?', *International and Comparative Law Quarterly* 67 (2017), 263–86.

[251] In addition to the UK (see Wright, 'The Modern Law of Self-Defence' 2017 (n. 176)), statements have been made by Australia, Canada, Turkey and the US (see n. 240).

[252] Some have claimed that the opinion and practice of certain, 'specially-affected' States has greater weight in the formation of customary international law rules than others. The International Law Commission has cast considerable doubt on this claim. See, Dire Tladi, 'Progressive Development and Codification of International Law: The Work of the International Law Commission During its Sixty-Sixth Session', *South African Yearbook of*

In 2016, for example, a joint committee of the British Parliament looking into the killing of Reyaad Khan provided this assessment of the international law on self-defence:

> State practice since 9/11 certainly supports the view that a State's right of self-defence includes the right to respond with force to an actual or imminent armed attack by a non-state actor, and the most recent UN Security Council Resolution 2249 (2015) lends support to this view. To be entitled to rely on self-defence against non-state actors, the State from whose territory the armed attack is being launched or prepared for must be unable or unwilling to prevent the attack.[253]

The Parliamentary committee did not rely on 'unable/unwilling' alone. It also referred to Security Council Resolution 2249. That resolution, too, however, is insufficient to justify the UK's attack in Syria. The Costa Rican scholar Nicolas Boeglin points out that the resolution falls well short of a Security Council authorisation for the use of force.[254] Without authorisation, the use of force in response to terrorism will be unlawful.[255] Boeglin believes France worked hard to convince its public that Resolution 2249 authorises the use of military force in Syria because it had no other possible justification. He further asks why France, the UK, the US and Australia have all made a considerable effort to expand the law of self-defence to permit force against non-State actors. He concludes that these efforts at expansion are a result of a pro-war mentality afflicting political leaders that biases them toward using military action, despite the poor results of armed conflict against non-State actors.[256] Boeglin rejects the view that violations of the Charter or of general principles of international law can yield new, permissive doctrines such as the unable/unwilling proposal.

None of the three doctrines reviewed here rest on persuasive arguments of legal change. US State Department Legal Advisor Egan said the US position rested on 'cases' without naming them. The UK Parliamentary Joint Committee asserted that State practice exists without listing any. Even the few examples of State practice that do exist are inconsistent. Much more is needed to anchor such highly indeterminate concepts as imminence,

---

International Law 28 (2013), 124–43 (129–30). Regardless, all States are 'specially-affected' when the issue is the use of force.

[253] UK House of Lords, House of Commons, Joint Committee on Human Rights, 'The Government's Policy on the Use of Drones for Targeted Killing' (n. 2).

[254] Nicolas Boeglin, 'La Résolution 2249 n'autorise pas à bombarder en Syrie', *Voltairenet.org*, 1 December 2015, available at www.voltairenet.org/article189496.html.

[255] *Ibid.*

[256] *Ibid.*

accumulation of events, inability and unwillingness. Even if the core features of the three doctrines were capable of incorporation in customary international law and sufficient State practice existed with an accompanying *opinio iuris*, customary rules may not derogate from a *ius cogens* norm. No one doubts this when it comes to norms such as the prohibition on genocide or slavery. Article 2(4) is also *ius cogens* and as such has a durability that contrary State practice, policy arguments, and even competing moral conceptions cannot undermine.

IV. THE PROHIBITION ON THE USE OF FORCE AS *IUS COGENS*

Humanity has turned to law as an alternative to violence and status in ordering social affairs. Controls on the use of force and principles such as equality, necessity and proportionality are, therefore, essential to any legal system, going to the very reason for law. Such principles are found in the categories of general principles and *ius cogens*, and, given their essential role, require an explanation different from the vast majority of rules, principles and procedures. Most law is made through agreement – positive action – in the form of treaties, statutes or practice. It may be unmade using the same legal processes. Not so with these essential norms. They are discerned, rather than created through positive law method. Humanity has only one explanatory theory for law other than positivism, and that is natural law theory. It is natural law theory, therefore, that provides the explanation of *ius cogens* and general principles. Yet, the study of natural law has been in decline for a century. Scholars are turning to it once again,[257] but this section cannot draw on a well-developed current body of scholarship to support the analysis. The aim must be limited to offering evidence of the importance of natural law to *ius cogens* and the general principles and to invite further research.

The peremptory norms of international law are understood to be the prohibitions on the use of force, genocide, slavery, apartheid, widespread extrajudicial killing, torture and intentional targeting of civilians in armed

---

[257] See e.g., Martti Koskenniemi, 'Transformations of Natural Law, Germany 1648–1815', in Anne Orford and Florian Hoffmann (eds.), *The Oxford Handbook of the Theory of International Law* (Oxford: Oxford University Press, 2016), 59–81; Antônio Augusto Cançado Trindade, *International Law for Humankind: Towards a New Jus Gentium* (Leiden: Martinus Nijhoff, 2nd edn., 2013), 139; and Christopher G. Weeramantry, *Universalizing International Law* (Leiden: Martinus Nijhoff, 2004). See also Mary Ellen O'Connell and Caleb Day, 'Sources and the Legality and Validity of International Law: Natural Law as Source of Extra-Positive Norms', in Samantha Besson and Jean D'Aspremont (eds.), *The Oxford Handbook on the Sources of International Law* (Oxford: Oxford University Press, 2017), 562–80.

conflict.[258] The list of inherent general principles is far longer. It includes principles associated with the proper administration of the law, such as equality, fairness and good faith, as well as principles associated with the operation of legal processes, such as necessity and proportionality. This section will discuss the meaning of *ius cogens* and inherent general principles and the implications for the law of self-defence that norms from these categories are seen as integral to the right of self-defence. Within the international legal community there is wide agreement that a category of norms exists known as '*ius cogens*' and that these are norms superior to the positive law. The wide agreement on *ius cogens* extends to including the prohibition on the use of force. This section will offer additions to these points in the form of several logical corollaries. These corollaries include approaches to interpretation, the operation of customary international law and the emergence of new rules.

The first subsection below provides further description and evidence of the *ius cogens* prohibition on the use of force and the general principles of necessity and proportionality. Subsection B reveals the ancient origins of treating resort to war as a matter of grave moral and legal import owing to the conflict between violence and law. The final subsection will draw out the implications of the *ius cogens* character of the prohibition on the use of force, especially with regard to the accurate interpretation of rules and the understanding of legal change.

A. *The Methodology of* Ius Cogens

1. Characteristics and Evidence of *Ius Cogens*

Descriptions of the character of *ius cogens* as well as evidence of the existence of particular *ius cogens* norms can be gathered from the work of the UN International Law Commission (ILC), decisions of the ICJ and other courts, and the work of scholars. The best-known characteristic of *ius cogens* is found in the VCLT, drafted by the ILC. The VCLT makes clear that a treaty or treaty provision in conflict with *ius cogens* is void *ab initio*.[259] A treaty provision that conflicts with an emerging norm will become void.[260] This characteristic gives *ius cogens* a type of superiority to other principles and rules. The *ius cogens* norms form a barrier to action but do not compel action. To the extent that *ius*

---

[258] For support of this list, see O'Connell and Day, 'Sources and the Legality and Validity of International Law' 2017 (n. 257).

[259] Article 53 VCLT. See also American Law Institute, *Restatement (Third) of the Foreign Relations Law of the United States* (St. Paul, Minn. 1987), §102, comment k.

[260] Article 64 VCLT.

cogens norms are similar to rights, they are more like negative rights, such as the right to be free of torture. They do not establish positive obligations that might require the expenditure of resources. They do entail the affirmative duty of respect attaching to all legal prohibitions. *Ius cogens* norms work like principles of public policy or *ordre public*. In the law of contracts, a judge may apply public policy to void a contract, but she generally cannot prescribe obligations not indicated in the agreement of the parties. The same logic applies to *ius cogens*.

In 2012, in *Jurisdictional Immunities of the State*, the ICJ acknowledged the existence of the *ius cogens* category and indicated that the core civilian protections in time of armed conflict are *ius cogens*.[261] States are absolutely prohibited from violating these norms. That, however, is the extent of the *ius cogens* effect. States have no affirmative duty to craft remedies in national law for *ius cogens* violations. The fact that Germany violated *ius cogens* norms during World War II in intentionally targeting, enslaving and deporting civilians did not serve to negate Germany's absolute sovereign immunity from national judicial process, which was the prevailing principle in the 1940s. Sovereign immunity is not, in itself, a violation of *ius cogens*. The applicants in the case tried to argue that *ius cogens* norms incorporate certain procedural rights to help secure remedies. The ICJ found this reasoning too attenuated. Every international legal principle is open to means of enforcement and remedies for violation. The doctrine of *ius cogens* does not require any specific remedy.

The ICJ has not discussed the source of *ius cogens* in any majority opinion. Contemporary scholarship appears divided between two views. One sees *ius cogens* as a form of 'super customary international law'.[262] To be 'super', however, implies something other than regular customary international law. The other view holds that understanding the difference between a peremptory norm and a regular rule of custom requires drawing on natural law.[263]

The most forthright evidence of *ius cogens* status for the prohibition on the use of force comes from the ILC. Drawing on the natural law tradition, the

---

[261]   ICJ, *Jurisdictional Immunities of the State* (n. 90), para. 93.
[262]   Hillary Charlesworth, 'Law-Making and Sources', in James Crawford and Martti Koskenniemi (eds.), *Cambridge Companion to International Law* (New York: Cambridge University Press, 2012), 187–202. See also, André de Hoogh, *Obligations Erga Omnes and International Crimes* (The Hague: Kluwer Law International, 1996), 44–8; R. Y. Jennings and A. Watts (eds.), *Oppenheim's International Law* (Oxford: Oxford University Press, 1992), 7–8; and Orakhelashvili, 'Changing Jus Cogens Through State Practice?' 2015 (n. 88), 166.
[263]   See O'Connell and Day, 'Sources and the Legality and Validity of International Law' 2017 (n. 257).

ILC developed the 1968 Vienna Convention on the Law of Treaties with two provisions, Articles 54 and 62, relating to *ius cogens*.[264] The commentary provides as an example of *ius cogens* 'the law of the Charter concerning the prohibition of the use of force'. The ILC found that Article 2(4) 'constitutes a conspicuous example of a rule in international law having the character of *ius cogens*'.[265] The ILC's 2001 commentary to the Articles on State Responsibility also includes a supportive reference, but to the somewhat narrower prohibition of aggression: 'It is generally agreed that the prohibition of aggression is to be regarded as peremptory.'[266]

The ICJ has been more cautious than the ILC in how it has referred to *ius cogens*, but it did say in the 1986 *Nicaragua* case: 'Article 2, paragraph 4, of the Charter of the United Nations ... is frequently referred to in statements by State representatives as being not only a principle of customary international law but also a fundamental or cardinal principle of such law.' The Court proceeded to cite the ILC's comment that Article 2(4) is a 'conspicuous example of a rule in international law having the character of *ius cogens*'.[267]

ICJ judges have been more expansive in their individual opinions in stating that the prohibition is *ius cogens*. For example, Judge Elaraby expressed his view in *The Wall* that '[t]he prohibition of the use of force ... is universally recognised as a *ius cogens* principle, a peremptory norm from which no derogation is permitted.'[268] In 1970, the ICJ made an indirect reference to *ius cogens* norms in its decision in the *Barcelona Traction* case. In listing *erga omnes* obligations, it included the international law 'outlawing of acts of aggression, and of genocide' as well as 'the principles and rules concerning the basic rights of the human person, including protection from slavery and racial discrimination'.[269]

Relying on the *American Law Institute's Restatement (Third) of Foreign Relations Law*, a US Federal court judge cited the prohibition on the use of force as *ius cogens* in a case brought by plaintiffs attempting to enforce US compliance with the *Nicaragua* judgment. 'The ... *Restatement*

---

[264] See, e.g., Carnegie Endowment for International Peace, European Centre, *The Concept of Jus Cogens in International Law – Lagonissi Conference: Papers and Proceedings* (Geneva: Carnegie Endowment for International Peace, 1967).

[265] ILC, 'Draft Articles on the Law of Treaties with Commentaries', *Yearbook of the International Law Commission* (1966), vol. II, 247, commentary to Article 50.

[266] ILC Articles on the Responsibility of States for Internationally Wrongful Acts (n. 118), 112 (commentary to Article 40, para. 4).

[267] ICJ, *Military and Paramilitary Activities* (n. 75), para. 190.

[268] ICJ, *Construction of a Wall* (n. 84), Separate Opinion of Judge Elaraby, ICJ Reports 2004, 122.

[269] ICJ, *Barcelona Traction, Light & Power Co.* (Belgium v. Spain), Jurisdiction, Judgment of 5 February 1970, ICJ Reports 1970, 3, para. 34.

acknowledges two categories of [*ius cogens*] norms: "the principles of the
United Nations Charter prohibiting the use of force", ... and fundamental
human rights law that prohibits genocide, slavery, murder, torture, prolonged
arbitrary detention, and racial discrimination ...'[270] Louis Henkin was the
chief reporter of the Restatement. He argued in other writing that the prohibition 'is the principal norm of international law of this century'.[271]
Orakhelashvili represents the consensus scholarly view in saying:
'The prohibition of the use of force by States undoubtedly forms part of *ius
cogens*.'[272]

Despite this evidence, some authors have questioned whether Article 2(4)
can be *ius cogens* if it has exceptions.[273] Their view, however, confuses the
substance of the norm with a derogation from it. Self-defence is part of what
constitutes the prohibition on the use of force. It is not a derogation from the
prohibition. Orakhelashvili has replied to this confusion by saying the whole
of the *ius ad bellum* is *ius cogens*.[274] He is also not entirely correct, however,
because necessity and proportionality are part of the *ius ad bellum* but are
general principles of law, not *ius cogens*. General principles are also non-
derogable but lack the substantive moral content of peremptory norms, as will
be discussed next.

2. General Principles of Necessity, Proportionality and State Responsibility

Certain general principles have similar characteristics to *ius cogens* but are
more procedural than ethical in nature. The general principles of necessity,
proportionality and attribution are general principles and essential compo-
nents of the lawful resort to force. These principles are discerned much as
peremptory norms are, through natural law method, discussed in more detail
in section IV below. General principles inherent to the law are distinguishable
from the general principles found by searching national legal systems to find

---

[270]   *Committee of US Citizens v. Reagan*, 859 Federal Reporter 2d (District Court of the District
        of Columbia 1988), 929–52 (939–42).
[271]   Henkin, 'The Use of Force' 1991 (n. 180), 38.
[272]   Alexander Orakhelashvili, *Peremptory Norms in International Law* (Oxford: Oxford
        University Press, 2006), 50, and Lauri Hannikainen, *Peremptory Norms (Jus Cogens) in
        International Law: Historical Development, Criteria, Present Status* (Helsinki:
        Lakimiesliiton Kustannus, 1988), 323, 356.
[273]   See James Green and others referred to in his article, James Green, 'Questioning the
        Peremptory Status of the Prohibition of the Use of Force', *Michigan Journal of
        International Law* 32 (2011), 215–57 (221 *et seq.*).
[274]   Orakhelashvili, *Peremptory Norms in International Law* 2006 (n. 272), 51.

a common rule, which tend to be based on national legislation, a consent-based or positivist source.

As mentioned above, the ICJ classified necessity and proportionality as rules of customary international law in the *Nuclear Weapons* case.[275] The Court provided no basis for this categorisation. It cited no State practice or *opinio iuris*. Nor are these the type of principles that could be eliminated from the law. For these reasons, they fit the category of general principles better than customary international law. Both Judith Gardam and Bin Cheng take the position that necessity and proportionality are general principles.[276] Like peremptory norms, inherent general principles are formed through means other than voluntary consent or other affirmative material acts. Peremptory norms are distinguishable in that general principles tend to condition processes, while *ius cogens* norms have ethical or moral content. The process of using force, for example, is regulated by necessity and proportionality.

When necessity and proportionality are correctly categorised as general principles, rather than rules of customary international law, it is possible to accurately assess their role in regulating the use of force. Necessity limits the use of force to a 'last resort after all peaceful means have failed'.[277] In addition, the principle requires that the party resorting to force must calculate that there is a high likelihood of success that force will accomplish the legitimate objective.[278] In this sense, Brownlie has called the principle of necessity 'innate in any genuine concept of self-defence'.[279]

Proportionality is equally innate. Force used in self-defence must not be excessive in relation to the injury. The ICJ has mentioned necessity and proportionality as conditions of the lawful resort to force in a number of its decisions. In the *Nicaragua* case, the Court said that even if the evidence proved a significant armed attack attributable to Nicaragua, the US response had to be necessary and proportionate.[280] In the *Oil Platforms* case, the US failed to prove that Iran was responsible for attacks on US ships. Even if it had proved Iran was responsible, the Court indicated that the US response was disproportionate.[281]

---

[275] ICJ, *Legality of the Threat or Use of Nuclear Weapons* (n. 82).
[276] Cheng, *General Principles of Law as Applied by International Courts and Tribunals* 1953 (n. 100) and Gardam, *Necessity, Proportionality and the Use of Military Force by States* 2004 (n. 100).
[277] Gardam, *Necessity, Proportionality and the Use of Military Force by States* 2004 (n. 100), 5.
[278] On likelihood of success, see Seth Lazar, 'War', in Edward N. Zalta (ed.), *The Stanford Encyclopedia of Philosophy* (Summer 2016 Edition), para. 2.5, available at https://plato .stanford.edu/entries/war.
[279] Brownlie, *International Law and the Use of Force by States* 1963 (n. 185), 434.
[280] ICJ, *Military and Paramilitary Activities* (n. 75), para. 194.
[281] ICJ, *Oil Platforms* (n. 83), paras. 74–8.

The US adhered more closely to the requirements of necessity in leading the coalition that liberated Kuwait from Iraq in 1991. In August 1990, Iraq invaded Kuwait, quickly overwhelming Kuwait's small military. The UN Security Council became involved and, after a period of attempting to use economic sanctions to persuade Iraq to withdraw, the Council authorised a coalition of States to use force to liberate Kuwait. The coalition forces quickly drove Iraq's armed forces out of the country and drove them beyond a swathe of territory that later became a demilitarised zone for Kuwait's security. Famously, the coalition did not proceed to Baghdad to remove Saddam Hussein from power, because doing so, in the view of coalition leaders, was not necessary to the liberation of Kuwait. Indeed, fighting unrelated to the liberation of Kuwait could not be justified under the principle of necessity, since it was clearly beyond the force required to remove the occupier. Failing to respect the principle of necessity would make any killing and destruction both unnecessary and disproportionate.[282]

In Afghanistan, after the Taliban fled the capital, Kabul, in December 2001, any further use of force was arguably unnecessary to accomplish self-defence.[283] By mid-2002, with Hamid Karzai's elevation to the leadership of Afghanistan, international forces shifted the purpose of fighting to supporting his government. The armed conflict in self-defence became a counter-insurgency or civil war.

US and UK drone operations since 2001 also raise the issue of compliance with the principles of necessity and proportionality. Scholars have debated the possible violations of the *ius ad bellum, ius in bello* and human rights norms involved in such operations that aim at killing individuals on a 'kill list' and are now referred to as 'targeted killing' operations.[284] Necessity and proportionality are rarely mentioned in the legal analyses. After a decade and a half of these operations, Al-Qaeda continues, and more virulent offshoots, such as ISIS and Boko Haram, have emerged. If the self-defence aim of targeted killing is to suppress these non-State actors, the record is one of consistent failure. The United Kingdom certainly had a heavy burden to meet in demonstrating

---

[282] Gardam is more critical of the amount of force used; Gardam, *Necessity, Proportionality and the Use of Military Force by States* 2004 (n. 100), 159–66. The focus here is the *ius ad bellum* and does not offer an assessment of *ius in bello* proportionality.

[283] David Usborne, 'UN Raps US Military, After Afghan Wedding "Cover Up"', *The Independent*, 30 July 2002, 9.

[284] Gray, 'Targeted Killings' 2013 (n. 19). See also Christine Gray, 'Targeted Killing Outside Armed Conflict: A New Departure for the UK?', *Journal on the Use of Force and International Law* 3 (2016), 198–204.

that killing Khan in 2015 was necessary and proportionate. The US had the same burden in the killing of Hussain.

Both States fell far short of meeting that burden. References were made only to the victims' past actions. The *Guardian* newspaper reported that in the announcement of the killings 'Cameron referred to Khan and Hussain planning an attack, but in its briefing to reporters later, Downing Street referred to events that had happened long before they were killed.'[285] The drone strike was not a response to violence happening at that moment. Thus, the attacks on Khan, Hussain and others have the character of unlawful reprisal attacks, not action in self-defence.[286] The right of self-defence is a right to use force to repel an attack in progress,[287] to prevent the near-time attacks that will occur as part of the attack in progress, or to reverse the consequences of an attack, such as ending an occupation. In these situations, necessity and proportionality can be calculated.

The 2011 intervention in Libya by NATO members and others further demonstrates the importance of compliance with necessity and proportionality. In March 2011, the Security Council authorised States to use military force to protect civilians in the Libyan civil war.[288] Virtually no attempt at negotiation was made and no alternatives to force were tried, such as protected corridors for refugees to move to safe areas. It seemed clear soon after NATO began attacks in Libya that the alliance's military objective was to oust Ghaddafi, not simply civilian protection.[289] Russia and China argued that fighting to change the regime exceeded the Security Council's mandate and was thus a resort to unlawful force.[290] As many as 30,000 people died – many, if not most, civilians – in about six months. With the fall of Ghaddafi, near anarchy erupted and more civilians died. If the principle of necessity had been taken seriously, such widespread fighting would not have been initiated, even if the Security Council had authorised it. As a general principle, all uses of

---

[285] Ewen MacAskill and Richard Norton-Taylor, 'How the UK Government Decided to Kill Reyaad Khan', *The Guardian*, 8 September 2015, available at www.theguardian.com/world/2015/sep/08/how-did-britain-decide-to-assassinate-uk-isis-fighter-reyaad-khan-drone-strike.

[286] See Stanimir A. Alexandrov, *Self-Defence against the Use of Force in International Law* (The Hague: Kluwer Law International, 1996), 17–18.

[287] 'Art. 51 clearly licenses at least one kind of resort to force by an individual member State: namely, the use of armed force to repel an armed attack'; Röling, 'The Ban on the Use of Force and the UN Charter' 1986 (n. 26), 3.

[288] Hugh Roberts, 'Who Said Ghaddafi Had to Go?', *London Review of Books* 33 (2011), 8–18 (8).

[289] *Ibid.*

[290] Patrick Goodenough, 'Russia, China Accuse West of Exceeding UN Resolution, Making Libyan Crisis Worse', *CNS News*, 29 March 2011, available at www.cnsnews.com/news/article/russia-china-accuse-west-exceeding-un-resolution-making-libyan-crisis-worse.

force must meet its requirements, whether in self-defence or with Security Council authorisation.[291]

South Korea has modelled compliance with necessity and proportionality. North Korea has attacked it with missiles and other forms of force many times since the end of the Korean War. Despite this, South Korean leaders have exercised restraint in launching counter-attacks, calculating they will have little positive effect. This was the case even prior to North Korea acquiring a nuclear weapon.[292]

B. History, Morality, Natural Law

The ancient prohibition on the use of force with its narrow allowance for self-defence in situations of necessity is found in the earliest discussions of law between communities. Prior to the European Enlightenment and the rise of positivism, legal theory explained the content of law as incorporating mostly positive law but within a frame of principles ordained by divine command. The *ius ad bellum* was one of the last areas that continued to be explained through natural law.[293] Then, just as the international legal community lost nearly all knowledge of natural law, scholars began again to argue that *ius cogens* principles as well as legal authority in general require more than positivism. The discussion below describes both the ancient origins of the prohibition on the use of force as a moral and legal precept and the reappearance of natural law along with the new interest in *ius cogens*.

Historians consistently find the earliest direct antecedents of today's prohibition on the use of force in the Christian Just War Doctrine that emerged in the fifth century and drew on Roman, Greek and Jewish teaching in addition to Christianity.[294] Proponents of the Just War Doctrine sought to end the early

---

[291]   I have argued elsewhere that the Security Council itself must take necessity into account in authorising a use of force. Mary Ellen O'Connell, 'Peace through Law and the Security Council: Modelling Law Compliance', in Jeremy Matam Farrall and Hilary Charlesworth (eds.), *Strengthening the Rule of Law through the UN Security Council* (Abingdon: Routledge, 2016), 255–69 (259–60).

[292]   For a history of North Korean actions against South Korea, see Hannah Fischer, *North Korean Provocative Actions, 1950–2007* (Washington, DC: Congressional Research Service, 2007). North Korea announced it had successfully tested a nuclear weapon in 2006. SC Res. 1718 of 14 October 2006.

[293]   Green, 'Questioning the Peremptory Status of the Prohibition of the Use of Force' 2001 (n. 273), 221 *et seq*. Conforti approached the Just War Doctrine through natural law theory into the 2000s; Benedetto Conforti, 'The Doctrine of "Just War" and Contemporary International Law', *Italian Yearbook of International Law* 12 (2002), 3–11 (3–4).

[294]   See e.g. Yoram Dinstein, *War, Aggression, and Self-Defence* (Cambridge: Cambridge University Press, 5th edn., 2011), 65–7.

Church's 'extreme pacifism'.[295] As Christianity became 'linked with the secular power of the Empire', Saint Augustine of Hippo presented theologically
based arguments for allowing limited resort to force in self-defence, as well as
to restore stolen property, to deter future wrongs and to promote
Christianity.[296] Some later Christian groups, including Quakers,
Mennonites and the Amish, returned to a commitment to total non-
violence, but most have followed Augustine. Over the centuries, a complete
reversal has occurred in some quarters. From a narrow exception for situations
of extremes, certain Just War theorists extol the virtue of war in good causes.[297]

Saint Thomas Aquinas systematised Just War teaching in the thirteenth
century into a set of law-like principles that required a declaration by a right
authority, a just cause, the right intention on the part of the authority, and
compliance with the principles of necessity and proportionality.[298] Self-
defence was among the just causes. Aquinas used natural law method in
developing his Just War principles. For him this method combined the use
of reason – informed by education, experience, and divine revelation – and
reflection on humanity's social nature and the observable order of the natural
world.[299]

Aquinas fused reason, openness to transcendence, and observation of nature
as sources of guidance and authority. This three-part, interconnected synthesis
for natural law method had evolved over centuries.[300] Aquinas understood
legitimate positive law to be consistent with norms derived from natural law

---

[295] Brownlie, *International Law and the Use of Force by States* 1963 (n. 185), 5 (citation omitted).

[296] Augustine's writing on Just War is found among his various letters and books. For the critical
point of the importance of peace, see his letter to St. Boniface, reproduced in
Leon Friedman, *The Law of War: A Documentary History* (New York: Random House,
1972). See also John Langan, 'The Elements of St. Augustine's Just War Theory', *Journal of
Religious Ethics* 12 (1984), 19–38, and Joachim von Elbe, 'The Evolution of the Concept of the
Just War in International Law', *American Journal of International Law* 33 (1939),
665–688 (665).

[297] See generally, for example, Nigel Biggar, *In Defence of War* (Oxford: Oxford University Press,
2013). For a critique of this development, see, Zehfuss, *War and the Politics of Ethics* 2018
(n. 23), 53–4. ('The contemporary discourse of war, which is permeated by just war thinking,
provides a frame of intelligibility; ethics is an essential part of this... [I]deas of ethics have
come to enable and enhance war.')

[298] Thomas Aquinas, *Summa Theologica* (Internet Sacred Texts Archive, Fathers of the English
Dominican Province, translation, 1947), I–II, Q.40, available at http://sacred-texts.com/chr/
aquinas/summa/index.htm. See also Wilhelm G. Grewe, *The Epochs of International Law*
(Berlin: De Gruyter, 2000), 108–11.

[299] Richard Horsley, 'The Law of Nature in Philo and Cicero', *The Harvard Theological Review*
71 (1978), 35–59 (48–9).

[300] O'Connell and Day, 'Sources and the Legality and Validity of International Law' 2017
(n. 257).

method and thereby with the good.[301] He explained that the vast majority of law is derived from positive sources – legislation and practice – but that it exists within a frame of natural law. The application of natural law method results in more complete explanations than are available in positive law theory, answering such questions as to why law has authority in society and what principles are essential and, therefore, unalterable through positive law method, including the restrictions on resort to war.[302]

Figures such as Hugo Grotius sought to retain natural law method without the intermediation of Catholic Church clergy. He argued, in distinction to other Protestants, such as Alberico Gentili, for a limit on individualistic determinations of ultimate morality. With respect to the Just War Doctrine, for example, Grotius argued for retaining the brief list of just causes used since Augustine as the chief means of restraining resort to war.[303] Grotius's seminal work, *On the Law of War and Peace* (1625) aimed at the Thirty Years' War and mitigating its barbarism. Grotius wanted to inspire greater humanity in the conduct of the war and encourage the establishment of a legal order superior to the warring factions after the war. A group of legally co-equal sovereign States did in fact emerge in Western Europe under the treaties known as the Peace of Westphalia (1648). Grotius's comprehensive treatise provided the legal blueprint for the new world order. In the prologue he made the decisive point that both allowed Europeans to move past their religious differences to agree to peace, but also contributed significantly to the undermining of natural law theory and the Just War Doctrine based upon it. To win the adherence of both Protestants and Catholics to one unified law, Grotius famously wrote:

> What we have been saying [about law] would have a degree of validity even if we should concede that which cannot be conceded without the utmost wickedness, that there is no God, or that the affairs of men are of no concern to him.[304]

It was this concept that began the process of eliminating reference to a divine basis of legal authority in the West. Grotius's proposition helped avoid theological disputes in winning adherents to international law, doing little

---

[301] Aquinas, *Summa Theologica* (n. 298), I–II, Q. 94, Art. 4.

[302] The term 'positive law' was put into wide philosophical circulation first by Aquinas. John Finnis, 'Natural Law Theories', in Edward N. Zalta (ed.), *The Stanford Encyclopedia of Philosophy* (Winter 2016), 1, available at https://plato.stanford.edu/archives/win2016/entries/natural-law-theories.

[303] Von Elbe, 'The Evolution of the Concept of the Just War in International Law' (n. 296), 678.

[304] Hugo Grotius, *De Jure Belli ac Pacis*, translated by Francis Kelsey (Buffalo, NY: Francis W. Kelsey, translation of the 1625 text, 1995), Prolegomena.

immediate harm as the Western conception of law continued to benefit from the centuries of association with belief in divine authority.

Each decade after Grotius, however, the assumed tradition supplying the frame of international law within which the positive law exists has thinned.[305] Some theorists view the move away from religion to be a move to greater sophistication and rationality.[306] Removing particular religious understandings of transcendence from natural law was a rational response to the new, more pluralist understanding of contemporary society.[307] However, without an alternative explanation as to why some legal principles are superior to positive law rules, misunderstanding was bound to arise. After Grotius, scholarship on the normativity of international law increasingly narrowed towards exclusively positivist theories. The Swiss jurist Emer de Vattel did great damage to the theory of law as superior to political communities or sovereigns by returning to the argument that the sovereign alone may judge the lawfulness of her own actions.[308] After Vattel, the concept grew steadily that law is what the sovereign wills, and international law could, therefore, be no more than the consensus of State will, unrelated to any higher source.

With the rise of positivism and sovereign absolutism, the reasons for adherence to the Just War Doctrine became increasingly unpersuasive. Nevertheless, the Doctrine did not disappear. European powers developed various justifications for waging wars to take and control colonies. Inconsistencies between actual practice and the Just War Doctrine grew, but States did, in fact, continue to proclaim the justice of their causes.[309] States attempted to avoid the implications of formally declaring war by engaging in force short of war or reprisals.[310] They presented arguments as to why the use of force met the requirements of necessity and proportionality.[311]

Proof of the continuing vitality of the Just War Doctrine through the nineteenth century is provided by the same correspondence over the 1837 *Caroline*

[305] See, e.g., Talal Asad, *Formations of the Secular: Christianity, Islam, Modernity* (Stanford, CA: Stanford University Press, 2003) and Charles Taylor, *A Secular Age* (Cambridge, MA: Belknap Press of Harvard University Press, 2007).
[306] Jean D'Aspremont and Jörg Kammerhofer, 'Introduction', in Besson and D'Aspremont (eds.), *The Oxford Handbook on the Sources of International Law* 2017 (n. 257), 12–13.
[307] Jean Porter, *Nature as Reason – A Thomistic Theory of the Natural Law* (Grand Rapids, MI: Eerdmans, 2005), 30.
[308] Emmerich de Vattel, *The Law of Nations or the Principles of Natural Law, Applied to the Conduct and to the Affairs of Nations and of Sovereigns* (Washington, DC: Carnegie Institute of Washington, Charles G. Fenwick translation of the 1758 edn., 1916), 189–92.
[309] Von Elbe, 'The Evolution of the Concept of the Just War in International Law' (n. 296), 684.
[310] Grewe, *The Epochs of International Law* 2000 (n. 298), 367–9.
[311] Gardam, *Necessity, Proportionality and the Use of Military Force by States* (n. 100), 32.

incident Bowett used to attempt to weaken the restrictions on the use of force. The correspondence between Webster and Ashburton was over the meaning of the law restricting resort to force outside of any treaty.[312]

Natural law teaching on war was also retained through transformation into positive law. The Paris Declaration on Maritime Law of 1856 had provisions regulating the conduct of maritime warfare, including outlawing privateering.[313] In 1899, States adopted the First Hague Peace Convention, which required States to seek alternatives to resort to force. In 1907, at the Second Hague Peace Conference, more conventions were adopted to prevent and mitigate armed conflict. The First Hague Peace Convention of 1907 on peaceful settlement of disputes expressed the purpose in Article 1 to be 'obviating as far as possible recourse to force in the relations between States' and 'to ensure the pacific settlement of international differences'.[314] These developments in positive law further occluded the gap in legal theory left through suppression of natural law.

Into the early twentieth century international law scholars continued to acknowledge a role for natural law, especially regarding resort to force. One of the most prominent international law scholars of the time, Lassa Oppenheim, felt the need to continue arguing against natural law and its proponents, who seemed to him to disagree about the most basic issues.[315] The 1906 edition of his influential treatise refers to peace activists as 'fanatics'.[316] Oppenheim's protests are just another indication, however, that in fact governments and scholars persisted in looking to the natural law doctrine of Just War. Those who saw it as their mission to rid the world of any vestige of natural law never in fact succeeded.[317]

---

[312]   Daniel Webster and Alexander B. Ashburton, *Correspondence between Mr Webster and Lord Ashburton*, Washington, 1842, United States Department of State, available at https://archive .org/details/correspondencebeo4unit.

[313]   Arthur Nussbaum, *A Concise History of the Law of Nations* (New York: MacMillan, rev. edn., 1962), 192.

[314]   Hague Convention (IV) Respecting the Laws and Customs of War on Land, 18 October 1907.

[315]   Lassa Oppenheim, 'The Science of International Law', *American Journal of International Law* 2 (1908), 313–56 (332).

[316]   Lassa Oppenheim, *International Law – vol. II: War and Neutrality* (London: Longmans Green, 1906), 55–6.

[317]   While some international law scholars considered references to natural law to be moral, not legal claims, and might have so characterised government invocations of the Just War Doctrine in the same way, there is little indication that governments seeking to justify resort to force had abandoned the classic natural law position that Just War principles reflect both law and morality. See, e.g., Amos S. Hershey, *The International Law and Diplomacy of the Russo-Japanese War* (New York: Macmillan, 1906), 67. Neff cites a list of international law scholars writing in the mid-nineteenth century who forthrightly supported the law–morality connection of the Just War Doctrine, including Halleck, Heffter, Bluntschli, Funck-

By the end of the First World War it was quite clear to some legal scholars that the theory of absolute sovereignty had gone too far. They were blaming the 'crude' positivism of the previous century for the understanding that no law existed above positive law made by States.[318] Positivism contained no explanation to use against the dictators emerging in Europe with aggressive designs on other States. Those designs were, after all, an exercise of State will. If a positive law obstacle stood in the way, such as The Hague Conventions, a State need only withdraw its consent to be free to act.[319]

Others, however, returned to natural law to revive some restraining principles superior to the will of States. Hans Kelsen, a critic of natural law, nevertheless incorporated key natural law concepts in his view of war and his theory of legal authority. Kelsen understood the sanction to be an integral part of any legal rule. For Kelsen, war and reprisals, subject to constraints, were the necessary legal sanctions of international law.[320] Kelsen responded to those who believed all war to be unlawful by saying that the only way to respond to unlawful war was with war. Logically all war could not, therefore, be considered unlawful.[321] War in the classic thinking of the Just War Doctrine could be lawful. Kelsen found positive evidence that the Just War Doctrine persisted in international law in provisions of the Treaty of Versailles, the Covenant of the League of Nations and the Kellogg–Briand Pact.[322] Kelsen interpreted all of these agreements as permitting the use of force to respond to unlawful war.

At the same time, the Just War Doctrine did not permit unfettered war. Kelsen credited Augustine, Aquinas and Grotius as developing the idea of war being forbidden except in a just cause.[323] The increasing rejection of the Just War Doctrine during the nineteenth century came in connection with the

---

Brentano and Sorel; Stephen C. Neff, *War and the Law of Nations* (New York: Cambridge University Press, 2005), 200. One of the leading theorists of the twentieth century, Hans Kelsen, considered the Just War Doctrine, as received from theologians Augustine, Aquinas and Grotius, to be part of international law. Hans Kelsen, *What is Justice? Law and Politics in the Mirror of Science: Collected Essays* (Berkeley, CA: University of California Press, 1957), 144.

[318] Nussbaum, *A Concise History of the Law of Nations* 1962 (n. 313), 276–8.

[319] *Ibid.*

[320] Hans Kelsen, *General Theory of Law and the State* (Cambridge, MA: Harvard University Press, Anders Wedberg translation, 1945; reprinted: Clark, NJ: The Lawbook Exchange, 1999, 2011), 330.

[321] *Ibid.*, 331–2.

[322] *Ibid.*, 333. Hans Kelsen, *Pure Theory of Law* (Berkeley, CA: University of California Press, Max Knight translation of the 2nd German edn., 1967; reprinted: Clark, NJ: The Lawbook Exchange, 2005), 322.

[323] Kelsen, *General Theory of Law and the State* 1945 (n. 320), 335–6.

emergence of theories promoting absolute State sovereignty.[324] Those theories challenged all international law, not just the limitation on war. They had to be rejected, and, in doing so, the main objection to restricting war disappeared too.[325] Kelsen was alert to the quixotic position of scholars like Oppenheim who took the view that while war could not be restricted, measures short of war or reprisals could be regulated.[326] After the Second World War, Kelsen described the UN Charter prohibition on the use of force as an instantiation of the Just War Doctrine.[327]

The catastrophe of World War II drew some others back to natural law. For German scholars Theodor Adorno and Gustav Radbruch, positivism, shorn of any connection to natural law, had played a significant role in persuading large populations of the legality of Fascist policies.[328] Adolf Hitler was elected ostensibly in compliance with the German constitution and was, therefore, the legitimate leader who could command obedience. The courts enforced the laws adopted by parliament. After the War, in the famous trial of the judges, a standard defence was that a judge's job is to enforce the law developed following legally instituted procedures. Judging morality is not the job of a positive law court.[329] Prosecuting German and Japanese leaders required confronting this defence. According to David Luban and co-authors, Article 8 of the Nuremberg Charter relies on natural law in restricting the defence of acting 'pursuant to an order of his government or a superior'.[330] Thus, natural law 'form[s] the most obvious

---

[324]   *Ibid.*, 336.

[325]   *Ibid.*

[326]   Hans Kelsen, *The Legal Process and International Order* (London: Constable, 1935), 13–14.

[327]   Kelsen, *Pure Theory of Law* 1967 (n. 322), 322.

[328]   Adorno critiqued how positivism reduces the sources of knowledge to the rational alone, much as Fascist ideology had done, repressing observation of nature, insights from emotion, and reactions to beauty. Theodor W. Adorno *et al.*, *The Positivist Dispute in German Sociology* (London: Heinemann Educational Books, 1976), 55–66. See also Theodor W. Adorno and Max Horkheimer, *Dialectic of Enlightenment* (Paolo Alto, CA: Stanford University Press, 1947; reprinted 2002).

Radbruch argued that positive law, which failed to conform with extra-positive or natural principles, in particular, justice, was invalid law. See, e.g., Gustav Radbruch, *Der Geist des Englischen Rechts* (Heidelberg: Adolf Rausch, 1947), 49. Radbruch inspired a return to natural law in post-war Germany. Vivian Grosswald Curran, 'Fear of Formalism: Indications from the Fascist Period in France and Germany of Judicial Methodology's Impact on Substantive Law', *Cornell International Law Journal* 35 (2001), 101–87 (135, fn. 141).

[329]   *United States v. Altstoetter (The Justice Case)*, in *Trials of War Criminals Before the Nuernberg Military Tribunals Under Control Council Law* No. 10 (Washington, DC: US Government Printing Office, 1951), vol. III, 983–6.

[330]   David Luban, Alan Strudler and David Wasserman, 'Moral Responsibility in the Age of Bureaucracy', *Michigan Law Review* 90 (1992), 2348–92 (2352).

justification for criminalizing "murder, extermination, enslavement, depor-
tation, and other inhumane acts" . . . whether or not in violation of domestic
law'.[331] The influence of natural law can also be seen in the Nuremberg
Tribunal's characterisation of aggression as the 'supreme international
crime'.[332]

In 1946, Sir Hersch Lauterpacht also re-presented law as a hybrid system of
positive and natural law.[333] Lauterpacht understood that all law consists of
both forms, but argued that while this fact could be merely assumed for
national legal systems, it had to be openly acknowledged in the case of
international law. International law has a unique role in regulating relations
in a system of diverse nations and cultures lacking regular governmental
institutions of courts, legislature and executive. At the international level,
'the function of natural law, whatever may be its form, must approximate
more closely to that of a direct source of law.'[334] Lauterpacht did not provide
an explanation of what exactly natural law is, or how it can approximate
a direct source of law. He did point to certain 'features' of natural law that
he considered essential to international law, including the comprehension of
law as superior to 'the totality of international relations'. He credited Grotius
with endowing international law with 'unprecedented dignity and authority by
making it part not only of a general system of jurisprudence but also of
a universal moral code'.[335]

ICJ Judge Kōtarō Tanaka also made a case for natural law in his dissenting
opinion in the 1966 *South West Africa* cases.[336] Other international law
theorists, such as Verdross, worked to revive natural law, providing the reasoning for acceptance today that the Charter prohibition on force and principles
related to it respecting the right to life and civilian protections in armed
conflict are *ius cogens*, peremptory norms. Writing recently, ICJ Judge
Antônio Augusto Cançado Trindade and former judge Christopher

[331] *Ibid.*
[332] 'The charges in the Indictment that the defendants planned and waged aggressive wars are
charges of the utmost gravity. War is essentially an evil thing. Its consequences are not
confined to the belligerent States alone, but affect the whole world. To initiate a war of
aggression, therefore, is not only an international crime; *it is the supreme international crime*
differing only from other war crimes in that it contains within itself the accumulated evil of
the whole'; International Military Tribunal (Nuremberg), Judgment and Sentences 1946
(n. 61), 186.
[333] Hersch Lauterpacht, 'The Grotian Tradition in International Law', *British Yearbook of
International Law* 23 (1946), 1–53 (22–3).
[334] *Ibid.*
[335] *Ibid.*, 51.
[336] ICJ, *South West Africa* (Ethiopia v. South Africa; Liberia v. South Africa), Second Phase,
Judgment of 18 July 1966, Dissenting Opinion of Judge Tanaka, ICJ Reports 1966, 298.

Weeramantry also support renewed understanding of natural law.[337] The important point for this discussion is that the peremptory norms and inherent general principles have a distinctive theoretical basis in international law. The ancient history of restraint on resort to force reflects deeply held moral precepts, moral precepts further reflected in the natural law method developed to account for non-derogable legal principles and the basis of legal authority. Using the approach of natural law, judges, delegates to a negotiating conference, or other representatives of the community with authority to participate in legal process continue to reflect the approach associated with Aquinas of discerning *ius cogens* by employing reason and reflecting on human nature and the natural world, while remaining open to transcendence.[338] Aquinas looked to revelation for understanding transcendence. Philosophers in our secular age see secular paths leading to the same concepts, especially in aesthetic philosophy, the study of beauty.[339]

C. The Implications of Ius Cogens Status for Self-Defence

Certain conclusions flow from the status of the prohibition on the use of force as a peremptory norm. One critical conclusion is that under international law, no other norms or values are superior. The other *ius cogens* norms are co-equal; all other norms and values are inferior. Inferior norms do not trump superior norms. Another conclusion is that peremptory norms require a conservative approach to interpretation of the norm itself and related provisions, such as Article 51 of the UN Charter. Indeed, the drafters of the Vienna Convention understood that interpreting *ius cogens* might require the intervention of the International Court of Justice and provided for that possibility in Article 66. These prohibitions are durable and impervious to diminution. Interpretation that permits conduct contrary to the established meaning of the norm is a form of derogation. State practice contrary to the prohibition cannot modify it; contrary practice is a violation of the prohibition.

Finally, peremptory norms are not 'frozen'. They may expand, reaching more conduct, such as the use of force to wage civil war. Again, the Vienna Convention points to the possibility of expansion in Article 64, which refers to the 'emergence' of new *ius cogens*. Expansion of peremptory norms is not impermissible derogation. It is consistent with the ethos of *ius cogens*.

---

[337]   Cançado Trindade, *International Law for Humankind* 2013 (n. 257); Weeramantry, *Universalizing International Law* 2004 (n. 257), 333.
[338]   Aquinas, *Summa Theologica* (n. 298), I–II, Q. 90.
[339]   See, e.g., Iris Murdoch, *The Sovereignty of Good* (London: Routledge/Keagan Paul, 1st edn., 1970), 32.

1. Peace as the Superior Moral and Legal Norm

Proponents of force against non-State actors, for humanitarian purposes, arms control, and other goals, often use arguments from morality to justify violating the prohibition on the use of force. The arguments parallel the standard civil disobedience reasoning that the moral rightness of using force excuses the legal violation. This line of thought seems to overlook that the prohibition on force is not a mere positive rule that is less important in the moral universe than the advocate's own normative goal. Peremptory norms prohibit conduct; they do not command it. No logical reason exists to violate one peremptory norm to advance another. No State could excuse the use of torture to advance the prohibition of genocide. The same is true of the prohibition on the use of force. In the case of a value such as national security, the argument is even stronger. The prohibition on the use of force is *ius cogens* and may not be violated to advance national security. Other ways must be found consistent with the norm.

In the issue area of use of force against non-State actors, the value being juxtaposed to the prohibition on force is typically security. The sort of argument has become familiar, owing to advocacy for humanitarian intervention. Supporters of humanitarian intervention tend to accept that they stand on weak legal grounds and seek to substitute moral arguments as supplementary legal ones. The great suffering of victims is used to argue for a lower quantity of evidence to support reinterpretation, modification or addition to the Charter exceptions for resort to force.[340] Without the moral argument, the legal argument would likely be dismissed out of hand. Another approach accepts that the legal basis for humanitarian intervention is weak but finds sufficient support to place humanitarian intervention in a 'grey area' of illegality.[341]

In the pursuit of security against non-State actors, Orna Ben-Naftali says States have developed a 'theology of security'.[342] This theology involves

---

[340] See Koh, 'Not Illegal: But Now the Hard Part Begins' (n. 23).

[341] The Independent Kosovo Commission declared that the use of force by NATO against Yugoslavia in 1999 was unlawful but nevertheless 'legitimate'. See Independent International Commission on Kosovo, *Kosovo Report: Conflict, International Response and Lessons Learned* (Oxford: Oxford University Press, 2000), 164; and see Robert Cryer *et al.*, *An Introduction to International Criminal Law and Procedure* (Cambridge: Cambridge University Press, 2nd edn., 2010), 326–7. But see Zehfuss, *War and the Politics of Ethics* 2018 (n. 23), for weaknesses in the post-Cold War ethical arguments in support of war.

[342] Orna Ben Naftali, Michael Sfard and Hedi Viterbo, *The ABC of the OPT: A Legal Lexicon of the Occupation of the Palestinian Territory* (Cambridge: Cambridge University Press, 2017), chapter X, citing Yael Berda, 'The Security Risk as a Security Risk: Notes on the Classification and Practices of the Israeli Security Services', in Abeer Baker and Anat Matar (eds.), *Threat: Palestinian Political Prisoners in Israel* (London: Pluto Press, 2011), 44–55; Nadera Shalhoub-

believing that an increase in one's own sense of security is acceptable even at
the cost of limiting the right to life of another, generally a person outside one's
community. This notion places security as a value ahead of the peremptory
norm prohibiting force. Advocates for expanding the legal right to resort to
force tend to ignore this basic legal fact. They also tend to begin analysis with
the exception to the prohibition in Article 51, rather than the prohibition, and
from Article 51 their argument continues with policy reasons why governments
should have a wide-open right to resort to military force against enemies,
whether the Irish Republican Army, Hezbollah, the PKK, Abu Sayyaf, the
FARC, Al-Qaeda, Al-Shabab, Boko Haram, ISIS, or others. The reason these
groups are or have been the enemy is because they use violence and violate the
right to life and other human rights in promoting their causes. The law against
force is in favour of the right to life and forms the very foundation of orderly life
in society.

As discussed above, the doctrine of *ius cogens* rejects the argument that
violating a peremptory norm is justifiable to promote another *ius cogens* or
other important norm.[343] Even if the prohibition on force were not *ius cogens*,
arguments based on national security, necessity, or even the protection of the
right to life would still fail. Inherent in such attempted justifications is the
contradiction that it is acceptable to kill and injure some, even wholly
innocent people, to preserve the human rights of others.[344] Ian Brownlie raised
concerns about believing in the use of military force to accomplish the
protection of human rights in the 1970s.

[T]hose making novel proposals need to produce more evidence. What is the
price in human terms of intervention? What were the casualty ratios in the
Stanleyville [Congo] operation in 1964, the Dominican Republic in 1965,
and other possible examples? How many were killed in order to 'save lives'?
To what extent does the typical intervention cause collateral harms by
exacerbating a civil war, introducing indiscriminate use of air power in
support operations, and so on?[345]

International law has other ways to counter terrorism and advance human
rights, including the right to life, without violating the prohibition on the
use of force. Proposing the expansion of the right to use force to these new

Kevorkian, *Security Theology, Surveillance and the Politics of Fear* (Cambridge: Cambridge
University Press, 2015), 16–20.
[343] Kelsen, *General Theory of Law and the State* 1945 (n. 320), 330.
[344] Ian Brownlie, 'Humanitarian Law', in John N. Moore (ed.), *Law and Civil War in the
Modern World* (Baltimore, MD: Johns Hopkins University Press, 1974), 217–28 (footnotes
omitted).
[345] *Ibid.*

causes reverses the assumption upon which the right to resort to force is tolerated in international law. Under the Charter, military force in self-defence is lawful to counter unlawful military force by or attributable to a State with a government and territory. The Charter does not expressly reach civil war, but international law principles in that context, too, are designed to apply to a contention among armed groups using military force to control territory.[346] The law of self-defence does not envision using military force to try to affect the kind of social change needed to supress terrorist crime or deter human rights violations. Whether or not the Security Council has the legal right to authorise such use of force is beyond the scope of this chapter. Suffice it to say here that the history and structure of law restricting the use of force supports the conclusion that violating the prohibition on the use of force is immoral and impractical regardless of the aim. The law supports seeking alternatives to military force under the justification of self-defence.

In any case of uncertainty, situations where a 'blurring of the lines between war ... and countering the crime of terrorism'[347] takes place, the logic of *ius cogens* requires adherence to peacetime law. The whole body of international law is structured to move toward eliminating war. The exceptions to the prohibition of force and in IHL are designed to apply in narrowly defined emergencies. The argument that it is too difficult to comply with the restrictions on the use of force is misleading. Nothing is easier than *not* killing. Pacifists are willing to be killed by an attacker rather than risk killing in an act of self-defence. The idea that *not* killing is hard has grown out of the false assumption that military force is an effective tool against terrorism and in support of human rights. Foreign policy realists, weapons manufacturers and even some academics advance this myth despite the substantial social science evidence to the contrary.[348]

---

[346] Additional Protocol II is based on an even narrower assumption that a non-State actor armed group has taken control of territory and not prior to that event. Protocol Additional to the Geneva Conventions of 12 August 1949, and Relating to the Protection of Victims of Non-International Armed Conflicts (Protocol II), 8 June 1977, 1125 UNTS 609, Article 1.

[347] See UK House of Lords, House of Commons, Joint Committee on Human Rights, 'The Government's Policy on the Use of Drones for Targeted Killing' (n. 2), 9.

[348] E.g., Audrey Kurth Cronin, 'The Strategic Implications of Targeted Drone Strikes for US Global Counterterrorism', in David Cortright (ed.), *Drones and the Future of Armed Conflict* (Chicago, IL: University of Chicago Press, 2015), 99–120 (119). Seth G. Jones and Martin C. Libicki, *How Terrorist Groups End, Lessons for Countering al Qa'ida* (Santa Monica,CA: RAND Corporation, 2008), available at www.rand.org/pubs/monographs/2008/RAND_MG741-1.pdf.

2. Peremptory Interpretation/Irrelevant State Practice

Little has been written on the proper approach to interpreting *ius cogens*. Expansionists attempt to use State practice to show that the Charter provisions have changed and are weaker, posing less of a barrier to State use of force.[349] Indeed, much of the standard work on self-defence looks to State practice, such as the use of force against non-State actors beyond armed conflict zones or the use of force without a territorial State's express consent, to argue that these law violations are capable of diluting the restrictions in Article 51.[350] Given the nature of peremptory prohibitions, however, valid interpretation must not result in a weaker norm. Logically, peremptory norms may expand, not contract.

As a theoretical matter, attempting to create a new treaty rule or a rule of customary law that derogates from a *ius cogens* prohibition may be distinctive from derogation through interpretation. As a practical matter, the two processes are indistinguishable. Indeed, it is sometimes difficult to tell whether an expansionist is invoking State practice as evidence of a new rule of customary international law or as subsequent practice relevant to rule interpretation.[351] When peremptory norms are newly discerned, the discovery may lead to invalidating existing treaties and rules of custom.[352] Similarly, interpretation can lead to greater restrictions where aggression, genocide, torture, or another peremptory prohibition is concerned, not lesser. In any case of doubt as to a prohibition's reach, the presumption favours treating more conduct as restricted, not less.[353] This means, for example, that reading Article 51 as

---

[349] Expansionists writing today include Bethlehem and Deeks; see above, n. 23 and n. 246. See also Claus Kress, 'Time for Decision: Some Thoughts on the Immediate Future of the Crime of Aggression', *European Journal of International Law* 20 (2009), 1129–46 (1140, fn. 42); Elena Chachko and Ashley Deeks, 'Who is on Board with "Unwilling or Unable"?', *Lawfare Blog*, 16 October 2016, available at www.lawfareblog.com/who-board-unwilling-or-unable.

[350] For an example, see Raphaël van Steenberghe, 'The Law of Self-Defence and the New Argumentative Landscape on the Expansionists' Side', *Leiden Journal of International Law* 29 (2016), 43–65; van Steenberghe, 'State Practice and the Evolution of the Law of Self-Defence' 2015 (n. 22), 81–96, and Reinold, 'State Weakness, Irregular Warfare, and the Right to Self-Defence Post 9/11' 2011 (n. 91), arguing that uses of force by the US, Russia, Turkey, Colombia, Israel and Uganda against weaker opponents has altered Article 51.

[351] See Christian J. Tams, 'Light Treatment of a Complex Problem: The Law of Self-Defence in the Wall Case', *European Journal of International Law* 16 (2005), 963–78 (964, 972–3).

[352] Article 64 VCLT.

[353] Presumptions within international law are an unstudied aspect of the field. Some presumptions are well known, such as the presumption in favour of civilian status in International Humanitarian Law or the presumption in favour of free trade in international trade law. See Geneva Convention Relative to the Treatment of Prisoners of War, 12 August 1949, 75 UNTS 135, Article 4; see also Protocol Additional to the Geneva Conventions of 12 August 1949, and relating to the Protections of Victims of International Armed Conflicts (Protocol I),

permitting self-defence before an armed attack occurs, as the inherent right doctrine permits, would be an incorrect reading, given the nature of the prohibition. The same may be said of removing the significance requirement respecting the armed attack and the attribution requirement for the target of military action in self-defence.

If Article 2(4) were just a treaty principle or rule of customary international law, standard interpretation rules would include subsequent practice as a guide to meaning, even to some extent meaning that changes over time.[354] As *ius cogens*, however, meaning is stable, and contrary State practice is of little relevance. States acknowledge that the prohibition on the use of force is *ius cogens* but overlook this point about interpretation and the impact of State practice. To avoid diluting Article 2(4), Article 51 must be interpreted to limit weakening the general prohibition. Only State practice indicating discernment toward a rule with wider reach is consistent with the 'no derogation'.

The general principles of necessity and proportionality that are part of the prohibition on the use of force must also be interpreted conservatively, as must the principles of State responsibility. State responsibility principles of attribution as well as consent require clear and convincing evidence provided openly for the members of the international community to assess.[355] Consent as a defence in the law of State responsibility is 'subject to the limitation codified in Article 26 of the Articles on State Responsibility (ASR): they may not be invoked against peremptory rules'.[356] The unable/unwilling doctrine substitutes the attacking State's subjective assessment that another State is not managing a problem of terrorism for the target State's consent. The better position in light of the peremptory status of the prohibition is that only express

---

8 June 1977, 1125 UNTS 3, Articles 43, 44 and 51. Both examples rest on core normative assumptions upon which the relevant regime is built. Peremptory norms are even more fundamental normative assumptions for law in general and, therefore, enjoy a presumption in their favour.

[354] Articles 31–32 VCLT; ICJ, *Dispute Regarding Navigational and Related Rights* (Costa Rica v. Nicaragua), Merits, Judgment of 13 July 2009, ICJ Reports 2009, 213.

[355] For the clear, convincing, and public standard of evidence as applicable to the international law on the use of force, see Mary Ellen O'Connell, 'Evidence of Terror', *Journal of Conflict and Security Law* 7 (2002), 19–36. While manipulation of facts by governments and other actors has always been a problem of international law, the need for a high standard of proof to deal with it seems all the more important in a time of 'alternative facts' and 'fake news'.

[356] Federica Paddeu, 'Excusing Humanitarian Intervention: A Reply to Jure Vidmar', *EJIL Talk!*, 27 April 2017, available at www.ejiltalk.org/excusing-humanitarian-intervention-a-reply-to-ju re-vidmar. See also, Zehfuss, *War and the Politics of Ethics* 2018 (n. 23), 9 ('The upshot is that, from the perspective of the West, war appears geographically distant but morally required and therefore unending').

and public consent is adequate to permit the lawful use of force on another State's territory. The *Nicaragua* case supports this position on consent.

Even if new interpretations could result in weakening the prohibition on the use of force, the current arguments aiming to do so tend to be insufficient to create valid, new interpretations, even of standard treaty and customary rules. The arguments are consistently a form of special pleading, intended for particular States and not the international community as a whole. Bowett states expressly that he had the Suez Crisis in mind in developing the 'inherent right' doctrine. Greenwood's approach to regard terrorist attacks as armed attacks was a defence of the US attack on Libya. Bethlehem focused in 2012 on American uses of military force in the terrorism context. Each was written after a use of force and each supplied a novel argument of *post hoc* justification.

These novel approaches to the law of self-defence seem to be designed for a few select States only.[357] The US and UK may resort to force when they deem another State 'unwilling' or 'unable' to respond adequately to terrorism but not others. The United Kingdom may use a drone-launched Hellfire missile to kill a person and bystanders in Syria to prevent a potential future terrorist attack at home, but China may not use the same weapon and rationale to kill an organised crime figure in Myanmar. The US claims a right to carry out drone strikes in Yemen against a man implicated in violent, anti-US propaganda because Yemen is unable or unwilling to control the suspect, but Russia cannot claim the same right to kill individuals considered a danger to the stability of its government living in the United Kingdom. This exceptionalism is an assumption of some government officials. An adviser to the former UK prime minister Tony Blair made the point as plainly as possible: 'The challenge ... is to get used to the idea of double standards. Among ourselves, we operate on the basis of laws ... But when dealing with more old-fashioned kinds of states ... we need to revert to the rougher methods of an earlier era – force, pre-emptive attack, deception.'[358]

A subtler approach relies on an idea related to customary international law formation that some States are 'specially affected' and that their practice and *opinio iuris* should have greater weight.[359] This idea has been used to assert

---

[357] Brunnée and Toope, 'Self-Defence against Non-State Actors' 2018 (n. 250) and accompanying text.

[358] Robert Cooper, 'The New Liberal Imperialism', *The Guardian*, 7 April 2002, available at www.theguardian.com/world/2002/apr/07/1.

[359] ICJ, *North Sea Continental Shelf* (Federal Republic of Germany/Denmark; Federal Republic of Germany/Netherlands), Judgment of 20 February 1969, ICJ Reports 1969, 44, para. 77.

that 'legal advisers from the defence, intelligence, and security services of reputable governments, should be accorded more weight because of these states' experiences countering new threats with new technologies that only these states possess.'[360] The rules that emerge advantage these States.

There is, however, no 'among ourselves' or States with greater weight when it comes to international law. States are equal before the law. Neither democracies, States with major military forces, nor any other has greater rights to resort to force. As Dire Tladi discusses in his chapter, the International Law Commission rejected a proposal to favour the 'specially affected' State in customary law formation.[361] Even if such a status existed, no State can claim to have exceptional rights based on being the victim of terrorism or in possession of high tech weapons like drones. The problem of terrorism is too widespread, and States do not retain monopolies on weapons technology. These arguments, once made with a Prime Minister Cameron or President Obama in mind, may appear quite differently to advocates when contemplating their use by a President Trump. Additionally, the poor results of using force in violation of the law continue to mount. It is a record of human tragedy that should undercut exceptionalist stances.[362]

3. Progressive Development Toward Peace

While diluting and contracting the prohibition on the use of force through interpretation is impermissible, discerning a broader prohibition is not. Interpreting the meaning of peremptory norms logically follows the principle of progression: the prohibitions on aggression, genocide, torture, and other egregious conduct may expand to reach more conduct in the future, not less.[363] This means that stretching analogies to allow more force is an invalid approach. The analogies between armed conflict and intermittent terrorist

[360]   Kattan, 'Furthering the "War on Terrorism" through International Law' 2017 (n. 248), 8.
[361]   Tladi, 'Progressive Development and Codification of International Law' 2013 (n 252). See also Peters and Marxsen, this volume, 272–4.
[362]   In addition to the dead and the injured, the tragedy involves the suffering of those displaced by armed conflict. See, e.g., UN News Centre, 'World's Forcibly Displaced Hit Record 38 Million, Prompting UN Appeal for "All-Out Effort" for Peace', 6 May 2015, available at www.un.org/apps/news/story.asp?NewsID=50785#.VZ050Usmz1p.
[363]   See Jorge Vinuales, 'The Paris Climate Agreement, An Initial Assessment (Part II of III)', *EJIL Talk!*, 8 February 2016, available at www.ejiltalk.org/the-paris-climate-agreement-an-initial-examination-part-ii-of-iii. Vinuales explains that the principle of progression was originally identified in relation to human rights. It is best categorized as a general principle as it concerns how certain norms function. Human rights, environmental protection principles, and *jus cogens* may regulate more conduct in the future but never less.

attacks or consent and implicit acquiescence because a State is 'unable or unwilling' to control terrorism are invalid.

One obvious area to expand the prohibition on the use of force is to reach civil war. The natural progression of the prohibition is to obligate non-State actors not to engage in military force. Non-State actors are already obligated not to kill under national criminal and international human rights law. Some may believe that once individuals form a group and struggle to secede or throw off an oppressive government, they are no longer bound by the national criminal law or the protection for the right to life. While it is true that, if such a group engages in fighting that has reached the level of armed conflict, aspects of IHL apply, no one has the right to initiate internal armed conflict by killing government forces or using excessive force against rebels. This principle could be incorporated into the *ius ad bellum*, raising the visibility and status of the prohibition on initiating military force. With greater awareness of the prohibition, non-State actors might be persuaded to adopt non-violent approaches.

Including initiation of civil war in the prohibition would also result in a limit on the right to assist governments fighting non-State actors within their own borders. The prohibition on the use of force in Article 2(4) by its plain terms prohibits assisting a government in fighting rebels. Presumably, any such use of force would require Security Council authorisation to be lawful. Nevertheless, governments have regularly intervened in internal conflicts in colonies and where a puppet government has been installed for the very purpose of making the invitation. The practice should end for all the normative reasons already discussed but also because the record of intervention on the side of governments is one of consistent failure. Consider the many interventions by France in former colonies – more than twenty within a period of forty years.[364] The intervention in the Central African Republic that began in 2013 has not only done little to improve stability, French troops were implicated in child sex abuse.[365] The record of intervention on the side of governments is one of extending conflict and keeping authoritarian, unpopular leaders in power.

---

[364] See Andrew Hansen, 'The French Military in Africa', *Council on Foreign Relations*, 8 February 2008, available at www.cfr.org/france/french-military-africa/p12578. Since the report was issued, France has undertaken major interventions in Syria, Mali and the Central African Republic.

[365] David Smith, 'France's Poisoned Legacy in the Central African Republic', *The Guardian*, 29 April 2015, available at www.theguardian.com/world/2015/apr/29/france-poisoned-legacy-central-african-republic.

This section has highlighted three significant implications that follow from the *ius cogens* status of the prohibition on the use of force. First, peremptory norms embody the international community's highest normative principles. Claims for the right to use military force outside the established limits of the prohibition by claiming a morally superior purpose must fail as a legal matter. Under international law, *ius cogens* norms are co-equal. One may not be violated in the pursuit of another, if that is even possible. Inferior norms do not trump superior ones.

The second implication is that peremptory norms require a conservative approach to interpretation. Contrary State practice does not open the way to new, more relaxed understandings of the prohibition. In terms of the three pernicious doctrines, the words 'if an armed attack occurs' cannot be read out of Article 51. Low-level, intermittent terrorist attacks do not satisfy the significant armed attack requirement, nor may the 'unable/unwilling' doctrine substitute for attribution or consent.

Finally, peremptory norms may be discerned to reach more conduct, not less. Expansion of peremptory norms is consistent with the ethos of *ius cogens*, expansion, for example, to prohibit the initiation of civil war under the *ius ad bellum*.

V. CONCLUSION

The purpose of law is peace. Law emerged in communities as an alternative to physical force, religion, and status for the settlement of disputes on the basis of the principle of fairness – of treating like cases alike. Sophisticated law builds on this foundation to foster not just negative peace – the absence of violence – but positive cooperation. Peace through law is the condition necessary for cooperation, trust and creativity. It is the necessary condition for the flourishing of all life on the planet.

These observations are as true of international law as they are for any other body of law. The very origins of international law lie in the struggle to regulate resort to force. To date, a limited right to use force in cases of self-defence or when authorised is considered consistent with a moral order built on peace. Those contributing to international law have ever since struggled between the poles of opening the law to greater acceptance of violence and retaining restrictions and even building on them. This centuries-old debate has reached us today in the form of legal prohibitions on the use of force that count among international law's highest norms as against a continuing effort to develop new legal formulas reducing the restrictions on certain States and actors in attaining their preferred goals. Three of these doctrines have been examined here –

inherent right/imminence, terrorist attack/armed attack, and unable/unwill-
ing – and found to be inconsistent not only with the general goal of greater
peace but even with the more limited ends that they espouse.

The reason non-State actors are or have been considered the enemy is
because they use violence in defiance of fundamental law, the very law the
three pernicious doctrines undermine. The three doctrines have many flaws as
a basic legal matter: they ignore the plain meaning of express treaty terms; they
ignore legal presumptions that bear on accurate interpretation; they ignore the
status of the prohibition of force as *ius cogens*; they ignore the long history of
struggle to create positive law norms restricting force; and they ignore the data
on the ineffectiveness of military force for most goals other than simple self-
defence, data which goes to the heart of determining the necessity of using
force. Despite these flaws, the three doctrines of self-defence examined here
make little common sense when seen as a part of a general rule of international
law applicable to all. The doctrines emerged to justify uses of force by the
US and UK after the fact. When used to justify force by other States, the deep
flaws are plain even to those sympathetic to them.

In response to the spectre of wider rights to use force, proponents of the
three doctrines point out that the fear of military retaliation by the UK or
US prevents the dangers predicted from materialising. In a world of military
power imbalance, fair and equal understanding of the rules is not needed.
The reason law has power, however, is the very fact it applies generally. Law
does not depend on physical or military strength. It does not depend on divine
revelation accessible to the enlightened or blessed among us. It does not
depend on being the friend or relative of a national leader. We develop law
through reason, drawing on our understanding of the natural world, as well as
transcendent inspiration engendered by beauty or faith. This approach to law
has led to the most fundamental principle of law, one uncontestably held
universally: the principle of fairness. In the West, Aristotle is credited for
defining fairness as the treatment of like cases alike. Fairness means the
subjects of the law are treated as equal before the law. Sovereign States are
the principal subjects of international law. If one has the right to go to war to
pre-empt an attack or because another State is unable or unwilling to do
something then all States have the same right.[366]

The three doctrines analysed in this chapter are exceptionalist views of the
law. They have been developed to justify unlawful uses of force by leaders of
States with major militaries and programmes of research into new weapons

---

[366] For more on the nature of law and the use of force, see Mary Ellen O'Connell, *The Art of Law in the International Community* (Cambridge: Cambridge University Press, 2019).

technology. These are States that have also enjoyed stature and prestige in the world for their commitment to the rule of law. The three doctrines paper over the law violations that gave rise to them. On close analysis, they make nonsense of the general prohibition on the use of force. If every government is free to decide to use force on the basis of any of these propositions, the use of force is for all practical purposes unrestricted. Without controls on violence, international law is no longer law. Instead of pouring effort into building such doctrines, the current generation of legal scholars is overdue to take up the progressive development of the law of peace. No advances have been made in this area since the drafting of the UN Charter in 1945 and the discernment at that time that significant violations of Article 2(4) violate a *ius cogens* norm.

Legal scholars interested in advancing the law of peace have clear challenges. Among them is the need to develop global law enforcement, not mere clearing houses for warrants like Interpol. A robust global law enforcement institution is essential and must have the best cybercrime fighting capacity possible and a thorough grounding in international law. The world also requires the revival of the practice of peaceful settlement of disputes, particularly a return to the ability to mediate an end of conflicts and a restoration of interest in the compulsory jurisdiction of the International Court of Justice. Finally, a new substantive prohibition on civil war is needed. The thinking that encourages the taking up of arms to overthrow dictatorial regimes as moral crusading can be replaced with the model of waging peaceful campaigns of non-violence.

These goals are consistent not only with the prohibition on the use of force, but with the legal presumption of peace, and with the human right to life. These are all norms the international community has preserved through the assaults of realists, humanitarian interventionists, and other militarists. It should be celebrated that these norms have been preserved.[367] They can also be renewed and re-prioritised in communities locally and globally. They are worthy of the efforts of the international legal community and the ideal of the rule of law.

This returns the discussion to the beginning and the targeted killings with military force in Syria of ISIS members Reyaad Khan and Junaid Hussain by the UK and US. The UK Prime Minister said that the killing of Khan and the people near him with drone-launched missiles was an exercise of the UK's

---

[367] Jeremy Waldron, 'Justifying Targeted Killing with a Neutral Principle? Three Possible Models', in Claire Finkelstein, Jens David Ohlin and Andrew Altman (eds.), *Targeted Killings: Law and Morality in an Asymmetrical World* (Oxford: Oxford University Press, 2012), 112–34.

'inherent' right of self-defence. In attempting to justify the killing, Prime Minister Cameron was reaching back to 1958 and the claim that States may use force in self-defence on the basis of necessity, even when no armed attack occurs. The claim is in clear conflict with the terms of the Charter and the peremptory norm prohibiting the use of force. States may invoke an exception to the prohibition for self-defence if the exercise of self-defence meets the terms of Article 51, which include the condition that an 'armed attack occurs'.

The US issued no specific justification for killing Hussain. Nine months after the attack, however, State Department Legal Adviser Brian Egan claimed a right of the US to use military force to kill people in States that are 'unable or unwilling' to control terrorists active within their border.[368] This is as close as the US has come to issuing a justification. After 9/11, the US attempted to argue it was in a 'global war' with terrorism. The Obama administration abandoned that position to argue the US is involved in a worldwide 'armed conflict with Al-Qaeda and associated forces'.[369] Both claims were built on the series of terrorist attacks Al-Qaeda members have carried out against the US starting in 1993. As terrorist attacks, however, they have been intermittent, often low-level, and unconnected with a State sponsor. They have been crimes, not armed attacks triggering the right of self-defence. Even the 9/11 attacks most likely lacked the requisite link to Afghanistan to support the exercise of self-defence against that State.[370] If Afghanistan was responsible, the use of force has been beyond anything necessary or proportionate to the 9/11 attacks.

Al-Qaeda and ISIS are enemies, which may explain why Egan proffered a new justification in 2016 for military attacks on ISIS members, like Hussain. In saying, however, that Syria is 'unable' or 'unwilling' to control ISIS and that that judgment gives rise to the right to attack individuals, Egan had to ignore critical facts as well as the law. At the time of Hussain's killing, Syria was fighting strenuously to defeat ISIS. Syria was clearly not 'unwilling' to counter it, and Syria might have had more success – been less 'unable' – had the US not been actively supporting non-State actors fighting to bring down the

---

[368] Egan, 'International Law, Legal Diplomacy, and the Counter-ISIL Campaign' 2016 (n. 241).
[369] Remarks of Harold Hongju Koh to the Annual Meeting of the American Society of International Law, 'The Obama Administration and International Law', 25 March 2010, available at www.state.gov/documents/organization/179305.pdf.
[370] The Taliban government of Afghanistan did bear responsibility for failing to comply with a Security Council mandate to extradite Osama bin Laden. See calls for extradition or condemnation for failure to extradite in SC Res. 1267 of 15 October 1999, SC Res. 1333 of 19 December 2000, and SC Res. 1378 of 14 November. That failure is not the same as being responsible for Al-Qaeda's terrorist attacks, which could support the US and UK claim of self-defence against Afghanistan.

Syrian government and thereby incidentally reducing the Syrian capacity to combat ISIS. These are the facts. On the law, the case is just as weak. The claim extrapolates from the State responsibility principle that a non-State actor controlled by a State incurs the State's own responsibility. An armed attack that can trigger Article 51 will be attributed to a State if carried out by a non-State actor controlled by the State. Syria does not control ISIS, even if it could be shown that ISIS had carried out the requisite attack on the US, a subjective American judgment that Syria is now responsible for ISIS attacks because it is unable or unwilling to control ISIS does not change the attribution principles. The principles of attribution are embedded in the very structure of international law and may not be simply ignored, however complex or inconvenient the duty of compliance. Law is often complicated and inconvenient. In this area, however, complexity offers no excuse for failing to comply. There is a straightforward alternative to the risk of violating the law: when in doubt find non-lethal alternative responses.

Attribution principles are general principles, and as such do not change based on contrary State practice. The UK and US may wish to hold Afghanistan or Syria responsible in order to have the legal basis for military attacks against them, but it needs to show control by those States of non-State actor conduct. Equally, the UK and US are barred from claiming that they may substitute the unable/unwilling concept for Syrian consent to kill Khan and Hussain.

In violating the prohibition on the use of force in the killing of these men, the UK and US have violated a *ius cogens* norm. It is a durable norm that will not fade under the pressure of contrary practice. Yet, neither will the scourge of terrorism. Success against terrorism has been won through upholding the rule of law, using law enforcement measures, and building successful communities – expanding the options for peace, not the excuses for war. Some may find these conclusions radical or even utopian. They are likely counter-cultural, but beyond that are no more than the findings which follow from comprehensively assessing the theory, law and facts of self-defence against non-State actors.

Conclusion

Self-Defence against Non-State Actors – The Way Ahead

Christian Marxsen and Anne Peters

This Trialogue has discussed whether and – if yes – under which conditions international law as it stands allows for self-defence against non-State actors on the territory of a non-consenting State. Unsurprisingly, it has not come up with *one* clear answer. Rather, it has come up with *three* distinct answers – the contrast and interplay of which illuminate the facets and intricate details of one of the most pressing problems of international peace and security law. Dire Tladi advocates an inter-State reading of self-defence based on a thorough investigation of the UN Charter framework and recent State practice and thus concludes that self-defence against an 'innocent' State is unlawful. Christian Tams arrives at the opposite result. Employing – as Tladi does – a principally positivist method, his finding is that the better interpretation of the law is open for self-defence against non-State actors. Mary Ellen O'Connell, by contrast, advocates an originalist and value-imbued reading of the UN Charter. Based on such an understanding of the Charter, O'Connell concurs with Tladi and adduces an interpretation of the law that categorically prohibits self-defence against non-State actors.

I. DIFFERENT MODES OF ENGAGING WITH THE INTERNATIONAL LAW ON SELF-DEFENCE

Pulling the strings of this Trialogue together, our first observation is that the chapters manifest different modes of engaging with international law. These modes unveil divergent expectations about the functions of law and of legal scholarship. The underlying mindset seems to inform how the authors tackle the more technical and specific aspects of legal interpretation. Dire Tladi and Mary Ellen O'Connell follow a more traditional legal approach in that they seek to determine what the law objectively provides for at a given moment in time, thus essentially raising the question as to what 'international law is on a given day'.[1] The binarity of the law (related to its task of distinguishing lawful from unlawful behaviour) is crucial for both authors. Indeed, the benchmarking-function is normally viewed to be the essential job of law as a mode of governance. By painstakingly seeking to identify this benchmark, the two chapters are apt to provide political practice with clear criteria for the legality and illegality of potential courses of action.

Christian Tams, by contrast, is concerned with nuances in the substance of the law over time. He uses legal debates to illustrate historical trends and incremental shifts in perceptions and interpretations. Thus, Tams engages with the law not so much as a binary system that paints a black and white picture but treats the law as a flexible device to accommodate legal and political developments. This type of analysis does not need to search for the tipping point at which a legal rule changes (or ceases to exist and gives way to a new one). Tams' method allows for a deep understanding of the matters, but does not strive for unequivocal answers to the complex questions surrounding self-defence. Depending on the perspective and interests of legal actors, notably practitioners, this approach can be either seen as suitable or not. It may be of little use in that it does not provide a clear answer to the question of what the law says at a concrete point in time, but it may be of some use for those (notably for practitioners such as legal advisers) who must develop legal arguments for justifying a certain course of action (e.g. of a government) and therefore study prior incidents seeking argumentative support in them.

Both perspectives (O'Connell's and Tladi's on the one hand, and Tams' on the other) manifest or reveal diverging assumptions about the functioning of international law. For Dire Tladi and Mary Ellen O'Connell, international law provides a rather static framework. Once we have identified what the law objectively provided for, we carefully have to analyse whether and when the strict requirements for legal change are met. From Christian Tams' perspective, the law provides a rather flexible framework. The emphasis is not on one objective content, but rather on the different legal positions that can be formulated within a legal discourse and which are neither a correct nor an incorrect reading of the law, but have 'degrees of legal merit'.[2] In that sense the law provides an argumentative resource in which legal views and the related nuances are preserved even when they are not the dominant reading of the law – and they can more easily be activated than within the static framework.

---

[1] James Crawford and Thomas Viles, 'International Law on a Given Day', in Konrad Ginther (ed.), *Völkerrecht zwischen normativem Anspruch und politischer Realität* (Berlin: Duncker & Humblot, 1994), 45–68.
[2] Tams in this volume, 93, quoting Hersch Lauterpacht, *The Development of International Law by the International Court* (London: Stevens, 1958), 398.

II. HANDLING THE SOURCES OF SELF-DEFENCE

An important focus of this Trialogue rests on doctrinal analyses of the state of the law. A first question is which sources are most relevant for the rules on self-defence: custom, treaty (the UN Charter), or a combination of both? While this question is controversial in international legal debates in general,[3] the authors of the Trialogue all – in one way or another – prefer to analyse self-defence under the UN Charter. According to Christian Tams, self-defence has, with the adoption of the UN-Charter, been shaped as a question of treaty law.[4] Dire Tladi agrees that treaty law is crucial, but assumes – in accordance with the position espoused by the ICJ in the *Nicaragua* case – that both sources – treaty and custom – have a parallel existence, and Tladi therefore also attributes significance to custom. In the end, however, he holds that the substantive content of the rules flowing from both sources is 'co-extensive and identical'.[5] Mary Ellen O'Connell is less explicit about the sources of the obligation, but the UN Charter plays a crucial role in her overall argument.

For Dire Tladi and Christian Tams, the legal debate pivots around the interpretation of Article 51 based on the familiar canons of interpretation, as articulated in Articles 31 and 32 of the Vienna Convention on the Law of Treaties,[6] and both authors focus their chapters on this point. This debate involves the usual questions of interpretation, addressing the 'ordinary meaning' of the terms 'armed attack', their context, object and purpose (Article 31(1) VCLT). Both authors then zoom in on 'subsequent practice', which must be taken into account when interpreting a treaty norm (Article 31(3) lit. b) VCLT). Although the examination of subsequent practice is mentioned in the VCLT as a means 'for the purpose of . . . interpretation' (Article 31(3) VCLT), such practice might – arguably – not only clarify but also modify the meaning of a treaty rule (in our case Article 51 of the UN Charter).[7] Along this vein, Tams' and Tladi's chapters address the following questions. How dense does the practice need to be, i.e. how many States must perform acts in order to constitute subsequent practice? What is the significance of the silence of the majority of States that do not actively support the potentially law-shaping State practice of other States, but do not articulate protest either? Which weight shall we attribute to practice that is not accompanied by an explicit *opinio iuris*?

---

[3]   See Tams in this volume, 104–8.
[4]   Tams in this volume, 106–8.
[5]   Tladi in this volume, 48.
[6]   Vienna Convention on the Law of Treaties, 23 May 1969, 1155 UNTS 331 (VCLT).
[7]   See also *infra*, section V.

Dire Tladi and Christian Tams give strikingly different answers to these questions and arrive at opposite conclusions. Tams places more emphasis on the practice of States, arguing that it has reached a sufficient density to allow for self-defence against non-State actors. Tladi acknowledges existing practice, but argues that this practice is not accompanied by an agreement of the parties[8] to the UN Charter and therefore not sufficient to allow for or even compel a broader interpretation of self-defence, especially since many States have not taken a position on the issue.[9] The difference of opinion between both positions manifests two divergent overall understandings of international law. The first is a consent- and intent-oriented conceptualisation of international law which emphasises that *all* parties to a treaty need to agree to a reinterpretation (or silent evolution) of legal provisions. Tladi subscribes to that requirement by writing that 'any expression of criticism or objection will most certainly inflict a deathblow' to attempts to reinterpret the Charter.[10] By contrast, the second view of international law – to which Tams leans – privileges the objectives and purposes of treaties over the original intent of the States concluding them. Treaty interpretation along that line tends to accord more importance to a treaty's intrinsic telos (to some extent detached from the views of the original drafters). Correspondingly, this interpretive approach places more emphasis on the practice of States than on their verbal statements, because non-verbal practice is a more malleable sign of the parties' 'agreement' (as required by Article 31(3) lit. a) and b) VCLT) than the States' utterances.[11]

Another question is whether the content of a formerly established rule may be said to have changed even if the exact contours of the presumable new rule have not taken shape yet. Postulating that the original rule allowed self-defence only against attacks led by States, can we assume that – in view of latest practice – self-defence against non-State actors has become permissible, although we do not (yet) know exactly under which legal conditions? Not even those States which have taken military action have espoused a consistent view on this point. As discussed in our Introduction, the interventions in Syria have been justified by some States with the 'unwilling or unable' standard, while other States, notably Belgium and Germany, have focused on the loss of

---

[8] Cf. Article 31(3) lit. a) and b) VCLT.
[9] Tladi in this volume, 77–81.
[10] Tladi in this volume, 51.
[11] This point is stressed by Olivier Corten when analysing the prohibition on the use of force under a customary international law perspective: Olivier Corten, 'The Controversies over the Customary Prohibition on the Use of Force: A Methodological Debate', *European Journal of International Law* 16 (2005), 803–22 (816).

effective control by Syria over parts of the State's territory.[12] Tladi negates that under such circumstances subsequent practice would be capable of reinterpreting (or modifying) the law, because we do not have 'a clear meeting of minds as to the interpretation of Article 51'.[13]

III. MORAL VALUES AND *IUS COGENS*

Mary Ellen O'Connell's chapter is less concerned with the practice of States. She espouses an originalist reading of the UN Charter, whose centrepiece is certain fundamental moral values, above all the right to life of the individual and the quest for peace. O'Connell argues that these moral values form the nucleus of the concept of *ius cogens*. The peremptory quality of the prohibition on use of force affects – so she claims – the possibility of development of the legal rule.

This touches a further legal issue related to the development (evolution or change) of international law:[14] how relevant is the concept of *ius cogens* for the involved rules' potential for legal development? While it is widely believed that at least parts of the legal regime on the use of force in fact constitute *ius cogens*,[15] the exact scope of this presumable *ius cogens* quality is a subject of controversy.[16] It is often acknowledged that the (assumed) peremptory character of the prohibition on the use of force has some impact on the possibility, modalities and thresholds of the evolution of this legal norm. According to Article 53 of the VCLT, 'a

---

[12] Introduction to this volume, 8 (n. 39).

[13] Tladi in this volume, 77.

[14] We here employ the terms 'development' and – synonymously – 'evolution' and 'change' as umbrella terms for progressive interpretation and modification, and both for treaty and customary rules (see also *infra* section V.). With regard to treaty norms, such a development can occur silently (without rewriting the treaty), and by amending the treaty text. The VCLT does not explicitly regulate modifications without textual changes. Moreover, legal development/evolution can be conceptualised as the modification of a surviving norm, or as 'death' and 'birth' of a new norm.

[15] See for doubts James Green, 'Questioning the Peremptory Status of the Prohibition of the Use of Force', *Michigan Journal of International Law* 32 (2011), 215–57.

[16] Some regard the prohibition on the (illegal) use of force to constitute *ius cogens* (see International Law Commission, Draft Articles on the Law of Treaties with Commentaries, Article 50 – Commentary, *Yearbook of the International Law Commission*, 1966, vol. II, 247), while others include the established exceptions such as self-defence in the *ius cogens* character (Alexander Orakhelashvili, *Peremptory Norms in International Law* (Oxford: Oxford University Press, 2006), 51). Yet others suggest that only the prohibition of aggression as a particularly grave form of the use of force constitutes *ius cogens* (Lauri Hannikainen, *Peremptory Norms (Jus Cogens) in International Law: Historical Development, Criteria, Present Status* (Helsinki: Lakimiesliiton Kustannus, 1988), 356).

peremptory norm of general international law ... can be *modified* only by a subsequent norm of general international law having the same [i.e., *ius cogens*] character."[17] Therefore, many observers who analyse the prohibition on the use of force as a customary rule (and who accept its peremptory quality) find that the threshold for its change is higher than for ordinary customary law.[18] In contrast, if we analyse the prohibition on the use of force only as a treaty norm, the requirements for legal development[19] differ, and the *ius cogens* character of a rule would not have any significant effect: the 'general rule regarding the amendment of treaties' is that 'a treaty may be amended by agreement between the parties' (Article 39 VCLT).[20] A novel interpretation of a treaty requires an 'agreement of the parties' regarding its interpretation (Article 31(3) lit a) and b) VCLT). This means that *all* parties need to agree on the amendment or reinterpretation of the law. This establishes a very high threshold, also for a 'silent' development of treaty norms (i.e. without a change of the treaty text).

Dire Tladi and Christian Tams, in their chapters, do not attribute significance to the issue of *ius cogens* in determining the lawfulness of self-defence against non-State actors. Their main argument is that even if the prohibition on the use of force might possess a *ius cogens* status, this status does not fix the exact substantive content or coverage of the norm. This coverage is determined by the interplay between the prohibition and the exception (self-defence).[21] Figuratively speaking, the extension of the exception shrinks the scope of the prohibition. Thus, if an action is justified as self-defence, the prohibition does not cover this action. Such an adjustment of

---

[17] Emphasis added.

[18] Anthea E. Roberts, 'Traditional and Modern Approaches to Customary International Law', *American Journal of International Law* 95 (2001), 757–91 (785); Michael Byers and Simon Chesterman, 'Changing the Rules about Rules? Unilateral Intervention and the Future of International Law', in Judith L. Holzgrefe and Robert O. Keohane (eds.), *Humanitarian Intervention: Ethical, Legal, and Political Dilemmas* (Cambridge: Cambridge University Press, 2003), 177–203 (180); Corten, 'The Controversies over the Customary Prohibition on the Use of Force' 2005 (n. 11), 819; Tom Ruys, *'Armed Attack' and Article 51 of the UN Charter: Evolutions in Customary Law and Practice* (Cambridge: Cambridge University Press, 2010), 28; Christian Henderson, *The Persistent Advocate and the Use of Force: The Impact of the United States upon the Jus ad Bellum in the Post-Cold War Era* (Farnham: Ashgate, 2010), 28–9.

[19] See for the term above n. 14. The following observations relate to 'development' in all variants: progressive interpretation, silent modification without textual change, and modification through rewriting of a treaty text. However, a textual change of the UN Charter is not in sight.

[20] See on the amendment of the UN Charter *infra* text with note 69.

[21] See Tladi, 26–7, and Tams, 110–11, in this volume.

the coverage of the rule would, in that conceptualisation, not even be a 'modification', in the terms of Article 53 of the VCLT quoted above. Or, one might say that self-defence co-determines the prohibition, that hence it partakes in its normative 'character' as a peremptory rule, and that therefore any expansion of self-defence is apt to change the rule even under the conditions formulated by Article 53 of the VCLT. Key to this understanding is a perception of the ban on the use of force and self-defence as communicating vessels.

Mary Ellen O'Connell's account departs from established positivist conceptions of *ius cogens*. She claims that *ius cogens* rules are 'discerned ... through natural law method'.[22] In her view, peace is the 'superior moral and legal norm'[23] as articulated in the *ius cogens* character of the prohibition on the use of force. Her conclusion is that peremptory norms can only develop in one direction, namely towards the greater realisation of the moral norm they aim to protect ('principle of progression').[24] Thus, O'Connell believes that contrary State practice may not dilute or undermine an established scope of the prohibition on the use of force. If self-defence against non-State actors was – as O'Connell holds – once illegal, it cannot become lawful, because this would create more legal opportunities for the use of force. This view implies but does not spell out a novel theory of legal change and raises difficult conceptual questions about the relationship between law and morality. On Martti Koskenniemi's spectrum between apology and utopia it is far on the utopian side.

IV. THE INDETERMINACY OF THE LAW ON SELF-DEFENCE

The chapters demonstrate how a seemingly narrow legal question (such as whether and under which conditions self-defence against non-State armed attacks is lawful) may be and often is answered differently, both in the abstract and when deciding a concrete case. International law (in all its shapes, including notably treaties and customary norms) is notoriously blurry and gives plenty of leeway to those interpreting and applying its rules.[25] The well-known phenomenon has been described with many terms, as the law's

---

[22] O'Connell in this volume, 232.
[23] O'Connell in this volume, 245.
[24] O'Connell in this volume, 251.
[25] We use the term 'rules' in a broad sense, synonymous to 'norms', not as a contrast to 'principles'.

'indeterminacy',[26] as 'uncertainty'[27], as 'vagueness',[28] and as 'ambiguity'.[29] We here use the term 'indeterminacy' to describe a characteristic feature of legal rules.[30] The term describes the fact that any person handling legal rules must make choices about which scope to give to the rule, and how to apply it to the given facts. Put differently, legal rules are indeterminate if they do not provide only one answer for deciding a controversial case but – on the contrary – various (not exactly predictable) answers can be given.[31]

The indeterminacy of the law and the resulting uncertainty in applying it have a number of causes. The two main causes are, firstly, the properties of the ordinary language (which is imprecise and malleable) that furnishes the technical language of the law and, secondly, the unforseeability of future situations to which the rules are designed to apply.

In the field of international relations, a frequent third cause of the indeterminacy of treaty provisions is deliberate compromises in the drafting stage that lead to a choice of wording which (due to its ambiguity or vagueness) can be understood differently by the negotiating parties. In this context, the treaty

[26] See *infra*, n. 31.

[27] Jörg Kammerhofer, 'Uncertainty in the Formal Sources of International Law: Customary International Law and Some of Its Problems', *European Journal of International Law* 15 (2004), 523–53; Jörg Kammerhofer, *Uncertainty in International Law: A Kelsenian Perspective* (Abingdon: Routledge, 2010), 1–4.

[28] Timothy A. O. Endicott, *Vagueness in Law* (Oxford: Oxford University Press, 2000); Andreas Kulick, 'From Problem to Opportunity? An Analytical Framework for Vagueness and Ambiguity in International Law', *German Yearbook of International Law* 59 (2016), 257–88.

[29] Michael Thaler, *Mehrdeutigkeit und juristische Auslegung* (Vienna: Springer, 1982), 1–7; Sanford Schane, 'Ambiguity and Misunderstanding in the Law', *Thomas Jefferson Law Review* 25 (2002), 167–94.

[30] The notions of 'ambiguity' and 'vagueness', by contrast, point towards the causes of indeterminacy. Ambiguous words have more than one meaning (as e.g. the term bank, which can either refer to a 'river bank' or the financial institution). A word or expression is vague when the objects or situations to which it refers are not precisely demarcated. For example, the expression 'use of force' refers to physical violence, and it might, at the borderline, also cover cyber-attacks.

[31] Ken Kress, 'Legal Indeterminacy', *California Law Review* 77 (1989), 283–337 (283); Timothy A. O. Endicott, 'Linguistic Indeterminacy', *Oxford Journal of Legal Studies* 16 (1996), 667–97 (669). See also Mark Tushnet, 'Defending the Indeterminacy Thesis', *Quinnipiac Law Review* 16 (1996), 339–56 (341). The term 'indeterminacy' has been famously used, though in a slightly different sense, by Martti Koskenniemi, From *Apology to Utopia: The Structure of International Legal Argument* (Cambridge: Cambridge University Press, 2nd edn., 2005), 590–1 and 595. Koskenniemi does not focus on semantic open-endedness or ambiguity of the words used in international legal texts but on structural indeterminacy, resulting from the diversity and (self-)contradiction of premises, political preferences, and priorities of the actors participating in the legal process. He does not consider this feature a deficit but an essential asset which secures international law's acceptability (*ibid.*, 591).

law's indeterminacy is intended by the drafters. This technique might be called 'constructive indeterminacy', because it pushes fundamental disagreement from the drafting stage to the stage of applying and implementing the law, opening a window of opportunity for consensus in a later point in time.[32]

A fourth cause of indeterminacy has to do with the 'sources' of international law, i.e. the shapes or forms in which international law comes (the traditional major ones being treaty and custom). We therefore face a 'second-order indeterminacy'[33] in international law. Myres McDougal and Michael Reisman highlight that beyond Article 38 of the ICJ Statute, 'all agreement among commentators [on sources] ends.'[34] With regard to the law on the use of force, Andrea Bianchi observes that 'the interpretive community is currently divided and is no longer able to agree on the method that must be used for interpreting the law.'[35] Or, should there be some amount of agreement on method, it is not robust enough to provide much guidance in controversial cases.

Specifically on the norm of self-defence, Georg Nolte and Albrecht Randelzhofer write: 'A significant amount of current disagreement over the proper interpretation of Article 51, both among States and among commentators, can ultimately be traced to underlying differences of opinion over the interpretation and application of the rules on the sources of international law.'[36] It is generally agreed that a customary norm on self-defence exists – the 'inherent right' as mentioned in Article 51 of the UN Charter. Unwritten rules, which are not fixed in verbal form, are even more indeterminate than written rules, because the starting points for discussions about their scope and application are even less agreed.[37] Additional insecurity flows from the

---

[32] Kulick, 'From Problem to Opportunity?' 2016 (n. 28), 283 (using the term 'constructive ambiguity').

[33] Cf. (with a different terminology) Frederick Schauer, 'Second-Order Vagueness in the Law', in Geert Keil and Ralf Poscher (eds.), *Vagueness and Law: Philosophical and Legal Perspectives* (Oxford: Oxford University Press, 2016), 177–88.

[34] Myres S. McDougal and W. Michael Reisman, 'The Prescribing Function in World Constitutive Process: How International Law is Made', *Yale Studies in World Public Order* 6 (1980), 249–84 (260).

[35] Andrea Bianchi, 'The international Regulation of the Use of Force: The Politics of the Interpretative Method', in Larissa van den Herik and Nico Schrijver (eds.), *Counter-Terrorism Strategies in a Fragmented International Legal Order* (Cambridge: Cambridge University Press, 2013), 283–316 (286). Bianchi understands by 'method' 'the intellectual matrix that provides the paradigms (legal categories and interpretative techniques) used to identify the state of the law on the use of force' (*ibid.*, 284).

[36] Georg Nolte and Albrecht Randelzhofer, 'Article 51', in Bruno Simma, Daniel-Erasmus Khan, Georg Nolte and Andreas Paulus (eds.), *The Charter of the United Nations – A Commentary* (Oxford: Oxford University Press, 3rd edn., 2012), vol. II, 1397–444 (para. 5).

[37] Cf. William Twining and David Miers, *How to do Things with Rules* (London: Butterworths, 4th edn., 1999), 180.

possible interplay of the customary rule with the Charter provision and from its possible quality of the rule as *ius cogens*. For example, the current practice on self-defence against non-State actors seems to constitute both a means of interpreting the Charter law (as 'subsequent practice' in the sense of Article 31(3) lit. b) VCLT) and the objective element of the customary rule.[38] In fact, as the Trialogue manifests, there is no full agreement on how to handle the complex legal questions in this constellation. The three chapters' analyses of these points diverge to some extent, although all focus on the UN Charter as opposed to custom.

Generally speaking, the methods for identifying and determining customary rules are undertheorised and lack rigour.[39] The poor understanding of the process of development of customary law and the paucity of guidance for the exact determination of the content of customary rules are highly relevant for the law of self-defence because of its (also) customary law quality. Methodological choices for norm-identification are, for example, whether to prioritise practice versus *opinio iuris*, and how to range *ius cogens*, as highlighted by Mary Ellen O'Connell. These choices co-determine the outcomes of legal reasoning, but they are themselves not entirely determined by law. Rather, they significantly depend on external factors, and they are informed by the theoretical, practical, geo-political and political background assumptions of those interpreting and applying the law. In this Trialogue, Dire Tladi makes this explicit. He acknowledges that he seeks to avoid 'an interpretation of law that facilitates the "de-constraining"' in the interest of those who enjoy much military power,[40] stressing that this position is not 'merely a policy preference', but one 'which is grounded in the law'.[41] O'Connell, on the other hand, builds

---

[38] See on subsequent practice the four ILC reports by Special Rapporteur Georg Nolte: UN Doc. A/CN.4/660, 19 March 2013; UN Doc. A/CN.4/671, 26 March 2014; UN Doc. A/CN.4/ 683, 7 April 2015; UN Doc. A/CN.4/694, 7 March 2016.

[39] The ILC has recently undertaken to offer guidance for the determination of the content of rules of customary law, but has not sought to explain the development of such rules (fourth report of UN Doc. A/CN.4/695 of 8 March 2016, para. 16). The ILC-reports are, in other words, exclusively concerned with law-application (for participants in the legal process) and not with reflections about the law and legal process (from an observer perspective). See further the five ILC reports by Special Rapporteur Sir Michael Wood: first report UN Doc. A/CN.4/663, 17 May 2013; second report UN Doc. A/CN.4/672, 22 May 2014; third report UN Doc. A/CN.4/ 682, 27 March 2015; fourth report UN Doc. A/CN.4/695, 8 March 2016; fifth report UN Doc. A/CN.4/717, 14 March 2018. See also the ILC Draft Conclusions with Commentary (*Yearbook of the International Law Commission*, vol. II, Part 2, chapter V: Identification of Customary International Law (UN Doc. A/71/10), report ILC 86th sess. of 2 May–10 June and 4 July–12 August 2016).

[40] Tladi in this volume, 21.

[41] *Ibid.*

her argument on strong normative convictions at the heart of which is a 'presumption of peace'[42] that is underpinned by a natural law theory.

The indeterminacy of the law and its application, including the methodological openness for reaching legal answers, is a problem both for legal practice and for legal scholarship. Because the legal findings presented by scholars or practitioners in the relevant legal debates can easily be called into question and refuted by opponents who favour a different substantive result,[43] such legal findings offer little practical guidance for the conduct of States and no stable knowledge-base on which further research can build.

Indeterminacy of the law is a matter of degree.[44] All legal rules are indeterminate to some extent. Problems arise when a rule is so extraordinarily indeterminate that it has only a weak capacity to coordinate, guide or 'govern' State behaviour. Extreme indeterminacy (or insufficient determinacy) corrodes the international rule of law because it leaves much space for arbitrary interpretations and applications of the rule. Moreover, insufficient determinacy saps a rule's legitimacy which in turn impacts on its compliance pull.[45]

The Trialogue has shown that the rules on self-defence are indeed extremely indeterminate. The law on the use of force is a prime example of methodological openness and indeterminacy on various levels (regarding the canons of interpretation, regarding the relevance of the sources and regarding the conceptualisation of legal development).[46] This is not meant to suggest a radical indeterminacy in the sense that no objective content of the international law of self-defence could be established and that therefore this body of rules could never constitute a yardstick for distinguishing lawful from unlawful employments of military force.[47] There is a core of certainty where

---

[42] O'Connell in this volume, 255.

[43] Martti Koskenniemi, 'The Politics of International Law', *European Journal of International Law* 1 (1990), 4–32 (28).

[44] Cf. Glanville L. Williams, 'Law and Language III', *Law Quarterly Review* 61 (1945), 293–303 (302).

[45] Thomas M. Franck, *The Power of Legitimacy among Nations* (Oxford: Oxford University Press, 1990), 50–90, on determinacy as a factor of legitimacy. As Franck has argued, '[t]he preeminent literary property affecting legitimacy is the rule text's *determinacy*: that which makes its message clear' (*ibid.*, 52; emphasis in original).

[46] This has been highlighted by Andrea Bianchi who called for the restoration of a societal consensus of the interpretive community of international lawyers (Andrea Bianchi, 'The International Regulation of the Use of Force', *Leiden Journal of International Law* 22 (2009), 651–76 (651)).

[47] But see Koskenniemi, *From Apology to Utopia* 2005 (n. 31), who argues 'that it is possible to defend *any* course of action – including deviation from a clear rule – by professionally impeccable legal arguments that look from rules to their underlying reasons, make choices between several rules as well as rules and exceptions, and interpret rules in the context of evaluative standards' (591, emphasis in the original). Although Koskenniemi does not base his

one State defends against the ongoing armed attack of another State. This core, however, is surrounded by a 'twilight zone'[48] of indeterminacy, in which the applicability of the rule is controversial, the case of self-defence against non-State actors being a focal point of contestation.

Although there is not one right answer to the question of whether and under which conditions self-defence against non-State actors is lawful, there are better and worse answers within the parameters of the legal discourse.[49] The better answer is not inevitably simply politics in disguise but can be a specifically *legal* answer.[50] The simple observation that legal discussants, such as the three participants of the Trialogue, in fact seriously struggle and disagree about a legal answer illustrates that there is a specifically legal sphere of the meaning of self-defence.

V. HOW DOES THE LAW OF SELF-DEFENCE CHANGE?

A key issue brought to light in this Trialogue is legal change. All three contributions explicitly or implicitly address the widespread assumption that the law of self-defence seems to be changing or has changed. As a political matter, the support for the old orthodoxy of State-centred self-defence has weakened. Apparently, a significant number of States opine that they need to act in self-defence against non-State actors on the territory of a non-consenting State. They therefore seek to loosen the State-nexus of self-defence. We find

indeterminacy argument on the semantic openness (590–1 and 595; see also above n. 31), his view leads to the same result as the strong linguistic indeterminacy thesis. Cf. also Lawrence B. Solum, 'On the Indeterminacy Crisis: Critiquing Critical Dogma', *University of Chicago Law Review* 54 (1987), 462–503(470 *et seq.*).

[48] Endicott, *Vagueness in Law* 2000 (n. 28), 8.

[49] Ralf Poscher, 'Ambiguity and Vagueness in Legal Interpretation', in Peter M. Tiersma and Lawrence Solan (eds.), *Oxford Handbook of Language and Law* (Oxford: Oxford University Press, 2012), 128–44 (138).

[50] Poscher here focuses on the steadying power of legal doctrine: '[A]lthough legal interpretation has to create law in cases of vagueness, the conditions under which law is created in adjudication distance it from politics, economics, and morality in a way that gives it a specifically legal ... character ... Doctrinally developed law ... creates a specifically legal sphere of meaning with its own content and structures. Since the creation of law through legal interpretation in hard cases must occur within this specifically legal sphere of meaning, it belongs to a different tradition, with different restraints and path dependencies from politics, economics, or morality.' (Poscher, 'Ambiguity and Vagueness in Legal Interpretation' 2012 (n. 49), 142). See also Twining and Miers, *How to do Things with Rules* 1999 (n. 37), 180, focusing on the social 'steadying factors' that reduce doubts and limit the choices of the law-interpreters and law-appliers 'such as the mental conditioning of lawyers, the prior identification and sharpening of the issues, accepted ways of handling authoritative sources of law and of presenting arguments in court, and the constraints of group decision-making and of publicity'.

ourselves in constant debates about whether the tipping point for the modification of a previously established norm on self-defence (or dissolution of the
old norm and the emergence of a new norm) has been reached or not.
The development (or evolution[51]) of the law of self-defence concerns both
legal sources, the treaty law (Article 51 of the UN Charter) and the 'inherent'
right mentioned in the Charter that is based on a customary rule.

The Trialogue authors address this matter in dissimilar terms and draw
different conclusions. Their divergence shows that the process and procedures
of the change of international law are still poorly conceptualised in legal
terms. This stands in contrast to studies in the field of international relations,
notably by social constructivists who have developed theories of norm change
since the 1990s, such as the 'cascade' model by Kathryn Sikkink,[52] the 'cyclic
theory' of norm change by Wayne Sandholtz[53] and the 'spiral' model by
Thomas Risse and others.[54]

A. Change of the Charter Law

The textually unrevised provision of Article 51 of the UN Charter might have
acquired or might be acquiring a new meaning. This could be conceptualised
either as a progressive interpretation or as an ('unwritten' or 'silent') modification without changing the text of the treaty. Put differently, the question arises
whether the understanding that an 'armed attack' might emanate from a non-
State actor would still be a legitimate form of *interpreting* the Charter rule, or
whether this would amount to a silent *modification* (an unwritten amendment
of the UN Charter). If it amounts to a modification, it might be more prone to
critique, notably as an illegitimate or even unlawful juridical operation.

Doctrinal international legal scholarship postulates a conceptual dividing
line between interpretation 'proper' and silent modification 'effected under
the pretext of interpretation' – although the writers agree that this line is
blurry.[55] Simplistically speaking, the interpretation of a legal rule is considered

---

[51] See for our terminology *supra*, n. 14.
[52] Kathryn Sikkink, *The Justice Cascade: Human Rights Prosecutions and World Politics*
(New York: W.W. Norton & Co., 2011).
[53] Wayne Sandholtz, *Prohibiting Plunder: How Norms Change* (Oxford: Oxford University Press,
2007).
[54] Thomas Risse, Stephen C. Ropp and Kathryn Sikkink (eds.), *The Persistent Power of Human
Rights: From Commitment to Compliance* (Cambridge: Cambridge University Press, 2013).
[55] ILC, Reports of the Commission to the General Assembly, *Yearbook of the International Law
Commission*, vol. 2 (1966), 236; Wolfram Karl, *Vertrag und spätere Praxis im Völkerrecht*
(Berlin: Springer, 1983), 21–46, 43, on the fluid boundary; Ian M. Sinclair, *The Vienna
Convention on the Law of Treaties* (Manchester: Manchester University Press, 2nd edn.,

to be somehow bounded (although it is not fully clear by what), whereas the modification of a rule is potentially unlimited. Also, an interpretation happens first of all for one single case (and lives on only through precedent), while a modification of a treaty provision will formally govern all future cases.[56]

The dichotomy between the dynamic interpretation of a treaty and its 'silent' modification does not withstand the insights of legal theory that every text needs interpretation, and that every interpretation creates new meanings.[57] And actually, the continuum between interpretation and silent modification of a legal text does not pose a normative problem when it is performed by the identical actors, and when no third parties are affected by the development of the law. Put differently, it is not always necessary to determine whether the members to a given treaty (such as the UN Charter) interpret that treaty or silently modify it.[58]

Nevertheless, the simplistic and perhaps even false dichotomy between the interpretation of a treaty and its amendment persists in practice. The Vienna Convention contains one section on 'Interpretation of Treaties' (in Part III) and another (Part IV) entitled 'Amendment and Modification of Treaties'. Both the case-law and treaty texts postulate that the interpretation and the modification of legal rules are two conceptually and legally distinct operations. The leading case is an ICJ Advisory Opinion on treaty interpretation of 1950 in which the Court stated that '[i]t is the duty of the Court to interpret the

---

1984), 138; Georg Nolte, 'Report 1 – Jurisprudence of the International Court of Justice and Arbitral Tribunals of Ad Hoc Jurisdiction Relating to Subsequent Agreements and Subsequent Practice', in Georg Nolte (ed.), *Treaties and Subsequent Practice* (Oxford: Oxford University Press, 2013), 169–209 (200). See specifically for the UN Charter Philip Kunig, 'United Nations Charter, Interpretation of', in *Max Planck Encyclopedia of Public International Law* (online edn.), September 2006, para. 20: '[T]he limit of the treaty interpretation begins where it goes beyond the provisions of the UN Charter and becomes in effect an amendment. The definition of the line between the two remains difficult.'

56   Karl, *Vertrag und spätere Praxis im Völkerrecht* 1983 (n. 55), 28 and 46.

57   Cf. Ludwig Wittgenstein, Philosophical Investigations, translated by G. E. M. Anscombe (Oxford: Basil Blackwell, 1958), 20: '43. For a large class of cases – though not for all – in which we employ the word "meaning" it can be defined thus: the meaning of a word is its use in the language.' See in legal scholarship Ingo Venzke, How Interpretation Makes International Law (Oxford: Oxford University Press, 2012), *passim*, e.g. 4, 10, 196.

58   See on a modification of Article 2 ECHR through member State practice ECtHR, *Al-Saadoon and Mufdhi v. The United Kingdom*, Application no. 61498/08, Judgment of 2 March 2010. The Court found the State practice on the death penalty as 'strongly indicative that Article 2 [ECHR] has been *amended* so as to prohibit the death penalty in all circumstances. Against this background, the Court does not consider that the wording of the second sentence of Article 2 § 1 continues to act as a bar to its *interpreting* the words "inhuman or degrading treatment or punishment" in Article 3 as including the death penalty' (para. 120, emphases added). The Court here confused interpretation and amendment through practice.

Treaties, not to revise them.'[59] This dictum has been picked up by further judgments[60] and by numerous arbitral awards.[61]

Article 3(2) of the WTO Dispute Settlement Understanding, which prohibits the Dispute Settlement Body (DSB) to add or diminish rights and obligation provided in the WTO agreements,[62] presupposes that the interpretation by the WTO Dispute Settlement Body of those treaties and their modification are two different things. The case-law and the mentioned legal provision bring us to the heart of the matter. The normative reason for upholding the dichotomy is a presumed separation of powers in the international legal process.[63] When States parties – and not international courts – are recognised as the primary law-makers and law-changers, it is necessary to draw a line between the operations of interpreting the law on the one hand and changing it on the other, because the operations might befit different actors. The normative question undergirding this separation of powers is *who* is entitled to shape

---

[59]   ICJ, *Interpretation of Peace Treaties* (Second Phase), Advisory Opinion of 18 July 1950, ICJ Reports 1950, 221, 229. See in that sense already PCIJ, *Acquisition of Polish Nationality*, Series B no. 7, 6–21, 20.

[60]   ICJ, *Rights of Nationals of the United States in Morocco* (France v. United States of America), Merits, Judgment of 27 August 1952, ICJ Reports 1952, 176, 196: 'In these circumstances, the Court can not adopt a construction by implication of the provisions of the Madrid Convention which would go beyond the scope of its declared purposes and objects. Further, this contention *would involve radical changes and additions* to the provisions of the Convention' (emphasis added); ICJ, *Case Concerning Kasikili/Sedudu Island* (Botswana v. Namibia), Judgment of 13 December 1999, Dissenting Opinion of Judge Parra-Aranguren, ICJ Reports 1999, 1212–13, para. 16: '[T]here may be a blurring of the line between the interpretation and the amendment of a treaty by subsequent practice, even though these two processes are legally quite distinct' (internal reference and quotation mark omitted).

[61]   *Dispute between Argentina and Chile concerning the Beagle Channel*, RIAA 21 (1977), 53–263 (231): 'Interpretation is thus a function determined and regulated by international law and not a task left simply to the discretion or whim of the judge. *He is not allowed to overstep the established limits, for then he would not be interpreting the law but revising it*' (emphasis added). See along this line also *Case Concerning the Delimitation of the Maritime Boundary between Guinea-Bissau and Senegal* (Guinea-Bissau v. Senegal), RIAA 10 (1989), 119–213, 151, para. 85. See also *Case Concerning a Boundary Dispute between Argentina and Chile Concerning the Delimitation of the Frontier Line between Boundary Post 62 and Mount Fitzroy*, RIAA 22 (1994), 3–149, 25, para. 75: 'Interpretation is a legal operation designed to determine the precise meaning of a rule, but it cannot change its meaning.'

[62]   Understanding on Rules and Procedures Governing the Settlement of Disputes, Marrakesh Agreement Establishing the World Trade Organization, Annex 2, 1869 UNTS 401, Article 3(2): 'Recommendations and rulings of the DSB cannot add to or diminish the rights and obligations provided in the covered agreements.'

[63]   The recurring reproaches against 'lawmaking' judges (as overstepping their mandate to apply and interpret the law) only make sense against the background of an (intuitive) distinction between interpretation and law-making (or, for our purposes, law-changing). If these intellectual and technical operations were indistinct, any critique against activist courts would be senseless.

the legal environment for third parties, notably for citizens who are subjected to the rules. The traditional answer, mainly motivated by the concern for State sovereignty, is that this job is assigned to the State parties. Arguably, democracy and the rule of law (comprising the principles of legal certainty and previsibility of the law) are also better safeguarded in treaty-making or amending processes than in judicial law-making.

The problem becomes apparent in a proceeding pending before the German Federal Constitutional Court which concerns self-defence actions against a non-State actor, namely the Islamic State of Iraq and Syria. The German parliamentary faction *Die Linke* in 2016 filed a complaint against the government's deployment decision in the context of the anti-ISIS-operation 'Inherent Resolve'. The applicant argues, inter alia, that the deployment is based on an over-extensive reading of Article 51 of the UN Charter that is no longer a legitimate interpretation of the UN Charter, but rather a modification. The constitutional law argument, then, is that this practice also oversteps the parliamentary statute approving of Germany's accession to the United Nations in 1973.[64]

The UN Charter, formally a treaty, may be interpreted (and re-reinterpreted) by 'taking into account' any 'subsequent agreement between the parties regarding the interpretation of the treaty' (Article 31(3) lit. a) VCLT) or by taking into account 'any subsequent practice in the application of the treaty which establishes the agreement of the parties regarding its interpretation' (Article 31(3) lit. b) VCLT). Past evolutions of the UN Charter without changing its text have arguably not amounted to modifications but have remained within the realms of progressive interpretation.[65] Indeed, it is often argued that the UN Charter is particularly prone to and in need of dynamic interpretation due to its constitutional character and due to the difficulty of formal amendment.[66]

A true change of the UN Charter, notably of its Article 51, under the guise of interpretation would pose additional problems. From the perspective of the VCLT, the required agreement between the parties could be completely informal, for example through practice.[67] But the VCLT provides only

---

[64]   *Organstreit*-proceeding, applicants' memo of 31 May 2016, at 110–20. The complaint is directed both against the German Federal government and against the *Bundestag* (Parliament) as respondents. The applicant seeks the declaration that the respondents, with their joint deployment decision (of 1 and 4 December 2015), violated competences of the *Bundestag* flowing from Article 24(2) in conjunction with Article 59(2) of the German Basic Law.

[65]   The best-known example is the evolution of Article 27(3) UN Charter: abstention of a veto power has come to be understood as not constituting a veto.

[66]   Philip Kunig, 'United Nations Charter, Interpretation of' (n. 55), paras. 4–5 and 19.

[67]   Article 39 sentence 2; Article 40(1) VCLT.

residual rules; treaty amendment is first of all subject to the rules of revision in the given treaty itself.[68] The UN Charter itself contains specific rules of procedure for its revision and amendment (Articles 108–9). 'Informal' amendments risk undermining the UN Charter's formal revision procedures which seek to safeguard institutional balance and legal clarity. The concern about circumventing procedures is exacerbated if the UN Charter is perceived as a constitutional document whose specific function as a repository of the most fundamental norms is put at risk by adding bits and pieces of 'constitutional by-law' whose extent and content is not clear and which cannot function as a guideline.[69] These reflections are in line with the chapters of both Mary Ellen O'Connell and Dire Tladi who find that the Charter law of self-defence has not been amended, and O' Connell even implies that such a change would not be legally possible.

B. Change of the Customary International Law on Self-Defence

The customary law of self-defence may have evolved through a change of practice and of *opinio iuris*.[70] However, in the face of more than a few isolated incidences of military action against non-State actors and accompanying legal assertions, it is hard and probably impossible to keep apart practice, which simply breaches the outlasting 'old' norm, from the advent of a novel, norm-generating practice. Christian Tams' chapter discusses this problem on the level of treaty law, but the similar difficulty exists with regard to the change of custom. So how to distinguish breaking from making the customary rule on self-defence?

Looking at the intensified military strikes against armed groups in the territory of a non-consenting State alone, we cannot tell whether the behaviour is aberrant, or whether the practice is 'right'. In order to find out whether the old customary law is being breached or whether – conversely – the formation of a new customary rule is going on, we need to examine the second element of customary law, the *opinio iuris* of the States involved. However, at the point in

---

[68] Cf. Article 40 VCLT.

[69] This is the main reason why Bardo Fassbender finds informal amendment of the Charter impermissible (Bardo Fassbender, The United Nations Charter as Constitution of the International Community (Leiden: Nijhoff, 2009), 136–7).

[70] See the ILC Draft Conclusions (n. 39), Conclusion 9, Requirement of Acceptance as Law (*opinio juris*): '1. The requirement, as a constituent element of customary international law, that the general practice be accepted as law (*opinio juris*) means that the practice in question must be undertaken with a sense of legal right or obligation. 2. A general practice that is accepted as law (*opinio juris*) is to be distinguished from mere usage or habit.' (UN Doc. A/71/10, Report ILC 86th sess. 2 May–10 June and 4 July–12 August 2016).

time when the customary law changes, the opinion of the legal subjects that their behaviour (in our case, for example, the US and allies conducting air strikes in Syria) is lawful can only be in error. The States cannot be (rightfully) convinced that they are acting in conformity with the law, that their behaviour is permitted or required by law, because such a legal rule does not (yet) stand. An *opinio iuris* in its strict sense (in the sense of a conviction that a permissive legal rule allows such self-defence independent of any attribution of the non-State actor's attack to the territorial State) cannot exist as a matter of logic.[71]

Legal scholars therefore concur that in this phase the States' attitudes cannot be more than a 'claim'[72] or 'signal'[73] to others and the acceptance of that claim. International Relations scholar Wayne Sandholtz, too, has highlighted that the norm change hinges on the justification of the new practice and on the reaction of other States.[74] A powerful State such as the United States might get away easier with breaking the law of self-defence. But if most other States condemn an action, a violation remains simply a violation, and the old rule is affirmed. Sandholtz argues that a violation can lead to new or modified rules in two scenarios. An only mild *pro forma* condemnation evidences that the old rule is weakening. If, in addition, apparent violation is followed by subsequent similar conduct, then the new pattern can be evidence of an emerging law: '[i]n that case, the initial non-compliant act would be seen as not just a violation but as the first step in defining a new rule. Of course, such judgements can only be made in retrospect.'[75]

In legal terms, the failure of other States to condemn the initial violations evidences a shift of *opinio iuris*.[76] Initially, that *opinio iuris* may exist (only) as to the immediate future. It may then take 'the form of a settled conviction as to what the law should be, and would be for the proclaiming state . . . One can without contradiction announce the intention to live by a certain rule, if one does live by it from that time.'[77]

---

[71] Hans Kelsen, 'Théorie du droit international coutumier', *Revue internationale de la théorie du droit* 1 (1939), 253–74 (263).

[72] Maurice H. Mendelson, 'The Formation of Customary International Law', *Recueil des Cours* 272 (1998), 155–410 (280).

[73] Pierre-Hugues Verdier and Erik Voeten, 'Precedent, Compliance and Change in Customary International Law: An Explanatory Theory', *American Journal of International Law* 108 (2014), 389–434 (418–19, on the seeming 'paradox' of a 'false' belief in an existing rule, especially at 416 and 418).

[74] Sandholtz, *Prohibiting Plunder* 2007 (n. 53), 19.

[75] *Ibid.*

[76] See Conclusion 10, Forms of Evidence of Acceptance as Law (*opinio juris*) of the ILC Draft Conclusions (n. 39). Conclusion 10(3) is especially pertinent: '3. Failure to react over time to a practice may serve as evidence of acceptance as law (*opinio juris*), provided that States were in a position to react and the circumstances called for some reaction.'

[77] Crawford and Viles, 'International Law on a Given Day' 1994 (n. 1), 67.

C. The Law in Transition

The difficulty for understanding and describing legal change is that – both for customary and for treaty law – the traditional doctrines on the sources of international law lack the vocabulary to capture the transitional period, during which the old law is still present, but during which a new rule has not yet taken shape.[78] The case of self-defence against non-State actors illustrates that during a protacted period of change an indeterminacy of the law reigns.

Such indeterminacy is often the result of a deliberate or welcome strategy of international actors. States, international organisations and other bodies carefully pursue strategies of indeterminacy that create and maintain a situation in which differences of legal interpretations can be upheld without one or the other view of the law being clearly endorsed or condemned. The legal meaning and value of States' statements and acts and their (non-)reaction remains obscure because many States avoid taking a clear position. The Security Council, too, sometimes employs tactics of indeterminacy. Resolutions 1368 and 1373 of 2001 in relation to Afghanistan, and Resolution 2249 of 2015 on Syria, use language which is apt to provide arguments for both sides: for 'restrictivists' and for 'expansionists'.[79] Finally, international courts also often pronounce judgments which contain vague and obscure passages, most likely due to compromises when reconciling different views on the bench during the judges' deliberations. The ICJ's landmark decisions dealing with self-defence, ranging from *Oil Platforms* to the *Wall* Advisory Opinion to the judgment in *Congo v. Uganda*, are written in a way that can be interpreted in different directions.[80]

Our claim is that such indeterminacy fulfils an important function for international law. With the help of vagueness, with widespread silence, and through moderation in their international reactions, States (and other international legal persons with law-making power) are continuously creating and upholding a 'regulatory sphere' in which the rules may be reinterpreted or even remade until a norm has taken sufficient shape and the point has been reached that it becomes widely accepted as being the law. This 'method' for developing international law is not explicit and not explicated, and therefore deserves the label 'method' only in quotation marks. Rather, it is tacit,

---

[78] It has been has observed that international law is short of a 'vocabulary to tackle that moment [of change] in the middle' (René Uruena, 'Temporariness and Change in Global Governance', *Netherlands Yearbook of International Law* 45 (2014), 19–40 (24)).

[79] This has been lucidly analysed by Dapo Akande and Marko Milanovic, 'The Constructive Ambiguity of the Security Council's ISIS Resolution', *EJIL Talk!*, 21 Nov 2015.

[80] See Tladi in this volume, 54–61; Tams in this volume, 156–8. See also the Introduction in this volume, 4–5.

intuitive, unstructured, pragmatic and politicised. On the plus side, it allows for incrementalism, which is often needed in order to allow for change to happen. This perspective means abandoning the purely static view on the law. Observers should accept and welcome the fact that, in order to be functional, law needs to be a living instrument. Once this dynamic vision is espoused, we must acknowledge that there will be a phase of uncertainty during a certain period of time. The emergence of the new rule will only be identifiable in hindsight. The exact turning point of legal change cannot be pinned down with precision. The disagreement among the Trialogue authors confirms the impression that we currently find ourselves in this 'grey' period.[81]

The downside of this 'method' of legal change is that it does not embrace open exchange of arguments and public debate, but significantly relies on indirectness, implicitness and reluctance. Moreover, while potentially beneficial for the consolidation and development of international law when limited to specific issues, this 'method' has the potential to dilute and eventually undermine the *ius contra bellum*'s regulatory function.[82] When States refrain from articulating their legal views, when they shy away from protesting against the use of doctrines such as the 'unwilling or unable' formula that lend themselves for arbitrary interpretations, we might witness a general dilution of the law's regulatory power.

VI. CONCLUSION

The indeterminacy of the law on self-defence is both opportunity and risk. It is an opportunity because it is the precondition and environment in which the law may develop towards greater clarity and in which it may adapt to new security threats that are caused by non-State actors. At the same time, it carries significant risks of abuse and the danger of an overall erosion of the existing security architecture. Indeterminacy becomes 'a deficit when it lends itself to arbitrariness' and when it allows actors 'to exempt their actions from the reason of law'.[83] The more indeterminate the law is, the more leeway it gives to political decisions and to those States that have the financial and military

---

[81] Cf. in this sense also Jutta Brunnée and Stephen J. Toope, 'Self-Defence against Non-State Actors: Are Powerful States Willing but Unable to Change International Law?', *International and Comparative Law Quarterly* 67 (2018), 263–86 (277): 'In our view, the rather mixed, and largely self-referential, practice of a small number of primarily Western States cannot suffice to shift customary law in the face of the silence of a majority of States on the operations against IS in Syria.'

[82] Helmut Philipp Aust and Mehrdad Payandeh, 'Praxis und Protest im Völkerrecht', *Juristen Zeitung* 73 (2018), 633–43 (638).

[83] Endicott, *Vagueness in Law* 2000 (n. 28), 203 (Endicott uses the term 'vagueness' at this point).

resources to act. For example, the 'unwilling or unable' standard – for identifying States from whose territory terror attacks have been launched and against which self-defensive action should then be allowed – would benefit mainly or exclusively the powerful States which arrogate themselves the privilege to apply this standard against others. But fully generalising the standard would create a high risk of escalating military actions. It therefore seems as if the concept could ultimately not become a general legal rule because this would deeply erode or even destroy international order.[84]

Unsurprisingly, proponents of Third-World approaches to international law have noted that indeterminacy in general 'very rarely works in favor of Third World interests. Ambiguities and uncertainties are invariably resolved by resort to broader legal principles, policy goals or social contexts, all of which are often shaped by colonial views of the world.'[85]

The danger of abuse of an extended reading of self-defence is particularly pressing when we take into account the broader context in which military action against non-State actors is taken. Mary Ellen O'Connell's 'three pernicious doctrines of expansive self-defence'[86] are important here. Each of these 'doctrines' in isolation seems manageable: terrorist acts might be reasonably qualified as armed attacks once a threshold of gravity is met; self-defence against imminent attacks might not pose a problem when it is based on strict and verifiable *indicia* for imminence as opposed to merely unsupported assertions of threats; and ultimately self-defence against non-State actors would – if sufficiently limited by legal criteria – appear containable, too.

It seems, however, as if exactly the interplay of all three 'doctrines' constitutes the danger O'Connell evokes. First, it lies in the nature of terrorist organisations that their armed attacks are clandestine and difficult to detect. Therefore, the type of objective evidence that can be furnished for upcoming State attacks is lacking here. States invoking terrorist attacks need to rely more often on intelligence sources which other States and the public cannot access and assess. Accepting, secondly, that such a lofty type of attack does not even have to be ongoing to trigger self-defence, but contending ourselves with an 'imminent' putative attack, gives all leeway to well-armed powerful States. So far we lack any standards for objectively establishing imminence, and such establishment again requires superior intelligence information. If the military reaction is, then, thirdly, directed against any State that has not countered this

---

[84] Cf. Brunée and Toope, 'Self-Defence against Non-State Actors' 2018 (n. 81), 285.

[85] Anthony Anghie and B. S. Chimni, 'Third World Approaches to International Law and Individual Responsibility in Internal Conflicts', *Chinese Journal of International Law* 2 (2003), 77–103 (101).

[86] O'Connell in this volume, 212–28.

potentially quite fanciful 'imminent attack', these three doctrines in combination can essentially furnish a justification for each and every intervention. The result is that we currently witness the morphing of the battle against allegedly imminent terrorist attacks into a generalised toleration of pre-emptive action against remote threats. The Turkish operation 'Olive Branch' against the region of Afrin in Northern Syria in March 2018, which simply asserted 'a clear and imminent threat of continuing attack from Daesh'[87] without proffering any evidence, illustrates this unwelcome trend.

The *de iure* acceptance of this practice as a genuine entitlement or allowance would – as Mary Ellen O'Connell and Dire Tladi warn – undermine the structure of multilateralism which forms the heart of the UN Charter. The danger is that a threat of terrorism is used as an argument for indefinite self-defence actions, thereby turning a special exception into a permanent authorisation. It is therefore necessary to develop criteria for operationalising notably the temporal dimension of self-defensive actions, including both their lawful starting point and the legal parameters demanding their termination.

So what could be the way ahead for the law on self-defence as applied to non-State actors? The best way which Christian Tams describes as the 'obvious cure'[88] would be to foster multilateral cooperation. We need multilateralism for the functioning of the system of collective security system and for allowing the Security Council to fulfil its mandate – this is the preferred way ahead for Mary Ellen O'Connell and Dire Tladi. Multilateralism would also be the ideal way to elucidate the substance of international law concerning self-defence. A definition of self-defence following the example of the General Assembly's Definition of Aggression could provide clarification. If such a definition were unanimously adopted by the General Assembly, such a resolution could qualify as a subsequent agreement in the sense of article 31(3) lit. a) of the VCLT. It could thus provide an authoritative interpretation of self-defence.[89] The contemporary climate of world politics, with its emphasis on *Realpolitik*, 'post-globalisation', a renewed focus on the nation State, and the crisis of multilateralism seem adverse to such an exercise for the time being. However, one should remember that the period in which States attempted to define aggression was by no means more favourable than it is today. Quite to the contrary: the Cold War was gaining momentum, with deep

---

[87] UN Doc. S/2018/53, 22 January 2018 (Turkey).
[88] Tams in this volume, 171.
[89] See Natalino Ronzitti, 'The Expanding Law of Self-Defence', *Journal of Conflict and Security Law* 11 (2006), 343–59 (358); Ruys, *'Armed Attack' and Article 51 of the UN Charter* 2010 (n. 18), 535–45.

cleavages between the two blocks showing up. It took almost twenty-five years from the first Soviet proposal of a definition of aggression tabled in 1950[90] to its actual adoption by the General Assembly in 1974. It is likely that such a timeframe would be needed to develop roughly shared positions on the law of self-defence and in particular on the issue of non-State actors. Hence, multilateral approaches will in any case, if they are at all feasible, not provide any short-term answers.

Therefore, the most likely scenario is the persistence of the indeterminacy of the law for some time to come. Along this line, Monica Hakimi states that '[e]fforts to clarify the law on the use of defensive force against non-State actors are premature' because of the 'ongoing struggle over the law's proper content'.[91]

However, while the questions of *whether* and under which conditions self-defence against non-State actors situated in another State is lawful are likely to remain controversial for some time, it will be crucial to not lose sight of the '*how* question'. Inquiries into the requirements of necessity and proportionality of self-defence actions against non-State actors need to be intensified, as advocated by Christian Tams: 'A more active, and more robust, debate about the necessity and proportionality of self-defence could help define the limits of forcible responses more clearly.'[92]

Such a sharpening of existing principles (and their transfer to the constellation of a non-State attack) could be bolstered by attempts to improve the procedural side of self-defence, as advocated by Larissa van den Herik.[93] Van den Herik suggests tightening the requirements on reporting of self-defence actions as demanded by Article 51 of the UN Charter. This could be done, for example, by holding routine debates once Article 51 is invoked, by setting up a database of Article 51 letters, by developing best practices about when and how often such letters should be submitted and what they should contain, by creating a subsidiary body that collects and monitors the submission of Article 51 letters, and by installing expert panels tasked with collecting and examining information and making *prima facie* evaluations.[94] Christian Tams also points in that direction by suggesting that international actors should insist more on

---

[90]   Duties of States in the Event of the Outbreak of Hostilities – USSR Draft Resolution on the Definition of Aggression, 4 November 1950, UN Doc. A/C.1/608.

[91]   Monica Hakimi, 'Defensive Force against Non-State Actors: The State of Play', *International Law Studies* 91 (2015), 1–31 (3).

[92]   Tams in this volume, 171.

[93]   Larissa van den Herik, '"Proceduralising" Article 51', *Heidelberg Journal of International Law* 77 (2017), 65–7.

[94]   *Ibid.*, 67.

the provision of 'credible evidence supporting self-defence claims' which 'could force reacting States into a public dialogue'.[95] Such a fortification of procedural requirements could in fact provide an institutional framework that would probably also contribute to the development of the substantive law.

It is hoped that the multiperspectivism of this volume contributes to a richer understanding not only of the law on self-defence but also of the dynamics of legal change in a pluralist world. Finally, the trialogical approach might be a pathway for teasing out universally acceptable legal answers which strike a fair balance in the tripolar tension between security demands of States, respect for all States' territorial integrity and the objective of containing military violence.

---

[95]   Tams in this volume, 171.

Index

Afghanistan, 3, 46, 66–9, 144, 152, 221, 234
African Union Non-Aggression and Common
  Defence Pact, 151
aggression, 133
  definition, 131–3
  indirect, 131
aiding or abetting, 86
Al Harithi, Abu Ali, 222
al-Awlaki, Anwar, 222, 223
Albania, 193
Algeria, 137
Al-Qaeda, 46
Aquinas, Thomas, 237–8, 244
armed attack, 23, 28, 44, 49, 65–6, 72, 81, 84, 87,
    112–15, 139, 164, 169, 172, 199, 210, 215, 253
  definition, 54–61, 165
  French definition, 182
  ICJ, 195–6
  State support for, 162–3, 168
  threshold question, 91
  treaty law, 93
armed bands, 141
armed conflict zones, outside of, 213
armed reprisals, as justification for
    response, 100
Articles on State Responsibility, 149
Ashburton, Lord, 23, 45, 53, 240
asymmetrical self-defence, 102–4, 134, 161
  case for recognising right of, 164
  claims of, 140
  harbouring, loss of control, 163
  number of claims, 147
  problem of, 97–8
  recognition of, 170
  risk of abuse, 169–71
  state supported attacks, 167

attribution, requirement of, 87, 198, 200, 202,
    207, 211, 212, 213, 224, 232, 249, 253, 257, 275
Augustine of Hippo, 237

Ban Ki-Moon, 191
Bellinger, John, 226
bellum iustum, 22
Bernadotte, Count Folke, 205
Bethlehem, Daniel, 213, 224–6, 250
Bethlehem's Principles, 40–2, 69, 76, 82,
    105, 217
Blair, Tony, 250
Boko Haram, 18
Buergenthal, Judge, 69, 157
Bush Administration (2001), 217, 220, 221

Cançado Trindade, Judge
    Antônio Augusto, 243
Caroline incident, 22, 44, 53
Chad, 147
Chatham House Principles, 5, 38, 39, 41, 42,
    62, 224
civil war, 252, 255
Clinton administration, 220
collective security system, 28, 38, 80, 83, 165
Colombia, 47, 146, 148, 150
Conclusion on the Identification of Customary
    International Law, 51
condemnations, 4, 67, 69, 150, 154, 193, 205, 275
Congo, 58–9, 202
consent, 202–5
control of territory, 200
countermeasures, to less than armed attack, 196
counter-terrorism
  law enforcement measures, 175
Cuban Missile Crisis, 208

customary international law, 49, 51, 52–4, 106,
274–7
dynamic nature of, 54
formation of, 50
relationship to treaty law, 106
right to self-defence, 44, 53
cyber operations, 265

Daesh. *See* ISIS
de lege ferenda proposals, 5
Deeks, Ashley, 225
Definition of Aggression, 135
Denmark, 154
Dispute Settlement Body, 272
Draft Conclusions on the Identification of
Customary International Law, 50

Egan, Brian, 225, 227, 256
El Salvador, 196
Ethiopia, 147, 152

framework-theory, xxii–xxiii
France, 124, 130, 137, 140, *See also* Suez Crisis
Friendly Relations Declaration, 131

Georgia, 47, 73
German Federal Constitutional Court
on self-defence against ISIS, 150–1
Germany, 186, 230
Goldsmith, Attorney General (UK), 215
Greece, 130
Greenwood, Judge, 212
Grotius, Hugo, 238–9, 243
Guatemala, 141

Hague Lectures, 55
harbouring of non-State actors, 138, 141,
147–8, 168
Hezbollah, 153–4
Higgins, Judge, 55, 114, 157, 200
hot pursuit
as justification for response, 100
asymmetry as part of, 102
Hussain, Junaid, 175, 199, 256

ICJ (International Court of Justice), 24, 25, 52,
67, 68, 70, 81, 84, 85, 86, 109, 133, 135,
156–8, 161, 166, 192–205, 255, 276
attacks attributable to States, 1
consent, 203
ius cogens, 230, 231

necessity and proportionality, 233
sources relied on for self-defence rulings,
204
Statute, 266
treaty interpretation, 271
IHL (International Humanitarian Law), 204,
247, 252
imminence, 222
indeterminacy, 264–9
India, 137, 140, 146
international law, xii
English language scholarship, xxiv
sources, 266, 274
universalisation, xx
universalism, xvi
*International Law and the Use of Force by
States*, 214
International Law Commission, 53, 111, 126,
128, 159–61, 167, 193, 230, 251
Interpol, 255
inter-State understanding of self-defence, 62,
64, 103, 129–35, 137, 138, 142, 156, 159, 258
UN Charter, 61, 97, 119, 128, 129–33
intervention by invitation, 151, 202–5
Iran, 146, 152
Iraq, 47, 70–1, 73, 152, 153, 189, 234
ISIS, 73–7, 150–1, 279
German Federal Constitutional Court on
self-defence against, 150–1
Islamic State. *See* ISIS
Israel, 47, 130, 138, 144, 153–4, 156, 157, 200, 216,
See also Suez Crisis
ius cogens, 229–32
doctrine of, 246
ICJ, 230, 231
prohibition on the use of force, 25–7, 48,
178

Japan, 186
Jennings, Judge, 133
Just War Doctrine, 236–40
rejection of, 241
justifications for use of force against non-State
actors, 245

Kashmir, 137
Kellogg–Briand Pact, 183–4
Kelsen, Hans, 241–2
Khan, Reyaad, 174–5, 199, 227, 255
Kooijmans, Judge, 58, 67, 157, 201
Korea, 205–6

284 *Index*

Kurdistan Workers Party, 47
Kuwait, 234

Larger Freedom, In, 65, 121, 155
Lauterpacht, Hersch, 243
law enforcement, 255
Law Enforcement Officials, 204
law, source of, 254
Lebanon, 47, 71–2, 153–4
Leiden Recommendations, 5, 6, 38, 39–40, 41, 42
Liberia, 147
Libya, 218–19, 235
loss of effective control, 148–9, 168
Luban, David, 242

mercenaries, 141
Morocco, 138, 140

national security, 245–6
nationals, rescue of, 225
natural law, 12, 228, 236, 237, 238, 240, 243, 244
necessity
  as justification for response, 99
  asymmetry as part of, 102
  principle of, 198–9
necessity and proportionality, 233
Nicaragua, 55, 194–7
Nigeria, 18
9/11, 3, 46, 220–1
  effect of, 159
Non-Aligned Movement, 154, 155, 162
non-consenting third States, 5, 10, 21, 42, 43, 46, 47, 48, 49, 54, 57, 63, 69, 74, 79, 81, 258, 269, 274
non-intervention, principle of, 197, 198, 202
North Korea, 236

Obama administration, 216, 217, 222–3
occupation law, 201
Occupied Palestinian Territories, 57
opinio iuris, 51
Oppenheim, Lassa, 240
Osirak, Iraq, 209

Pakistan, 137
perspectivism, xv
pirates, 1
Portugal, 137, 141

positive law, 237, 240–1
post truth age, xviii
proportionality, principle of, 198–9

Reagan administration, 219
requirement to report, 36
responsibility, 149
right to respond to armed attacks that could be attributed to another State, 134
Rio Treaty Organization, 185
Russia, 47, 72, 73, 74, 75, 146, 148
Rwanda, 146, 150

Scelle, George, xix
Schwebel, Judge, 55, 59, 68
self-defence
  alternative justifications, 99
  as exception, 100–1
  conditions of, 101
  legitimacy, 100
  source of, 105
  UN Charter, 62
Self-Defence in International Law, 214
Senegal, 146, 152
Shultz doctrine, 138
Simma, Judge, 58, 67, 157, 201
Sofaer, Judge Abraham, 219–20
Somalia, 152
sources, for self-defence, 165
South Africa, 100, 137, 139, 140, 175
South Korea, 236
Soviet Union, 124, 205–6
State attack, 104, 115, 120, 122, 124, 142, 154, 156, 157, 161, 164, 185, 278
  definition, 103
State nexus, 104, 113, 115, 142, 156
State-centric view of self-defence, 96, 97, 98, 111, 114, 116, 119, 120, 122, 125, 129, 131, 156
  changes, 161–4, 165
States
  definition of state attack, 103
  duty of toleration, 103
  responsibility, 134
  unable/unwilling, 212, 224–8, 250, 252, 254, 256, 257
Sudan, 47, 73, 147, 152
Suez Crisis, 206–8, 214, 250
Syria, 7–8, 73–7
system of collective security
  effectiveness and unilateral use of force, 34

Tajikistan, 146, 148, 152
Tanaka, Judge, 243
targeted killing, 174–7, 213, 218, 234–5
terrorism, 18, 215, 217, 218–24, 246, 247, 250
 as criminal act, 205
terrorist organizations, 1
terrorism, 246
Thailand, 146, 152
threshold question, 94
Tomka, Judge, 158
treaty interpretation, 261
triggering attack, 101, 182, 199, 256
Tunisia, 137
Turkey, 70–1, 138, 144, 148, 152

Uganda, 57, 58–9, 146, 156, 157
unable or unwilling test, 9, 90, 149, 212, 224–8,
 250, 252, 253, 254, 256, 257
unilateralism, 88, 89
United Kingdom, 124, 174, 175–6, 177–8, 234–5,
 250, *See also* Suez Crisis
United Nations, 155
 Article 51, 280
 collective security system, 125
United Nations Charter, 2, 4, 14, 22, 23–4,
 165–6, 179–80, 190–1
 Article 2(4), 64, 65, 95, 115–16, 181, 184–5,
  188
 Article 2(4), as *ius cogens* norm, 249
 Article 3(g), 159
 Article 39, 64
 Article 42, 64
 Article 51, 36, 48–9, 52, 76–8, 84, 104, 105,
  106, 124, 128, 129, 166, 168, 182–3, 185, 186,
  266–7
 Article 51, context, 109–12
 Article 51, reliance on, 146
 Chapter VII, 119
 inter-State reading of, 61, 62, 64, 97, 119, 128,
  129–33
 purpose of, 120–5
 self defence, 30–6
 travaux préparatoires, 123–4
 use of force, 20
United Nations General Assembly, 31–4, 131,
 135, 166, 187–92, 205
United Nations Secretary General, 189–91

United Nations Security Council, 30, 32, 33,
 34, 69, 74, 84–5, 87, 141, 162, 205–12, 215,
 235, 247
 international terrorism, 85
 ISIS, 150
 non-State actors, 118
 on 9/11 self-defence, 46
 on attacks by non-State actors, 140
 political restraints, 85
 right to self-defence, 4
 Syria, 7
United States, 124, 138, 144, 175, 176–7, 183–5,
 194–7, 205–6, 218–24, 234–5, 250, 275,
 See also Suez Crisis
 Iraq, 189, 234
 Syria, 76
 war in Afghanistan, 66–9, 152, 163
universality
 as mode of power, xxi
use of force
 collective, 15
 customary international law, 11, 18, 25, 43, 44,
  52–4, 72, 95, 100, 107, 193, 197, 199, 202,
  214, 231, 233
 in self defence, 54
 less grave forms, 24
 prohibition of, 22–8
 UN Charter, 20
 unilateral, 15
USS Cole, 220

Vattel, Emer de, 239
VCLT (Vienna Convention on the Law of
 Treaties), 49, 51–2, 61–6, 77, 81, 108, 125,
 126, 231, 262, 264, 273, 279
 Articles 31–33, 110
 ius cogens, 229

war, elimination of, 247
World Trade Center 1993, 220
Wright, Attorney General Jeremy (UK), 212,
 216, 217

Yemen, 220, 221, 222

Zaire, 141
Zimbabwe, 137, 139